Philosophical Skepticism

BLACKWELL READINGS IN PHILOSOPHY

Series Editor: Steven M. Cahn

Blackwell Readings in Philosophy are concise, chronologically arranged collections of primary readings from classical and contemporary sources. They represent core positions and important developments with respect to key philosophical concepts. Edited and introduced by leading philosophers, these volumes provide valuable resources for teachers and students of philosophy, and for all those interested in gaining a solid understanding of central topics in philosophy.

Philosophical Skepticism

Edited by
Charles Landesman
and
Roblin Meeks

Blackwell
Publishing

350 Main Street, Malden, MA 02148-5018, USA
108 Cowley Road, Oxford OX4 1JF, UK
550 Swanston Street, Carlton South, Melbourne, Victoria 3053, Australia
Kurfürstendamm 57, 10707 Berlin, Germany

First published 2003 by Blackwell Publishers Ltd,
a Blackwell Publishing company

Library of Congress Cataloging-in-Publication Data

Philosophical Skepticism / edited by Charles Landesman and Roblin Meeks.
p. cm.—(Blackwell readings in philosophy ; 6)
Includes bibliographical references and index.
ISBN 0–631–21353–8 (alk. paper)—ISBN 0–631–21354–6 (pbk.: alk. paper)
1. Skepticism. I. Landesman, Charles. II. Meeks, Roblin. III. Series.

B837 .S567 2002   149'.73—dc21   2002066428

A catalogue record for this title is available from the British Library.

Set in 10/12.5pt Palatino
by Kolam Information Services Pvt. Ltd, Pondicherry, India

For further information on
Blackwell Publishing, visit our website:
http://www.blackwellpublishing.com

For Emily Jayne, not yet a skeptic,
and
For Yen, dispeller of doubts

Contents

Acknowledgments

The editors and publishers gratefully acknowledge the following for permission to reproduce copyright material:

J. L. Austin, *Sense and Sensibilia*, ed. G. J. Warnock (Oxford University Press, 1962). © Oxford University Press 1962. Reprinted by permission of Oxford University Press.

Cicero, *De Natura Deorum*, Loeb Classical Library Volume XIX, trans. H. Rackham (Cambridge, Mass.: Harvard University Press 1933). The Loeb Classical Library ® is a registered trademark of the President and Fellows of Harvard College.

René Descartes, Meditations I, II, III, and VI, from *A Discourse on Method and Selected Writings*, trans. John Veitch (E. P. Dutton and Co., 1951).

Martin Heidegger, from *Being and Time*, trans. John Macquarrie and Edward Robinson (SCM Press Ltd, 1962), pp. 89–90, 246–7. © SCM Press Ltd 1962.

Immanuel Kant, *Prolegomena to Any Future Metaphysics*, trans. Paul Carus (La Salle, Ill.: Open Court, 1902) and *Critique of Pure Reason*, trans. F. Max Müller (1881).

Søren Kierkegaard, *Concluding Unscientific Postscript*, trans. Louis Pojman. Permission granted by Louis Pojman.

Diogenes Laertius, "Pyrrho," from *Lives of Eminent Philosophers*, Loeb Classical Library Volume II, trans. R. D. Hicks (Cambridge, Mass.: Harvard University Press, 1925). The Loeb Classical Library ® is a registered trademark of the President and Fellows of Harvard College.

Norman Malcolm, "Knowledge of Other Minds," from *The Journal of Philosophy* LV, 23 (1958). © Cornell University 1958. Reprinted by permission of the publisher.

Jean-Baptiste Molière, *The Forced Marriage*, from *One Act Comedies of Molière*, trans. Albert Bermel (Frederick Ungar, 1975).

Michel de Montaigne, "Apology for Raymond Sebond," from *The Complete Essays of Montaigne*, trans. Donald M. Frame. © the Board of Trustees of the Leland Stanford Junior University 1958.

G. E. Moore, "Proof of an External World". Reprinted by permission of Timothy Moore.

Thomas Nagel, *The View from Nowhere*. © Thomas Nagel 1986. Reprinted by permission of Oxford University Press, Inc.

Thomas Nagel, *What Does it all Mean? A Very Short Introduction to Philosophy*. © Thomas Nagel 1987. Reprinted by permission of Oxford University Press, Inc.

Friedrich Nietzsche, *Beyond Good and Evil: Prelude to a Philosophy of the Future*, trans R. J. Hollingdale (Penguin Classics 1973; revised edition 1990). © R. J. Hollingdale 1973, 1990.

Blaise Pascal, "Contradictions" and "Wager," in *Pensées*, trans. A. J. Krailsheimer (Penguin Classics, 1966) © A. J. Krailsheimer 1966.

Plato, "Apology," in *The Last Days of Socrates*, trans. H. Tredennick, revised translation by Harold Tarrant (Penguin Classics 1954, third revised edition 1993). © Hugh Tredennick, 1954, 1959, 1969; © Harold Tarrant 1993.

W. V. Quine, *A Logical Point of View: Nine Logico-Philosophical Essays* (Harvard University Press, 1980), pp. 42–6. Reprinted by permission of the publisher. © the President and Fellows of Harvard College 1980, renewed 1989 by W. V. Quine.

W. V. Quine, "Epistemology Naturalized," from *Ontological Relativity and Other Essays* (Columbia University Press, 1969). Reprinted by permission of the publisher.

Hans Reichenbach, "The Theory of Probability," (University of California Press, 1949), pp. 470–5, 480–2. Reprinted by permission of Dr Maria Reichenbach.

Richard Rorty, "Solidarity or Objectivity?" from *Objectivity, Relativism and Truth: Philosophical Papers*, vol. 1 (Cambridge University Press, 1991). Reprinted by permission of Columbia University Press.

Bertrand Russell, *Human Knowledge: Its Scope and Limits* (Routledge, 1948). Reprinted by permission of the publisher and the Bertrand Russell Peace Foundation.

Sextus Empiricus, *Outlines of Pyrrhonism*, Loeb Classical Library Volume I, trans. R. G. Bury (Cambridge, Mass.: Harvard University Press, 1933). The Loeb Classical Library ® is a registered trademark of the President and Fellows of Harvard College.

W. T. Stace, "Refutation of Realism," *Mind* 53 (1934).

Peter Unger, "A Defense of Skepticism," *Philosophical Review* 80 (1971). © Cornell University 1971. Reprinted by permission of the publisher.

Ludwig Wittgenstein, *Tractatus Logico-Philosophicus*, trans. D. F. Pears and B. F. McGuiness (Routledge and Kegan Paul 1961), 5.6–5.641.

The following essays can be found in the public domain: chs 6, 18, 19, 24, 28, and 29.

Michael Levin's essay, ch. 13, was written especially for this volume.

The publishers apologize for any errors or omissions in the above list and would be grateful to be notified of any corrections that should be incorporated in the next edition or reprint of this book.

Introduction

The purpose of this anthology is to provide a selection of texts drawn from the skeptical tradition of Western philosophy as well as texts written by opponents of skepticism and by others who have skeptical leanings but who wish to travel a different path. Together, these texts clearly illustrate the profound influence that skeptical stances and questions have had, and continue to have, on the branch of philosophy known as epistemology, or the study of how we come to possess knowledge, including whether we can possess it at all.

The original meaning of the Greek word from which "skeptic" is derived denotes one who inquires into the truth of things or who wishes to gain knowledge about some subject matter. The term came to characterize those whose inquiries convinced them that the knowledge they sought was not to be attained, so that "skeptic" came to mean one who doubts that certainty, knowledge, or perhaps even justified belief is possible. We find, for example, that in some of Plato's dialogues, Socrates raises important questions about the nature of virtue, piety, or even knowledge itself, but ultimately fails to find an answer that satisfies him. In other dialogues, Plato ascribes definite opinions to Socrates, and hence we cannot tell from his writings whether or not the real Socrates can be properly classified as a skeptic. But the dialogues that end without definite answer to the questions they raise are among the first texts in the skeptical tradition, and so some of the ancient skeptics thought of Socrates as a kindred spirit. However we classify him, in the selection from the *Apology* included below, we see that Socrates promotes the value of acknowledging the limits of human wisdom, including, perhaps most importantly, one's own.

Although we have referred to the skeptical tradition, the various strands of skepticism running through Western philosophy should not be construed as a simple, highly unified system of thought. Doubt about whether knowledge is attainable by human efforts is common to all versions, and they all likewise attempt to base their doubts upon rigorous arguments, many of which are still thought to be convincing by contemporary philosophers who still wrestle with the same doubts. But skeptics differed among themselves in the arguments they employed and in the conclusions they drew from their inability to achieve knowledge. Those ancient skeptics, who called themselves Pyrrhonists, claimed that for any proposition asserted, the arguments supporting it are no better and no worse than the arguments against it, and hence they recommended suspending judgment altogether. Moreover, the Pyrrhonists claimed to discover that such turning away from philosophical, religious, and ethical disputes led to inner tranquility or peace of mind. Accordingly, for them, skepticism provided a route to the contented life that proved superior to the proposals offered by rival schools such as Stoicism, Aristotelianism, and Epicureanism.

Although the skeptical philosophers of Ancient Greece produced an enormous body of writings, only a few have survived. Our knowledge of their thought is based upon a few surviving texts, such as Diogenes Laertius' *Life of Pyrrho*, Cicero's *Academica*, and Sextus Empiricus' *Outlines of Pyrrhonism*, selections from which are included in this volume. On the basis of recent research, we have no reason to believe that these skeptical ideas had a significant impact upon philosophy in medieval times. In fact, these texts were largely unavailable until they were recovered in the fifteenth and sixteenth centuries. The writings of Sextus Empiricus, which contain the richest and most interesting presentation of ancient skeptical thought, appeared for the first time in Latin translation in the mid-sixteenth century, and it was these texts that contributed most to the revival of interest in skepticism in early modern philosophy, as reflected especially in the works of the great French philosophers Michel de Montaigne and René Descartes, but in many others as well.

For Montaigne, skepticism did not lead to suspension of belief; in fact, he was not reluctant to express his opinions on a wide variety of topics. However, in his longest essay, "Apology for Raymond Sebond," he makes use of Pyrrhonist arguments to undermine the ability of reason to provide a basis for religious belief. Because conclusions founded on rational argument "are subject to uncertainty and debate," we must rely upon faith in God's grace to lead us to appropriate belief.

Descartes, on the other hand, argued that reason was the source of all knowledge. He claimed to have discovered conclusive arguments for God's existence as well as for the distinction between mind or self and body. He aimed at achieving certainty and believed that he was successful in this quest. Although he was by no means a skeptic, at the outset of his most influential work, *Meditations on First Philosophy*, Descartes put forward several powerful arguments intended to remove opinions that could be doubted so that he could begin with and build up from an indubitable base of knowledge. He argued, for example, that since we possess no criterion for distinguishing waking life from dreams, we cannot tell with certainty when our experiences are the products of our slumber or of an objectively existing world, and thus the evidence of the senses is not immune from doubt. Though your senses tell you that you are currently reading this book, you might in fact be safely at home asleep. Descartes further entertained the possibility that we might be continuously deceived by a powerful evil demon, and hence any conclusion we would normally assent to could be false, including truths about mathematics such as $2 + 3 = 5$. Descartes undertook to rebut these arguments, claiming that he was the first philosopher to overcome skepticism. He professed to have discovered a criterion of certainty – perceiving something clearly and distinctly – the application of which yields unimpeachable knowledge of the existence of God and of the external world. In the end, we are entitled to trust our senses, and we no longer have to worry that life might be just a dream or that we might be at the mercy of an omnipotent deceiver.

However, most philosophers after Descartes concluded that his antiskeptical arguments were not successful and that other ways must be found to cope with skeptical challenges – including those challenges he himself raised. Nevertheless, Descartes did succeed in placing the epistemological problems raised by the skeptical tradition near the top of the agenda of modern philosophy. In fact, epistemology itself, as it has evolved after Descartes, is primarily an attempt to deal with skeptical arguments like those raised by providing an understanding of how knowledge is possible. The lack of consensus on epistemological problems in modern and contemporary philosophy, and the wide variety of conflicting opinions offered by philosophers concerning the issues raised by skepticism, imply that the agenda is far from being completed.

Most post-Cartesian philosophers tried to refute skepticism and to substantiate our common claims to possess knowledge. David Hume, however, embraced skeptical arguments and conclusions, ultimately developing aspects of skepticism such as doubts about induction and self-knowledge that had not been given special consideration. Unlike the ancient Pyrrhonists, however, Hume did not recommend that we suspend judgment for the simple reason that our inborn natural propensities made that impossible. For example, our minds are so constructed that, upon experiencing two things constantly going together, if we should then experience the first, we will expect the second to occur. This is a form of induction, but it is not based upon reason, or upon any experience of a connection between the two events, but upon custom or habit. Although Hume was not a Pyrrhonist, he did recommend a kind of mitigated skepticism in which we limit our inquiries "to such subjects as are best adapted to the narrow capacity of human understanding." The proper approach "confines itself to common life and to such subjects as fall under daily practice and experience." Of any book containing theological or metaphysical discussion, Hume famously remarks, "Commit it then to the flames: for it can contain nothing but sophistry and illusion." It is as if he advocates a controlled dose of skepticism to inoculate us against the more virulent, crippling forms of Pyrrhonian doubt.

Part I of this volume includes some of the major texts of what we call *global skepticism*. By this term, we mean the thought that we are mistaken about all or almost all the knowledge claims we make in daily life, in science, and in other areas of human concern. Take the example that G. E. Moore discussed at length: he raised his hands and moved them about and said "Here is one hand and here is another." He takes his hands to belong to the external world, by which he means the domain of objects and events that exist independently of his perceptions and thoughts about them. This, Moore thinks, is an example of the sort of statement that we frequently know to be true. But, for the global skeptic, such an assertion relies upon our sense experience, which may be illusory and which may exist even if there were no hands there at all. Global skeptics agree that we have beliefs about the external world but doubt whether the evidence of the senses provides a sufficient basis for knowledge or even for justified belief. Some global skeptics will admit that we do have some knowledge, most frequently knowledge of the experiences we are having at the moment we are having them. But they see no way to go beyond our experience to the world of things as they are in themselves. The texts in Part I present a variety of approaches to global skepticism, representing a sample of the radical side of the skeptical tradition from Ancient Greek philosophy to the contemporary world.

Not all skeptical doubts are global, however. Some concern particular ways of forming beliefs and particular classes of assertions, and in Part II we present a selection of texts on some of these topics of unusual philosophical interest. The selections on perception discuss the issue of whether evidence provided by the senses suffices to provide us with knowledge of the external world. The section on induction offers two replies to Hume's inductive skepticism. Following that, we include a series of texts concerned with the question whether there is any reason at all to believe that there exist other persons who have minds, thoughts, and experiences much like our own, even though one cannot apprehend them directly. What these three problems have in common is the effort to find a rationale for inferences that are not deductively valid – the inference from sense experience to an external world, the inference from past experience to the future, and the inference from the experience of the behavior of others to the existence of their thoughts and experiences.

But skepticism does not seem limited to concerns about our ability to know the external world. In the section on self-knowledge, we include the work of philosophers who raise doubts about our knowledge of the "internal world," or whether one can gain knowledge of oneself. Intuitively, one doesn't seem to infer one's beliefs and desires from observations of one's behavior. But philosophers have questioned our awareness of the supposed owner of experiences, whether such an owner can be known at all, whether that owner is an immaterial mind or a physical body, or even whether the supposition of a self that possesses experiences but is distinct from them is even intelligible. Here again we locate the source of this debate primarily in the work of Descartes and Hume. Descartes claims that the mind is transparent to itself: thinking alone suffices for knowledge of the essential nature of the subject and the contents of one's mind that is far more certain than knowledge of the body. Hume, in contrast, questions whether the subject of our perceptions can be known at all, for "gazing inward" reveals distinct perceptions but no perceiver.

The final section in Part II concerns the foundations of religious belief. One of the standard meanings of the term "skeptic" refers to one who doubts the existence of God or the claims of a particular religion. A number of philosophers have followed Montaigne in using skeptical arguments to undermine the capacity of reason to verify the existence of God and to conclude that belief in God must be based upon faith or, in the case of Pascal, upon prudential considerations. Others have argued that faith independent of reason provides no basis for thinking that one religious belief is any better justified than others. This section includes selections on these and other uses of skepticism in the philosophy of religion.

Part III includes a variety of responses and reactions to the skeptical tradition. It includes efforts to refute skepticism (Descartes, Reid, and Heidegger), efforts to show how to maintain both philosophical poise as well as a normal life while at the same time accepting the soundness of skeptical arguments (Hume), and efforts to find ways around skepticism (Kant, Quine, and Rorty). The papers by Quine and Rorty, in particular, show how the philosophy of pragmatism has been revived in recent years as a way of coming to terms with the skeptical tradition. They illustrate how other philosophical traditions have been impressed by skeptical arguments and have attempted to absorb skeptical conclusions into the foundations of their systems. As Quine eloquently puts it in his selection included below, "The Humean predicament is the human predicament."

In any case, philosophical skepticism is alive and well. In recent years there has been a revival of interest in the question of the soundness of skeptical arguments, and lively debates currently rage in the journals and in a variety of new books. The material in this volume provides a more than sufficient background to allow the student and general reader to engage in further study of skepticism both from classical as well as contemporary sources.

Charles Landesman
Roblin Meeks

Part I

Global Skepticism

1

Plato, from *Apology*

One of the most influential figures in Western philosophy is Socrates (470–399 BCE), the Ancient Greek philosopher who was put to death for allegedly corrupting the youth of Athens by teaching them his method of relentless questioning. What follows is an excerpt from the dialogue *Apology*, beautifully and powerfully written by his student, the likewise enormously influential philosopher Plato (428–347 BCE). In it, we witness Socrates' defense of his "occupation" – his systematical inquiry into the depth of his fellow citizens' knowledge and the degree to which they recognize their own ignorance.

In his words to the jury, we discover that Socrates was deemed the wisest man by the oracle of Delphi. Since he believed that he knew very little, Socrates sets out to untangle this riddle. In seeking out those who claimed to have extensive knowledge (politicians, artists, and craftsmen), he discovered that they instead possessed an inflated sense of themselves. In the end, Socrates concludes that his wisdom lies in his knowledge of the limits of human wisdom, that he – unlike his fellow Athenians – did not claim to know what he in fact did not know.

The defense of Socrates sets the standard for philosophical inquiry – namely, a general attitude where no belief is immune from a call for justification, where one must constantly submit one's beliefs to a healthy dose of skepticism, and where difficult but central questions concerning such things as the nature of justice, virtue, and goodness demand incredible effort to address and to answer. Perhaps most important, however, is the maxim that "the unexamined life is not worth living." Socrates teaches that self-examination proves essential, for out of it comes the humility of ignorance and the desire to know. In other words, we see in Socrates the definition of "philosopher": one who loves wisdom.

[...] Here perhaps one of you might interrupt me and say, But what is it that you do, Socrates? How is it that you have been mis-represented like this? Surely all this talk and gossip about you would never have arisen if you had confined yourself to ordinary activities, but only if your behavior was abnormal. Tell us the explanation, if you do not want us to invent it for ourselves.

This seems to me to be a reasonable request, and I will try to explain to you what it is that has given me this false notoriety. So please give me your attention. Perhaps some of you will think that I am not being serious, but I assure you that I am going to tell you the whole truth.

I have gained this reputation, gentlemen, from nothing more or less than a kind of wisdom. What kind of wisdom do I mean? Human wisdom, I suppose. It seems that I really am wise in this limited sense. Presumably the geniuses whom I mentioned just now are wise in a wisdom that is more than human. I do not know how else to account for it. I certainly have no knowledge of such wisdom, and anyone who says that I have is a liar and willful slanderer. Now, gentlemen, please do not interrupt me if I seem to make an extravagant claim, for what I am going to tell you is not my own opinion. I am going to refer you to an unimpeachable authority. I shall call as witness to my wisdom, such as it is, the god at Delphi.

You know Chaerephon, of course. He was a friend of mine from boyhood, and a good democrat who played his part with the rest of you in the recent expulsion and restoration. And you know what he was like, how enthusiastic he was over anything that he had once undertaken. Well, one day he actually went to Delphi and asked this question of the god – as I said before, gentlemen, please do not interrupt – he asked whether there was anyone wiser than myself. The priestess replied that there was no one. As Chaerephon is dead, the evidence for my statement will be supplied by his brother, who is here in court.

Please consider my object in telling you this. I want to explain to you how the attack upon my reputation first started. When I heard about the oracle's answer, I said to myself, What does the god mean? Why does he not use plain language? I am only too conscious that I have no claim to wisdom, great or small. So what can he mean by asserting that I am the wisest man in the world? He cannot be telling a lie; that would not be right for him.

After puzzling about it for some time, I set myself at last with considerable reluctance to check the truth of it in the following way. I went to interview a man with a high reputation for wisdom, because I felt that here if anywhere I should succeed in disproving the oracle and pointing out to my divine authority, You said that I was the wisest of men, but here is a man who is wiser than I am.

Well, I gave a thorough examination to this person – I need not mention his name, but it was one of our politicians that I was studying when I had this experience – and in conversation with him I formed the impression that although in many people's opinion, and especially in his own, he appeared to be wise, in fact he was not. Then when I began to try to show him that he only thought he was wise and was not really so, my efforts were resented both by him and by many of the other people present. However, I reflected as I walked away, Well, I am certainly wiser than this man. It is only too likely that neither of us has any knowledge to boast of, but he thinks that he knows something which he does not know, whereas I am quite conscious of my ignorance. At any rate it seems that I am wiser than he is to this small extent, that I do not think that I know what I do not know.

After this I went on to interview a man with an even greater reputation for wisdom, and I formed the same impression again, and here too I incurred the resentment of the man himself and a number of others.

From that time on I interviewed one person after another. I realized with distress and alarm that I was making myself unpopular, but I felt compelled to put my religious duty first. Since I was trying to find out the meaning of the oracle, I was bound to interview everyone who had a reputation for knowledge. And by dog, gentlemen, for I must be frank with you, my honest impression was this. It seemed to me, as I pursued my investigation at the god's command, that the people with the greatest reputations were almost entirely deficient, while others who were supposed to be their inferiors were much better qualified in practical intelligence.

I want you to think of my adventures as a sort of pilgrimage undertaken to establish the truth of the oracle once for all. After I had finished with the politicians I turned to the poets, dramatic, lyric, and all the rest, in the belief that here I should expose myself as a comparative ignoramus. I used to pick up what I thought were some of their most perfect works and question them closely about the meaning of what they had written, in the hope of incidentally enlarging my own knowledge. Well, gentlemen, I hesitate to tell you the truth, but it must be told. It is hardly an exaggeration to say that any of the bystanders could have explained those poems better than their actual authors. So I soon made up my mind about the poets too. I decided that it was not wisdom that enabled them to write their poetry, but a kind of instinct or inspiration, such as you find in seers and prophets who deliver all their sublime messages without knowing in the least what they mean. It seemed clear to me that the poets were in much the same case, and I also observed that the very fact that they were poets made them think that they had a perfect understanding of all other subjects, of which they were totally ignorant. So I left that line of inquiry too with the same sense of advantage that I had felt in the case of the politicians.

Last of all I turned to the skilled craftsmen. I knew quite well that I had practically no technical qualifications myself, and I was sure that I should find them full of impressive knowledge. In this I was not disappointed. They understood things which I did not, and to that extent they were wiser than I was. But, gentlemen, these professional experts seemed to share the same failing which I had noticed in the poets. I mean that on the strength of their technical proficiency they claimed a perfect understanding of every other subject, however important, and I felt that this error more than outweighed their positive wisdom. So I made myself spokesman for the oracle, and asked myself whether I would rather be as I was – neither wise with their wisdom nor stupid with their stupidity – or possess both qualities as they did. I replied through myself to the oracle that it was best for me to be as I was.

The effect of these investigations of mine, gentlemen, has been to arouse against me a great deal of hostility, and hostility of a particularly bitter and persistent kind, which has resulted in various malicious suggestions, including the description of me as a professor of wisdom. This is due to the fact that whenever I succeed in disproving another person's claim to wisdom in a given subject, the bystanders assume that I know everything about that subject myself. But the truth of the matter, gentlemen, is pretty certainly this, that real wisdom is the property of God, and this oracle is his way of telling us that human wisdom has little or no value. It seems to me that he is not referring literally to Socrates, but has merely taken my name as an example, as if he would say to us, The wisest of you men is he who has realized, like Socrates, that in respect of wisdom he is really worthless.

That is why I still go about seeking and searching in obedience to the divine command, if I think that anyone is wise, whether citizen or stranger, and when I think that any person is not wise, I try to help the cause of God by proving that he is not. This occupation has kept me too busy to do much either in politics or in my own affairs. In fact, my service to God has reduced me to extreme poverty.

There is another reason for my being unpopular. A number of young men with wealthy fathers and plenty of leisure have deliberately attached themselves to me because they enjoy hearing other people cross-questioned. These often take me as their model, and go on to try to question other persons. Whereupon, I suppose, they find an unlimited number of people who think that they know something, but really know little or nothing. Consequently their victims become annoyed, not with themselves but with me, and they complain that there is a pestilential busybody called Socrates who fills young people's heads with wrong ideas. If you ask them what he does, and what he teaches that has this effect, they have no answer, not knowing what to say. But as they do not want to admit their confusion, they fall back on the stock charges against any philosopher, that he teaches his pupils about things in the heavens and below the earth, and to disbelieve in gods, and to make the weaker argument defeat the stronger. They would be very loath, I fancy, to admit the truth – which is that they are being convicted of pretending to knowledge when they are entirely ignorant. So, jealous, I suppose, for their own reputation, and also energetic and numerically strong, and provided with a plausible and carefully worked-out case against me, these people have been dinning into your ears for a long time past their violent denunciations of myself.

There you have the causes which led to the attack upon me by Meletus and Anytus and Lycon, Meletus being aggrieved on behalf of the poets, Anytus on behalf of the professional men and politicians, and Lycon on behalf of the orators. So, as I said at the beginning, I should be surprised if I were able, in the short time that I have, to rid your minds of a misconception so deeply implanted.

There, gentlemen, you have the true facts, which I present to you without any concealment or suppression, great or small. I am fairly certain that this plain speaking of mine is the cause of my unpopularity, and this really goes to prove that my statements are true, and that I have described correctly the nature and the grounds of the calumny which has been brought against me. Whether you inquire into them now or later, you will find the facts as I have just described them. [...]

[...] But perhaps someone will say, Do you feel no compunction, Socrates, at having followed a line of action which puts you in danger of the death penalty?

I might fairly reply to him, You are mistaken, my friend, if you think that a man who is worth anything ought to spend his time weighing up the prospects of life and death. He has only one thing to consider in performing any action – that is, whether he is acting rightly or wrongly, like a good man or a bad one. On your view the heroes who died at Troy would be poor creatures, especially the son of Thetis. He, if you remember, made light of danger in comparison with incurring dishonor when his goddess mother warned him, eager as he was to kill Hector, in some such words as these, I fancy: My son, if you avenge your comrade Patroclus' death and kill Hector, you will die yourself – 'Next after Hector is thy fate prepared.' When he heard this warning, he made light of his death and danger, being much more afraid of an ignoble life and of failing to avenge his friends. 'Let me die forthwith,' said he, 'when I have requited the villain, rather than remain here by the beaked ships to be mocked, a burden on the ground.'[1] Do you suppose that he gave a thought to death and danger?

The truth of the matter is this, gentlemen. Where a man has once taken up his stand, either because it seems best to him or in obedience to his orders, there I believe he is bound to remain and face the danger, taking no account of death or anything else before dishonor.

This being so, it would be shocking inconsistency on my part, gentlemen, if, when the officers whom you chose to command me assigned me my position at Potidaea and Amphipolis and Delium, I remained at my post like anyone else and faced death, and yet afterward, when God appointed me, as I supposed and believed, to the duty of leading the philosophical life, examining myself and others, I were then through fear of death or of any other danger to desert my post. That would indeed be shocking, and then I might really with justice be summoned into court for not believing in the gods, and disobeying the oracle, and being afraid of death, and thinking that I am wise when I am not. For let me tell you, gentlemen, that to be afraid of death is only another form of thinking that one is wise when one is not; it is to think that one knows what one does not know. No one knows with regard to death whether it is not really the greatest blessing that can happen to a man, but people dread it as though they were certain that it is the greatest evil, and this ignorance, which thinks that it knows what it does not, must surely be ignorance most culpable. This, I take it, gentlemen, is the degree, and this the nature of my advantage over the rest of mankind, and if I were to claim to be wiser than my neighbor in any respect, it would be in this – that not possessing any real knowledge of what comes after death, I am also conscious that I do not possess it. But I do know that to do wrong and to disobey my superior, whether God or man, is wicked and dishonorable, and so I shall never feel more fear or aversion for something which, for all I know, may really be a blessing, than for those evils which I know to be evils.

Suppose, then, that you acquit me, and pay no attention to Anytus, who has said that either I should not have appeared before this court at all, or, since I have appeared here, I must be put to death, because if I once escaped your sons would all immediately become utterly demoralized by putting the teaching of Socrates into practice. Suppose that, in view of this, you said to me, Socrates, on this occasion we shall disregard Anytus and acquit you, but only on one condition, that you give up spending your time on this quest and stop philosophizing. If we catch you going on in the same way, you shall be put to death.

Well, supposing, as I said, that you should offer to acquit me on these terms, I should reply, Gentlemen, I am your very grateful and devoted servant, but I owe a greater obedience to God than to you, and so long as I draw breath and have my faculties, I shall never stop practicing philosophy and exhorting you and elucidating the truth for everyone that I meet. I shall go on saying, in my usual way, My very good friend, you are an Athenian and belong to a city which is the greatest and most famous in the world for its wisdom and strength. Are you not ashamed that you give your attention to acquiring as much money as possible, and similarly with reputation and honor, and give no attention or thought to truth and understanding and the perfection of your soul?

And if any of you disputes this and professes to care about these things, I shall not at once let him go or leave him. No, I shall question him and examine him and test him; and if it appears that in spite of his profession he has made no real progress toward goodness, I shall reprove him for neglecting what is of supreme importance, and giving his attention to trivialities. I shall do this to everyone that I meet, young or old, foreigner or fellow citizen, but especially to you, my fellow citizens, inasmuch as you are closer to me in kinship. This, I do assure you, is what my God commands, and it is my belief that no greater good has ever befallen you in this city than my service to my God. For I spend all my time going about trying to persuade you, young and old, to make your first and chief concern not for your bodies nor for your possessions, but for the highest welfare of your souls, proclaiming as I go, Wealth does not bring goodness, but goodness brings wealth and every other blessing, both to the individual and to the state.

Now if I corrupt the young by this message, the message would seem to be harmful, but if anyone says that my message is different from this, he is talking nonsense. And so, gentlemen, I would say, You can please yourselves whether you listen to Anytus or not, and whether you acquit me or not. You know that I am not going to alter my conduct, not even if I have to die a hundred deaths.

Order, please, gentlemen! Remember my request to give me a hearing without interruption. Besides, I believe that it will be to your advantage to listen. I am going to tell you something else, which may provoke a storm of protest, but please restrain yourselves. I assure you that if I am what I claim to be, and you put me to death, you will harm yourselves more than me. Neither Meletus nor Anytus can do me any harm at all; they would not have the power, because I do not believe that the law of God permits a better man to be harmed by a worse. No doubt my accuser might put me to death or have me banished or deprived of civic rights, but even if he thinks – as he probably does, and others too, I dare say – that these are great calamities, I do not think so. I believe that it is far worse to do what he is doing now, trying to put an innocent man to death. For this reason, gentlemen, so far from pleading on my own behalf, as might be supposed, I am really pleading on yours, to save you from misusing the gift of God by condemning me. If you put me to death, you will not easily find anyone to take my place. It is literally true, even if it sounds rather comical, that God has specially appointed me to this city, as though it were a large thorough-bred horse which because of its great size is inclined to be lazy and needs the stimulation of some stinging fly. It seems to me that God has attached me to this city to perform the office of such a fly, and all day long I never cease to settle here, there, and everywhere, rousing, persuading, reproving every one of you. You will not easily find another like me, gentlemen, and if you take my advice you will spare my life. I suspect, however, that before long you will awake from your drowsing, and in your annoyance you will take Anytus' advice and finish me off with a single slap, and then you will go on sleeping till the end of your days, unless God in his care for you sends someone to take my place. [...]

[*The jury now gives its verdict of guilty, and Meletus asks for the penalty of death.*]

There are a great many reasons, gentlemen, why I am not distressed by this result – I mean your condemnation of me – but the chief reason is that the result was not unexpected. What does surprise me is the number of votes cast on the two sides. I should never have believed that it would be such a close thing, but now it seems that if a mere thirty votes had gone the other way, I should have been acquitted. Even as it is, I feel that so far as Meletus' part is concerned I have been acquitted, and not only that, but anyone can see that if Anytus and Lycon had not come forward to accuse me, Meletus would actually have forfeited his one thousand drachmas for not having obtained one fifth of the votes.

However, we must face the fact that he demands the death penalty. Very good. What alternative penalty shall I propose to you, gentlemen? Obviously it must be adequate. Well, what penalty do I deserve to pay or suffer, in view of what I have done?

I have never lived an ordinary quiet life. I did not care for the things that most people care about – making money, having a comfortable home, high military or civil rank, and all the other activities, political appointments, secret societies, party organizations, which go on in our city. I thought that I was really too strict in my principles to survive if I went in for this sort of thing. So instead of taking a course which would have done no good either to you or to me, I set myself to do you individually in private what I hold to be the greatest possible service. I tried to persuade each one of you not to think more of practical advantages than of his mental and moral well-being, or in general to think more of advantage than of well-being in the case of the state or of anything else. What do I deserve for behaving in this way? Some reward, gentlemen, if I am bound to suggest what I really deserve, and what is more, a reward which would be appropriate for myself. Well, what is appropriate for a poor man who is a public benefactor and who requires leisure for giving you moral encouragement? Nothing could be more appropriate for such a person than free maintenance at the state's expense. He deserves it much more than any victor in the races at Olympia, whether he wins with a single horse or a pair or a team of four. These people give you the semblance of success, but I give you the reality; they do not need maintenance, but I do. So if I am to suggest an appropriate penalty which is strictly in accordance with justice, I suggest free maintenance by the state.

Perhaps when I say this I may give you the impression, as I did in my remarks about exciting sympathy and making passionate appeals, that I am showing a deliberate perversity. That is not so, gentlemen. The real position is this. I am convinced that I never wrong anyone intentionally, but I cannot convince you of this, because we have had so little time for discussion. If it was your practice, as it is with other nations, to give not one day but several to the hearing of capital trials, I believe that you might have been convinced, but under present conditions it is not easy to dispose of grave allegations in a short space of time. So, being convinced that I do no wrong to anybody, I can hardly be expected to wrong myself by asserting that I deserve something bad, or by proposing a corresponding penalty. Why should I? For fear of suffering this penalty proposed by

Meletus, when, as I said, I do not know whether it is a good thing or a bad? Do you expect me to choose something which I know very well is bad by making my counterproposal? Imprisonment? Why should I spend my days in prison, in subjection to the periodically appointed officers of the law? A fine, with imprisonment until it is paid? In my case the effect would be just the same, because I have no money to pay a fine. Or shall I suggest banishment? You would very likely accept the suggestion.

I should have to be desperately in love with life to do that, gentlemen. I am not so blind that I cannot see that you, my fellow citizens, have come to the end of your patience with my discussions and conversations. You have found them too irksome and irritating, and now you are trying to get rid of them. Will any other people find them easy to put up with? That is most unlikely, gentlemen. A fine life I should have if I left this country at my age and spent the rest of my days trying one city after another and being turned out every time! I know very well that wherever I go the young people will listen to my conversation just as they do here, and if I try to keep them off, they will make their elders drive me out, while if I do not, the fathers and other relatives will drive me out of their own accord for the sake of the young.

Perhaps someone may say, But surely, Socrates, after you have left us you can spend the rest of your life in quietly minding your own business.

This is the hardest thing of all to make some of you understand. If I say that this would be disobedience to God, and that is why I cannot 'mind my own business,' you will not believe that I am serious. If on the other hand I tell you that to let no day pass without discussing goodness and all the other subjects about which you hear me talking and examining both myself and others is really the very best thing that a man can do, and that life without this sort of examination is not worth living, you will be even less inclined to believe me. Nevertheless that is how it is, gentlemen, as I maintain, though it is not easy to convince you of it. Besides, I am not accustomed to think of myself as deserving punishment. If I had money, I would have suggested a fine that I could afford, because that would not have done me any harm. As it is, I cannot, because I have none, unless of course you like to fix the penalty at what I could pay. I suppose I could probably afford a mina. I suggest a fine of that amount.

One moment, gentlemen. Plato here, and Crito and Critobulus and Apollodorus, want me to propose thirty minas, on their security. Very well, I agree to this sum, and you can rely upon these gentlemen for its payment.

Well, gentlemen, for the sake of a very small gain in time you are going to earn the reputation – and the blame from those who wish to disparage our city – of having put Socrates to death, 'that wise man' – because they will say I am wise even if I am not, these people who want to find fault with you. If you had waited just a little while, you would have had your way in the course of nature. You can see that I am well on in life and near to death. I am saying this not to all of you but to those who voted for my execution, and I have something else to say to them as well.

No doubt you think, gentlemen, that I have been condemned for lack of the arguments which I could have used if I had thought it right to leave nothing unsaid or undone to secure my acquittal. But that is very far from the truth. It is not a lack of arguments that has caused my condemnation, but a lack of effrontery and impudence, and the fact that I have refused to address you in the way which would give you most pleasure. You would have liked to hear me weep and wail, doing and saying all sorts of things which I regard as unworthy of myself, but which you are used to hearing from other people. But I did not think then that I ought to stoop to servility because I was in danger, and I do not regret now the way in which I pleaded my case. I would much rather die as the result of this defense than live as the result of the other sort. In a court of law, just as in warfare, neither I nor any other ought to use his wits to escape death by any means. In battle it is often obvious that you could escape being killed by giving up your arms and throwing yourself upon the mercy of your pursuers, and in every kind of danger there are plenty of devices for avoiding death if you are unscrupulous enough to stick at nothing. But I suggest, gentlemen, that the difficulty is not so much to escape death; the real difficulty is to escape from doing wrong, which is far more fleet of foot. In this present instance I, the slow old man, have been overtaken by the slower of the two, but my accusers, who are clever and quick, have been overtaken by the faster – by iniquity. When I leave this court I shall go away condemned by you to death, but they will go away convicted by truth herself of depravity and wickedness. And they accept their sentence even as I accept mine. No doubt it was bound to be so, and I think that the result is fair enough.

Having said so much, I feel moved to prophesy to you who have given your vote against me, for I am now at that point where the gift of prophecy comes most readily to men – at the point of death. I tell you, my executioners, that as soon as I am dead, vengeance shall fall upon you with a punishment far more painful than your killing of me. You have brought about my death in the belief that through it you will be delivered from submitting your conduct to criticism, but I say that the result will be just the opposite. You will have more critics, whom up till now I have restrained without your knowing it, and being younger they will be harsher to you and will cause you more annoyance. If you expect to stop denunciation of your wrong way of life by putting people to death, there is something amiss with your reasoning. This way of escape is neither possible nor creditable. The best and easiest way is not to stop the mouths of others, but to make yourselves as good men as you can. This is my last message to you who voted for my condemnation.

As for you who voted for my acquittal, I should very much like to say a few words to reconcile you to the result, while the officials are busy and I am not yet on my way to the place where I must die. I ask you, gentlemen, to spare me these few moments. There is no reason why we should not exchange fancies while the law permits. I look upon you as my friends, and I want you to understand the right way of regarding my present position.

Gentlemen of the jury – for *you* deserve to be so called – I have had a remarkable experience. In the past the prophetic voice to which I have become accustomed has always been my constant companion, opposing me even in quite trivial things if I was going to take the wrong course. Now something has happened to me, as you can see, which might be thought and is commonly considered to be a supreme calamity; yet neither when I left home this morning, nor when I was taking my place here in the court, nor at any point in any part of my speech did the divine sign oppose me. In other discussions it has often checked me in the middle of a sentence, but this time it has never opposed me in any part of this business in anything that I have said or done. What do I suppose to be the explanation? I will tell you. I suspect that this thing that has happened to me is a blessing, and we are quite mistaken in supposing death to be an evil. I have good grounds for thinking this, because my accustomed sign could not have failed to oppose me if what I was doing had not been sure to bring some good result.

We should reflect that there is much reason to hope for a good result on other grounds as well. Death is one of two things. Either it is annihilation, and the dead have no consciousness of anything, or, as we are told, it is really a change – a migration of the soul from this place to another. Now if there is no consciousness but only a dreamless sleep, death must be a marvelous gain. I suppose that if anyone were told to pick out the night on which he slept so soundly as not even to dream, and then to compare it with all the other nights and days of his life, and then were told to say, after due consideration, how many better and happier days and nights than this he had spent in the course of his life – well, I think that the Great King himself, to say nothing of any private person, would find these days and nights easy to count in comparison with the rest. If death is like this, then, I call it gain, because the whole of time, if you look at it in this way, can be regarded as no more than one single night. If on the other hand death is a removal from here to some other place, and if what we are told is true, that all the dead are there, what greater blessing could there be than this, gentlemen? If on arrival in the other world, beyond the reach of our so-called justice, one will find there the true judges who are said to preside in those courts, Minos and Rhadamanthus and Aeacus and Triptolemus and all those other half-divinities who were upright in their earthly life, would that be an unrewarding journey? Put it in this way. How much would one of you give to meet Orpheus and Musaeus, Hesiod and Homer? I am willing to die ten times over if this account is true. It would be a specially interesting experience for me to join them there, to meet Palamedes and Ajax, the son of Telamon, and any other heroes of the old days who met their death through an unfair trial, and to compare my fortunes with theirs – it would be rather amusing, I think. And above all I should like to spend my time there, as here, in examining and searching people's minds, to find out who is really wise among them, and who only thinks that he is. What would one not give, gentlemen, to be able to question the leader of that great host against Troy, or Odysseus, or Sisyphus, or the thousands of other men and women whom one could mention, to talk and mix and argue with whom would be unimaginable happiness? At any rate I presume that they do not put one to death there for such conduct, because apart from the other happiness in which their world surpasses ours, they are now immortal for the rest of time, if what we are told is true.

You too, gentlemen of the jury, must look forward to death with confidence, and fix your minds on this one belief, which is certain – that nothing can harm a good man either in life or after death, and his fortunes are not a matter of indifference to the gods. This present experience of mine has not come about mechanically. I am quite clear that the time had come when it was better for me to die and be released from my distractions. That is why my sign never turned me back. For my own part I bear no grudge at all against those who condemned me and accused me, although it was not with this kind intention that they did so, but because they thought that they were hurting me; and that is culpable of them. However, I ask them to grant me one favor. When my sons grow up, gentlemen, if you think that they are putting money or anything else before goodness, take your revenge by plaguing them as I plagued you; and if they fancy themselves for no reason, you must scold them just as I scolded you, for neglecting the important things and thinking that they are good for something when they are good for nothing. If you do this, I shall have had justice at your hands, both I myself and my children.

Now it is time that we were going, I to die and you to live, but which of us has the happier prospect is unknown to anyone but God.

Note

1   *Iliad* 18.96 sq.

2

Diogenes Laertius, from *Pyrrho*

The following selection is taken from the life of Pyrrho included in *The Lives and Opinions of Eminent Philosophers* by Diogenes Laertius. Diogenes probably lived in the third century CE. His *Lives* is a compilation of stories, facts, and ideas culled from many sources, few of which are extant. His use of these sources appears to be quite uncritical, and, for this reason, his accuracy has been frequently questioned. His text was recovered and translated into Latin in the fifteenth century and was used as an authority by many subsequent writers. Even if nothing he says about Pyrrho is true, the ideas he presents have had extraordinary influence on modern thought.

Pyrrho is thought to have lived in the fourth century BCE. It seems that he wrote nothing, and there is little reliable information about him. Subsequent writers have used the term "Pyrrhonism" to refer to a set of skeptical ideas that have become associated with his name. Whether or not the selection below is an accurate rendition of what Pyrrho really thought, it contains an outline of the basic tenets of a skeptical philosophy that had a significant impact upon modern philosophy.

According to Diogenes' account, the Pyrrhonists or skeptics rejected the dogmas of all the philosophical schools, and they formulated no dogmas of their own. They claimed that each view put forward on a philosophical problem is no more or no less probable than contrary views. They offered many arguments to support their doubts, including the ten modes of perplexity and the five additional modes said to be added by Agrippa. Because the appearances produced by the senses are relative to the conditions of perception, they cannot be relied upon to reveal the underlying nature of material things. The Pyrrhonists also adopted a form of ethical relativism according to which moral values vary according to the customs of the country. They also provided powerful arguments to show that there could be no reliable criterion of truth and reality and that there is no non-circular way of establishing the truth of anything by means of proof. Their dogmatic opponents made them aware that their doubts about everything tended to undermine their own arguments, and so they tried to formulate their point of view to avoid this effort at self-referential refutation. The Pyrrhonists concluded that although one can have knowledge about how things appear, one can know nothing about the underlying reality; therefore one should simply suspend judgment, from which tranquillity of mind will follow.

The Sceptics, then, were constantly engaged in overthrowing the dogmas of all schools, but enuntiated none themselves; and though they would go so far as to bring forward and expound the dogmas of the others, they themselves laid down nothing definitely, not even the laying down of nothing. So much so that they even refuted their laying down of nothing, saying, for instance, "We determine nothing," since otherwise they would have been betrayed into determining; but we put forward, say they, all the theories for the purpose of indicating our unprecipitate attitude, precisely as we might have done if we had actually assented to them. [...]

Thus the Pyrrhonean principle, as Aenesidemus says in the introduction to his *Pyrrhonics*, is but a report on phenomena or on any kind of judgement, a report in which all things are brought to bear on one another, and in the comparison are found to present much anomaly and confusion. As to the contradictions in their doubts, they would first show the ways in which things gain credence, and then by the same methods they would destroy belief in them; for they say those things gain credence which either the senses are agreed upon or which never or at least rarely change, as well as things which become habitual or are determined by law and those which please or excite wonder. They showed, then, on the basis of that which is contrary to what induces belief, that the probabilities on both sides are equal.

Perplexities arise from the agreements between appearances or judgements, and these perplexities they distinguished under ten different modes in which the subjects in question appeared to vary. The following are the ten modes laid down.

The *first* mode relates to the differences between living creatures in respect of those things which give them pleasure or pain, or are useful or harmful to them. By this it is inferred that they do not receive the same impressions from the same things, with the result that such a conflict necessarily leads to suspension of judgement. For some creatures multiply without intercourse, for example, creatures that live in fire, the Arabian phoenix and worms; others by union, such as man and the rest. Some are distinguished in one way, some in another, and for this reason they differ in their senses also, hawks for instance being most keen-sighted, and dogs having a most acute sense of smell. It is natural that if the senses, e.g. eyes, of animals differ, so also will the impressions produced upon them; so to the goat vine-shoots are good to eat, to man they are bitter; the quail thrives on hemlock, which is fatal to man; the pig will eat ordure, the horse will not.

The *second* mode has reference to the natures and idiosyncrasies of men; for instance, Demophon, Alexander's butler, used to get warm in the shade and shiver in the sun. Andron of Argos is reported by Aristotle to have travelled across the waterless deserts of Libya without drinking. Moreover, one man fancies the profession of medicine, another farming, and another commerce; and the same ways of life are injurious to one man but beneficial to another; from which it follows that judgement must be suspended.

The *third* mode depends on the differences between the sense-channels in different cases, for an apple gives the impression of being pale yellow in colour to the sight, sweet in taste and fragrant in smell. An object of the same shape is made to appear different by differences in the mirrors reflecting it. Thus it follows that what appears is no more such and such a thing than something different.

The *fourth* mode is that due to differences of condition and to changes in general; for instance, health, illness, sleep, waking, joy, sorrow, youth, old age, courage, fear, want, fullness, hate, love, heat, cold, to say nothing of breathing freely and having the passages obstructed. The impressions received thus appear to vary according to the nature of the conditions. Nay, even the state of madmen is not contrary to nature; for why should their state be so more than ours? Even to our view the sun has the appearance of standing still. And Theon of Tithorea used to go to bed and walk in his sleep, while Pericles' slave did the same on the housetop.

The *fifth* mode is derived from customs, laws, belief in myths, compacts between nations and dogmatic assumptions. This class includes considerations with regard to things beautiful and ugly, true and false, good and bad, with regard to the gods, and with regard to the coming into being and the passing away of the world of phenomena. Obviously the same thing is regarded by some as just and by others as unjust, or as good by some and bad by others. Persians think it not unnatural for a man to marry his daughter; to Greeks it is unlawful. The Massagetae, acording to Eudoxus in the first book of his *Voyage round the World*, have their wives in common; the Greeks have not. The Cilicians used to delight in piracy; not so the Greeks. Different people believe in different gods; some in providence, others not. In burying their dead, the Egyptians embalm them; the Romans burn them; the Paeonians throw them into lakes. As to what is true, then, let suspension of judgement be our practice.

The *sixth* mode relates to mixtures and participations, by virtue of which nothing appears pure in and by itself, but only in combination with air, light, moisture, solidity, heat, cold, movement, exhalations and other forces. For purple shows different tints in sunlight, moonlight, and lamplight; and our own complexion does not appear the same at noon and when the sun is low. Again, a rock which in air takes two men to lift is easily moved about in water, either because, being in reality heavy, it is lifted by the water or because, being light, it is made heavy by the air. Of its own inherent property we know nothing, any more than of the constituent oils in an ointment.

The *seventh* mode has reference to distances, positions, places and the occupants of the places. In this mode things which are thought to be large appear small, square things round; flat things appear to have projections, straight things to be bent, and colourless coloured. So the sun, on account of its distance, appears small, mountains when far away appear misty and smooth, but when near at hand rugged. Furthermore, the sun at its rising has a certain appearance, but has a dissimilar appearance when in mid-heaven, and the same body one appearance in a wood and another in open country. The image again varies according to the position of the object, and a dove's neck according to the way it is turned. Since, then, it is not possible to observe these things apart from places and positions, their real nature is unknowable.

The *eighth* mode is concerned with quantities and qualities of things, say heat or cold, swiftness or slowness, colourlessness or variety of colours. Thus wine taken in moderation strengthens the body, but too much of it is weakening; and so with food and other things.

The *ninth* mode has to do with perpetuity, strangeness, or rarity. Thus earthquakes are no surprise to those among whom they constantly take place; nor is the sun, for it is seen every day. This ninth mode is put eighth by Favorinus and tenth by Sextus and Aenesidemus; moreover the tenth is put eighth by Sextus and ninth by Favorinus.

The *tenth* mode rests on inter-relation, e.g. between light and heavy, strong and weak, greater and less, up and down. Thus that which is on the right is not so by nature, but is so understood in virtue of its position with respect to something else; for, if that change its position, the thing is no longer on the right. Similarly father and brother are relative terms, day is relative to the sun, and all things relative to our mind. Thus relative terms are in and by themselves unknowable. These, then, are the ten modes of perplexity.

But Agrippa and his school add to them five other modes, resulting respectively from disagreement, extension *ad infinitum*, relativity, hypothesis and reciprocal inference. The mode arising from disagreement proves, with regard to any inquiry whether in philosophy or in everyday life, that it is full of the utmost contentiousness and confusion. The mode which involves extension *ad infinitum* refuses to admit that what is sought to be proved is firmly established, because one thing furnishes the ground for belief in another, and so on *ad infinitum*. The mode derived from relativity declares that a thing can never be apprehended in and by itself, but only in connexion with something else. Hence all things are unknowable. The mode resulting from hypothesis arises when people suppose that you must take the most elementary of things as of themselves entitled to credence, instead of postulating them: which is useless, because some one else will adopt the contrary hypothesis. The mode arising from reciprocal inference is found whenever that which should be confirmatory of the thing requiring to be proved itself has to borrow credit from the latter, as, for example, if anyone seeking to establish the existence of pores on the ground that emanations take place should take this (the existence of pores) as proof that there are emanations.

They would deny all demonstration, criterion, sign, cause, motion, the process of learning, coming into being, or that there is anything good or bad by nature. For all demonstration, say they, is constructed out of things either already proved or indemonstrable. If out of things already proved, those things too will require some demonstration, and so on *ad infinitum*; if out of things indemonstrable, then, whether all or some or only a single one of the steps are the subject of doubt, the whole is indemonstrable. If you think, they add, that there are some things which need no demonstration, yours must be a rare intellect, not to see that you must first have demonstration of the very fact that the things you refer to carry conviction in themselves. Nor must we prove that the elements are four from the fact that the elements are four. Besides, if we discredit particular demonstrations, we cannot accept the generalization from them. And in order that we may know that an argument constitutes a demonstration, we require a criterion; but again, in order that we may know that it is a criterion we require a demonstration; hence both the one and the other are incomprehensible, since each is referred to the other. How then are we to grasp the things which are uncertain, seeing that we know no demonstration? For what we wish to ascertain is not whether things appear to be such and such, but whether they are so in their essence. . . .

We must not assume that what convinces us is actually true. For the same thing does not convince every one, nor even the same people always. Persuasiveness sometimes depends on external circumstances, on the reputation of the speaker, on his ability as a thinker or his artfulness, on the familiarity or the pleasantness of the topic.

Again, they would destroy the criterion by reasoning of this kind. Even the criterion has either been critically determined or not. If it has not, it is definitely untrustworthy, and in its purpose of distinguishing is no more true than false. If it has, it will belong to the class of particular judgements, so that one and the same thing determines and is determined, and the criterion which has determined will have to be determined by another, that other by another, and so on *ad infinitum*. In addition to this there is disagreement as to the criterion, some holding that man is the criterion, while for some it is the senses, for others reason, for others the apprehensive presentation. Now man disagrees with man and with himself, as is shown by differences of laws and customs. The senses deceive, and reason says different things. Finally, the apprehensive presentation is judged by the mind, and the mind itself changes in various ways. Hence the criterion is unknowable, and consequently truth also.

The dogmatists answer them by declaring that the Sceptics themselves do apprehend and dogmatize; for when they are thought to be refuting their hardest they do apprehend, for at the very same time they are asseverating and dogmatizing. Thus even when they declare that they determine nothing, and that to every argument there is an opposite argument, they are actually determining these very points and dogmatizing. The others reply, "We confess to human weaknesses; for we recognize that it is day and that we are alive, and many other apparent facts in life; but with regard to the things about which our opponents argue so positively, claiming to have definitely apprehended them, we suspend our judgement because they are not certain, and confine knowledge to our impressions. For we admit that we see, and we recognize that we think this or that, but how we see or how we think we know not. And we say in conversation that a certain thing appears white, but we are not positive that it really is white. As to our 'We determine nothing' and the like, we use the expressions in an undogmatic sense, for they are not like the assertion that the world is spherical. Indeed the latter statement is not certain, but the others are mere admissions. Thus in saying 'We determine nothing,' we are *not* determining even that."

Again, the dogmatic philosophers maintain that the Sceptics do away with life itself, in that they reject all that life consists in. The others say this is false, for they do not deny that we see; they only say that they do not know how we see. "We admit the apparent fact," say they, "without admitting that it really is what it appears to be." We also perceive that fire burns; as to whether it is its nature to burn, we suspend our judgement. We see that a man moves, and that he perishes; how it happens we do not know. We merely object to accepting the unknown substance behind phenomena.

3

Cicero, from *Academica*

Marcus Tullius Cicero (106–43 BCE) was a Roman statesman, orator, and philosopher. He wrote many philosophical works on a variety of topics. The selection below consists of a few passages from his *Academica*, a work whose main purpose is to defend against criticisms a version of skepticism associated with the New Academy, so called because of its alleged continuity with the Academy of Plato and the skepticism of Socrates. The argument against the possibility of knowledge that is cited on a number of occasions within this text is that it is possible that any sense experience that we think represents the world correctly exactly resembles one that does not; therefore, our sense experiences provide no certainty with regard to our beliefs about external reality because we have no way of distinguishing between true and false appearances. According to Cicero, although the New Academy denies the possibility of certainty, it does accept probability as a basis for conduct.

It was entirely with Zeno, so we have been told [...] that Arcesilas set on foot his battle, not from obstinacy or desire for victory, as it seems to me at all events, but because of the obscurity of the facts that had led Socrates to a confession of ignorance, as also previously his predecessors Democritus, Anaxagoras, Empedocles, and almost all the old philosophers, who utterly denied all possibility of cognition or perception or knowledge, and maintained that the senses are limited, the mind feeble, the span of life short, and that truth (in Democritus's phrase) is sunk in an abyss, opinion and custom are all-prevailing, no place is left for truth, all things successively are wrapped in darkness. Accordingly Arcesilas said that there is nothing that can be known, not even that residuum of knowledge that Socrates had left himself – the truth of this very dictum: so hidden in obscurity did he believe that everything lies, nor is there anything that can be perceived or understood, and for these reasons, he said, no one must make any positive statement or affirmation or give the approval of his assent to any proposition, and a man must always restrain his rashness and hold it back from every slip, as it would be glaring rashness to give assent either to a falsehood or to something not certainly known, and nothing is more disgraceful than for assent and approval to outstrip knowledge and perception. His practice was consistent with this theory – he led most of his hearers to accept it by arguing against the opinions of all men, so that when equally weighty reasons were found on opposite sides on the same subject, it was easier to withhold assent from either side. They call this school the New Academy – to me it seems old, at all events if we count Plato a member of the Old Academy, in whose books nothing is stated positively and there is much arguing both *pro* and *contra*, all things are inquired into and no certain statement is made; but nevertheless let the Academy that you expounded be named the Old and this one the New. [...]

No presentation proceeding from a true object is such that a presentation proceeding from a false one might not also be of the same form. This is the one argument that has held the field down to the present day. [...] There are four heads of argument intended to prove that there is nothing that can be known, perceived or comprehended, which is the subject of all this debate: the first of these arguments is that there is such a thing as a false presentation; the second, that a false presentation cannot be perceived; the third, that of presentations between which there is no difference it is impossible for some to be able to be perceived and others not; the fourth, that there is no true presentation originating from sensation with which there is not ranged another presentation that precisely corresponds to it and that cannot be perceived. The second and third of these four arguments are admitted by everybody; the first is not granted by Epicurus, but you with whom we are dealing admit that one too; the entire battle is about the fourth. If therefore a person looking at Publius Servilius Geminus used to think he saw Quintus, he was encountering a presentation of a sort that could not be perceived, because there was no mark to distinguish a true presentation from a false one; and if that mode of distinguishing were removed, what mark would he have, of such a sort that it could not be false, to help him to recognize Gaius Cotta, who was twice consul with Geminus? You say that so great a degree of resemblance does not exist in the world. You show fight, no doubt, but you have an easy-going opponent; let us grant by all means that it does not exist, but undoubtedly it can appear to exist, and therefore it will cheat the sense, and if a single case of resemblance has done that, it will have made everything doubtful; for when that proper canon of recognition has been removed, even if the man himself whom you see is the man he appears to you to be, nevertheless you will not make that judgement, as you say it ought to be made, by means of a mark of such a sort that a false likeness could not have the same character. [. . .]

Even many sense-percepts must be deemed probable, if only it be held in mind that no sense-presentation has such a character as a false presentation could not also have without differing from it at all. Thus the wise man will make use of whatever apparently probable presentation he encounters, if nothing presents itself that is contrary to that probability, and his whole plan of life will be charted out in this manner. In fact even the person whom your school brings on the stage as the wise man follows many things probable, that he has not grasped nor perceived nor assented to but that possess verisimilitude; and if he were not to approve them, all life would be done away with. Another point: when a wise man is going on board a ship surely he has not got the knowledge already grasped in his mind and perceived that he will make the voyage as he intends? how can he have it? But if for instance he were setting out from here to Puteoli, a distance of four miles, with a reliable crew and a good helmsman and in the present calm weather, it would appear probable that he would get there safe. He will therefore be guided by presentations of this sort to adopt plans of action and of inaction. [. . .]

For you see now that I do admit the existence of some truth, nevertheless I deny that they are grasped and perceived. [. . .] But I return to the mind and the body. Pray are we sufficiently acquainted with the nature of the sinews and the veins? do we grasp what mind is, where it is, and in fine whether it exists, or, as Dicaearchus held, does not even exist at all? If it does, do we know if it has three parts, as Plato held, reason, passion and appetite, or is a simple unity? if simple, whether it is fire or breath or blood, or, as Xenocrates said, an incorporeal numerical formula (a thing the very nature of which is almost unintelligible)? and whatever it is, whether it is mortal or everlasting? for many arguments are put forward on both sides. Some part of these matters seems to your wise man to be certain, but ours has not a notion even what part is most probable, to such an extent do most of these matters contain equal reasons for contrary theories. [. . .]

Do you people therefore suppose that when I am listening to these and countless other things, I am quite unaffected? I am just as much affected as you are, Lucullus, pray don't think that I am less a human being than yourself. The only difference is that whereas you, when you have been deeply affected, acquiesce, assent, approve, hold that the fact is certain, comprehended, perceived, ratified, firm, fixed, and are unable to be driven or moved away from it by any reason, I on the contrary am of the opinion that there is nothing of such a kind that if I assent to it I shall not often be assenting to a falsehood, since truths are not separated from falsehoods by any distinction, especially as those logical criteria of yours are non-existent.

4

Sextus Empiricus, from *Outlines of Pyrrhonism*

Hardly anything is known about the life of Sextus Empiricus. It is surmised that he lived in the second century CE. He wrote in Greek. He identified his views with those of the Pyrrhonist tradition of skepticism, and his best-known work, *Outlines of Pyrrhonism*, from which these selections are taken, contains a collection of almost all the arguments that skeptics have ever offered to show that we do not possess the knowledge we think we possess, together with a critique of the major dogmatic philosophies of his time, particularly Stoicism and Epicureanism. The *Outlines* was not known to medieval philosophers but surfaced in the sixteenth century and had an enormous impact on subsequent philosophy. Although Sextus' writings are not ranked by historians of philosophy alongside such philosophical peaks as the works of Plato and Aristotle, the *Outlines* is a great work of philosophy and contains a coherent skeptical point of view. It is also one of the principal sources for our knowledge of the other traditions that Sextus classified as dogmatic.

For Sextus, Pyrrhonism is not just an epistemological doctrine but a way of life based upon reflection about the possibility of knowledge. In attempting to determine which of the competing doctrines offered by dogmatic systems of philosophy is correct, the Pyrrhonist discovers that any argument that supports any particular doctrine is matched by arguments that refute it. This equality of arguments pro and con applies not only to philosophical disagreements, but also to our religious, ethical, and common-sense beliefs. Whatever supports any belief is canceled by considerations that tend to refute it.

The Pyrrhonist concludes that the only thing for him to do is to suspend his judgment, since there is no more reason to assent to any proposition than to deny it. He discovers that as soon as he gives up trying to discover the truth about anything, he becomes tranquil, his anxieties disappear, and he finds peace of mind and contentment. Instead of trying to support a conception of human well-being by developing a theory of the nature of reality, as the dogmatic philosophers did, the skeptic comes upon well-being by shedding all such theories.

The dogmatic philosophers reply by trying to show that skepticism itself is a theory, that it makes assertions and assents to various propositions, and that it thereby contradicts itself. After all, the skeptic seems to be saying that we do not possess the knowledge we think we have, so he assents to this proposition at least, and thus contradicts his refusal to assent to anything. Sextus replies that skepticism is not a theory about anything; the skeptic asserts nothing except that things appear puzzling to him. Skepticism is an account of how things appear to the skeptic after he has surveyed the arguments pro and con for any belief. Sextus allows that we have knowledge about how things appear to us, about our sense impressions and other subjective states, but refuses to assent to any proposition about external realities. In fact, he sometimes questions whether any such proposition is intelligible.

In the selections below, in addition to a general characterization of the skeptical outlook, we find texts about the unreliability of sense-perception and of inductive inference; we find reasons for thinking that we cannot establish any criterion of truth; we find arguments in favor of ethical relativism; and there is even a passage about dreams that anticipates the skeptical use of dreams that we find later in Montaigne and Descartes.

Scepticism is an ability, or mental attitude, which opposes appearances to judgements in any way whatsoever, with the result that, owing to the equipollence of the objects and reasons thus opposed, we are brought firstly to a state of mental suspense and next to a state of "unperturbedness" or quietude. Now we call it an "ability" not in any subtle sense, but simply in respect of its "being able." By "appearances" we now mean the objects of sense-perception, whence we contrast them with the objects of thought or "judgements." The phrase "in any way whatsoever" can be connected either with the word "ability," to make us take the word "ability," as we said, in its simple sense, or with the phrase "opposing appearances to judgements"; for inasmuch as we oppose these in a variety of ways – appearances to appearances, or judgements to judgements, or *alternando* appearances to judgements – in order to ensure the inclusion of all these antitheses we employ the phrase "in any way whatsoever." Or, again, we join "in any way whatsoever" to "appearances and judgements" in order that we may not have to inquire how the appearances appear or how the thought-objects are judged, but may take these terms in the simple sense. The phrase "opposed judgements" we do not employ in the sense of negations and affirmations only but simply as equivalent to "conflicting judgements." "Equipollence" we use of equality in respect of probability and improbability, to indicate that no one of the conflicting judgements takes precedence of any other as being more probable. "Suspense" is a state of mental rest owing to which we neither deny nor affirm anything. "Quietude" is an untroubled and tranquil condition of soul. And how quietude enters the soul along with suspension of judgement we shall explain in our chapter (XII.) "Concerning the End." [...]

The originating cause of Scepticism is, we say, the hope of attaining quietude. Men of talent, who were perturbed by the contradictions in things and in doubt as to which of the alternatives they ought to accept, were led on to inquire what is true in things and what false, hoping by the settlement of this question to attain quietude. The main basic principle of the Sceptic system is that of opposing to every proposition an equal proposition; for we believe that as a consequence of this we end by ceasing to dogmatize.

When we say that the Sceptic refrains from dogmatizing we do not use the term "dogma," as some do, in the broader sense of "approval of a thing" (for the Sceptic gives assent to the feelings which are the necessary results of sense-impressions, and he would not, for example, say when feeling hot or cold "I believe that I am not hot or cold"); but we say that "he does not dogmatize" using "dogma" in the sense, which some give it, of "assent to one of the non-evident objects of scientific inquiry"; for the Pyrrhonean philosopher assents to nothing that is non-evident. Moreover, even in the act of enunciating the Sceptic formulae concerning things non-evident – such as the formula "No more (one thing than another)," or the formula "I determine nothing," or any of the others which we shall presently mention – he does not dogmatize. For whereas the dogmatizer posits the things about which he is said to be dogmatizing as really existent, the Sceptic does not posit these formulae in any absolute sense; for he conceives that, just as the formula "All things are false" asserts the falsity of itself as well as of everything else, as does the formula "Nothing is true," so also the formula "No more" asserts that itself, like all the rest, is "No more (this than that)," and thus cancels itself along with the rest. And of the other formulae we say the same. If then, while the dogmatizer posits the matter of his dogma as substantial truth, the Sceptic enunciates his formulae so that they are virtually cancelled by themselves, he should not be said to dogmatize in his enunciation of them. And, most important of all, in his enunciation of these formulae he states what appears to himself and announces his own impression in an undogmatic way, without making any positive assertion regarding the external realities. [...]

We follow the same lines in replying to the question "Has the Sceptic a doctrinal rule?" For if one defines a "doctrinal rule" as "adherence to a number of dogmas which are dependent both on one another and on appearances," and defines "dogma" as "assent to a non-evident proposition," then we shall say that he has not a doctrinal rule. But if one defines "doctrinal rule" as "procedure which, in accordance with appearance, follows a certain line of reasoning, that reasoning indicating how it is possible to seem to live rightly (the word 'rightly' being taken, not as referring to virtue only, but in a wider sense) and tending to enable one to suspend judgement," then we say that he has a doctrinal rule. For we follow a line of reasoning which, in accordance with appearances, points us to a life conformable to the customs of our country and its laws and institutions, and to our own instinctive feelings. [...]

Those who say that "the Sceptics abolish appearances," or phenomena, seem to me to be unacquainted with the statements of our School. For, as we said above, we do not overthrow the affective sense-impressions which induce our assent involuntarily; and these impressions are "the appearances." And when we question whether the underlying object is such as it appears, we grant the fact that it appears, and our doubt does not concern the appearance itself but the account given of that appearance – and that is a different thing from questioning the appearance itself. For example, honey appears to us to be sweet (and this we grant, for we perceive sweetness through the senses), but whether it is also sweet in its essence is for us a matter of doubt, since this is not an appearance but a judgement regarding the appearance. And even if we do actually argue against the appearances, we do not propound such arguments with the intention of abolishing appearances, but by way of pointing out the rashness of the Dogmatists; for if reason is such a trickster as to all but snatch away the appearances from under our very eyes, surely we should view it with suspicion in the case of things non-evident so as not to display rashness by following it.

That we adhere to appearances is plain from what we say about the Criterion of the Sceptic School. The word "Criterion" is used in two senses: in the one it means "the standard regulating belief in reality or unreality" (and this we shall discuss in our refutation); in the other it denotes the standard of action by conforming to which in the conduct of life we perform some actions and abstain from others; and it is of the latter that we are now speaking. The criterion, then, of the Sceptic School is, we say, the appearance, giving this name to what is virtually the sense-presentation. For since this lies in feeling and involuntary affection, it is not open to question. Consequently, no one, I suppose, disputes that the underlying object has this or that appearance; the point in dispute is whether the object is in reality such as it appears to be.

Adhering, then, to appearances we live in accordance with the normal rules of life, undogmatically, seeing that we cannot remain wholly inactive. And it would seem that this regulation of life is fourfold, and that one part of it lies in the guidance of Nature, another in the constraint of the passions, another in the tradition of laws and customs, another in the instruction of the arts. Nature's guidance is that by which we are naturally capable of sensation and thought; constraint of the passions is that whereby hunger drives us to food and thirst to drink; tradition of customs and laws, that whereby we regard piety in the conduct of life as good, but impiety as evil; instruction of the arts, that whereby we are not inactive in such arts as we adopt. But we make all these statements undogmatically.

Our next subject will be the End of the Sceptic system. Now an "End" is "that for which all actions or reasonings are undertaken, while it exists for the sake of none"; or, otherwise, "the ultimate object of appetency." We assert still that the Sceptic's End is quietude in respect of matters of opinion and moderate feeling in respect of things unavoidable. For the Sceptic, having set out to philosophize with the object of passing judgement on the sense-impressions and ascertaining which of them are true and which false, so as to attain quietude thereby, found himself involved in contradictions of equal weight, and being unable to decide between them suspended judgement; and as he was thus in suspense there followed, as it happened, the state of quietude in respect of matters of opinion. For the man who opines that anything is by nature good or bad is for ever being disquieted: when he is without the things which he deems good he believes himself to be tormented by things naturally bad and he pursues after the things which are, as he thinks, good; which when he has obtained he keeps falling into still more perturbations because of his irrational and immoderate elation, and in his dread of a change of fortune he uses every endeavour to avoid losing the things which he deems good. On the other hand, the man who determines nothing as to what is naturally good or bad neither shuns nor pursues anything eagerly; and, in consequence, he is unperturbed.

The Sceptic, in fact, had the same experience which is said to have befallen the painter Apelles. Once, they say, when he was painting a horse and wished to represent in the painting the horse's foam, he was so unsuccessful that he gave up the attempt and flung at the picture the sponge on which he used to wipe the paints off his brush, and the mark of the sponge produced the effect of a horse's foam. So, too, the Sceptics were in hopes of gaining quietude by means of a decision regarding the disparity of the objects of sense and of thought, and being unable to effect this they suspended judgement; and they found that quietude, as if by chance, followed upon their suspense, even as a shadow follows its substance. We do not, however, suppose that the Sceptic is wholly untroubled; but we say that he is troubled by things unavoidable; for we grant that he is cold at times and thirsty, and suffers various affections of that kind. But even in these cases, whereas ordinary people are afflicted by two circumstances – namely, by the affections themselves and, in no less a degree, by the belief that these conditions are evil by nature – the Sceptic, by his rejection of the added belief in the natural badness of all these conditions, escapes here too with less discomfort. Hence we say that, while in regard to matters of opinion the Sceptic's End is quietude, in regard to things unavoidable it is "moderate affection." But some notable Sceptics have added the further definition "suspension of judgement in investigations." [...]

But if the same things appear different owing to the variety in animals, we shall, indeed, be able to state our own impressions of the real object, but as to its essential nature we shall suspend judgement. For we cannot ourselves judge between our own impressions and those of the other animals, since we ourselves are involved in the dispute and are, therefore, rather in need of a judge than competent to pass judgement ourselves. [...]

Seeing, then, that choice and avoidance depend on pleasure and displeasure, while pleasure and displeasure depend on sensation and sense-impression, whenever some men choose the very things which are avoided by others, it is logical for us to conclude that they are also differently affected by the same things, since otherwise they would all alike have chosen or avoided the same things. But if the same objects affect men differently owing to the differences in the men, then, on this ground also, we shall reasonably be led to suspension of judgement. For while we are, no doubt, able to state what each of the underlying objects appears to be, relatively to each difference, we are incapable of explaining what it is in reality. For we shall have to believe either all men or some. But if we believe all, we shall be attempting the impossible and accepting contradictories; and if some, let us be told whose opinions we are to endorse. For the Platonist will say "Plato's"; the Epicurean, "Epicurus's"; and so on with the rest; and thus by their unsettled disputations they will bring us round again to a state of suspense. Moreover, he who maintains that we ought to assent to the majority is making a childish proposal, since no one is able to visit the whole of mankind and determine what pleases the majority of them; for there may possibly be races of whom we know nothing amongst whom conditions rare with us are common, and conditions common with us rare – possibly, for instance, most of them feel no pain from the bites of spiders, though a few on rare occasions feel such pain; and so likewise with the rest of the "idiosyncrasies" mentioned above. Necessarily, therefore, the differences in men afford a further reason for bringing in suspension of judgement. [...]

Let us imagine a man who possesses from birth the senses of touch, taste and smell, but can neither hear nor see. This man, then, will assume that nothing visible or audible has any existence, but only those three kinds of qualities which he is able to apprehend. Possibly, then, we also, having only our five senses, perceive only such of the apple's qualities as we are capable of apprehending; and possibly it may possess other underlying qualities which affect other sense-organs, though we, not being endowed with those organs, fail to apprehend the sense-objects which come through them.

"But," it may be objected, "Nature made the senses commensurate with the objects of sense." What kind of "Nature"? we ask, seeing that there exists so much unresolved controversy amongst the Dogmatists concerning the reality which belongs to Nature. For he who decides the question as to the existence of Nature will be discredited by them if he is an ordinary person, while if he is a philosopher he will be a party to the controversy and therefore himself subject to judgement and not a judge. If, however, it is possible that only those qualities which we seem to perceive subsist in the apple, or that a greater number subsist, or, again, that not even the qualities which affect us subsist, then it will be non-evident to us what the nature of the apple really is. And the same argument applies to all the other objects of sense. But if the senses do not apprehend external objects, neither can the mind apprehend them;

hence, because of this argument also, we shall be driven, it seems, to suspend judgement regarding the external underlying objects. [...]

Sleeping and waking, too, give rise to different impressions, since we do not imagine when awake what we imagine in sleep, nor when asleep what we imagine when awake; so that the existence or non-existence of our impressions is not absolute but relative, being in relation to our sleeping or waking condition. Probably, then, in dreams we see things which to our waking state are unreal, although not wholly unreal; for they exist in our dreams, just as waking realities exist although non-existent in dreams. [...]

In another way, too, the disagreement of such impressions is incapable of settlement. For he who prefers one impression to another, or one "circumstance" to another, does so either uncritically and without proof or critically and with proof; but he can do this neither without these means (for then he would be discredited) nor with them. For if he is to pass judgement on the impressions he must certainly judge them by a criterion; this criterion, then, he will declare to be true, or else false. But if false, he will be discredited; whereas, if he shall declare it to be true, he will be stating that the criterion is true either without proof or with proof. But if without proof, he will be discredited; and if with proof, it will certainly be necessary for the proof also to be true, to avoid being discredited. Shall he, then, affirm the truth of the proof adopted to establish the criterion after having judged it or without judging it? If without judging, he will be discredited; but if after judging, plainly he will say that he has judged it by a criterion; and of that criterion we shall ask for a proof, and of that proof again a criterion. For the proof always requires a criterion to confirm it, and the criterion also a proof to demonstrate its truth; and neither can a proof be sound without the previous existence of a true criterion nor can the criterion be true without the previous confirmation of the proof. So in this way both the criterion and the proof are involved in the circular process of reasoning, and thereby both are found to be untrustworthy; for since each of them is dependent on the credibility of the other, the one is lacking in credibility just as much as the other. Consequently, if a man can prefer one impression to another neither without a proof and a criterion nor with them, then the different impressions due to the differing conditions will admit of no settlement; so that as a result of this Mode also we are brought to suspend judgement regarding the nature of external realities. [...]

Since, then, all apparent objects are viewed in a certain place, and from a certain distance, or in a certain position, and each of these conditions produces a great divergency in the sense-impressions, as we mentioned above, we shall be compelled by this Mode also to end up in suspension of judgement. For in fact anyone who purposes to give the preference to any of these impressions will be attempting the impossible. For if he shall deliver his judgement simply and without proof, he will be discredited; and should he, on the other hand, desire to adduce proof, he will confute himself if he says that the proof is false, while if he asserts that the proof is true he will be asked for a proof of its truth, and again for a proof of this latter proof, since it also must be true, and so on *ad infinitum*. But to produce proofs to infinity is impossible; so that neither by the use of proofs will he be able to prefer one sense-impression to another. If, then, one cannot hope to pass judgement on the afore-mentioned impressions either with or without proof, the conclusion we are driven to is suspension; for while we can, no doubt, state the nature which each object appears to possess as viewed in a certain position or at a certain distance or in a certain place, what its real nature is we are, for the foregoing reasons, unable to declare. [...]

There is a *Tenth Mode*, which is mainly concerned with Ethics, being based on rules of conduct, habits, laws, legendary beliefs, and dogmatic conceptions. A rule of conduct is a choice of a way of life, or of a particular action, adopted by one person or many – by Diogenes, for instance, or the Laconians. A law is a written contract amongst the members of a State, the transgressor of which is punished. A habit or custom (the terms are equivalent) is the joint adoption of a certain kind of action by a number of men, the transgressor of which is not actually punished; for example, the law proscribes adultery, and custom with us forbids intercourse with a woman in public. Legendary belief is the acceptance of unhistorical and fictitious events, such as, amongst others, the legends about Cronos; for these stories win credence with many. Dogmatic conception is the acceptance of a fact which seems to be established by analogy or some form of demonstration, as, for example, that atoms are the elements of existing things, or homoeomeries, or *minima*, or something else.

And each of these we oppose now to itself, and now to each of the others. For example, we oppose habit to habit in this way: some of the Ethiopians tattoo their children, but we do not; and while the Persians think it seemly to wear a brightly dyed dress reaching to the feet, we think it unseemly; and whereas the Indians have intercourse with their women in public, most other races regard this as shameful. And law we oppose to law in this way: among the Romans the man who renounces his father's property does not pay his father's debts, but among the Rhodians he always pays them; and among the Scythian Tauri it was a law that strangers should be sacrificed to Artemis, but with us it is forbidden to slay a human being at the altar. And we oppose rule of conduct to rule of conduct, as when we oppose the rule of Diogenes to that of Aristippus or that of the Laconians to that of the Italians. And we oppose legendary belief to legendary belief when we say that whereas in one story the father of men and gods is alleged to be Zeus, in another he is Oceanos – "Ocean sire of the gods, and Tethys the mother that bare them." And we oppose dogmatic conceptions to one another when we say that some declare that there is one element only, others an infinite number; some that the soul is mortal, others that it is immortal; and some that human affairs are controlled by divine Providence, others without Providence. [. . .]

The phrase "I suspend judgement" we adopt in place of "I am unable to say which of the objects presented I ought to believe and which I ought to disbelieve," indicating that the objects appear to us equal as regards credibility and incredibility. As to whether they are equal we make no positive assertion; but what we state is what appears to us in regard to them at the time of observation. And the term "suspension" is derived from the fact of the mind being held up or "suspended" so that it neither affirms nor denies anything owing to the equipollence of the matters in question. [. . .]

When we say "To every argument an equal argument is opposed," we mean "to every argument" that has been investigated by us, and the word "argument" we use not in its simple sense, but of that which establishes a point dogmatically (that is to say with reference to what is non-evident) and establishes it by any method, and not necessarily by means of premises and a conclusion. We say "equal" with reference to credibility or incredibility, and we employ the word "opposed" in the general sense of "conflicting"; and we supply therewith in thought the phrase "as appears to me." So whenever I say "To every argument an equal argument is opposed," what I am virtually saying is "To every argument investigated by me which establishes a point dogmatically, it seems to me there is opposed another argument, establishing a point dogmatically, which is equal to the first in respect of credibility and incredibility"; so that the utterance of the phrase is not a piece of dogmatism, but the announcement of a human state of mind which is apparent to the person experiencing it. [. . .]

Of those, then, who have treated of the criterion some have declared that a criterion exists – the Stoics, for example, and certain others – while by some its existence is denied, as by the Corinthian Xeniades, amongst others, and by Xenophanes of Colophon, who says – "Over all things opinion bears sway"; while we have adopted suspension of judgement as to whether it does or does not exist. This dispute, then, they will declare to be either capable or incapable of decision; and if they shall say it is incapable of decision they will be granting on the spot the propriety of suspension of judgement, while if they say it admits of decision, let them tell us whereby it is to be decided, since we have no accepted criterion, and do not even know, but are still inquiring, whether any criterion exists. Besides, in order to decide the dispute which has arisen about the criterion, we must possess an accepted criterion by which we shall be able to judge the dispute; and in order to possess an accepted criterion, the dispute about the criterion must first be decided. And when the argument thus reduces itself to a form of circular reasoning the discovery of the criterion becomes impracticable, since we do not allow them to adopt a criterion by assumption, while if they offer to judge the criterion by a criterion we force them to a regress *ad infinitum*. And furthermore, since demonstration requires a demonstrated criterion, while the criterion requires an approved demonstration, they are forced into circular reasoning. [...]

Nor, again, is it possible to assert that the soul apprehends external realities by means of the affections of sense owing to the similarity of the affections of the senses to the external real objects. For how is the intellect to know whether the affections of the senses are similar to the objects of sense when it has not itself encountered the external objects, and the senses do not inform it about their real nature but only about their own affections, as I have argued from the Modes of Suspension? For just as the man who does not know Socrates but has seen a picture of him does not know whether the picture is like Socrates, so also the intellect when it gazes on the affections of the senses but does not behold the external objects will not so much as know whether the affections of the senses are similar to the external realities. So that not even on the ground of resemblance will he be able to judge these objects according to the presentation. [...]

It is also easy, I consider, to set aside the method of induction. For, when they propose to establish the universal from the particulars by means of induction, they will effect this by a review either of all or of some of the particular instances. But if they review some, the induction will be insecure, since some of the particulars omitted in the induction may contravene the universal; while if they are to review all, they will be toiling at the impossible, since the particulars are infinite and indefinite. Thus on both grounds, as I think, the consequence is that induction is invalidated.

5

René Descartes, "Meditation I"

Perhaps the most widely discussed example of radical global skepticism comes from the French mathematician and philosopher René Descartes (1596–1650). Descartes is often called the father of modern philosophy because of his huge influence in setting the agenda and method for much of the philosophical discourse that takes place even today. Hardly a philosopher writing in these times can avoid speaking to the problems he raises in his *Meditations on First Philosophy* and other writings.

In the first meditation, included below, Descartes reasons that a solid foundation of scientific knowledge requires holding only true beliefs. Since he admits that he has held erroneous beliefs in the past, he must find some way of distinguishing those beliefs he should keep from those he should not. Considering one's beliefs individually would require an almost infinite amount of time to complete, and he instead undertakes to cast doubt on the principles that underlie sets of beliefs. The goal is certainty; hence, Descartes intends to withhold belief from any proposition infected with even the slightest bit of doubt.

Accordingly, to overthrow completely all his former opinions, Descartes systematically engages in increasingly expansive exercises in doubt. The occurrence of optical illusions and the like indicates that our senses can mislead us, he argues, but illusions alone don't give us reason to doubt normal cases of perception. Still, we can cast doubt on normal cases by considering that what we currently experience as real could be nothing more than a dream. Since any possible test we could perform to distinguish between dreams and reality could be dreamt, all sensory information becomes dubious and must therefore be discarded.

Even without relying upon the senses, Descartes further argues, a class of beliefs remains intact – namely those of arithmetic, geometry, and similar sciences. How can we doubt something so certain as the truth of $2 + 2 = 4$? In perhaps his most enduring skeptical image, Descartes imagines an evil demon capable of deceiving him at every instant into thinking erroneously, for example, that squares have four sides, that the material world exists, or even that he has a corporeal body. In the end, then, it seems that nothing that he has once believed remains removed from the possibility of doubt, and hence no current beliefs can be relied upon to form the foundation of scientific knowledge.

By the end of the *Meditations*, Descartes believed that he had put to rest the profound doubt he raises in these first few pages. The degree to which he actually succeeded in doing so remains a subject of some debate. In any event, attempts to answer the challenge that our experience might be but a dream or to dispel Descartes' evil genius require careful investigation into how we come to know things.

Of the Things of which We May Doubt

Several years have now elapsed since I first became aware that I had accepted, even from my youth, many false opinions for true, and that consequently what I afterwards based on such principles was highly doubtful; and from that time I was convinced of the necessity of undertaking once in my life to rid myself of all the opinions I had adopted, and of commencing anew the work of building from the foundation, if I desired to establish a firm and abiding superstructure in the sciences. But as this enterprise appeared to me to be one of great magnitude, I waited until I had attained an age so mature as to leave me no hope that at any stage of life more advanced I should be better able to execute my design. On this account, I have delayed so long that I should henceforth consider I was doing wrong were I still to consume in deliberation any of the time that now remains for action. Today, then, since I have opportunely freed my mind from all cares [and am happily disturbed by no passions],[1] and since I am in the secure possession of leisure in a peaceable retirement, I will at length apply myself earnestly and freely to the general overthrow of all my former opinions. But, to this end, it will not be necessary for me to show that the whole of these are false – a point, perhaps, which I shall never reach; but as even now my reason convinces me that I ought not the less carefully to withhold belief from what is not entirely certain and indubitable, than from what is manifestly false, it will be sufficient to justify the rejection of the whole if I shall find in each some ground for doubt. Nor for this purpose will it be necessary even to deal with each belief individually, which would be truly an endless labour; but, as the removal from below of the foundation necessarily involves the downfall of the whole edifice, I will at once approach the criticism of the principles on which all my former beliefs rested.

All that I have, up to this moment, accepted as possessed of the highest truth and certainty, I received either from or through the senses. I observed, however, that these sometimes misled us; and it is the part of prudence not to place absolute confidence in that by which we have even once been deceived.

But it may be said, perhaps, that, although the senses occasionally mislead us respecting minute objects, and such as are so far removed from us as to be beyond the reach of close observation, there are yet many other of their informations (presentations), of the truth of which it is manifestly impossible to doubt; as for example, that I am in this place, seated by the fire, clothed in a winter dressing-gown, that I hold in my hands this piece of paper, with other intimations of the same nature. But how could I deny that I possess these hands and this body, and withal escape being classed with persons in a state of insanity, whose brains are so disordered and clouded by dark bilious vapours as to cause them pertinaciously to assert that they are monarchs when they are in the greatest poverty; or clothed [in gold] and purple when destitute of any covering; or that their head is made of clay, their body of glass, or that they are gourds? I should certainly be not less insane than they, were I to regulate my procedure according to examples so extravagant.

Though this be true, I must nevertheless here consider that I am a man, and that, consequently, I am in the habit of sleeping, and representing to myself in dreams those same things, or even sometimes others less probable, which the insane think are presented to them in their waking moments. How often have I dreamt that I was in these familiar circumstances – that I was dressed, and occupied this place by the fire, when I was lying undressed in bed? At the present moment, however, I certainly look upon this paper with eyes wide awake; the head which I now move is not asleep; I extend this hand consciously and with express purpose, and I perceive it; the occurrences in sleep are not so distinct as all this. But

I cannot forget that, at other times, I have been deceived in sleep by similar illusions; and, attentively considering those cases, I perceive so clearly that there exist no certain marks by which the state of waking can ever be distinguished from sleep, that I feel greatly astonished; and in amazement I almost persuade myself that I am now dreaming.

Let us suppose, then, that we are dreaming, and that all these particulars – namely, the opening of the eyes, the motion of the head, the forth-putting of the hands – are merely illusions; and even that we really possess neither an entire body nor hands such as we see. Nevertheless, it must be admitted at least that the objects which appear to us in sleep are, as it were, painted representations which could not have been formed unless in the likeness of realities; and, therefore, that those general objects, at all events – namely, eyes, a head, hands, and an entire body – are not simply imaginary, but really existent. For, in truth, painters themselves, even when they study to represent sirens and satyrs by forms the most fantastic and extraordinary, cannot bestow upon them natures absolutely new, but can only make a certain medley of the members of different animals; or if they chance to imagine something so novel that nothing at all similar has ever been seen before, and such as is, therefore, purely fictitious and absolutely false, it is at least certain that the colours of which this is composed are real.

And on the same principle, although these general objects, viz. [a body], eyes, a head, hands, and the like, be imaginary, we are nevertheless absolutely necessitated to admit the reality at least of some other objects still more simple and universal than these, of which, just as of certain real colours, all those images of things, whether true and real, or false and fantastic, that are found in our consciousness (*cogitatio*), are formed.

To this class of objects seem to belong corporeal nature in general and its extension; the figure of extended things, their quantity or magnitude, and their number, as also the place in, and the time during, which they exist, and other things of the same sort. We will not, therefore, perhaps reason illegitimately if we conclude from this that physics, astronomy, medicine, and all the other sciences that have for their end the consideration of composite objects, are indeed of a doubtful character; but that arithmetic, geometry, and the other sciences of the same class, which regard merely the simplest and most general objects, and scarcely inquire whether or not these are really existent, contain somewhat that is certain and indubitable: for whether I am awake or dreaming, it remains true that two and three make five, and that a square has but four sides; nor does it seem possible that truths so apparent can ever fall under a suspicion of falsity [or incertitude].

Nevertheless, the belief that there is a God who is all-powerful, and who created me, such as I am, has for a long time, obtained steady possession of my mind. How, then, do I know that he has not arranged that there should be neither earth, nor sky, nor any extended thing, nor figure, nor magnitude, nor place, providing at the same time, however, for [the rise in me of the perceptions of all these objects, and] the persuasion that these do not exist otherwise than as I perceive them? And further, as I sometimes think that others are in error respecting matters of which they believe themselves to possess a perfect knowledge, how do I know that I am not also deceived each time I add together two and three, or number the sides of a square, or form some judgment still more simple, if more simple indeed can be imagined? But perhaps Deity has not been willing that I should be thus deceived, for he is said to be supremely good. If, however, it were repugnant to the goodness of Deity to have created me subject to constant deception, it would seem likewise to be contrary to his goodness to allow me to be occasionally deceived; and yet it is clear that this is permitted. Some, indeed, might perhaps be found who would be disposed rather to deny the existence of a being so powerful than to believe that there is nothing certain. But let us for the present refrain from opposing this opinion, and grant that all which is here said of a Deity is fabulous: nevertheless, in whatever way it be supposed that I reached the state in which I exist, whether by fate, or chance, or by an endless series of antecedents and consequents, or by any other means, it is clear (since to be deceived and to err is a certain defect) that the probability of my being so imperfect as to be the constant victim of deception, will be increased exactly in proportion as the power possessed by the cause, to which they assign my origin, is lessened. To these reasonings I have assuredly nothing to reply, but am constrained at last to avow that there is nothing at all that I formerly believed to be true of which it is impossible to doubt, and that not through thoughtlessness or levity, but from cogent and maturely considered reasons; so that henceforward, if I desire to discover anything certain, I ought not the less carefully to refrain from assenting to those same opinions than to what might be shown to be manifestly false.

But it is not sufficient to have made these observations; care must be taken likewise to keep them in remembrance. For those old and customary opinions perpetually recur – long and familiar usage giving them the right of occupying my mind, even almost against my will, and subduing my belief; nor will I lose the habit of deferring to them and confiding in them so long as I shall consider them to be what in truth they are, viz., opinions to some extent doubtful, as I have already shown, but still highly probable, and such as it is much more reasonable to believe than deny. It is for this reason I am persuaded that I shall not be doing wrong, if, taking an opposite judgment of deliberate design, I become my own deceiver, by supposing, for a time, that all those opinions are entirely false and imaginary, until at length, having thus balanced my old by my new prejudices, my judgment shall no longer be turned aside by perverted usage from the path that may conduct to the perception of truth. For I am assured that, meanwhile, there will arise neither peril nor error from this course, and that I cannot for the present yield too much to distrust, since the end I now seek is not action but knowledge.

I will suppose, then, not that Deity, who is sovereignly good and the fountain of truth, but that some malignant demon, who is at once exceedingly potent and deceitful, has employed all his artifice to deceive me; I will suppose that the sky, the air, the earth, colours, figures, sounds, and all external things, are nothing better than the illusions of dreams, by means of which this being has laid snares for my credulity; I will consider myself as without hands, eyes, flesh, blood, or any of the senses, and as falsely believing that I am possessed of these; I will continue resolutely fixed in this belief, and if indeed by this means it be not in my power to arrive at the knowledge of truth, I shall at least do what is in my power, viz. [suspend my judgment], and guard with settled purpose against giving my assent to what is false, and being imposed upon by this deceiver, whatever be his power and artifice.

But this undertaking is arduous, and a certain indolence insensibly leads me back to my ordinary course of life; and just as the captive, who, perchance, was enjoying in his dreams an imaginary liberty, when he begins to suspect that it is but a vision, dreads awakening, and conspires with the agreeable illusions that the deception may be prolonged; so I, of my own accord, fall back into the train of my former beliefs, and fear to arouse myself from my slumber, lest the time of laborious wakefulness that would succeed this quiet rest, in place of bringing any light of day, should prove inadequate to dispel the darkness that will arise from the difficulties that have now been raised.

Note

1 The square brackets in this chapter mark Descartes' own additions to the revised French translation (Eds).

6

David Hume, from *An Enquiry concerning Human Understanding*

David Hume (1711–76), Scottish philosopher, historian, and essayist, is best known for his youthful philosophical work *A Treatise of Human Nature* (1739–40), in which he attempts to develop a complete science of human nature, including theories on the foundations of knowledge, morals, and politics. His theory of knowledge, based on the principle that all the materials of thought are abstracted from impressions of sense and inner experience, came to the conclusion that most of what we believe cannot be rationally justified.

In particular, our judgments about causal necessity are ultimately founded upon correlations among experienced events, and the alleged necessity of the causal connection consists merely of the uniformity or constancy of the correlation together with the habit of mind engendered by this experience of associating one event with another. When it comes to predicting the future (inductive inference), we have nothing more to rely upon than past correlations. Inductive inference is nothing but the extrapolation of the past into the future. According to Hume, the mere occurrence of past correlations is insufficient to justify our beliefs about the future, and any attempt to justify them by introducing some general principle that ties the past to the future, such as the uniformity of nature, is ultimately circular. So induction cannot be justified by any process of rational argument; the principle in human nature on which it depends is not reason, but custom or habit. Hume is sympathetic to the global skepticism of the Pyrrhonist tradition, but feels that its results are excessive and need to be corrected and tempered by common sense. The result is a point of view he calls "mitigated scepticism," which limits "our enquiries to such subjects as are best adapted to the narrow capacity of human understanding."

Because his *Treatise* was not well received, Hume recast its central portions into two separate works, *An Enquiry concerning Human Understanding* (1748), and *An Enquiry concerning the Principles of Morals* (1751). The following selections consist of the bulk of sections IV, V, and XII from the first *Enquiry* and contain the mature formulations of his analysis of inductive inference and his overall skeptical philosophy.

Section IV   Sceptical Doubts concerning the Operations of the Understanding

Part I

All the objects of human reason or enquiry may naturally be divided into two kinds, to wit, *Relations of Ideas*, and *Matters of Fact*. Of the first kind are the sciences of Geometry, Algebra, and Arithmetic; and in short, every affirmation, which is either intuitively or demonstratively certain. *That the square of the hypothenuse is equal to the square of the two sides*, is a proposition, which expresses a relation between these figures. *That three times five is equal to the half of thirty*, expresses a relation between these numbers. Propositions of this kind are discoverable by the mere operation of thought, without dependence on what is any where existent in the universe. Though there never were a circle or triangle in nature, the truths, demonstrated by Euclid, would for ever retain their certainty and evidence.

Matters of fact, which are the second objects of human reason, are not ascertained in the same manner; nor is our evidence of their truth, however great, of a like nature with the foregoing. The contrary of every matter of fact is still possible; because it can never imply a contradiction, and is conceived by the mind with the same facility and distinctness, as if ever so conformable to reality. *That the sun will not rise tomorrow* is no less intelligible a proposition, and implies no more contradiction, than the affirmation, *that it will rise*. We should in vain, therefore, attempt to demonstrate its falsehood. Were it demonstratively false, it would imply a contradiction, and could never be distinctly conceived by the mind.

It may, therefore, be a subject worthy of curiosity, to enquire what is the nature of that evidence, which assures us of any real existence and matter of fact, beyond the present testimony of our senses, or the records of our memory. This part of philosophy, it is observable, has been little cultivated, either by the ancients or moderns; and therefore our doubts and errors, in the prosecution of so important an enquiry, may be the more excusable; while we march through such difficult paths, without any guide or direction. They may even prove useful, by exciting curiosity, and destroying that implicit faith and security, which is the bane of all reasoning and free enquiry. The discovery of defects in the common philosophy, if any such there be, will not, I presume, be a discouragement, but rather an incitement, as is usual, to attempt something more full and satisfactory, than has yet been proposed to the public.

All reasonings concerning matter of fact seem to be founded on the relation of *Cause and Effect*. By means of that relation alone we can go beyond the evidence of our memory and senses. If you were to ask a man, why he believes any matter of fact, which is absent; for instance, that his friend is in the country, or in France; he would give you a reason; and this reason would be some other fact; as a letter received from him, or the knowledge of his former resolutions and promises. A man, finding a watch or any other machine in a desert island, would conclude, that there had once been men in that island. All our reasonings concerning fact are of the same nature. And here it is constantly supposed, that there is a connexion between the present fact and that which is inferred from it. Were there nothing to bind them together, the inference would be entirely precarious. The hearing of an articulate voice and rational discourse in the dark assures us of the presence of some person: Why? because these are the effects of the human make and fabric, and closely connected with it. If we anatomize all the other reasonings of this nature, we shall find, that they are founded on the relation of cause and effect, and that this relation is either near or remote, direct or collateral. Heat and light are collateral effects of fire, and the one effect may justly be inferred from the other.

If we would satisfy ourselves, therefore, concerning the nature of that evidence, which assures us of matters of fact, we must enquire how we arrive at the knowledge of cause and effect.

I shall venture to affirm, as a general proposition, which admits of no exception, that the knowledge of this relation is not, in any instance, attained by reasonings *a priori*; but arises entirely from experience, when we find, that any particular objects are constantly conjoined with each other. Let an object be presented to a man of ever so strong natural reason and abilities; if that object be entirely new to him, he will not be able, by the most accurate examination of its sensible qualities, to discover any of its causes or effects. Adam, though his rational faculties be supposed, at the very first, entirely perfect, could not have inferred from the fluidity, and transparency of water, that it would suffocate him, or from the light and warmth of fire, that it would consume him. No object ever discovers, by the qualities which appear to the senses, either the causes which produced it, or the effects which will arise from it; nor can our reason, unassisted by experience, ever draw any inference concerning real existence and matter of fact.

This proposition, *that causes and effects are discoverable, not by reason, but by experience*, will readily be admitted with regard to such objects, as we remember to have once been altogether unknown to us; since we must be conscious of the utter inability, which we then lay under, of foretelling, what would arise from them. Present two smooth pieces of marble to a man, who has no tincture of natural philosophy; he will never discover, that they will adhere together, in such a manner as to require great force to separate them in a direct line, while they make so small a resistance to a lateral pressure. Such events, as bear little analogy to the common course of nature, are also readily confessed to be known only by experience; nor does any man imagine that the explosion of gunpowder, or the attraction of a loadstone, could ever be discovered by arguments *a priori*. In like manner, when an effect is supposed to depend upon an intricate machinery or secret structure of parts, we make no difficulty in attributing all our knowledge of it to experience. Who will assert, that he can give the ultimate reason, why milk or bread is proper nourishment for a man, not for a lion or a tiger?

But the same truth may not appear, at first sight, to have the same evidence with regard to events, which have become familiar to us from our first appearance in the world, which bear a close analogy to the whole course of nature, and which are supposed to depend on the simple qualities of objects, without any secret structure of parts. We are apt to imagine, that we could discover these effects by the mere operation of our reason, without experience. We fancy, that were we brought, on a sudden, into this world, we could at first have inferred, that one Billiard-ball would communicate motion to another upon impulse; and that we needed not to have waited for the event, in order to pronounce with certainty concerning it. Such is the influence of custom, that, where it is strongest, it not only covers our natural ignorance, but even conceals itself, and seems not to take place, merely because it is found in the highest degree.

But to convince us, that all the laws of nature, and all the operations of bodies without exception, are known only by experience, the following reflections may, perhaps, suffice. Were any object presented to us, and were we required to pronounce concerning the effect, which will result from it, without consulting past observation; after what manner, I beseech you, must the mind proceed in this operation? It must invent or imagine some event, which it ascribes to the object as its effect; and it is plain that this invention must be entirely arbitrary. The mind can never possibly find the effect in the supposed cause, by the most accurate scrutiny and examination. For the effect is totally different from the cause, and consequently can never be discovered in it. Motion in the second Billiard-ball is a quite distinct event from motion in the first; nor is there any thing in the one to suggest the smallest hint of the other. A stone or piece of metal raised into the air, and left without any support, immediately falls: But to consider the matter *a priori*, is there any thing we discover in this situation, which can beget the idea of a downward, rather than an upward, or any other motion, in the stone or metal?

And as the first imagination or invention of a particular effect, in all natural operations, is arbitrary, where we consult not experience; so must we also esteem the supposed tie or connexion between the cause and effect, which binds them together, and renders it impossible, that any other effect could result from the operation of that cause. When I see, for instance, a Billiard-ball moving in a straight line towards another; even suppose motion in the second ball should by accident be suggested to me, as the result of their contact or impulse; may I not conceive, that a hundred different events might as well follow from that cause? May not both these balls remain at absolute rest? May not the first ball return in a straight line, or leap off from the second in any line or direction? All the suppositions are consistent and conceivable. Why then should we give the preference to one, which is no more consistent or conceivable than the rest? All our reasonings *a priori* will never be able to show us any foundation for this preference.

In a word, then, every effect is a distinct event from its cause. It could not, therefore, be discovered in the cause, and the first invention or conception of it, *a priori*, must be entirely arbitrary. And even after it is suggested, the conjunction of it with the cause must appear equally arbitrary; since there are always many other effects, which, to reason, must seem fully as consistent and natural. In vain, therefore, should we pretend to determine any single event, or infer any cause or effect, without the assistance of observation and experience.

Hence we may discover the reason, why no philosopher, who is rational and modest, has ever pretended to assign the ultimate cause of any natural operation, or to show distinctly the action of that power, which produces any single effect in the universe. It is confessed, that the utmost effort of human reason is, to reduce the principles, productive of natural phenomena, to a greater simplicity, and to resolve the many particular effects into a few general causes, by means of reasonings from analogy, experience, and observation. But as to the causes of these general causes, we should in vain attempt their discovery; nor shall we ever be able to satisfy ourselves, by any particular explication of them. These ultimate springs and principles are totally shut up from human curiosity and enquiry. Elasticity, gravity, cohesion of parts, communication of motion by impulse; these are probably the ultimate causes and principles which we shall ever discover in nature; and we may esteem ourselves sufficiently happy, if, by accurate enquiry and reasoning, we can trace up the particular phenomena to, or near to, these general principles. The most perfect philosophy of the natural kind only staves off our ignorance a little longer: As perhaps the most perfect philosophy of the moral or metaphysical kind serves only to discover larger portions of it. Thus the observation of human blindness and weakness is the result of all philosophy, and meets us, at every turn, in spite of our endeavours to elude or avoid it.

Nor is geometry, when taken into the assistance of natural philosophy, ever able to remedy this effect, or lead us into the knowledge of ultimate causes, by all that accuracy of reasoning, for which it is so justly celebrated. Every part of mixed mathematics proceeds upon the supposition, that certain laws are established by nature in her operations; and abstract reasonings are employed, either to assist experience in the discovery of these laws, or to determine their influence in particular instances, where it depends upon any precise degree of distance and quantity. Thus, it is a law of motion, discovered by experience, that the moment or force of any body in motion is in the compound ratio or proportion of its solid contents and its velocity; and consequently, that a small force may remove the greatest obstacle or raise the greatest weight, if, by any contrivance or machinery, we can increase the velocity of that force, so as to make it an overmatch for its antagonist. Geometry assists us in the application of this law, by giving us the just dimensions of all the parts and figures, which can enter into any species of machine; but still the discovery of the law itself is owing merely to experience, and all the abstract reasonings in the world could never lead us one step towards the knowledge of it. When we reason *a priori*, and consider merely any object or cause, as it appears to the mind, independent of all observation, it never could suggest to us the notion of any distinct object, such as its effect; much less, show us the inseparable and inviolable connection between them. A man must be very sagacious, who could discover by reasoning, that crystal is the effect of heat, and ice of cold, without being previously acquainted with the operation of these qualities.

Part II

But we have not, yet, attained any tolerable satisfaction with regard to the question first proposed. Each solution still gives rise to a new question as difficult as the foregoing, and leads us on to farther enquiries. When it is asked, *What is the nature of all our reasonings concerning matter of fact?* the proper answer seems to be, that they are founded on the relation of cause and effect. When again it is asked, *What is the foundation of all our reasonings and conclusions concerning that relation?* it may be replied in one word, Experience. But if we still carry on our sifting humour, and ask, *What is the foundation of all conclusions from experience?* this implies a new question, which may be of more difficult solution and explication. Philosophers, that give themselves airs of superior wisdom and sufficiency, have a hard task, when they encounter persons of inquisitive dispositions, who push them from every corner, to which they retreat, and who are sure at last to bring them to some dangerous dilemma. The best expedient to prevent this confusion, is to be modest in our pretensions; and even to discover the difficulty ourselves before it is objected to us. By this means, we may make a kind of merit of our very ignorance.

I shall content myself, in this section, with an easy task, and shall pretend only to give a negative answer to the question here proposed. I say then, that, even after we have experience of the operations of cause and effect, our conclusions from that experience are *not* founded on reasoning, or any process of the understanding. This answer we must endeavour, both to explain and to defend.

It must certainly be allowed, that nature has kept us at a great distance from all her secrets, and has afforded us only the knowledge of a few superficial qualities of objects; while she conceals from us those powers and principles, on which the influence of these objects entirely depends. Our senses inform us of the colour, weight, and consistence of bread; but neither sense nor reason can ever inform us of those qualities, which fit it for the nourishment and support of a human body. Sight or feeling conveys an idea of the actual motion of bodies; but as to that wonderful force or power, which would carry on a moving body for ever in a

continued change of place, and which bodies never lose but by communicating it to others; of this we cannot form the most distant conception. But
notwithstanding this ignorance of natural powers and principles, we
always presume, when we see like sensible qualities, that they have like
secret powers, and expect, that effects, similar to those which we have
experienced, will follow from them. If a body of like colour and consistence with that bread, which we have formerly eat, be presented to us, we
make no scruple of repeating the experiment, and foresee, with certainty,
like nourishment and support. Now this is a process of the mind or
thought, of which I would willingly know the foundation. It is allowed
on all hands, that there is no known connexion between the sensible
qualities and the secret powers; and consequently, that the mind is not
led to form such a conclusion concerning their constant and regular
conjunction, by any thing which it knows of their nature. As to past
Experience, it can be allowed to give *direct* and *certain* information of
those precise objects only, and that precise period of time, which fell
under its cognizance: But why this experience should be extended to
future times, and to other objects, which for aught we know, may be
only in appearance similar; this is the main question on which I would
insist. The bread, which I formerly eat, nourished me; that is, a body of
such sensible qualities, was, at that time, endued with such secret
powers: But does it follow, that other bread must also nourish me at
another time, and that like sensible qualities must always be attended
with like secret powers? The consequence seems nowise necessary. At
least, it must be acknowledged, that there is here a consequence drawn
by the mind; that there is a certain step taken; a process of thought, and
an inference, which wants to be explained. These two propositions are far
from being the same, *I have found that such an object has always been attended
with such an effect*, and *I foresee, that other objects, which are, in appearance,
similar, will be attended with similar effects*. I shall allow, if you please, that
the one proposition may justly be inferred from the other: I know in fact,
that it always is inferred. But if you insist, that the inference is made by a
chain of reasoning, I desire you to produce that reasoning. The connexion
between these propositions is not intuitive. There is required a medium,
which may enable the mind to draw such an inference, if indeed it be
drawn by reasoning and argument. What that medium is, I must confess,
passes my comprehension; and it is incumbent on those to produce it,
who assert, that it really exists, and is the origin of all our conclusions
concerning matter of fact.

   This negative argument must certainly, in process of time, become
altogether convincing, if many penetrating and able philosophers shall

turn their enquiries this way; and no one be ever able to discover any connecting proposition or intermediate step, which supports the understanding in this conclusion. But as the question is yet new, every reader may not trust so far to his own penetration, as to conclude, because an argument escapes his enquiry, that therefore it does not really exist. For this reason it may be requisite to venture upon a more difficult task; and enumerating all the branches of human knowledge, endeavour to show, that none of them can afford such an argument.

All reasonings may be divided into two kinds, namely demonstrative reasoning, or that concerning relations of ideas, and moral reasoning, or that concerning matter of fact and existence. That there are no demonstrative arguments in the case, seems evident; since it implies no contradiction, that the course of nature may change, and that an object, seemingly like those which we have experienced, may be attended with different or contrary effects. May I not clearly and distinctly conceive, that a body, falling from the clouds, and which, in all other respects, resembles snow, has yet the taste of salt or feeling of fire? Is there any more intelligible proposition than to affirm, that all the trees will flourish in December and January, and decay in May and June? Now whatever is intelligible, and can be distinctly conceived, implies no contradiction, and can never be proved false by any demonstrative argument or abstract reasoning *a priori*.

If we be, therefore, engaged by arguments to put trust in past experience, and make it the standard of our future judgment, these arguments must be probable only, or such as regard matter of fact and real existence, according to the division above mentioned. But that there is no argument of this kind, must appear, if our explication of that species of reasoning be admitted as solid and satisfactory. We have said, that all arguments concerning existence are founded on the relation of cause and effect; that our knowledge of that relation is derived entirely from experience; and that all our experimental conclusions proceed upon the supposition, that the future will be conformable to the past. To endeavour, therefore, the proof of this last supposition by probable arguments, or arguments regarding existence, must be evidently going in a circle, and taking that for granted, which is the very point in question.

In reality, all arguments from experience are founded on the similarity, which we discover among natural objects, and by which we are induced to expect effects similar to those, which we have found to follow from such objects. And though none but a fool or madman will ever pretend to dispute the authority of experience, or to reject that great guide of human life; it may surely be allowed a philosopher to have so much curiosity at least, as to examine the principle of human nature, which gives this mighty authority to experience, and makes us draw advantage from that similarity, which nature has placed among different objects. From causes, which appear *similar*, we expect similar effects. This is the sum of all our experimental conclusions. Now it seems evident, that, if this conclusion were formed by reason, it would be as perfect at first, and upon one instance, as after ever so long a course of experience. But the case is far otherwise. Nothing so like as eggs; yet no one, on account of this appearing similarity, expects the same taste and relish in all of them. It is only after a long course of uniform experiments in any kind, that we attain a firm reliance and security with regard to a particular event. Now where is that process of reasoning, which, from one instance, draws a conclusion, so different from that which it infers from a hundred instances, that are nowise different from that single one? This question I propose as much for the sake of information, as with an intention of raising difficulties. I cannot find, I cannot imagine any such reasoning. But I keep my mind still open to instruction, if any one will vouchsafe to bestow it on me.

Should it be said, that, from a number of uniform experiments, we *infer* a connexion between the sensible qualities and the secret powers; this, I must confess, seems the same difficulty, couched in different terms. The question still recurs, on what process of argument this *inference* is founded? Where is the medium, the interposing ideas, which join propositions so very wide of each other? It is confessed, that the colour, consistence, and other sensible qualities of bread appear not, of themselves, to have any connexion with the secret powers of nourishment and support. For otherwise we could infer these secret powers from the first appearance of these sensible qualities, without the aid of experience; contrary to the sentiment of all philosophers, and contrary to plain matter of fact. Here then is our natural state of ignorance with regard to the powers and influence of all objects. How is this remedied by experience? It only shows us a number of uniform effects, resulting from certain objects, and teaches us, that those particular objects, at that particular time, were endowed with such powers and forces. When a new object, endowed with similar sensible qualities, is produced, we expect similar powers and forces, and look for a like effect. From a body of like colour and consistence with bread, we expect like nourishment and support. But this surely is a step or progress of the mind, which wants to be explained. When a man says, *I have found, in all past instances, such sensible qualities conjoined with such secret powers*: And when he says, *similar sensible qualities will always be conjoined with similar secret powers*; he is not guilty of a tautology, nor are these propositions in any respect the same. You say that the one proposition is an inference from the other. But you must confess that the inference is not intuitive; neither is it demonstrative: Of what nature is it then? To say it is experimental, is begging the question. For all inferences from experience suppose, as their foundation, that the future will resemble the past, and that similar powers will be conjoined with similar sensible qualities. If there be any suspicion, that the course of nature may change, and that the past may be no rule for the future, all experience becomes useless, and can give rise to no inference or conclusion. It is impossible, therefore, that any arguments from experience can prove this resemblance of the past to the future; since all these arguments are founded on the supposition of that resemblance. Let the course of things be allowed hitherto ever so regular; that alone, without some new argument or inference, proves not, that, for the future, it will continue so. In vain do you pretend to have learned the nature of bodies from your past experience. Their secret nature, and consequently, all their effects and influence, may change, without any change in their sensible qualities. This happens sometimes, and with regard to some objects: Why may it not happen always, and with regard to all objects? What logic, what process of argument secures you against this supposition? My practice, you say, refutes my doubts. But you mistake the purport of my question. As an agent, I am quite satisfied in the point; but as a philosopher, who has some share of curiosity, I will not say scepticism, I want to learn the foundation of this inference. No reading, no enquiry has yet been able to remove my difficulty, or give me satisfaction in a matter of such importance. Can I do better than propose the difficulty to the public, even though, perhaps, I have small hopes obtaining a solution? We shall at least, by this means, be sensible of our ignorance, if we do not augment our knowledge.

I must confess, that a man is guilty of unpardonable arrogance, who concludes, because an argument has escaped his own investigation, that therefore it does not really exist. I must also confess, that, though all the learned, for several ages, should have employed themselves in fruitless search upon any subject, it may still, perhaps, be rash to conclude positively, that the subject must, therefore, pass all human comprehension. Even though we examine all the sources of our knowledge, and conclude them unfit for such a subject, there may still remain a suspicion, that the enumeration is not complete, or the examination not accurate. But with regard to the present subject, there are some considerations, which seem to remove all this accusation of arrogance or suspicion of mistake.

It is certain, that the most ignorant and stupid peasants, nay infants, nay even brute beasts, improve by experience, and learn the qualities of natural objects, by observing the effects, which result from them. When a child has felt the sensation of pain from touching the flame of a candle, he will be careful not to put his hand near any candle; but will expect a similar effect from a cause, which is similar in its sensible qualities and appearance. If you assert, therefore, that the understanding of the child is led into this conclusion by any process of argument or ratiocination, I may justly require you to produce that argument; nor have you any pretence to refuse so equitable a demand. You cannot say, that the argument is abstruse, and may possibly escape your enquiry; since you confess, that it is obvious to the capacity of a mere infant. If you hesitate, therefore, a moment, or if, after reflection, you produce any intricate or profound argument, you, in a manner, give up the question, and confess, that it is not reasoning which engages us to suppose the past resembling the future, and to expect similar effects from causes, which are, to appearance, similar. This is the proposition which I intended to enforce in the present section. If I be right, I pretend not to have made any mighty discovery. And if I be wrong, I must acknowledge myself to be indeed a very backward scholar; since I cannot now discover an argument, which, it seems, was perfectly familiar to me, long before I was out of my cradle.

Section V   Sceptical Solution of these Doubts

Part I

The passion for philosophy, like that for religion, seems liable to this inconvenience, that, though it aims at the correction of our manners, and extirpation of our vices, it may only serve, by imprudent management, to foster a predominant inclination, and push the mind, with more determined resolution, towards that side, which already *draws* too much, by the biass and propensity of the natural temper. It is certain, that, while we aspire to the magnanimous firmness of the philosophic sage, and endeavour to confine our pleasures altogether within our own minds, we may, at last, render our philosophy like that of Epictetus, and other *Stoics*, only a more, refined system of selfishness, and reason ourselves out of all virtue, as well as social enjoyment. While we study with attention the vanity of human life, and turn all our thoughts towards the empty and transitory nature of riches and honours, we are, perhaps, all the while, flattering our natural indolence, which, hating the bustle of the world, and drudgery of business, seeks a pretence of reason, to give itself a full and uncontrolled indulgence. There is, however, one species of philosophy, which seems little liable to this inconvenience, and that because it strikes in with no disorderly passion of the human mind, nor can mingle itself with any natural affection or propensity; and that is the Academic or Sceptical philosophy. The academics always talk of doubt and suspense of judgment, of danger in hasty determinations, of confining to very narrow bounds the enquiries of the understanding, and of renouncing all speculations which lie not within the limits of common life and practice. Nothing, therefore, can be more contrary than such a philosophy to the supine indolence of the mind, its rash arrogance, its lofty pretensions, and its superstitious credulity. Every passion is mortified by it, except the love of truth; and that passion never is, nor can be carried to too high a degree. It is surprising, therefore, that this philosophy, which, in almost every instance, must be harmless and innocent, should be the subject of so much groundless reproach and obloquy. But, perhaps, the very circumstance, which renders it so innocent, is what chiefly exposes it to the public hatred and resentment. By flattering no irregular passion, it gains few partizans: By opposing so many vices and follies, it raises to itself abundance of enemies, who stigmatize it as libertine, profane, and irreligious.

Nor need we fear, that this philosophy, while it endeavours to limit our enquiries to common life, should ever undermine the reasonings of common life, and carry its doubts so far as to destroy all action, as well as speculation. Nature will always maintain her rights, and prevail in the end over any abstract reasoning whatsoever. Though we should conclude, for instance, as in the foregoing section, that, in all reasonings from experience, there is a step taken by the mind, which is not supported by any argument or process of the understanding, there is no danger, that these reasonings, on which almost all knowledge depends, will ever be affected by such a discovery. If the mind be not engaged by argument to make this step, it must be induced by some other principle of equal weight and authority; and that principle will preserve its influence as long as human nature remains the same. What that principle is, may well be worth the pains of enquiry.

Suppose a person, though endowed with the strongest faculties of reason and reflection, to be brought on a sudden into this world; he would, indeed, immediately observe a continual succession of objects, and one event following another; but he would not be able to discover any thing farther. He would not, at first, by any reasoning, be able to reach the idea of cause and effect; since the particular powers, by which all natural operations are performed, never appear to the senses; nor is it reasonable to conclude, merely because one event, in one instance, precedes another, that therefore the one is the cause, the other the effect. Their conjunction may be arbitrary and casual. There may be no reason to infer the existence of one from the appearance of the other. And in a word, such a person, without more experience, could never employ his conjecture or reasoning concerning any matter of fact, or be assured of any thing beyond what was immediately present to his memory and senses.

Suppose again, that he has acquired more experience, and has lived so long in the world as to have observed similar objects or events to be constantly conjoined together; what is the consequence of this experience? He immediately infers the existence of one object from the appearance of the other. Yet he has not, by all his experience, acquired any idea or knowledge of the secret power, by which the one object produces the other; nor is it, by any process of reasoning, he is engaged to draw this inference. But still he finds himself determined to draw it: And though he should be convinced, that his understanding has no part in the operation, he would nevertheless continue in the same course of thinking. There is some other principle, which determines him to form such a conclusion.

This principle is Custom or Habit. For wherever the repetition of any particular act or operation produces a propensity to renew the same act or operation, without being impelled by any reasoning or process of the understanding; we always say, that this propensity is the effect of *Custom*. By employing that word, we pretend not to have given the ultimate reason of such a propensity. We only point out a principle of human nature, which is universally acknowledged, and which is well known by its effects. Perhaps, we can push our enquiries no farther, or pretend to give the cause of this cause; but must rest contented with it as the ultimate principle, which we can assign, of all our conclusions from experience. It is sufficient satisfaction, that we can go so far; without repining at the narrowness of our faculties, because they will carry us no farther. And it is certain we here advance a very intelligible proposition at least, if not a true one, when we assert, that, after the constant conjunction of two objects, heat and flame, for instance, weight and solidity, we are determined by custom alone to expect the one from the appearance of the other. This hypothesis seems even the only one, which explains the difficulty, why we draw, from a thousand instances, an inference, which we are not able to draw from one instance, that is, in no respect, different from them. Reason is incapable of any such variation. The conclusions, which it draws from considering one circle, are the same which it would form upon surveying all the circles in the universe. But no man, having seen only one body move after being impelled by another, could infer, that every other body will move after a like impulse. All inferences from experience, therefore, are effects of custom, not of reasoning.

Custom, then, is the great guide of human life. It is that principle alone, which renders our experience useful to us, and makes us expect, for the future, a similar train of events with those which have appeared in the past. Without the influence of custom, we should be entirely ignorant of every matter of fact, beyond what is immediately present to the memory and senses. We should never know how to adjust means to ends, or to employ our natural powers in the production of any effect. There would be an end at once of all action, as well as of the chief part of speculation.

But here it may be proper to remark, that though our conclusions from experience carry us beyond our memory and senses, and assure us of matters of fact, which happened in the most distant places and most remote ages; yet some fact must always be present to the senses or memory, from which we may first proceed in drawing these conclusions. A man, who should find in a desert country the remains of pompous buildings, would conclude, that the country had, in ancient times, been cultivated by civilized inhabitants; but did nothing of this nature occur to him, he could never form such an inference. We learn the events of former ages from history; but then we must peruse the volumes, in which this instruction is contained, and thence carry up our inferences from one testimony to another, till we arrive at the eye-witnesses and spectators of these distant events. In a word, if we proceed not upon some fact, present to the memory or senses, our reasonings would be merely hypothetical; and however the particular links might be connected with each other, the whole chain of inferences would have nothing to support it, nor could we ever, by its means, arrive at the knowledge of any real existence. If I ask, why you believe any particular matter of fact, which you relate, you must tell me some reason; and this reason will be some other fact, connected with it. But as you cannot proceed after this manner, *in infinitum*, you must at last terminate in some fact, which is present to your memory or senses; or must allow that your belief is entirely without foundation.

What then is the conclusion of the whole matter? A simple one; though, it must be confessed, pretty remote from the common theories of philosophy. All belief of matter of fact or real existence is derived merely from some object, present to the memory or senses, and a customary conjunction between that and some other object. Or in other words; having found, in many instances, that any two kinds of objects, flame and heat, snow and cold, have always been conjoined together; if flame or snow be presented anew to the senses, the mind is carried by custom to expect heat or cold, and to *believe*, that such a quality does exist, and will discover itself upon a nearer approach. This belief is the necessary result of placing the mind in such circumstances. It is an operation of the soul, when we are so situated, as unavoidable as to feel the passion of love, when we receive benefits; or hatred, when we meet with injuries. All these operations are a species of natural instincts, which no reasoning or process of the thought and understanding is able, either to produce, or to prevent.

[...]

Section XII   Of the Academical or Sceptical Philosophy

Part I

There is not a greater number of philosophical reasonings, displayed upon any subject, than those, which prove the existence of a Deity, and refute the fallacies of *Atheists*; and yet the most religious philosophers still dispute whether any man can be so blinded as to be a speculative atheist. How shall we reconcile these contradictions? The knights-errant, who wandered about to clear the world of dragons and giants, never entertained the least doubt with regard to the existence of these monsters.

The *Sceptic* is another enemy of religion, who naturally provokes the indignation of all divines and graver philosophers; though it is certain, that no man ever met with any such absurd creature, or conversed with a man, who had no opinion or principle concerning any subject, either of action or speculation. This begets a very natural question; What is meant by a sceptic? And how far it is possible to push these philosophical principles of doubt and uncertainty?

There is a species of scepticism, *antecedent* to all study and philosophy, which is much inculcated by Descartes and others, as a sovereign preservative against error and precipitate judgment. It recommends an universal doubt, not only of all our former opinions and principles, but also of our very faculties; of whose veracity, say they, we must assure ourselves, by a chain of reasoning, deduced from some original principle, which cannot possibly be fallacious or deceitful. But neither is there any such original principle, which has a prerogative above others, that are self-evident and convincing: Or if there were, could we advance a step beyond it, but by the use of those very faculties, of which we are supposed to be already diffident. The Cartesian doubt, therefore, were it ever possible to be attained by any human creature (as it plainly is not) would be entirely incurable; and no reasoning could ever bring us to a state of assurance and conviction upon any subject.

It must, however, be confessed, that this species of scepticism, when more moderate, may be understood in a very reasonable sense, and is a necessary preparative to the study of philosophy, by preserving a proper impartiality in our judgments, and weaning our mind from all those prejudices, which we may have imbibed from education or rash opinion. To begin with clear and self-evident principles, to advance by timorous and sure steps, to review frequently our conclusions, and examine accurately all their consequences; though by these means we shall make both a slow and a short progress in our systems; are the only methods, by which we can ever hope to reach truth, and attain a proper stability and certainty in our determinations.

There is another species of scepticism, *consequent* to science and enquiry, when men are supposed to have discovered, either the absolute fallaciousness of their mental faculties, or their unfitness to reach any fixed determination in all those curious subjects of speculation, about which they are commonly employed. Even our very senses are brought into dispute, by a certain species of philosophers; and the maxims of common life are subjected to the same doubt as the most profound principles or conclusions of metaphysics and theology. As these paradoxical tenets (if they may be called tenets) are to be met with in some philosophers, and the refutation of them in several, they naturally excite our curiosity, and make us enquire into the arguments, on which they may be founded.

I need not insist upon the more trite topics, employed by the sceptics in all ages, against the evidence of *sense*; such as those which are derived from the imperfection and fallaciousness of our organs, on numberless occasions; the crooked appearance of an oar in water; the various aspects of objects, according to their different distances; the double images which arise from the pressing one eye; with many other appearances of a like nature. These sceptical topics, indeed, are only sufficient to prove, that the senses alone are not implicitly to be depended on; but that we must correct their evidence by reason, and by considerations, derived from the nature of the medium, the distance of the object, and the disposition of the organ, in order to render them, within their sphere, the proper *criteria* of truth and falsehood. There are other more profound arguments against the senses, which admit not of so easy a solution.

It seems evident, that men are carried, by a natural instinct or prepossession, to repose faith in their senses; and that, without any reasoning, or even almost before the use of reason, we always suppose an external universe, which depends not on our perception, but would exist, though we and every sensible creature were absent or annihilated. Even the animal creation are governed by a like opinion, and preserve this belief of external objects, in all their thoughts, designs, and actions.

It seems also evident, that, when men follow this blind and powerful instinct of nature, they always suppose the very images, presented by the senses, to be the external objects, and never entertain any suspicion, that the one are nothing but representations of the other. This very table, which we see white, and which we feel hard, is believed to exist, independent of our perception, and to be something external to our mind, which perceives it. Our presence bestows not being on it: Our absence does not annihilate it. It preserves its existence uniform and entire, independent of the situation of intelligent beings, who perceive or contemplate it.

But this universal and primary opinion of all men is soon destroyed by the slightest philosophy, which teaches us, that nothing can ever be present to the mind but an image or perception, and that the senses are only the inlets, through which these images are conveyed, without being able to produce any immediate intercourse between the mind and the object. The table, which we see, seems to diminish, as we remove farther from it: But the real table, which exists independent of us, suffers no alteration: It was, therefore, nothing but its image, which was present to the mind. These are the obvious dictates of reason; and no man, who reflects, ever doubted, that the existences, which we consider, when we say, *this house* and *that tree*, are nothing but perceptions in the mind, and fleeting copies or representations of other existences, which remain uniform and independent.

So far, then, are we necessitated by reasoning to contradict or depart from the primary instincts of nature, and to embrace a new system with regard to the evidence of our senses. But here philosophy finds herself extremely embarrassed, when she would justify this new system, and obviate the cavils and objections of the sceptics. She can no longer plead the infallible and irresistible instinct of nature: For that led us to a quite different system, which is acknowledged fallible and even erroneous. And to justify this pretended philosophical system, by a chain of clear and convincing argument, or even any appearance of argument, exceeds the power of all human capacity.

By what argument can it be proved, that the perceptions of the mind must be caused by external objects, entirely different from them, though resembling them (if that be possible) and could not arise either from the energy of the mind itself, or from the suggestion of some invisible and unknown spirit, or from some other cause still more unknown to us? It is acknowledged, that, in fact, many of these perceptions arise not from any thing external, as in dreams, madness, and other diseases. And nothing can be more inexplicable than the manner, in which body should so operate upon mind as ever to convey an image of itself to a substance, supposed of so different, and even contrary a nature.

It is a question of fact, whether the perceptions of the senses be produced by external objects, resembling them: How shall this question be determined? By experience surely; as all other questions of a like nature. But here experience is, and must be entirely silent. The mind has never any thing present to it but the perceptions, and cannot possibly reach any experience of their connexion with objects. The supposition of such a connexion is, therefore, without any foundation in reasoning.

To have recourse to the veracity of the supreme Being, in order to prove the veracity of our senses, is surely making a very unexpected circuit. If his veracity were at all concerned in this matter, our senses would be entirely infallible; because it is not possible that he can ever deceive. Not to mention, that, if the external world be once called in question, we shall be at a loss to find arguments, by which we may prove the existence of the Being or any of his attributes.

This is a topic, therefore, in which the profounder and more philosophical sceptics will always triumph, when they endeavour to introduce an universal doubt into all subjects of human knowledge and enquiry. Do you follow the instincts and propensities of nature, may they say, in assenting to the veracity of sense? But these lead you to believe, that the very perception or sensible image is the external object. Do you disclaim this principle, in order to embrace a more rational opinion, that the perceptions are only representations of something external? You here depart from your natural propensities and more obvious sentiments; and yet are not able to satisfy your reason, which can never find any convincing argument from experience to prove, that the perceptions are connected with any external objects.

There is another sceptical topic of a like nature, derived from the most profound philosophy; which might merit our attention, were it requisite to dive so deep, in order to discover arguments and reasonings, which can so little serve to any serious purpose. It is universally allowed by modern enquirers, that all the sensible qualities of objects, such as hard, soft, hot, cold, white, black, etc., are merely secondary, and exist not in the objects themselves, but are perceptions of the mind, without any external archetype or model, which they represent. If this be allowed, with regard to secondary qualities, it must also follow, with regard to the supposed primary qualities of extension and solidity; nor can the latter be any more entitled to that denomination than the former. The idea of extension is entirely acquired from the senses of sight and feeling; and if all the qualities, perceived by the senses, be in the mind, not in the object, the same conclusion must reach the idea of extension, which is wholly dependent on the sensible ideas or the ideas of secondary qualities. Nothing can save us from this conclusion, but the asserting, that the ideas of those primary qualities are attained by *Abstraction*; an opinion, which, if we examine it accurately, we shall find to be unintelligible, and even absurd. An extension, that is neither tangible nor visible, cannot possibly be conceived: And a tangible or visible extension, which is neither hard nor soft, black nor white, is equally beyond the reach of human conception. Let any man try to conceive a triangle in general, which is neither *Isoceles* nor *Scalenum*, nor has any particular length or proportion of sides; and he will soon perceive the absurdity of all the scholastic notions with regard to abstraction and general ideas.[1]

Thus the first philosophical objection to the evidence of sense or to the opinion of external existence consists in this, that such an opinion, if rested on natural instinct, is contrary to reason, and if referred to reason, is contrary to natural instinct, and at the same time carries no rational evidence with it, to convince an impartial enquirer. The second objection goes farther, and represents this opinion as contrary to reason: at least, if it be a principle of reason, that all sensible qualities are in the mind, not in the object. Bereave matter of all its intelligible qualities, both primary and secondary, you in a manner annihilate it, and leave only a certain unknown, inexplicable *something*, as the cause of our perceptions; a notion so imperfect, that no sceptic will think it worth while to contend against it.

Part II

It may seem a very extravagant attempt of the sceptics to destroy *reason* by argument and ratiocination; yet is this the grand scope of all their enquiries and disputes. They endeavour to find objections, both to our abstract reasonings, and to those which regard matter of fact and existence.

The chief objection against all *abstract* reasonings is derived from the ideas of space and time; ideas, which, in common life and to a careless view, are very clear and intelligible, but when they pass through the scrutiny of the profound sciences (and they are the chief object of these sciences) afford principles, which seem full of absurdity and contradiction. No priestly *dogmas*, invented on purpose to tame and subdue the rebellious reason of mankind, ever shocked common sense more than the doctrine of the infinite divisibility of extension, with its consequences; as they are pompously displayed by all geometricians and metaphysicians, with a kind of triumph and exultation. A real quantity, infinitely less than any finite quantity, containing quantities infinitely less than itself, and so on *in infinitum*; this is an edifice so bold and prodigious, that it is too weighty for any pretended demonstration to support, because it shocks the clearest and most natural principles of human reason. But what renders the matter more extraordinary, is, that these seemingly absurd opinions are supported by a chain of reasoning, the clearest and most natural; nor is it possible for us to allow the premises without admitting the consequences. Nothing can be more convincing and satisfactory than all the conclusions concerning the properties of circles and triangles; and yet, when these are once received, how can we deny, that the angle of contact between a circle and its tangent is infinitely less than any rectilineal angle, that as you may increase the diameter of the circle *in infinitum*, this angle of contact becomes still less, even *in infinitum*, and that the angle of contact between other curves and their tangents may be infinitely less than those between any circle and its tangent, and so on, *in infinitum*? The demonstration of these principles seems as unexceptionable as that which proves the three angles of a triangle to be equal to two right ones, though the latter opinion be natural and easy, and the former big with contradiction and absurdity. Reason here seems to be thrown into a kind of amazement and suspense, which, without the suggestions of any sceptic, gives her a diffidence of herself, and of the ground on which she treads. She sees a full light, which illuminates certain places; but that light borders upon the most profound darkness. And between these she is so dazzled and confounded, that she scarcely can pronounce with certainty and assurance concerning any one object.

The absurdity of these bold determinations of the abstract sciences seems to become, if possible, still more palpable with regard to time than extension. An infinite number of real parts of time, passing in succession, and exhausted one after another, appears so evident a contradiction, that no man, one should think, whose judgment is not corrupted, instead of being improved, by the sciences, would ever be able to admit of it.

Yet still reason must remain restless, and unquiet, even with regard to that scepticism, to which she is driven by these seeming absurdities and contradictions. How any clear, distinct idea can contain circumstances, contradictory to itself, or to any other clear, distinct idea, is absolutely incomprehensible; and is, perhaps, as absurd as any proposition, which can be formed. So that nothing can be more sceptical, or more full of doubt and hesitation, than this scepticism itself, which arises from some of the paradoxical conclusions of geometry or the science of quantity.[2]

The sceptical objections to *moral* evidence, or to the reasonings concerning matter of fact, are either *popular* or *philosophical*. The popular objections are derived from the natural weakness of human understanding; the contradictory opinions, which have been entertained in different ages and nations; the variations of our judgment in sickness and health, youth and old age, prosperity and adversity; the perpetual contradiction of each particular man's opinions and sentiments; with many other topics of that kind. It is needless to insist farther on this head. These objections are but weak. For as, in common life, we reason every moment concerning fact and existence, and cannot possibly subsist, without continually employing this species of argument, any popular objections, derived from thence, must be insufficient to destroy that evidence. The great subverter of *Pyrrhonism*, or the excessive principles of scepticism, is action, and employment, and the occupations of common life. These principles may flourish and triumph in the schools; where it is, indeed, difficult, if not impossible, to refute them. But as soon as they leave the shade, and by the presence of the real objects, which actuate our passions and sentiments, are put in opposition to the more powerful principles of our nature, they vanish like smoke, and leave the most determined sceptic in the same condition as other mortals.

The sceptic, therefore, had better keep within his proper sphere, and display those *philosophical* objections, which arise from more profound researches. Here he seems to have ample matter of triumph; while he justly insists, that all our evidence for any matter of fact, which lies beyond the testimony of sense or memory, is derived entirely from the relation of cause and effect; that we have no other idea of this relation than that of two objects, which have been frequently *conjoined* together; that we have no argument to convince us, that objects, which have, in our experience, been frequently conjoined, will likewise, in other instances, be conjoined in the same manner; and that nothing leads us to this inference but custom or a certain instinct of our nature; which it is indeed difficult to resist, but which, like other instincts, may be fallacious and deceitful. While the sceptic insists upon these topics, he shows his force, or rather, indeed, his own and our weakness; and seems, for the time at least, to destroy all assurance and conviction. These arguments might be displayed at greater length, if any durable good or benefit to society could ever be expected to result from them.

For here is the chief and most confounding objection to *excessive* scepticism, that no durable good can ever result from it; while it remains in its full force and vigour. We need only ask such a sceptic, *What his meaning is? And what he proposes by all these curious researches?* He is immediately at a loss, and knows not what to answer. A Copernican or Ptolemaic, who supports each his different system of astronomy, may hope to produce a conviction, which will remain constant and durable, with his audience. A Stoic or Epicurean displays principles, which may not only be durable, but which have an effect on conduct and behaviour. But a Pyrrhonian cannot expect, that his philosophy will have any constant influence on the mind: Or if it had, that its influence would be beneficial to society. On the contrary, he must acknowledge, if he will acknowledge any thing, that all human life must perish, were his principles universally and steadily to prevail. All discourse, all action would immediately cease; and men remain in a total lethargy, till the necessities of nature, unsatisfied, put an end to their miserable existence. It is true; so fatal an event is very little to be dreaded. Nature is always too strong for principle. And though a Pyrrhonian may throw himself or others into a momentary amazement and confusion by his profound reasonings; the first and most trivial event in life will put to flight all his doubts and scruples, and leave him the same, in every point of action and speculation, with the philosophers of every other sect, or with those who never concerned themselves in any philosophical researches. When he awakes from his dream, he will be the first to join in the laugh against himself, and to confess, that all his objections are mere amusement, and can have no other tendency than to show the whimsical condition of mankind, who must act and reason and believe though they are not able, by their most diligent enquiry, to satisfy themselves concerning the foundation of these operations, or to remove the objections, which may be raised against them.

Part III

There is, indeed, a more *mitigated* scepticism or *academical* philosophy, which may be both durable and useful, and which may, in part, be the result of this Pyrrhonism, or *excessive* scepticism, when its undistinguished doubts are, in some measure, corrected by common sense and reflection. The greater part of mankind are naturally apt to be affirmative and dogmatical in their opinions; and while they see objects only on one side, and have no idea of any counterpoising argument, they throw themselves precipitately into the principles, to which they are inclined;

nor have they any indulgence for those who entertain opposite sentiments. To hesitate or balance perplexes their understanding, checks their
passion, and suspends their action. They are, therefore, impatient till they
escape from a state, which to them is so uneasy; and they think, that they
can never remove themselves far enough from it, by the violence of their
affirmations and obstinacy of their belief. But could such dogmatical
reasoners become sensible of the strange infirmities of human understanding, even in its most perfect state, and when most accurate and
cautious in its determinations; such a reflection would naturally inspire
them with more modesty and reserve, and diminish their fond opinion of
themselves, and their prejudice against antagonists. The illiterate may
reflect on the disposition of the learned, who, amidst all the advantages of
study and reflection, are commonly still diffident in their determinations:
And if any of the learned be inclined, from their natural temper, to
haughtiness and obstinacy, a small tincture of Pyrrhonism might abate
their pride, by showing them, that the few advantages, which they may
have attained over their fellows, are but inconsiderable, if compared with
the universal perplexity and confusion, which is inherent in human
nature. In general, there is a degree of doubt, and caution, and modesty,
which, in all kinds of scrutiny and decision, ought for ever to accompany
a just reasoner.

Another species of *mitigated* scepticism, which may be of advantage to
mankind, and which may be the natural result of the Pyrrhonian doubts
and scruples, is the limitation of our enquiries to such subjects as are best
adapted to the narrow capacity of human understanding. The *imagination*
of man is naturally sublime, delighted with whatever is remote and
extraordinary, and running, without control, into the most distant parts
of space and time in order to avoid the objects, which custom has
rendered too familiar to it. A correct *Judgment* observes a contrary
method, and avoiding all distant and high enquiries, confines itself to
common life, and to such subjects as fall under daily practice and experience; leaving the more sublime topics to the embellishment of poets and
orators, or to the arts of priests and politicians. To bring us to so salutary
a determination, nothing can be more serviceable, than to be once thoroughly convinced of the force of the Pyrrhonian doubt, and of the impossibility, that any thing, but the strong power of natural instinct, could free
us from it. Those who have a propensity of philosophy, will still continue
their researches; because they reflect, that, besides the immediate pleasure, attending such an occupation, philosophical decisions are nothing
but the reflections of common life, methodized and corrected. But they
will never be tempted to go beyond common life, so long as they consider

the imperfection of those faculties which they employ, their narrow reach, and their inaccurate operations. While we cannot give a satisfactory reason, why we believe, after a thousand experiments, that a stone will fall, or fire burn; can we ever satisfy ourselves concerning any determination, which we may form, with regard to the origin of worlds, and the situation of nature, from, and to eternity?

This narrow limitation, indeed, of our enquiries, is, in every respect, so reasonable, that it suffices to make the slightest examination into the natural powers of the human mind, and to compare them with their objects, in order to recommend it to us. We shall then find what are the proper subjects of science and enquiry.

It seems to me, that the only objects of the abstract sciences or of demonstration are quantity and number, and that all attempts to extend this more perfect species of knowledge beyond these bounds are mere sophistry and illusion. As the component parts of quantity and number are entirely similar, their relations become intricate and involved; and nothing can be more curious, as well as useful, than to trace, by a variety of mediums, their equality or inequality, through their different appearances. But as all other ideas are clearly distinct and different from each other, we can never advance farther, by our utmost scrutiny, than to observe this diversity, and, by an obvious reflection, pronounce one thing not to be another. Or if there by any difficulty in these decisions, it proceeds entirely from the undeterminate meaning of words, which is corrected by juster definitions. That *the square of the hypothenuse is equal to the squares of the other two sides*, cannot be known, let the terms be ever so exactly defined, without a train of reasoning and enquiry. But to convince us of this proposition, *that where there is no property, there can be no injustice*, it is only necessary to define the terms, and explain injustice to be a violation of property. This proposition is, indeed, nothing but a more imperfect definition. It is the same case with all those pretended syllogistical reasonings, which may be found in every other branch of learning, except the sciences of quantity and number; and these may safely, I think, be pronounced the only proper objects of knowledge and demonstration.

All other enquiries of men regard only matter of fact and existence; and these are evidently incapable of demonstration. Whatever *is* may *not be*. No negation of a fact can involve a contradiction. The non-existence of any being, without exception, is as clear and distinct an idea as its existence. The proposition, which affirms it not to be, however false, is no less conceivable and intelligible, than that which affirms it to be. The case is different with the sciences, properly so called. Every proposition, which is not true, is there confused and unintelligible. That the cube root of 64 is equal to the half of 10, is a false proposition, and can never be distinctly conceived. But that Caesar, or the angel Gabriel, or any being never existed, may be a false proposition, but still is perfectly conceivable, and implies no contradiction.

The existence, therefore, of any being can only be proved by arguments from its cause or its effect; and these arguments are founded entirely on experience. If we reason *a priori*, any thing may appear able to produce any thing. The falling of a pebble may, for aught we know, extinguish the sun; or the wish of a man control the planets in their orbits. It is only experience, which teaches us the nature and bounds of cause and effect, and enables us to infer the existence of one object from that of another. Such is the foundation of moral reasoning, which forms the greater part of human knowledge, and is the source of all human action and behaviour.

Moral reasonings are either concerning particular or general facts. All deliberations in life regard the former; as also all disquisitions in history, chronology, geography, and astronomy.

The sciences, which treat of general facts, are politics, natural philosophy, physic, chymistry, etc. where the qualities, causes and effects of a whole species of objects are enquired into.

Divinity or Theology, as it proves the existence of a Deity, and the immortality of souls, is composed partly of reasonings concerning particular, partly concerning general facts. It has a foundation in *reason*, so far as it is supported by experience. But its best and most solid foundation is *faith* and divine revelation.

Morals and criticism are not so properly objects of the understanding as of taste and sentiment. Beauty, whether moral or natural, is felt, more properly than perceived. Or if we reason concerning it, and endeavour to fix its standard, we regard a new fact, to wit, the general taste of mankind, or some such fact, which may be the object of reasoning and enquiry.

When we run over libraries, persuaded of these principles, what havoc must we make? If we take in our hand any volume; of divinity or school metaphysics, for instance; let us ask, *Does it contain any abstract reasoning concerning quantity or number?* No. *Does it contain any experimental reasoning concerning matter of fact and existence?* No. Commit it then to the flames: For it can contain nothing but sophistry and illusion.

Notes

1 This argument is drawn from Dr. Berkeley; and indeed most of the writings of that very ingenious author form the best lessons of scepticism, which are to be found either among the ancient or modern philosophers, Bayle not excepted. He professes, however, in his title-page (and undoubtedly with great truth) to have composed his book against the sceptics as well as against the atheists and free-thinkers. But that all his arguments, though otherwise intended, are, in reality, merely sceptical, appears from this, *that they admit of no answer and produce no conviction.* Their only effect is to cause that momentary amazement and irresolution and confusion, which is the result of scepticism.

2 It seems to me not impossible to avoid these absurdities and contradictions, if it be admitted, that there is no such thing as abstract or general ideas, properly speaking; but that all general ideas are, in reality, particular ones, attached to a general term, which recalls, upon occasion, other particular ones, that resemble, in certain circumstances, the idea, present to the mind. Thus when the term Horse, is pronounced, we immediately figure to ourselves the idea of a black or a white animal, of a particular size or figure: But as that term is also usually applied to animals of other colours, figures and sizes, these ideas, though not actually present to the imagination, are easily recalled; and our reasoning and conclusion proceed in the same way, as if they were actually present. If this be admitted (as seems reasonable) it follows that all the ideas of quantity, upon which mathematicians reason, are nothing but particular, and such as are suggested by the senses and imagination, and consequently, cannot be infinitely divisible. It is sufficient to have dropped this hint at present, without prosecuting it any farther. It certainly concerns all lovers of science not to expose themselves to the ridicule and contempt of the ignorant by their conclusions; and this seems the readiest solution of these difficulties.

7

Thomas Nagel, from *The View from Nowhere*

This selection is an excerpt from Thomas Nagel's *The View from Nowhere*. According to Nagel (1937–), our epistemic aim in science and in everyday life is to achieve objective knowledge, a grasp of "objective reality." This aim presupposes the truth of realism, which is the idea that the way the world is is independent of how it seems to us. Believing does not make it so. We try to transcend our particular point of view, to correct and modify it so as to improve our understanding of the world as it exists independently of our cognitive strivings. We think that we have the capacity "to escape the limits of the original human situation," to discount and to explain away the deceptions and illusions introduced by the subjective point of view and our human constitution. However, the skeptical doubts such as those introduced by Descartes "cannot be finally laid to rest." The skeptical possibilities always remain open; there can be no assurance that our views of the world correspond to the ways things are actually constituted. Our views "might be correct," but we can never know it. They are, at best, provisional, and we can never foreclose the possibility of subsequent falsification.

1. Skepticism

The objective self is responsible both for the expansion of our understanding and for doubts about it that cannot be finally laid to rest. The extension of power and the growth of insecurity go hand in hand, once we place ourselves inside the world and try to develop a view that accommodates this recognition fully.

The most familiar scene of conflict is the pursuit of objective knowledge, whose aim is naturally described in terms that, taken literally, are unintelligible: we must get outside of ourselves, and view the world from nowhere within it. Since it is impossible to leave one's own point of view behind entirely without ceasing to exist, the metaphor of getting outside ourselves must have another meaning. We are to rely less and less on certain individual aspects of our point of view, and more and more on something else, less individual, which is also part of us. But if initial appearances are not in themselves reliable guides to reality, why should the products of detached reflection be different? Why aren't they either equally doubtful or else valid only as higher-order impressions? This is an old problem. The same ideas that make the pursuit of objectivity seem necessary for knowledge make both objectivity and knowledge seem, on reflection, unattainable.

Objectivity and skepticism are closely related: both develop from the idea that there is a real world in which we are contained, and that appearances result from our interaction with the rest of it. We cannot accept those appearances uncritically, but must try to understand what our own constitution contributes to them. To do this we try to develop an idea of the world with ourselves in it, an account of both ourselves and the world that includes an explanation of why it initially appears to us as it does. But this idea, since it is we who develop it, is likewise the product of interaction between us and the world, though the interaction is more complicated and more self-conscious than the original one. If the initial appearances cannot be relied upon because they depend on our constitution in ways that we do not fully understand, this more complex idea should be open to the same doubts, for whatever we use to understand certain interactions between ourselves and the world is not itself the object of that understanding. However often we may try to step outside of ourselves, something will have to stay behind the lens, something in us will determine the resulting picture, and this will give grounds for doubt that we are really getting any closer to reality.

The idea of objectivity thus seems to undermine itself. The aim is to form a conception of reality which includes ourselves and our view of things among its objects, but it seems that whatever forms the conception will not be included by it. It seems to follow that the most objective view we can achieve will have to rest on an unexamined subjective base, and that since we can never abandon our own point of view, but can only alter it, the idea that we are coming closer to the reality outside it with each successive step has no foundation.

All theories of knowledge are responses to this problem. They may be divided into three types: *skeptical, reductive,* and *heroic.*

Skeptical theories take the contents of our ordinary or scientific beliefs about the world to go beyond their grounds in ways that make it impossible to defend them against doubt. There are ways we might be wrong that we can't rule out. Once we notice this unclosable gap we cannot, except with conscious irrationality, maintain our confidence in those beliefs.

Reductive theories grow out of skeptical arguments. Assuming that we do know certain things, and acknowledging that we could not know them if the gap between content and grounds were as great as the skeptic thinks it is, the reductionist reinterprets the content of our beliefs about the world so that they claim less. He may interpret them as claims about possible experience or the possible ultimate convergence of experience among rational beings, or as efforts to reduce tension and surprise or to increase order in the system of mental states of the knower, or he may even take some of them, in a Kantian vein, to describe the limits of all possible experience: an inside view of the bars of our mental cage. In any case on a reductive view our beliefs are not about the world as it is in itself – if indeed that means anything. They are about the world as it appears to us. Naturally not all reductive theories succeed in escaping skepticism, for it is difficult to construct a reductive analysis of claims about the world which has any plausibility at all, without leaving gaps between grounds and content – even if both are within the realm of experience.

Heroic theories acknowledge the great gap between the grounds of our beliefs about the world and the contents of those beliefs under a realist interpretation, and they try to leap across the gap without narrowing it. The chasm below is littered with epistemological corpses. Examples of heroic theories are Plato's theory of Forms together with the theory of recollection, and Descartes' defense of the general reliability of human knowledge through an a priori proof of the existence of a nondeceiving God.[1]

I believe, first of all, that the truth must lie with one or both of the two realist positions – skepticism and heroism. My terminology reflects a realistic tendency: from the standpoint of a reductionist, heroic epistemology would be better described as quixotic. But I believe that skeptical problems arise not from a misunderstanding of the meaning of standard knowledge claims, but from their actual content and the attempt to transcend ourselves that is involved in the formation of beliefs about the world. The ambitions of knowledge and some of its achievements are heroic, but a pervasive skepticism or at least provisionality of commitment is suitable in light of our evident limitations.

Though a great deal of effort has been expended on them recently, definitions of knowledge cannot help us here. The central problem of epistemology is the first-person problem of what to believe and how to justify one's beliefs – not the impersonal problem of whether, given my beliefs together with some assumptions about their relation to what is actually the case, I can be said to have knowledge. Answering the question of what knowledge is will not help me decide what to believe. We must decide what our relation to the world actually is and how it can be changed.

Since we can't literally escape ourselves, any improvement in our beliefs has to result from some kind of self-transformation. And the thing we can do which comes closest to getting outside of ourselves is to form a detached idea of the world that includes us, and includes our possession of that conception as part of what it enables us to understand about ourselves. We are then outside ourselves in the sense that we appear inside a conception of the world that we ourselves possess, but that is not tied to our particular point of view. The pursuit of this goal is the essential task of the objective self. I shall argue that it makes sense only in terms of an epistemology that is significantly rationalist.

The question is how limited beings like ourselves can alter their conception of the world so that it is no longer just the view from where they are but in a sense a view from nowhere, which includes and comprehends the fact that the world contains beings which possess it, explains why the world appears to them as it does prior to the formation of that conception, and explains how they can arrive at the conception itself. This idea of objective knowledge has something in common with the program of Descartes, for he attempted to form a conception of the world in which he was contained, which would account for the validity of that conception and for his capacity to arrive at it. But his method was supposed to depend only on propositions and steps that were absolutely certain, and the method of self-transcendence as I have described it does not necessarily have this feature. In fact, such a conception of the world need not be developed by proofs at all, though it must rely heavily on a priori conjecture.[2]

In discussing the nature of the process and its pitfalls, I want both to defend the possibility of objective ascent and to understand its limits. We should keep in mind how incredible it is that such a thing is possible at all. We are encouraged these days to think of ourselves as contingent organisms arbitrarily thrown up by evolution. There is no reason in advance to expect a finite creature like that to be able to do more than accumulate information at the perceptual and conceptual level it occupies by nature. But apparently that is not how things are. Not only can we form the pure idea of a world that contains us and of which our impressions are a part, but we can give this idea a content which takes us very far from our original impressions.

The pure idea of realism – the idea that there is a world in which we are contained – implies nothing specific about the relation between the appearances and reality, except that we and our inner lives are part of reality. The recognition that this is so creates pressure on the imagination to recast our picture of the world so that it is no longer the view from here. The two possible forms this can take, skepticism and objective knowledge, are products of one capacity: the capacity to fill out the pure idea of realism with more or less definite conceptions of the world in which we are placed. The two are intimately bound together. The search for objective knowledge, because of its commitment to a realistic picture, is inescapably subject to skepticism and cannot refute it but must proceed under its shadow. Skepticism, in turn, is a problem only because of the realist claims of objectivity.

Skeptical possibilities are those according to which the world is completely different from how it appears to us, and there is no way to detect this. The most familiar from the literature are those in which error is the product of deliberate deception by an evil demon working on the mind, or by a scientist stimulating our brain in vitro to produce hallucinations. Another is the possibility that we are dreaming. In the latter two examples the world is not totally different from what we think, for it contains brains and perhaps persons who sleep, dream, and hallucinate. But this is not essential: we can conceive of the possibility that the world is different from how we believe it to be in ways that we cannot imagine, that our thoughts and impressions are produced in ways that we cannot conceive, and that there is no way of moving from where we are to beliefs about the world that are substantially correct. This is the most abstract form of skeptical possibility, and it remains an option on a realist view no matter what other hypotheses we may construct and embrace.

2.   Antiskepticism

Not everyone would concede either this skepticism or the realism on which it depends. Recently there has been a revival of arguments against the possibility of skepticism, reminiscent of the ordinary language arguments of the fifties which claimed that the meanings of statements about the world are revealed by the circumstances in which they are typically used, so that it couldn't be the case that most of what we ordinarily take to be true about the world is in fact false.

In their current versions these arguments are put in terms of reference rather than meaning.[3] What we refer to by the terms in our statements about the external world, for example – what we are really talking about – is said to be whatever *actually* bears the appropriate relation to the generally accepted use of those terms in our language. (This relation is left undefined, but it is supposed to be exemplified in the ordinary world by the relation between my use of the word "tree" and actual trees, if there are such things.)

The argument against the possibility of skepticism is a *reductio*. Suppose that I am a brain in a vat being stimulated by a mischievous scientist to think I have seen trees, though I never have. Then my word "tree" refers not to what we now call trees but to whatever the scientist usually uses to produce the stimulus which causes me to think, "There's a tree." So when I think that, I am usually thinking something true. I cannot use the word "tree" to form the thought that the scientist would express by saying I have never seen a tree, or the words "material object" to form the thought that perhaps I have never seen a material object, or the word "vat" to form the thought that perhaps I am a brain in a vat. If I were a brain in a vat, then my word "vat" would not refer to vats, and my thought, "Perhaps I am a brain in a vat," would not be true. The original skeptical supposition is shown to be impossible by the fact that if it were true, it would be false. The conditions of reference permit us to think that there are no trees, or that we are brains in a vat, only if this is not true.

This argument is no better than its predecessors. First, I can use a term which fails to refer, provided I have a conception of the conditions under which it would refer – as when I say there are no ghosts. To show that I couldn't think there were no trees if there were none, it would have to be shown that this thought could not be accounted for in more basic terms which would be available to me even if all my impressions of trees had been artificially produced. (Such an analysis need not describe my *conscious* thoughts about trees.) The same goes for "physical object". The skeptic may not be able to produce on request an account of these terms which is independent of the existence of their referents, but he is not refuted unless reason has been given to believe such an account impossible. This has not been attempted and seems on the face of it a hopeless enterprise.

A skeptic does not hold that all his terms fail to refer; he assumes, like the rest of us, that those that do not refer can be explained at some level in terms of those that do. When he says, "Perhaps I have never seen a physical object," he doesn't mean (holding up his hand), "Perhaps *this*, whatever it is, doesn't exist!" He means, "Perhaps I have never seen anything with the spatiotemporal and mind-independent characteristics necessary to be a physical object – nothing of the kind that I take physical objects to be." It has to be shown that he couldn't have *that* thought if it were true. Clearly we will be pushed back to the conditions for the possession of very general concepts. Nothing here is obvious, but it seems clear at least that a few undeveloped assumptions about reference will not enable one to prove that a brain in a vat or a disembodied spirit couldn't have the concept of mind-independence, for example. The main issue simply hasn't been addressed.

Second, although the argument doesn't work it wouldn't refute skepticism if it did. If I accept the argument, I must conclude that a brain in a vat can't think truly that it is a brain in a vat, even though others can think this about it. What follows? Only that I can't express my skepticism by saying, "Perhaps I'm a brain in a vat." Instead I must say, "Perhaps I can't even *think* the truth about what I am, because I lack the necessary concepts and my circumstances make it impossible for me to acquire them!" If this doesn't qualify as skepticism, I don't know what does.

The possibility of skepticism is built into our ordinary thoughts, in virtue of the realism that they automatically assume and their pretensions to go beyond experience. Some of what we believe must be true in order for us to be able to think at all, but this does not mean we couldn't be wrong about vast tracts of it. Thought and language have to latch onto the world, but they don't have to latch onto it directly at every point, and a being in one of the skeptic's nightmare situations should be able to latch onto enough of it to meet the conditions for formulating his questions.[4]

Critics of skepticism bring against it various theories of how the language works – theories of verifiability, causal theories of reference, principles of charity. I believe the argument goes in the opposite direction.[5] Such theories are refuted by the evident possibility and intelligibility of skepticism, which reveals that by "tree" I don't mean just anything that is causally responsible for my impressions of trees, or anything that looks and feels like a tree, or even anything of the sort that I and others have traditionally called trees. Since those things could conceivably not be trees, any theory that says they have to be is wrong.

The traditional skeptical possibilities that we can imagine stand for limitless possibilities that we can't imagine. In recognizing them we recognize that our ideas of the world, however sophisticated, are the products of one piece of the world interacting with part of the rest of it in ways that we do not understand very well. So anything we come to believe must remain suspended in a great cavern of skeptical darkness.

Once the door is open, it can't be shut again. We can only try to make our conception of our place in the world more complete – essentially developing the objective standpoint. The limit to which such development must tend is presumably unreachable: a conception that closes over itself completely, by describing a world that contains a being that has precisely that conception, and explaining how the being was able to reach that conception from its starting point within the world. Even if we did arrive at such a self-transcendent idea, that wouldn't guarantee its correctness. It would recommend itself as a possibility, but the skeptical possibilities would also remain open. The best we can do is to construct a picture that might be correct. Skepticism is really a way of recognizing our situation, though it will not prevent us from continuing to pursue something like knowledge, for our natural realism makes it impossible for us to be content with a purely subjective view.

3. Self-transcendence

To provide an alternative to the imaginable and unimaginable skeptical possibilities, a self-transcendent conception should ideally explain the following four things: (1) what the world is like; (2) what we are like; (3) why the world appears to beings like us in certain respects as it is and in certain respects as it isn't; (4) how beings like us can arrive at such a conception. In practice, the last condition is rarely met. We tend to use our rational capacities to construct theories, without at the same time constructing epistemological accounts of how those capacities work. Nevertheless, this is an important part of objectivity. What we want is to reach a position as independent as possible of who we are and where we started, but a position that can also explain how we got there.

In a sense, these conditions could also be satisfied by a conception of the world and our place in it that was developed by other beings, different from us; but in that case the fourth element would not involve self-referential understanding, as it does in the understanding of ourselves. The closest we can come to an external understanding of our relation to the world is to develop the self-referential analogue of an external understanding. This leaves us in no worse position than an external observer, for any being who viewed us from outside would have to face the problem of self-understanding in its own case, to be reasonably secure in its pretensions to understand us or anything else. The aim of objectivity would be to reach a conception of the world, including oneself, which involved one's own point of view not essentially, but only instrumentally, so to speak: so that the form of our understanding would be specific to ourselves, but its content would not be.

The vast majority of additions to what we know do not require any advance in objectivity: they merely add further information at a level that already exists. When someone discovers a previously undetected planet, or the chemical composition of a hormone, or the cause of a disease, or the early influences on a historical figure, he is essentially filling in a framework of understanding that is already given. Even something as fruitful as the discovery of the structure of DNA is in this category. It merely extended the methods of chemistry into genetics. Discoveries like this may be difficult to make, but they do not involve fundamental alterations in the idea of our epistemic relation to the world. They add knowledge without objective advance.

An advance in objectivity requires that already existing forms of understanding should themselves become the object of a new form of understanding, which also takes in the objects of the original forms. This is true of any objective step, even if it does not reach the more ambitious goal of explaining itself. All advances in objectivity subsume our former understanding under a new account of our mental relation to the world.

Consider for example the distinction between primary and secondary qualities, the precondition for the development of modern physics and chemistry. This is a particularly clear example of how we can place ourselves in a new world picture. We realize that our perceptions of external objects depend both on their properties and on ours, and that to explain both their effects on us and their interactions with each other we need to attribute to them fewer types of properties than they may initially appear to have.

Colin McGinn has argued convincingly that this is in the first instance an a priori philosophical discovery, not an empirical scientific one. Things have colors, tastes, and smells in virtue of the way they appear to us: to be red simply *is* to be the sort of thing that looks or would look red to normal human observers in the perceptual circumstances that normally obtain in the actual world. To be square, on the other hand, is an independent property which can be used to explain many things about an object, including how it looks and feels. (McGinn, *The Subjective View* (Oxford University Press, 1983), ch. 7.)

Once this is recognized and we consider how the various perceptible properties of objects are to be explained, it becomes clear that the best account of the appearance of colors will not involve the ascription to things of intrinsic color properties that play an ineliminable role in the explanation of the appearances: the way in which the appearances vary with both physical and psychological conditions makes this very implausible. Objective shape and size, on the other hand, enter naturally into an account of variable appearance of shape and size. So much is evident even if we have only a very rough idea of how as perceivers we are acted upon by the external world – an idea having to do primarily with the type of peripheral impact involved. It is then a short step to the conjecture that the appearances of secondary qualities are caused by other primary qualities of objects, which we can then try to discover.

The pressure to make an objective advance comes, here as elsewhere, from the incapacity of the earlier view of the world to include and explain itself – that is, to explain why things appear to us as they do. This makes us seek a new conception that can explain both the former appearances and the new impression that it itself is true. The hypothesis that objects have intrinsic colors in addition to their primary qualities would conspicuously fail this test, for it provides a poorer explanation of why they appear to have colors, and why those appearances change under internal and external circumstances, than the hypothesis that the primary qualities of objects and their effects on us are responsible for all the appearances.

Consider another example. Not all objective advances have been so widely internalized as this, and some, like general relativity and quantum mechanics, are advances beyond already advanced theories that are not generally accessible. But one huge step beyond common appearance was taken by Einstein with the special theory of relativity. He replaced the familiar idea of unqualified temporal and spatial relations between events, things, and processes by a relativistic conception according to which events are not without qualification simultaneous or successive, objects are not without qualification equal or unequal in size, but only with respect to a frame of reference. What formerly seemed to be an objective conception of absolute space and time was revealed to be a mere appearance, from the perspective of one frame of reference, of a world whose objective description from no frame of reference is not given in a four-dimensional coordinate system of independent spatial and temporal dimensions at all. Instead, events are objectively located in relativistic space-time, whose division into separate spatial and temporal dimensions depends on one's point of view. In this case it was reflection on electrodynamic phenomena rather than ordinary perception that revealed that the appearances had to be transcended. There was also, as with the primary-secondary quality distinction, an important philosophical element in the discovery that absolute simultaneity of spatially separated events was not a well-defined notion, in our ordinary system of concepts.

These examples illustrate the human capacity to escape the limits of the original human situation, not merely by traveling around and seeing the world from different perspectives, but by ascending to new levels from which we can understand and criticize the general forms of previous perspectives. The step to a new perspective is the product of epistemological insight in each case.

Of course it is also the product in some cases of new observations that can't be accommodated in the old picture. But the satisfactoriness of a new external perspective depends on whether it can place the internal perspective within the world in a way that enables one to occupy both of them simultaneously, with a sense that the external perspective gives access to an objective reality that one's subjective impressions are impressions of. Experience is not the sole foundation of our knowledge of the world, but a place must be found for it as part of the world, however different that world may be from the way it is depicted in experience.

Only objectivity can give meaning to the idea of intellectual progress. We can see this by considering any well-established objective advance, like the examples discussed already, and asking whether it could be reversed. Could a theory which ascribed intrinsic colors, tastes, smells, feels, and sounds to things account for the appearance that these are to be explained as the effects on our senses of primary qualities? Could a theory of absolute space and time explain the appearance that we occupy relativistic space-time? In both cases the answer is no. An objective advance may be superseded by a further objective advance, which reduces it in turn to an appearance. But it is not on the same level as its predecessors, and may well have been essential as a step on the route to its successors.

Still, the fact that objective reality is our goal does not guarantee that our pursuit of it succeeds in being anything more than an exploration and reorganization of the insides of our own minds. On a realist view this always remains a possibility, at least in the abstract, even if one isn't thinking of a specific way in which one might be deceived. A less radical point is that whatever we may have achieved we are only at a passing stage of intellectual development, and much of what we now believe will be overthrown by later discoveries and later theories.

A certain expectation of further advance and occasional retreat is rational: there have been enough cases in which what was once thought a maximally objective conception of reality has been included as appearance in a still more objective conception so that we would be foolish not to expect it to go on. Indeed, we should want it to go on, for we are evidently just at the beginning of our trip outward, and what has so far been achieved in the way of self-understanding is minimal.

Notes

1 A fourth reaction is to turn one's back on the abyss and announce that one is now on the other side. This was done by G. E. Moore.
2 The idea is much closer to what Bernard Williams calls the absolute conception of reality, which is a more general description of Descartes' idea of knowledge. See Williams, *Descartes. The Project of Pure Inquiry* (Harmondsworth: Penguin, 1978).
3 See for example Hilary Putnam, *Reason, Truth and History* (Cambridge University Press, 1981), Ch. 1.
4 There is perhaps one form of radical skepticism which could be ruled out as unthinkable, by an argument analogous to the *cogito*: skepticism about whether I am the kind of being who can have thoughts *at all*. If there were possible beings whose nature and relation to the world was such that nothing they did could constitute thinking, whatever went on inside them, then I could not wonder whether I was such a being, because if I were, I wouldn't be thinking, and even to consider the possibility that I may not be thinking is to think. But most forms of skepticism are not this extreme.
5 This is a theme of Thompson Clarke's and Barry Stroud's work on skepticism. See Stroud, *The Significance of Philosophical Skepticism* (Oxford University Press, 1984), pp. 205–6. Stroud's book is a highly illuminating discussion of skepticism and the inadequacy of most responses to it. He is nevertheless slightly more optimistic than I am about the possibility of finding something wrong with skepticism–and with the desire for an objective or external understanding of our position in the world that leads to it.

8

Peter Unger, "A Defense of Skepticism"

In "A Defense of Skepticism" Peter Unger (1942–), currently professor of philosophy at New York University, offers an interesting and powerful argument for accepting a strong global skepticism. Unger wants to motivate the claim that any given person knows hardly anything at all. Though one may quickly ask how we know Unger's own thesis to be correct, he is just as quick to say that he thinks he can provide grounds to think that it is true.

At the heart of Unger's argument lie observations about the nature of terms we use widely in common discourse, including those used to express knowledge claims. If we look at a term such as "flat" we see that for something truly to be flat is for it to be absolutely flat – that is, it must have absolutely no bumps or curves. Unger calls such terms absolute terms, and certain ones such as "flat" and "certain" are basic, since they require no further definition by other absolute terms. Just as few things in the world are truly flat, few people are truly certain of anything, for absolute certainty requires that one cannot be more certain of anything else. Since Unger argues that knowledge requires certainty, it follows that a particular person knows few things, if any.

Though Unger's case certainly proves compelling, we might wonder why a notion so central to our daily discourse, such as knowledge, actually applies according to what seems to be a superhuman standard. If we each know but a few things – perhaps only the conviction that we exist meets the test of absolute certainty – what of our more pedestrian beliefs that, for example, Albany is the capital of New York or that $2 + 2 = 4$? If we side with Unger, we must, at best, rest content merely to believe such things to be true.

The skepticism that I will defend is a negative thesis concerning what we know. I happily accept the fact that there is much that many of us correctly and reasonably believe, but much more than that is needed for us to know even a fair amount. Here I will not argue that nobody knows anything about anything, though that would be quite consistent with the skeptical thesis for which I will argue. The somewhat less radical thesis which I will defend is this one: every human being knows, at best, hardly anything to be so. More specifically, I will argue that hardly anyone knows that 45 and 56 are equal to 101, if anyone at all. On this skeptical thesis, no one will know the thesis to be true. But this is all right. For I only want to argue that it may be reasonable for us to suppose the thesis to be true, not that we should ever know it to be true.

Few philosophers now take skepticism seriously. With philosophers, even the most powerful of traditional skeptical argument has little force to tempt them nowadays. Indeed, nowadays, philosophers tend to think skepticism interesting only as a formal challenge to which positive accounts of our common-sense knowledge are the gratifying responses. Consequently, I find it at least somewhat natural to offer a defense of skepticism.[1]

My defense of skepticism will be quite unlike traditional arguments for this thesis. This is largely because I write at a time when there is a common faith that, so far as expressing truths is concerned, all is well with the language that we speak. Against this common, optimistic assumption, I shall illustrate how our language habits might serve us well in practical ways, even while they involve us in saying what is false rather than true. And this often does occur, I will maintain, when our positive assertions contain terms with special features of a certain kind, which I call *absolute* terms. Among these terms, "flat" and "certain" are *basic* ones. Due to these terms' characteristic features, and because the world is not so simple as it might be, we do not speak truly, at least as a rule, when we say of a real object, "That has a top which is flat" or when we say of a real person, "He is certain that it is raining." And just as basic absolute terms generally fail to apply to the world, so other absolute terms, which are at least partially defined by the basic ones, will fail to apply as well. Thus, we also speak falsely when we say of a real object or person, "That is a cube" or "He knows that it is raining." For an object is a cube only if it has surfaces which are flat, and, as I shall argue, a person knows something to be so only if he is certain of it.

I.   Sophisticated Worries about What Skepticism Requires

The reason contemporary sophisticated philosophers do not take skepticism seriously can be stated broadly and simply. They think that skepticism implies certain things which are, upon a bit of reflection, quite impossible to accept. These unacceptable implications concern the functioning of our language.

Concerning our language and how it functions, the most obvious requirement of skepticism is that some common terms of our language will involve us in error systematically. These will be such terms as "know" and "knowledge," which may be called the "terms of knowledge." If skepticism is right, then while we go around saying "I know," "He knows," and so on, and while we believe what we say to be true, all the while what we say and believe will actually be false. If our beliefs to the effect that we know something or other are so consistently false, then the terms of knowledge lead us into error systematically. But if these beliefs really are false, should we not have experiences which force the realization of their falsity upon us, and indeed abandon these beliefs? Consequently, shouldn't our experiences get us to stop thinking in these terms which thus systematically involve us in error? So, as we continue to think in the terms of knowledge and to believe ourselves to know all sorts of things, this would seem to show that the beliefs are not false ones and the terms are responsible for no error. Isn't it only reasonable, then, to reject a view which requires that such helpful common terms as "knows" and "knowledge" lead us into error systematically?

So go some worrisome thoughts which might lead us to dismiss skepticism out of hand. But it seems to me that there is no real need for our false beliefs to clash with our experiences in any easily noticeable way. Suppose, for instance, that you falsely believe that a certain region of space is a vacuum. Suppose that, contrary to your belief, the region does contain some gaseous stuff, though only the slightest trace. Now, for practical purposes, we may suppose that, so far as gaseous contents go, it is not important whether that region really is a vacuum or whether it contains whatever gaseous stuff it does contain. Once this is supposed, then it is reasonable to suppose as well that, for practical purposes, it makes no important difference whether you falsely believe that the region is a vacuum or truly believe this last thing – namely, that, for practical purposes, it is not important whether the region is a vacuum or whether it contains that much gaseous stuff.

We may notice that this supposed truth is entailed by what you believe but does not entail it. In other words, a region's being a vacuum entails that, for practical purposes, there is no important difference between whether the region is a vacuum or whether it contains whatever gaseous stuff it does contain. For, if the region *is* a vacuum, whatever gas it contains is nil, and so there is no difference at all, for any sort of purpose, between the region's being a vacuum and its having that much gaseous stuff. But the entailment does not go the other way, and this is where we may take a special interest. For while a region may not be a vacuum, it may contain so little gaseous stuff that, so far as gaseous contents go, for practical purposes there is no important difference between the region's being a vacuum and its containing whatever gaseous stuff it does contain. So if this entailed truth lies behind the believed falsehood, your false belief, though false, may not be harmful. Indeed, generally, it may even be helpful for you to have this false belief rather than having none and rather than having almost any other belief about the matter that you might have. On this pattern, we may have many false beliefs about regions being vacuums even while these beliefs will suffer no important clash with the experiences of life.

More to our central topic, suppose that, as skepticism might have it, you falsely believe that you *know* that there are elephants. As before, there is a true thing which is entailed by what you falsely believe and which we should notice. The thing here, which presumably you do not actually believe, is this: that, with respect to the matter of whether there are elephants, for practical purposes there is no important difference between whether you know that there are elephants or whether you are in that position with respect to the matter that you actually are in. This latter, true thing is entailed by the false thing you believe – namely, that you know that there are elephants. For if you do know, then, with respect to the matter of the elephants, there is no difference at all, for any purpose of any sort, between your knowing and your being in the position you actually are in. On the other hand, the entailment does not go the other way and, again, this is where our pattern allows a false belief to be helpful. For even if you do not really know, still, it may be that for practical purposes you are in a position with respect to the matter (of the elephants) which is not importantly different from knowing. If this is so, then it may be better, practically speaking, for you to believe falsely that you know than to have no belief at all here. Thus, not only with beliefs to the effect that specified regions are vacuums, but also with beliefs to the effect that we know certain things, it may be that there are very many of them which, though false, it is helpful for us to have. In both cases, the beliefs will not noticeably clash with the experiences of life. Without some further reason for doing so, then, noting the smooth functioning of our "terms of knowledge" gives us no powerful reason for dismissing the thesis of skepticism.

There is, however, a second worry which will tend to keep sophisticates far from embracing skepticism, and this worry is, I think, rather more profound than the first. Consequently, I shall devote most of the remainder to treating this second worry. The worry to which I shall be so devoted is this: that, if skepticism is right, then the terms of knowledge, unlike other terms of our language, will never or hardly ever be used to make simple, positive assertions that are true. In other words, skepticism will require the terms of knowledge to be isolated freaks of our language. But even with familiar, persuasive arguments for skepticism, it is implausible to think that our language is plagued by an isolated little group of troublesome freaks. So, by being so hard on knowledge alone, skepticism seems implausible once one reflects on the exclusiveness of its persecution.

II.   Absolute Terms and Relative Terms

Against the worry that skepticism will require the terms of knowledge to be isolated freaks, I shall argue that, on the contrary, a variety of other terms is similarly troublesome. As skepticism becomes more plausible with an examination of the terms of knowledge, so other originally surprising theses become more plausible once their key terms are critically examined. When all of the key terms are understood to have essential features in common, the truth of any of these theses need not be felt as such a surprise.

The terms of knowledge, along with many other troublesome terms, belong to a class of terms that is quite pervasive in our language. I call these terms *absolute terms*. The term "flat," in its central, literal meaning, is an absolute term. (With other meanings, as in "His voice is flat" and "The beer is flat," I have no direct interest.) To say that something is flat is no different from saying that it is absolutely, or perfectly, flat. To say that a surface is flat is to say that some things or properties *which are matters of degree* are *not* instanced in the surface *to any degree at all*. Thus, something which is flat is not at all bumpy, and not at all curved. Bumpiness and curvature are matters of degree. When we say of a surface that it is bumpy, or that it is curved, we use the *relative terms* "bumpy" and "curved" to talk about the surface. Thus, absolute terms and relative terms go together, in at least one important way, while other terms, like "unmarried," have only the most distant connections with terms of either of these two sorts.

There seems to be a syntactic feature which is common to relative terms and to certain absolute terms, while it is found with no other terms. This feature is that each of these terms may be modified by a variety of terms that serve to indicate (matters of) degree. Thus, we find "The table is *very* bumpy" and "The table is *very* flat" but not "The lawyer is *very* unmarried." Among those absolute terms which admit such qualification are all those absolute terms which are *basic* ones. A basic absolute term is an absolute term which is not (naturally) defined in terms of some other absolute term, not even partially so. I suspect that "straight" is such a term, and perhaps "flat" is as well. But in its central (geometrical) meaning, "cube" quite clearly is not a basic absolute term even though it is an absolute term. For "cube" means, among other things, "having edges that are *straight* and surfaces which are *flat*": and "straight" and "flat" are absolute terms. While "cube" does not admit of qualification of degree, "flat" and "straight" do admit of such qualification. Thus, all relative terms and all basic absolute terms admit of constructions of degree. While this is another way in which these two sorts of terms go together, we must now ask: how may we distinguish terms of the one sort from those of the other?

But is there now anything to distinguish here? For if absolute terms admit of degree construction, why think that any of these terms is not a relative term, why think that they do not purport to predicate things or properties which are, as they now look to be, matters of degree? If we may say that a table is very flat, then why not think flatness a matter of degree? Isn't this essentially the same as our saying of a table that it is very bumpy, with bumpiness being a matter of degree? So perhaps "flat," like "bumpy" and like all terms that take degree constructions, is, fittingly, a relative term. But basic absolute terms may be distinguished from relatives even where degree constructions conspire to make things look otherwise.

To advance the wanted distinction, we may look to a procedure for paraphrase. Now, we have granted that it is common for us to say of a surface that it is pretty, or very, or extremely, flat. And it is also common for us to say that, in saying such things of surfaces, we are saying *how* flat the surfaces are. What we say here seems of a piece with our saying of a surface that it is pretty, or very, or extremely, bumpy, and our then saying that, in doing this, we are saying *how* bumpy the surface is. But, even intuitively, we may notice a difference here. For only with our talk about "flat," we have the idea that these locutions are only convenient means for saying how closely a surface approximates, or *how close it comes to being*, a surface which is (absolutely) flat. Thus, it is intuitively plausible, and far from being a nonsensical interpretation, to paraphrase things so our result with our "flat" locutions is this: what we have said of a surface is that it is pretty *nearly* flat, or very *nearly* flat, or extremely *close to being* flat and, in doing that, we have said, not simply how flat the surface is, but rather *how close* the surface is *to being* flat. This form of paraphrase gives a plausible interpretation of our talk of flatness while allowing the term "flat" to lose its appearance of being a relative term. How will this form of paraphrase work with "bumpy," where, presumably, a genuine relative term occurs in our locutions?

What do we say when we say of a surface that it is pretty bumpy, or very bumpy, or extremely so? Of course, it at least appears that we say *how* bumpy the surface is. The paraphrase has it that what we are saying is that the surface is pretty *nearly* bumpy, or very *nearly* bumpy, or extremely *close to being* bumpy. In other words, according to the paraphrase, we are saying *how close* the surface is *to being* bumpy. But anything of this sort is, quite obviously, a terribly poor interpretation of what we are saying about the surface. Unfortunately for the paraphrase, if we say that a surface is very bumpy it is entailed by what we say that the surface is bumpy, while if we say that the surface is very close to being bumpy it is entailed that the surface is *not* bumpy. Thus, unlike the case with "flat," our paraphrase cannot apply with "bumpy." Consequently, by means of our paraphrase we may distinguish between absolute terms and relative ones.

Another way of noticing how our paraphrase lends support to the distinction between absolute and relative terms is this: the initial data are that such terms as "very," which standardly serve to indicate that there is a great deal of something, serve with opposite effect when they modify terms like "flat" – terms which I have called basic absolute terms. That is, when we say, for example, that something is (really) very flat, then, so far as flatness is concerned, we seem to say less of the thing than when we say, simply, that it is (really) flat. The augmenting function of "very" is turned on its head so that the term serves to diminish. What can resolve this conflict? It seems that our paraphrase can. For on the paraphrase, what we are saying of the thing is that it is very *nearly* flat, and so, by implication, that it is *not* flat (but only very nearly so). Once the paraphrase is exploited, the term "very" may be understood to have its standard augmenting function. At the same time, "very" functions without conflict with "bumpy." Happily, the term "very" is far from being unique here; we get the same results with other augmenting modifiers: "extremely," "especially," and so on.

For our paraphrastic procedure to be comprehensive, it must work with contexts containing explicitly comparative locutions. Indeed, with these contexts, we have a common form of talk where the appearance of relativeness is most striking of all. What shall we think of our saying, for example, that one surface is not *as* flat as another, where things strikingly look to be a matter of degree? It seems that we must allow that in such a suggested comparison, the surface which is said to be the *flatter* of the two may be, so far as logic goes, (absolutely) flat. Thus, we should *not* paraphrase this comparative context as "the one surface is not as *nearly* flat as the other." For this form of paraphrase would imply that the second surface is not flat, and so it gives us a poor interpretation of the original, which has no such implication. But then, a paraphrase with no bad implications is not far removed. Instead of simply inserting our "nearly" or our "close to being," we may allow for the possibility of (absolute) flatness by putting things in a way which is only somewhat more complex. For we may paraphrase our original by saying: the first surface is *either not flat though the second is, or else it is* not as *nearly* flat as the second. Similarly, where we say that one surface is flatter than another, we may paraphrase things like this: the first surface is *either flat though the second is not or else it is closer to being flat* than the second. But in contrast to all this, with comparisons of bumpiness, no paraphrase is available. To say that one surface is not as bumpy as another is not to say either that the first surface is not bumpy though the second is, or else that it is not as nearly bumpy as the second one.

Our noting the availability of degree constructions allows us to class together relative terms and basic absolute terms, as against any other terms. And our noting that only with the absolute terms do our constructions admit of our paraphrase allows us to distinguish between the relative terms and the basic absolute terms. Now that these terms may be quite clearly distinguished, we may restate without pain of vacuity those ideas on which we relied to introduce our terminology. Thus, to draw the *connection* between terms of the two sorts we may now say this: every basic absolute term, and so every absolute term whatever, may be defined, at least partially, by means of certain relative terms. The defining conditions presented by means of the relative terms are negative ones; they say that what the relative term purports to denote is *not* present *at all*, or *in the least*, where the absolute term correctly applies. Thus, these negative conditions are logically necessary ones for basic absolute terms, and so for absolute terms which are defined by means of the basic ones. Thus, something is flat, in the central, literal sense of "flat," only if it is not at all, or not in the least, curved or bumpy. And similarly, something is a cube, in the central, literal sense of "cube," only if it has surfaces which are not at all, or not in the least, bumpy or curved. In noting these demanding *negative relative requirements*, we may begin to appreciate, I think, that a variety of absolute terms, if not all of them, might well be quite troublesome to apply, perhaps even failing consistently in application to real things.

In a final general remark about these terms, I should like to motivate my choice of terminology for them. A reason I call terms of the one sort "absolute" is that, at least in the case of the basic ones, the term may always be modified, grammatically, with the term "absolutely." And indeed, this modification fits so well that it is, I think, always redundant. Thus, something is flat if and only if it is absolutely flat. In contrast, the term "absolutely" never gives a standard, grammatical modification for any of our relative terms: nothing which is bumpy is absolutely bumpy. On the other hand, each of the relative terms takes "relatively" quite smoothly as a grammatical modifier. (And, though it is far from being clear, it is at least arguable, I think, that this modifier is redundant for these terms. Thus, it is at least arguable that something is bumpy if and only if it is relatively bumpy.) In any event, with absolute terms, while "relatively" is grammatically quite all right as a modifier, the construction thus obtained must be understood in terms of our paraphrase. Thus, as before, something is relatively flat if and only if it is relatively close to being (absolutely) flat, and so only if it is not flat.

In this terminology, and in line with our linguistic tests, I think that the first term of each of the following pairs is a relative term while the second is an absolute one: "wet" and "dry," "crooked" and "straight," "important" and "crucial," "incomplete" and "complete," "useful" and "useless," and so on. I think that both "empty" and "full" are absolute terms, while "good" and "bad," "rich" and "poor," and "happy" and "unhappy" are all relative terms. Finally, I think that, in the sense defined by our tests, each of the following is neither an absolute term nor a relative one: "married" and "unmarried," "true" and "false," and "right" and "wrong". In other plausible senses, though, some or all of this last group might be called "absolute."

III.   On Certainty and Certain Related Things

Certain terms of our language are standardly followed by propositional clauses, and, indeed, it is plausible to think that wherever they occur they *must* be followed by such clauses on pain of otherwise occurring in a sentence which is elliptical or incomplete. We may call terms which take these clauses *propositional terms* and we may then ask: are some propositional terms absolute ones, while others are relative terms? By means of our tests, I will argue that "certain" is an absolute term, while "confident," "doubtful," and "uncertain" are all relative terms.

With regard to being certain, there are two ideas which are important: first, the idea of something's being certain, where that which is certain is *not* certain *of* anything, and, second, the idea of a being's being certain, where that which is certain *is* certain *of* something. A paradigm context for the first idea is the context "It is certain that it is raining" where the term "it" has no apparent reference. I will call such contexts *impersonal* contexts, and the idea of certainty which they serve to express, thus, the impersonal idea of certainty. In contrast, a paradigm context for the second idea is this one: "He is certain that it is raining" – where, of course, the term "he" purports to refer as clearly as one might like. In the latter context, which we may call the *personal* context, we express the personal idea of certainty. This last may be allowed, I think, even though in ordinary conversations we may speak of dogs as being certain; presumably, we treat dogs there the way we typically treat persons.

Though there are these two important sorts of context, I think that "certain" must mean the same in both. In both cases, we must be struck by the thought that the presence of certainty amounts to the complete absence of doubt, or doubtfulness. This thought leads me to say that "It is certain that p" means, within the bounds of nuance, "It is not at all doubtful that p." The idea of personal certainty may then be defined accordingly; we relate what is said in the impersonal form to the mind of the person, or subject, who is said to be certain of something. Thus, "He is certain that p" means, within the bounds of nuance, "*In his mind*, it is not at all doubtful that p." Where a man is certain of something, then, concerning that thing, all doubt is absent in that man's mind. With these definitions available, we may now say this: connected negative definitions of certainty suggest that, in its central, literal meaning, "certain" is an absolute term.

But we should like firmer evidence for thinking that "certain" is an absolute term. To be consistent, we turn to our procedure for paraphrase. I will exhibit the evidence for personal contexts and then say a word about impersonal ones. In any event, we want contrasting results for "certain" as against some related relative terms. One term which now suggests itself for contrast is, of course, "doubtful." Another is, of course, "uncertain." And we will get the desired results with these terms. But it is, I think, more interesting to consider the term "confident."

In quick discussions of these matters, one might speak indifferently of a man's being confident of something and of his being certain of it. But on reflection there is a difference between confidence and certainty. Indeed, when I say that I am certain of something, I tell you that I am not confident of it but that I am *more than* that. And if I say that I am confident that so-and-so, I tell you that I am *not so much as* certain of the thing. Thus, there is an important difference between the two. At least part of this difference is, I suggest, reflected by our procedure for paraphrase.

We may begin to apply our procedure by resolving the problem of augmenting modifiers. Paradoxically, when I say that I am (really) very certain of something, I say *less* of myself, so far as certainty is concerned, than I do when I say, simply, that I am (really) certain of the thing. How may we resolve this paradox? Our paraphrase explains things as before. In the first case, what I am really saying is that I am very *nearly* certain, and so, in effect, that I am not really certain. But in the second case, I say that I really am. Further, we may notice that, in contrast, in the case of "confident" and "uncertain," and "doubtful" as well, no problem with augmenting arises in the first place. For when I say that I am very confident of something, I say more of myself, so far as confidence is concerned, than I do when I simply say that I am confident of the thing. And again our paraphrastic procedure yields us the lack of any problems here. For the augmented statement cannot be sensibly interpreted as saying that I am very nearly confident of the thing. Indeed, with any modifier weaker than "absolutely," our paraphrase works well with "certain" but produces only a nonsensical interpretation with "confident" and other contrasting terms. For example, what might it mean to say of someone that he was rather confident of something? Would this be to say that he was rather close to being confident of the thing? Surely not.

Turning to comparative constructions, our paraphrase separates things just as we should expect. For example, from "He is more certain that p than he is that q" we get "He is either certain that p while not certain that q, or else he is more nearly certain that p than he is that q." But from "He is more confident that p than he is that q" we do *not* get "He is either confident that p while not confident that q, or else he is more nearly confident that p than he is that q." For he may well already be confident of both things. Further comparative constructions are similarly distinguished when subjected to our paraphrase. And no matter what locutions we try, the separation is as convincing with impersonal contexts as it is with personal ones, so long as there are contexts which are comparable. Of course, "confident" has no impersonal contexts; we cannot say "It is confident that *p*," where the "it" has no purported reference. But where comparable contexts do exist, as with "doubtful" and "uncertain," further evidence is available. Thus, we may reasonably assert that "certain" is an absolute term while "confident," "doubtful," and "uncertain" are relative terms.

IV.   The Doubtful Applicability of Some Absolute Terms

If my account of absolute terms is essentially correct, then, at least in the case of some of these terms, fairly reasonable suppositions about the world make it somewhat doubtful that the terms properly apply. (In certain contexts, generally where what we are talking about divides into discrete units, the presence of an absolute term need cause no doubts. Thus, considering the absolute term "complete," the truth of "His set of steins is now complete" may be allowed without hesitation, but the truth of "His explanation is now complete" may well be doubted. It is with the latter, more interesting contexts, I think, that we shall be concerned in what follows.) For example, while we say of many surfaces of physical things that they are flat, a rather reasonable interpretation of what we do observe makes it at least somewhat doubtful that these surfaces actually *are* flat. When we look at a rather smooth block of stone through a powerful microscope, the observed surface appears to us to be rife with irregularities. And this irregular appearance seems best explained, not by being taken as an illusory optical phenomenon, but by taking it to be a finer, more revealing look of a surface which is, in fact, rife with smallish bumps and crevices. Further, we account for bumps and crevices by supposing that the stone is composed of much smaller things, molecules and so on, which are in such a combination that, while a large and sturdy stone is the upshot, no stone with a flat surface is found to obtain.

Indeed, what follows from my account of "flat" is this: that, as a matter of logical necessity, if a surface is flat, then there never is any surface which is flatter than it is. For on our paraphrase, if the second surface is flatter than the first, then either the second surface is flat while the first is not, or else the second is more nearly flat than the first, neither surface being flat. So if there is such a second, flatter surface, then the first surface is not flat after all, contrary to our supposition. Thus there cannot be any second, flatter surface. Or in other words, if it is logically possible that there be a surface which is flatter than a given one, then that given surface is not really a flat one. Now, in the case of the observed surface of the stone, owing to the stone's irregular composition, the surface is *not* one such that it is logically impossible that there be a flatter one. (For example, we might veridically observe a surface through a microscope of the same power which did not appear to have any bumps or crevices.) Thus it is only reasonable to suppose that the surface of this stone is not really flat.

Our understanding of the stone's composition, that it is composed of molecules and so on, makes it reasonable for us to suppose as well that any similarly sized or larger surfaces will fail to be flat just as the observed surface fails to be flat. At the same time, it would be perhaps a bit rash to suppose that much smaller surfaces would fail to be flat as well. Beneath the level of our observation perhaps there are small areas of the stone's surface which are flat. If so, then perhaps there are small objects that have surfaces which are flat, like this area of the stone's surface: for instance, chipping off a small part of the stone might yield such a small object. So perhaps there are physical objects with surfaces which are flat, and perhaps it is not now reasonable for us to assume that there are no such objects. But even if this strong assumption is not now reasonable, one thing which does seem quite reasonable for us now to assume is this: we should at least suspend judgment on the matter of whether there are any physical objects with flat surfaces. That there are such objects is something it is not now reasonable for us to believe.

It is at least somewhat doubtful, then, that "flat" ever applies to actual physical objects or to their surfaces. And the thought must strike us that if "flat" has no such application, this must be due in part to the fact that "flat" is an absolute term. We may then do well to be a bit doubtful about the applicability of any other given absolute term and, in particular, about the applicability of the term "certain." As in the case of "flat," our paraphrase highlights the absolute character of "certain." As a matter of logical necessity, if someone is certain of something, then there never is anything of which he is more certain. For on our paraphrase, if the person is more certain of any other thing, then either he is certain of the other thing while not being certain of the first, or else he is more nearly certain of the other thing than he is of the first; that is, he is certain of neither. Thus, if it is logically possible that there be something of which a person might be more certain than he now is of a given thing, then he is not really certain of that given thing.

Thus it is reasonable to suppose, I think, that hardly anyone, if anyone at all, is certain that 45 and 56 are 101. For it is reasonable to suppose that hardly anyone, if anyone at all, is so certain of that particular calculation that it is impossible for there to be anything of which he might be yet more certain. But this is not surprising; for hardly anyone *feels* certain that those two numbers have that sum. What, then, about something of which people commonly do feel absolutely certain – say, of the existence of automobiles?

Is it reasonable for us now actually to believe that many people are certain that there are automobiles? If it is, then it is reasonable for us to believe as well that for each of them it is not possible for there to be anything of which he might be more certain than he now is of there being automobiles. In particular, we must then believe of these people that it is impossible for any of them ever to be more certain of his own existence than all of them now are of the existence of automobiles. While these people *might* all actually be as certain of the automobiles as this, just as each of them *feels* himself to be, I think it somewhat rash for us actually to believe that they *are* all so certain. Certainty being an absolute and our understanding of people being rather rudimentary and incomplete, I think it more reasonable for us now to suspend judgment on the matter. And, since there is nothing importantly peculiar about the matter of the automobiles, the same cautious position recommends itself quite generally: so far as actual human beings go, the most reasonable course for us now is to suspend judgment as to whether any of them is certain of more than hardly anything, if anything at all.[2]

V. Does Knowing Require Being Certain?

One tradition in philosophy holds that knowing requires being certain. As a matter of logical necessity, a man knows something only if he is certain of the thing. In this tradition, certainty is not taken lightly; rather, it is equated with absolute certainty. Even that most famous contemporary defender of common sense, G. E. Moore, is willing to equate knowing something with knowing the thing with absolute certainty.[3] I am rather inclined to hold with this traditional view, and it is now my purpose to argue that this view is at least a fairly reasonable one.

To a philosopher like Moore, I would have nothing left to say in my defense of skepticism. But recently some philosophers have contended that not certainty, but only belief, is required for knowing.[4] According to these thinkers, if a man's belief meets certain conditions not connected with his being certain, that mere belief may properly be counted as an instance or a bit of knowledge. And even more recently some philosophers have held that not even so much as belief is required for a man to know that something is so.[5] Thus, I must argue for the traditional view of knowing. But then what has led philosophers to move further and further away from the traditional strong assertion that knowing something requires being certain of the thing?

My diagnosis of the situation is this. In everyday affairs we often speak loosely, charitably, and casually; we tend to let what we say pass as being true. I want to suggest that it is by being wrongly serious about this casual talk that philosophers (myself included) have come to think it rather easy to know things to be so. In particular, they have come to think that certainty is not needed. Thus typical in the contemporary literature is this sort of exchange. An examiner asks a student when a certain battle was fought. The student fumbles about and, eventually, unconfidently says what is true: "The Battle of Hastings was fought in 1066." It is supposed, quite properly, that this correct answer is a result of the student's reading. The examiner, being an ordinary mortal, allows that the student knows the answer; he judges that the student knows that the Battle of Hastings was fought in 1066. Surely, it is suggested, the examiner is correct in his judgment even though this student clearly is not certain of the thing; therefore, knowing does not require being certain. But is the examiner really correct in asserting that the student knows the date of this battle? That is, do such exchanges give us good reason to think that knowing does not require certainty?

My recommendation is this. Let us try focusing on just those words most directly employed in expressing the concept whose conditions are our object of inquiry. This principle is quite generally applicable and, I think, quite easily applied. We may apply it by suitably juxtaposing certain terms, like "really" and "actually," with the terms most in question (here, the term "knows"). More strikingly, we may *emphasize* the terms in question. Thus, instead of looking at something as innocent as "He knows that they are alive," let us consider the more relevant "He (really) *knows* that they are alive."

Let us build some confidence that this principle is quite generally applicable, and that it will give us trustworthy results. Toward this end, we may focus on some thoughts about definite descriptions – that is, about expressions of the form "the so-and-so." About these expressions, it is a tradition to hold that they require uniqueness, or unique satisfaction, for their proper application. Thus, just as it is traditional to hold that a man knows something only if he is certain of it, so it is also traditional to hold that there is something which is the chair with seventeen legs only if there is exactly one chair with just that many legs. But, again, by being wrongly serious about our casual everyday talk, philosophers may come to deny the traditional view. They may do this by being wrongly serious, I think, about the following sort of ordinary exchange. Suppose an examiner asks a student, "Who is the father of Nelson Rockefeller, the present Governor of New York State?" The student replies, "Nelson Rockefeller is the son of John D. Rockefeller, Jr." No doubt, the examiner will allow that, by implication, the student got the right answer; he will judge that what the student said is true even though the examiner is correctly confident that the elder Rockefeller sired other sons. Just so, one might well argue that definite descriptions, like "the son of X," do not require uniqueness. But against this argument from the everyday flow of talk, let us insist that we focus on the relevant conception by employing our standard means for emphasizing the most directly relevant term. Thus, while we might feel nothing contradictory at first in saying, "Nelson Rockefeller is the son of John D. Rockefeller, Jr., and so is Winthrop Rockefeller," we must confess that even initially we would have quite different feelings about our saying "Nelson Rockefeller is actually *the* son of John D. Rockefeller, Jr., and so is Winthrop Rockefeller." With the latter, where emphasis is brought to bear, we cannot help but feel that what is asserted is inconsistent. And, with this, we feel differently about the original remark, feeling it to be essentially the same assertion and so inconsistent as well. Thus, it seems that when we focus on things properly, we may assume that definite descriptions do require uniqueness.

Let us now apply our principle to the question of knowing. Here, while we might feel nothing contradictory at first in saying "He knows that it is raining, but he isn't certain of it," we would feel differently about our saying "He really *knows* that it is raining, but he isn't certain of it." And, if anything, this feeling of contradiction is only enhanced when we further emphasize, "He really *knows* that it is raining, but he isn't actually *certain* of it." Thus it is plausible to suppose that what we said at first is actually inconsistent, and so that knowing does require being certain.

For my defense of skepticism, it now remains only to combine the result we have just reached with that at which we arrived in the previous section. Now, I have argued that each of two propositions deserves, if not our acceptance, at least the suspension of our judgment:

> That, in the case of every human being, there is hardly anything, if anything at all, of which he is certain.
> That (as a matter of necessity), in the case of every human being, the person knows something to be so only if he is certain of it.

But I think I have done more than just that. For the strength of the arguments given for this position on each of these two propositions is, I think, sufficient for warranting a similar position on propositions which are quite obvious consequences of the two of them together. One such consequential proposition is this:

> That, in the case of every human being, there is hardly anything, if anything at all, which the person knows to be so.

And so this third proposition, which is just the thesis of skepticism, also deserves, if not our acceptance, at least the suspension of our judgment. If this thesis is not reasonable to accept, then neither is its negation, the thesis of "common sense."

VI. A Prospectus and a Retrospective

I have argued that we know hardly anything, if anything, because we are certain of hardly anything, if anything. My offering this argument will strike many philosophers as peculiar, even many who have some sympathy with skepticism. For it is natural to think that, except for the requirement of the truth of what is known, the requirement of "attitude," in this case of personal certainty, is the *least* problematic requirement of knowing. Much more difficult to fulfill, one would think, would be requirements about one's justification, about one's grounds, and so on. And, quite candidly, I am inclined to agree with these thoughts. Why, then, have I chosen to defend skepticism by picking on what is just about the easiest requirement of knowledge? My thinking has been this: the requirement of being certain will, most likely, not be independent of more difficult requirements; indeed, any more difficult requirement will entail this simpler one. Thus one more difficult requirement might be that the knower be completely *justified* in being certain, which entails the requirement that the man be certain. And, in any case, for purposes of establishing some clarity, I wanted this defense to avoid the more difficult requirements because they rely on normative terms–for example, the term "justified." The application of normative terms presents problems which, while worked over by many philosophers, are still too difficult to handle at all adequately. By staying away from more difficult requirements, and so from normative terms, I hoped to raise doubts in a simpler, clearer context. When the time comes for a more powerful defense of skepticism, the more difficult requirements will be pressed. Then normative conditions will be examined and, for this examination, declared inapplicable. But these normative conditions will, most likely, concern one's being certain; no justification of mere belief or confidence will be the issue in the more powerful defenses. By offering my defense, I hoped to lay part of the groundwork for more powerful defenses of skepticism.

I would end with this explanation but for the fact that my present views contradict claims I made previously, and others have discussed critically these earlier claims about knowledge.[6] Before, I strove to show that knowledge was rather easy to come by, that the conditions of knowledge could be met rather easily. To connect my arguments, I offered a unified analysis:

> For any sentential value of *p*, (at a time *t*) a man knows that *p* if and only if (at *t*) it is not at all accidental that the man is right about its being the case that *p*.

And, in arguing for the analysis, I tried to understand its defining condition just so liberally that it would allow men to know things rather easily. Because I did this, I used the analysis to argue against skepticism – that is, against the thesis which I have just defended.

Given my present views, while I must find the criticisms of my earlier claims more interesting than convincing, I must find my analysis to be more accurate than I was in my too liberal application of it. For, however bad the analysis might be in various respects, it does assert that knowledge is an absolute. In terms of my currently favored distinctions, "accidental" is quite clearly a relative term, as are other terms which I might have selected in its stead: "coincidental," "matter of luck," "lucky," and so on. Operating on these terms with expressions such as "not at all" and "not in the least degree" will yield us absolute expressions, the equivalent of absolute terms. Thus, the condition that I offered is not at all likely to be one that is easily met. My main error, then, was not that of giving too vague or liberal a defining condition, but rather that of too liberally interpreting a condition which is in fact strict.

But I am quite uncertain that my analysis is correct in any case, and even that one can analyze knowledge. Still, so far as analyzing knowledge goes, the main plea of this paper must be this: whatever analysis of knowledge is adequate, if any such there be, it must allow that the thesis of skepticism be at least fairly plausible. For this plea only follows from my broader one: that philosophers take skepticism seriously and not casually suppose, as I have often done, that this unpopular thesis simply must be false.[7]

Notes

1   Among G. E. Moore's most influential papers against skepticism are "A Defense of Common Sense," "Four Forms of Scepticism," and "Certainty." These papers are now available in Moore's *Philosophical Papers* (New York, 1962). More recent representatives of the same anti-skeptical persuasion include A. J. Ayer's *The Problem of Knowledge* (Baltimore, 1956) and two books by Roderick M. Chisholm: *Perceiving* (Ithaca, 1957) and *Theory of Knowledge* (Englewood Cliffs, NJ, 1966). Among the many recent journal articles against skepticism are three papers of my own: "Experience and Factual Knowledge," *Journal of Philosophy*, vol. 64, no. 5 (1967), "An Analysis of Factual Knowledge," *Journal of Philosophy*, vol. 65, no. 6 (1968), and "Our Knowledge of the Material World," *Studies in the Theory of Knowledge, American Philosophical Quarterly Monograph*, no. 4 (1970). At the same time, a survey of the recent journal literature reveals very few papers where skepticism is defended or favored. With recent papers which do favor skepticism, however, I can mention at least two. A fledgling skepticism is persuasively advanced by Brian Skyrms in his "The Explication of 'X Knows that *p*,'" *Journal of Philosophy*, vol. 64, no. 12 (1967). And in William W. Rozeboom's "Why I Know So Much More Than You Do," *American Philosophical Quarterly*, vol. 4, no. 4 (1967), we have a refreshingly strong statement of skepticism in the context of recent discussion.

2   For an interesting discussion of impersonal certainty, which in some ways is rather in line with my own discussion while in other ways against it, one might see Michael Anthony Slote's "Empirical Certainty and the Theory of Important Criteria," *Inquiry*, vol. 10 (1967). Also, Slote makes helpful references to other writers in the philosophy of certainty.

3   See Moore's cited papers, especially "Certainty," p. 232.

4   An influential statement of this view is Roderick M. Chisholm's, to be found in the first chapter of each of his cited books. In "Experience and Factual Knowledge," I suggest a very similar view.

5   This view is advanced influentially by Colin Radford in "Knowledge by Examples," *Analysis*, 27 (October, 1966). In "An Analysis of Factual Knowledge," and especially in "Our Knowledge of The Material World," I suggest this view.

6   See my cited papers and these interesting discussions of them: Gilbert H. Harman, "Unger on Knowledge," *Journal of Philosophy*, 64 (1967), 353–9; Ruth Anna Putnam, "On Empirical Knowledge," *Boston Studies in the Philosophy of Science*, IV, 392–410; Arthur C. Danto, *Analytical Philosophy of Knowledge* (Cambridge, 1968), pp. 130 ff. and 144 ff.; Keith Lehrer and Thomas Paxson, Jr., "Knowledge: Undefeated Justified True Belief," *Journal of Philosophy*, 66 (1969), 225–37; J. L. Mackie, "The Possibility of Innate Knowledge," *Proceedings of the Aristotelian Society* (1970), pp. 245–57.

7   Ancestors of the present paper were discussed in philosophy colloquia at the following schools: Brooklyn College of The City University of New York, The University of California at Berkeley, Columbia University, The University of Illinois at Chicago Circle, The Rockefeller University, Stanford University, and The University of Wisconsin at Madison. I am thankful to those who participated in the discussion. I would also like to thank each of these many people for help in getting to the present defense: Peter M. Brown, Richard Cartwright, Fred I. Dretske, Hartry Field, Bruce Freed, H. P. Grice, Robert Hambourger, Saul A. Kripke, Stephen Schiffer, Michael A. Slote, Sydney S. Shoemaker, Dennis W. Stampe, Julius Weinberg, and Margaret Wilson, *all* of whom remain at least somewhat skeptical. Finally, I would like to thank the Graduate School of The University of Wisconsin at Madison for financial assistance during the preparation of this defense.

Part II
Skeptical Topics

Perception

9

W. T. Stace, "The Refutation of Realism"

The following selection is a paper published in 1934 by W. T. Stace, "The Refutation of Realism." By realism, Stace understands the common-sense view that there is an external world made up of objects that usually continue to exist even when no one is perceiving them. He undertakes to show that that "we do *not* know that any single entity exists unexperienced." Neither perception nor reasoning is competent to provide the grounds necessary for such knowledge. Realism, according to Stace, cannot even be shown to be probable. Our belief in the reality of unperceived objects is just a fiction or assumption that serves to simplify our view of the universe. But this assumption is "groundless;" it "ought not be believed."

More than thirty years have now elapsed since Prof. Moore published in *Mind* his famous article, "The Refutation of Idealism". Therewith the curtain rose upon the episode of contemporary British realism. After three decades perhaps the time is now ripe for the inauguration of another episode. And it is but fitting that "The Refutation of Realism" should appear on the same stage as its famous predecessor.

I shall not gird at realism because its exponents disagree among themselves as to what precisely their philosophy teaches. But disagreements certainly exist, and they make it difficult for a would-be refuter to know precisely what is the proposition which he ought to refute. It is far from certain that all idealists would agree that the idealism which Prof. Moore purported to refute represented adequately, or even inadequately, their views. And it may be that a similar criticism will be urged by realists against what I shall here have to say. But I must take my courage in my hands. Realists, it seems to me, agree in asserting that "some entities sometimes exist without being experienced by any finite mind". This, at any rate, is the proposition which I shall undertake to refute.

I insert the word "finite" in this formula because if I wrote "some entities exist without being experienced by any mind", it might be objected that the proposition so framed would imply that some entities exist of which God is ignorant, if there is such a being as God, and that it is not certain that all realists would wish to assert this. I think that we can very well leave God out of the discussion. In front of me is a piece of paper. I assume that the realist believes that this paper will continue to exist when it is put away in my desk for the night, and when no finite mind is experiencing it. He *may* also believe that it will continue to exist even if God is not experiencing it. But he must *at least* assert that it will exist when no finite mind is experiencing it. That, I think, is essential to his position. And therefore to refute that proposition will be to refute realism. In what follows, therefore, when I speak of minds I must be understood as referring to finite minds.

Possibly I shall be told that although realists probably do as a matter of fact believe that some entities exist unexperienced, yet this is not the essence of realism. Its essence, it may be said, is the belief that the relation between knowledge and its object is such that the knowledge makes no difference to the object, so that the object *might* exist without being known, whether as a matter of fact it does so exist or not.

But it would seem that there could be no point in asserting that entities *might* exist unexperienced, unless as a matter of fact they at least sometimes do so exist. To prove that the universe *might* have the property X, if as a matter of fact the universe has no such property, would seem to be a useless proceeding which no philosophy surely would take as its central contribution to truth. And I think that the only reason why realists are anxious to show that objects are such, and that the relation between knowledge and object is such, that objects might exist unexperienced, is that they think that this will lead on to the belief that objects actually do exist unexperienced. They have been anxious to prove that the existence of objects is not dependent on being experienced by minds because they wished to draw the conclusion that objects exist unexperienced. Hence I think that I am correct in saying that the essential proposition of realism, which has to be refuted, is that "some entities sometimes exist without being experienced by any finite mind".

Now, lest I should be misunderstood, I will state clearly at the outset that I cannot prove that no entities exist without being experienced by minds. For all I know completely unexperienced entities may exist, but what I shall assert is that we have not the slightest reason for believing that they do exist. And from this it will follow that the realistic position that they do exist is perfectly groundless and gratuitous, and one which ought not to be believed. It will be in exactly the same position as the proposition "there is a unicorn on the planet Mars". I cannot prove that there is no unicorn on Mars. But since there is not the slightest reason to suppose that there is one, it is a proposition which ought not to be believed.

And still further to clarify the issue, I will say that I shall not be discussing in this paper whether sense-objects are "mental". My personal opinion is that this question is a pointless one, but that if I am forced to answer it with a "yes" or "no", I should do so by saying that they are not mental; just as, if I were forced to answer the pointless question whether the mind is an elephant, I should have to answer that it is not an elephant. I will, in fact, assume for the purposes of this paper that sense-objects, whether they be colour patches or other sense-data, or objects, are not mental. My position will then be as follows: There is absolutely no reason for asserting that these non-mental, or physical, entities ever exist except when they are being experienced, and the proposition that they do so exist is utterly groundless and gratuitous, and one which ought not to be believed.

The refutation of realism will therefore be sufficiently accomplished if it can be shown that we do *not* know that any single entity exists unexperienced. And that is what I shall in this paper endeavour to show. I shall inquire how we could possibly know that unexperienced entities exist, even if, as a matter of fact, they do exist. And I shall show that there is no possible way in which we could know this, and that therefore we do *not* know it, and have no reason to believe it.

For the sake of clearness, let us take once again the concrete example of the piece of paper. I am at this moment experiencing it, and at this moment it exists, but how can I know that it existed last night in my desk when, so far as I know, no mind was experiencing it? How can I know that it will continue to exist tonight when there is no one in the room? The knowledge of these alleged facts is what the realists assert that they possess. And the question is, Whence could such knowledge have been obtained, and how can it be justified? What I assert is that it is absolutely impossible to have any such knowledge.

There are only two ways in which it could be asserted that the existence of any sense-object can be established. One is by sense-perception, the other by inference from sense-perception. I know of the existence of this paper *now* because I see it. I am supposed to know of the existence of the other side of the moon, which no one has ever seen, by inference from various actual astronomical observations, that is, by inference from things actually experienced. There are no other ways of proving the existence of a sense-object. Is either of them possible in the present case?

1. *Sense-perception.* I obviously cannot know by perception the existence of the paper when no one is experiencing it. For that would be self-contradictory. It would amount to asserting that I can experience the unexperienced.

2. *Inference.* Nor is it possible to prove by inference the existence of the paper when no mind is experiencing it. For how can I possibly pass by inference from the particular fact of the existence of the paper now, when I am experiencing it, to the quite different particular fact of the existence of the paper yesterday or tomorrow, when neither I nor any other mind is experiencing it? Strictly speaking, the onus of proving that such an inference is impossible is not on me. The onus of proving that it is possible is upon anyone who asserts it, and I am entitled to sit back and wait until someone comes forward with such an alleged proof. Many realists who know their business admit that no valid inference from an experienced to an unexperienced existence is possible. Thus Mr Russell says, "Belief in the existence of things outside my own biography must, from the standpoint of theoretical logic, be regarded as a prejudice, not as a well-grounded theory."[1]

I might therefore adopt the strategy of masterly inaction. But I prefer to carry the war into the enemy's camp. I propose to *prove* that no proof of the existence of unexperienced objects is possible.

It is clear in the first place that any supposed reasoning could not be inductive. Inductive reasoning proceeds always upon the basis that what has been found in certain observed cases to be true will also be true in unobserved cases. But there is no single case in which it has been observed to be true that an experienced object continues to exist when it is not being experienced; for, by hypothesis, its existence when it is not being experienced cannot be observed. Induction is generalisation from observed facts, but there is not a single case of an unexperienced existence having been observed on which could be based the generalisation that entities continue to exist when no one is experiencing them. And there is likewise not a single known instance of the existence of an unexperienced entity which could lead me to have even the slightest reason for supposing that this paper ever did exist, or will exist, when no one is experiencing it.

Since inductive reasoning is ruled out, the required inference, if there is to be an inference, must be of a formal nature. But deductive inference of all kinds depends upon the principle of consistency. If $P \supset Q$, then we can only prove Q, *if* P is admitted. From $P \supset Q$, therefore, all that can be deduced is that P and not-Q are inconsistent, and that we cannot hold both P and not-Q together, though we may hold either of them separately.

Hence, if it is alleged that a deductive inference can be drawn from the existence of the paper now, when I am experiencing it, to its existence when no one is experiencing it, this can only mean that to assert together the two propositions, (1) that it exists now, and (2) that it does not exist when no one is experiencing it, is an internally inconsistent position. But there is absolutely no inconsistency between these two propositions. If I believe that nothing whatever exists or ever did or will exist, except my own personal sense-data, this may be a view of the universe which no one would ever hold, but there is absolutely nothing internally inconsistent in it. Therefore, no deductive inference can prove the existence of an unexperienced entity. Therefore, by no reasoning at all, inductive or deductive, can the existence of such an entity be proved.

Nevertheless, arguments have been put forward from time to time by realists which are apparently intended to prove this conclusion. I will deal shortly with those with which I am acquainted. I am not bound to do this, since I have already proved that no proof of the realists' conclusion is possible. And for the same reason, if there are any arguments of this kind with which I am not acquainted, I am under no obligation to disprove them. But it will be better to meet at least the most well-known arguments.

a. It was Mr Perry, I believe, who invented the phrase "egocentric predicament". The egocentric predicament was supposed to indicate where lay a fallacy committed by idealists. It consisted in arguing from the fact that it is impossible to discover anything which is not known to the conclusion that all things are known. That any competent idealist ever did use such an argument may well be doubted, but I will waive that point. Mr Perry's comment was that the egocentric predicament, as employed by idealists, appeared to imply that from our ignorance of unexperienced entities we could conclude to their nonexistence, and that to do so is a fallacy.

No doubt such a procedure would be a fallacy. But though Mr Perry's argument may refute a supposed idealistic argument, *it does not prove anything whatever in favour of realism*. It would be a fallacy to argue that, because we have never observed a unicorn on Mars, therefore there is no unicorn there; but by pointing out this fallacy, one does not prove the existence of a unicorn there. And by pointing out that our ignorance of the existence of unexperienced entities does not prove their nonexistence, one does nothing whatever towards proving that unexperienced entities do exist. As regards the unicorn on Mars, the correct position, as far as logic is concerned, is obviously that if anyone asserts that there is a unicorn there, the onus is on him to prove it; and that until he does prove it, we ought not to believe it to be true. As regards the unexperienced entities, the correct position, as far as logic is concerned, is that if realists assert their existence, the onus is on them to prove it; and that until they do prove it, we ought not to believe that they exist. Mr Perry's argument, therefore, proves nothing whatever in favour of realism.

Possibly all this is admitted and understood by realists. But there seems, nevertheless, to have been a tendency to think that the overthrow of the supposed idealistic argument was a very important matter in forwarding the interests of realism. To point out, therefore, that it actually accomplishes nothing seems desirable.

b. Mr Lovejoy, in his recent book, *The Revolt Against Dualism*, argues that we can infer, or at least render probable, the existence of things during interperceptual intervals by means of the law of causation. He writes, "The same uniform causal sequences of natural events which may be observed within experience appear to go on in the same manner when not experienced. You build a fire in your grate of a certain quantity of coal, of a certain chemical composition. Whenever you remain in the room there occurs a typical succession of sensible phenomena according to an approximately regular schedule of clock-time; in, say, half an hour the coal is half consumed; at the end of the hour the grate contains only ashes. If you build a fire of the same quantity of the same material under the same conditions, leave the room, and return after any given time has elapsed, you get approximately the same sense-experiences as you would have had at the corresponding moment if you had remained in the room. You infer, therefore, that the fire has been burning as usual during your absence, and that being perceived is not a condition necessary for the occurrence of the process."[2]

This argument is simply a *petitio principii*. It assumes that we must believe that the law of causality continues to operate in the universe when no one is observing it. But the law of causality is, it is clear, one aspect of the universe, the unobserved existence of which is the very thing to be proved.

Why must we believe that causation continues to operate during interperceptual intervals? Obviously, the case as regards unexperienced processes and laws is in exactly the same position as the case regarding unexperienced *things*. Just as we cannot perceive unexperienced things, so we cannot perceive unexperienced processes and laws. Just as we cannot infer from anything which we experience the existence of unexperienced things, so we cannot infer from anything we experience the existence of unexperienced processes and laws. There is absolutely no evidence (sense-experience) to show that the fire went on burning during your absence, nor is any inference to that alleged fact possible. Any supposed inference will obviously be based upon our belief that the law of causation operates continuously through time whether observed or unobserved. But this is one of the very things which has to be proved. Nor is there the slightest logical inconsistency in believing that, when you first observe the phenomena, unburnt coal existed, that there followed an interval in which nothing existed, not even a law, and that at the end of the interval ashes began to exist.

No doubt this sounds very absurd and contrary to what we usually believe, but that is nothing to the point. We usually believe that things go on existing when no one is aware of them. But if we are enquiring how this can be *proved*, we must, of course, begin from the position that we do not know it, and therefore that it might not be true.

c. The distinction between sense-data and our awareness of them, which was first emphasized, so far as I know, by Prof. Moore, has been made the basis of an argument in favour of realism. Green, it is said, is not the same thing as awareness of green. For if we compare a green sense-datum with a blue sense-datum, we find a common element, namely awareness. The awareness must be different from the green because awareness also exists in the case of awareness of blue, and *that* awareness, at any rate, is not green. Therefore, since green is not the same thing as awareness of green, green might exist without awareness. Connected with this argument, too, is the assertion of a special kind of relationship between the awareness and the green.

Possibly this argument proves that green is not "mental". I do not know whether it proves this or not, but the point is unimportant, since I have already admitted that sense-data are not "mental". But whatever the argument proves, it certainly does *not* prove that unexperienced entities exist. For suppose that it proves that green has the predicate x (which may be "non-mental" or "independent of mind", or anything else you please), it still can only prove that green has the predicate x during the period when green is related to the awareness in the alleged manner, that is, when some mind is aware of the green. It cannot possibly prove anything about green when no mind is aware of it. Therefore, it cannot prove that green exists when no mind is aware of it.

For the sake of clearness, I will put the same point in another way. Suppose we admit that green and awareness of green are two quite different things, and suppose we admit that the relation between them is *r* – which may stand for the special relation asserted in the argument. Now it is not in any way inconsistent with these admissions to hold that green begins to exist only when awareness of green begins to exist, and that when awareness of green ceases to exist, green ceases to exist. It may be the case that these two quite different things always co-exist, always accompany each other, and are co-terminous in the sense that they always begin and end simultaneously, and that while they co-exist, they have the relation *r*. And this will be so *whatever* the relation *r* may be. And not only is this supposition that they always co-exist not at all absurd or arbitrary. It is on the contrary precisely the conclusion to which such evidence as we possess points. For we never have evidence that green exists except when some mind is aware of green. And it will not be asserted that awareness of green exists when green does not exist.

The argument from the distinction between green and the awareness of it, therefore, does nothing whatever towards proving the realist conclusion that some entities exist unexperienced.

d. It has also been argued that if we identify a green or a square sense-datum with our awareness of it, then, since awareness is admittedly a state of mind, we shall have to admit that there exist green and square states of mind.

This argument is merely intended to support the previous argument that a sense-datum is different from our awareness of it. And as it has already been shown that this proposition, even if admitted, proves nothing in favour of realism, it is not necessary to say anything further about the present argument.

I will, however, add the following. It is not by any means certain, as is here assumed, that awareness is a state of mind, or indeed that such a thing as a *state* of mind exists. For the mind is not static. It is active. And what exists in it are *acts* of mind. Now the *attention* involved in being aware of a sense-datum is certainly an act of mind. But it is certainly arguable that *bare* awareness of a sense-datum (if there is such a thing as *bare* awareness) would be identical with the sense-datum and would not be an act of mind. For such bare awareness would be purely passive. In that case, the conclusion that there must exist green or square states of mind would not follow.

Moreover, even if we admit that there exist green and square states of mind, what then? I can see no reason why we should not admit it, except that (1) it is an unusual and unexplored view, and (2) it seems to smack of materialism, although I do not believe that it does really involve materialism. This shows that the whole argument is not really a logical argument at all. It is merely an attempt to throw dust in our eyes by appealing to the popular prejudices against (1) unfamiliar views, and (2) materialism.

It is not possible in the brief space at my disposal to make plausible the suggestions contained in the last two paragraphs. A full discussion of them would be necessary and this I have endeavoured to give elsewhere. In the present place, therefore, I must rely upon the strict logical position, which is, that this argument, since it is merely intended to support argument (c) above, and since argument (c) has already been refuted, proves nothing in favour of realism.

By the preceding discussion, I claim to have proved (1) that the existence of an unexperienced entity cannot be known by perception, (2) that it cannot be known by reasoning, and (3) that the arguments commonly relied upon by realists to prove it are all fallacies.

I think it is not worth while to discuss the possible suggestion that the arguments in favour of realism, although not proving their conclusion rigorously, render that conclusion probable. For what has been shown is that no valid reasoning of *any* kind can possibly exist in favour of this conclusion. Any conceivable reasoning intended to prove that unexperienced entities exist must, it has been shown, be *totally* fallacious. It cannot, therefore, lead even to a probable conclusion. The position, therefore, is that we have not even the faintest reason for believing in the existence of unexperienced entities.

That this is the correct logical position seems to be dimly perceived by many realists themselves, for it is common among them to assert that our belief in unexperienced existences is a "primitive belief", or is founded upon "instinctive belief", or upon "animal faith". This suggestion is obviously based upon the realisation that we cannot obtain a knowledge of unexperienced existences either from perception or from reasoning. Since this is so, realists are compelled to appeal to instinctive beliefs.

Such a weak position seems hardly to require discussion. A "primitive belief" is merely a belief which we have held for a long time, and may well be false. An "instinctive belief" is in much the same case. An "instinct", so far as I know, is some kind of urge to *action*, not an urge to believe a proposition. And it is therefore questionable whether there are such things as instinctive beliefs in any strict sense, although, of course, no one will deny that we have beliefs the grounds of which are only dimly, or not at all, perceived. Certainly the psychology of such alleged instinctive beliefs has not been adequately investigated. And certainly we have no good ground for supposing that an instinctive belief (if any such exists) might not be false.

And if we have such an instinctive or primitive belief in unexperienced existences, the question must obviously be asked How, When, and Why such a belief arose in the course of our mental evolution. Will it be alleged that the amoeba has this belief? And if not, why and when did it come into existence? Or did it at some arbitrarily determined stage in our evolution descend suddenly upon us out of the blue sky, like the immortal soul itself?

Is it not obvious that to base our belief in unexperienced existences on such grounds is a mere gesture of despair, an admission of the bankruptcy of realism in its attempt to find a rational ground for our beliefs?

Strictly speaking, I have here come to the end of my argument. I have refuted realism by showing that we have absolutely no good reason for believing in its fundamental proposition that entities exist unexperienced. Nothing I have said, of course, goes any distance towards proving that entities do *not* exist unexperienced. That, in my opinion, cannot be proved. The logically correct position is as follows. We have no reason whatever to believe that unexperienced entities exist. We cannot prove that they do not exist. The onus of proof is on those who assert that they do. Therefore, as such proof is impossible, the belief ought not to be entertained, any more than the belief that there is a unicorn on Mars ought to be entained.

It is no part of the purpose of this essay to do more than arrive at this negative result. But lest it should be thought that this thinking necessarily leads to nothing but a negative result, or to a pure scepticism, I will indicate in no more than a dozen sentences that there is the possibility of a positive and constructive philosophy arising from it. That positive philosophy I have attempted to work out in detail in another place. Here, I will say no more than the following. Since our belief in unexperienced existences is not to be explained as either (1) a perception, or (2) an inference, or (3) an "instinctive belief", how is it to be explained? I believe that it can only be explained as a mental construction or fiction, a pure assumption which has been adopted, not because there is the slightest evidence for it, but solely because it simplifies our view of the universe. How it simplifies our view of the universe, and by what detailed steps it has arisen, I cannot discuss in this place. But the resulting conception is that, in the last analysis, nothing exists except minds and their sense-data (which are not "mental"), and that human minds have, out of these sense-data, slowly and laboriously constructed the rest of the solid universe of our knowledge. Unexperienced entities can only be said to exist in the sense that minds have chosen by means of a fiction to project them into the void of interperceptual intervals, and thus to construct or create their existence in imagination.

Notes

1   Bertrand Russell, *Analysis of Mind* (London: Allen and Unwin, 1921), p. 133.
2   Arthur Lovejoy, *The Revolt against Dualism* (LaSalle, Illinois: Open Court, 1929), p. 268.

10

G. E. Moore, from "Proof of an External World"

Throughout much of his long philosophical career, G. E. Moore (1873–1958) undertook to defend common sense against skepticism. There are, he claims, many things that we know even if we are in no position to prove that we know them. The selection that follows is taken from his paper "Proof of an External World," in which he attempts to prove the existence of an external world by holding up his two hands and saying "Here is one hand and here is another." Although the direct object of Moore's criticism is idealism – the claim that there are no material objects – nevertheless, it also attacks skepticism, since Moore asserts that he knows "Here is one hand and here is another" to be true.

In the preface to the second edition of Kant's *Critique of Pure Reason* some words occur, which, in Professor Kemp Smith's translation, are rendered as follows:

> It still remains a scandal to philosophy...that the existence of things outside of us...must be accepted merely on *faith*, and that, if anyone thinks good to doubt their existence, we are unable to counter his doubts by any satisfactory proof.[1]

It seems clear from these words that Kant thought it a matter of some importance to give a proof of 'the existence of things outside of us' or perhaps rather (for it seems to me possible that the force of the German words is better rendered in this way) of 'the existence of *the* things outside of us'; for had he not thought it important that a proof should be given, he would scarcely have called it a 'scandal' that no proof had been given. And it seems clear also that he thought that the giving of such a proof was a task which fell properly within the province of philosophy; for, if it did not, the fact that no proof had been given could not possibly be a scandal to *philosophy*.

Now, even if Kant was mistaken in both of these two opinions, there seems to me to be no doubt whatever that it is a matter of some importance and also a matter which falls properly within the province of philosophy, to discuss the question what sort of proof, if any, can be given of 'the existence of things outside of us'. And to discuss this question was my object when I began to write the present lecture. But I may say at once that, as you will find, I have only, at most, succeeded in saying a very small part of what ought to be said about it.

The words 'it . . . remains a scandal to philosophy . . . that we are unable . . .' would, taken strictly, imply that, at the moment at which he wrote them, Kant himself was unable to produce a satisfactory proof of the point in question. But I think it is unquestionable that Kant himself did not think that he personally was at the time unable to produce such a proof. On the contrary, in the immediately preceding sentence, he has declared that he has, in the second edition of his *Critique*, to which he is now writing the Preface, given a 'rigorous proof' of this very thing; and has added that he believes this proof of his to be 'the only possible proof'. It is true that in this preceding sentence he does not describe the proof which he has given as a proof of 'the existence of things outside of us' or of 'the existence of the things outside of us', but describes it instead as a proof of 'the objective reality of outer intuition'. But the context leaves no doubt that he is using these two phrases, 'the objective reality of outer intuition' and 'the existence of things (*or* 'the things') outside of us', in such a way that whatever is a proof of the first is also necessarily a proof of the second. We must, therefore, suppose that when he speaks as if *we* are unable to give a satisfactory proof, he does not mean to say that he himself, as well as others, is *at the moment* unable; but rather that, until he discovered the proof which he has given, both he himself and everybody else *were* unable. Of course, if he is right in thinking that he has given a satisfactory proof, the state of things which he describes came to an end as soon as his proof was published. As soon as that happened, anyone who read it was able to give a satisfactory proof by simply repeating that which Kant had given, and the 'scandal' to philosophy had been removed once for all.

If, therefore, it were certain that the proof of the point in question given by Kant in the second edition is a satisfactory proof, it would be certain that at least one satisfactory proof can be given; and all that would remain of the question which I said I proposed to discuss would be, firstly, the question as to what *sort* of a proof this of Kant's is, and secondly the question whether (contrary to Kant's own opinion) there may not perhaps be other proofs, of the same or of a different sort, which are also satisfactory. But I think it is by no means certain that Kant's proof is satisfactory. I think it is by no means certain that he did succeed in removing once for all the state of affairs which he considered to be a scandal to philosophy. And I think, therefore, that the question whether it is possible to give *any* satisfactory proof of the point in question still deserves discussion. [...]

It seems to me that, so far from its being true, as Kant declares to be his opinion, that there is only one possible proof of the existence of things outside of us, namely the one which he has given, I can now give a large number of different proofs, each of which is a perfectly rigorous proof; and that at many other times I have been in a position to give many others. I can prove now, for instance, that two human hands exist. How? By holding up my two hands, and saying, as I make a certain gesture with the right hand, 'Here is one hand', and adding, as I make a certain gesture with the left, 'and here is another'. And if, by doing this, I have proved *ipso facto* the existence of external things, you will all see that I can also do it now in numbers of other ways: there is no need to multiply examples.

But did I prove just now that two human hands were then in existence? I do want to insist that I did; that the proof which I gave was a perfectly rigorous one; and that it is perhaps impossible to give a better or more rigorous proof of anything whatever. Of course, it would not have been a proof unless three conditions were satisfied; namely (1) unless the premiss which I adduced as proof of the conclusion was different from the conclusion I adduced it to prove; (2) unless the premiss which I adduced was something which I *knew* to be the case, and not merely something which I believed but which was by no means certain, or something which, though in fact true, I did not know to be so; and (3) unless the conclusion did really follow from the premiss. But all these three conditions were in fact satisfied by my proof. (1) The premiss which I adduced in proof was quite certainly different from the conclusion, for the conclusion was merely 'Two human hands exist at this moment'; but the premiss was something far more specific than this – something which I expressed by showing you my hands, making certain gestures, and saying the words 'Here is one hand, and here is another'. It is quite obvious that the two were different, because it is quite obvious that the conclusion might have been true, even if the premiss had been false. In asserting the premiss I was asserting much more than I was asserting in asserting the conclusion. (2) I certainly did at the moment *know* that which I expressed by the combination of certain gestures with saying the words 'There is one hand and here is another'. I *knew* that there was one hand in the place indicated by combining a certain gesture with my first utterance of 'here' and that there was another in the different place indicated by combining a certain gesture with my second utterance of 'here'. How absurd it would be to suggest that I did not know it, but only believed it, and that perhaps it was not the case! You might as well suggest that I do not know that I am now standing up and talking – that perhaps after all I'm not, and that it's not quite certain that I am! And finally (3) it is quite certain that the conclusion did follow from the premiss. This is as certain as it is that if there is one hand here and another here *now*, then it follows that there are two hands in existence *now*.

My proof, then, of the existence of things outside of us did satisfy three of the conditions necessary for a rigorous proof. Are there any other conditions necessary for a rigorous proof, such that perhaps it did not satisfy one of them? Perhaps there may be; I do not know; but I do want to emphasize that, so far as I can see, we all of us do constantly take proofs of this sort as absolutely conclusive proofs of certain conclusions – as finally settling certain questions, as to which we were previously in doubt. Suppose, for instance, it were a question whether there were as many as three misprints on a certain page in a certain book. A says there are, B is inclined to doubt it. How could A prove that he is right? Surely he *could* prove it by taking the book, turning to the page, and pointing to three separate places on it, saying 'There's one misprint here, another here, and another here': surely that is a method by which it *might* be proved! Of course, A would not have proved, by doing this, that there were at least three misprints on the page in question, unless it was certain that there was a misprint in each of the places to which he pointed. But to say that he *might* prove it in this way, is to say that it *might* be certain that there was. And if such a thing as that could ever be certain, then assuredly it was certain just now that there was one hand in one of the two places I indicated and another in the other.

I did, then, just now, give a proof that there were *then* external objects; and obviously, if I did, I could *then* have given many other proofs of the same sort that there were external objects *then*, and could now give many proofs of the same sort that there are external objects *now*.

But, if what I am asked to do is to prove that external objects have existed *in the past*, then I can give many different proofs of this also, but proofs which are in important respects of a different *sort* from those just given. And I want to emphasize that, when Kant says it is a scandal not to be able to give a proof of the existence of external objects, a proof of their existence in the past would certainly *help* to remove the scandal of which he is speaking. He says that, if it occurs to anyone to question their existence, we ought to be able to confront him with a satisfactory proof. But by a person who questions their existence, he certainly means not merely a person who questions whether any exist at the moment of speaking, but a person who questions whether any have *ever* existed; and a proof that some have existed in the past would certainly therefore be relevant to *part* of what such a person is questioning. How then can I prove that there have been external objects in the past? Here is one proof. I can say: 'I held up two hands above this desk not very long ago; therefore two hands existed not very long ago; therefore at least two external objects have existed at some time in the past, Q.E.D.' This is a perfectly good proof, provided I *know* what is asserted in the premiss. But I *do* know that I held up two hands above this desk not very long ago. As a matter of fact, in this case you all know it too. There's no doubt whatever that I did. Therefore I have given a perfectly conclusive proof that external objects have existed in the past; and you will all see at once that, if this is a conclusive proof, I could have given many others of the same sort, and could now give many others. But it is also quite obvious that this sort of proof differs in important respects from the sort of proof I gave just now that there were two hands existing *then*.

I have, then, given two conclusive proofs of the existence of external objects. The first was a proof that two human hands existed at the time when I gave the proof; the second was a proof that two human hands had existed at a time previous to that at which I gave the proof. These proofs were of a different sort in important respects. And I pointed out that I could have given, then, many other conclusive proofs of both sorts. It is also obvious that I could give many others of both sorts now. So that, if these are the sort of proof that is wanted, nothing is easier than to prove the existence of external objects.

But now I am perfectly well aware that, in spite of all that I have said, many philosophers will still feel that I have not given any satisfactory proof of the point in question. And I want briefly, in conclusion, to say something as to why this dissatisfaction with my proofs should be felt.

One reason why, is, I think, this. Some people understand 'proof of an external world' as including a proof of things which I haven't attempted to prove and haven't proved. It is not quite easy to say *what* it is that they want proved – *what* it is that is such that unless they got a proof of it, they would not say that they had a proof of the existence of external things;

but I can make an approach to explaining what they want by saying that if I had proved the propositions which I used as *premisses* in my two proofs, then they would perhaps admit that I had proved the existence of external things, but, in the absence of such a proof (which, of course, I have neither given nor attempted to give), they will say that I have not given what they mean by a proof of the existence of external things. In other words, they want a proof of what I assert *now* when I hold up my hands and say 'Here's one hand and here's another'; and, in the other case, they want a proof of what I assert *now* when I say 'I did hold up two hands above this desk just now'. Of course, what they really want is not merely a proof of these two propositions, but something like a general statement as to how *any* propositions of this sort may be proved. This, of course, I haven't given; and I do not believe it can be given: if this is what is meant by proof of the existence of external things, I do not believe that any proof of the existence of external things is possible. Of course, in some cases what might be called a proof of propositions which seem like these can be got. If one of you suspected that one of my hands was artificial he might be said to get a proof of my proposition 'Here's one hand, and here's another', by coming up and examining the suspected hand close up, perhaps touching and pressing it, and so establishing that it really was a human hand. But I do not believe that any proof is possible in nearly all cases. How am I to prove now that 'Here's one hand, and here's another'? I do not believe I can do it. In order to do it, I should need to prove for one thing, as Descartes pointed out, that I am not now dreaming. But how can I prove that I am not? I have, no doubt, conclusive reasons for asserting that I am not now dreaming; I have conclusive evidence that I am awake: but that is a very different thing from being able to prove it. I could not tell you what all my evidence is; and I should require to do this at least, in order to give you a proof.

But another reason why some people would feel dissatisfied with my proofs is, I think, not merely that they want a proof of something which I haven't proved, but that they think that, if I cannot give such extra proofs, then the proofs that I have given are not conclusive proofs at all. And this, I think, is a definite mistake. They would say: 'If you cannot prove your premiss that here is one hand and here is another, then you do not know it. But you yourself have admitted that, if you did not know it, then your proof was not conclusive. Therefore your proof was not, as you say it was, a conclusive proof.' This view that, if I cannot prove such things as these, I do not know them, is, I think, the view that Kant was expressing in the sentence which I quoted at the beginning of this lecture, when he implies that so long as we have no proof of the existence of external things, their existence must be accepted merely on *faith*. He means to say, I think, that if I cannot prove that there is a hand here, I must accept it merely as a matter of faith – I cannot know it. Such a view, though it has been very common among philosophers, can, I think, be shown to be wrong – though shown only by the use of premisses which are not known to be true, unless we do know of the existence of external things. I can know things, which I cannot prove; and among things which I certainly did know, even if (as I think) I could not prove them, were the premisses of my two proofs. I should say, therefore, that those, if any, who are dissatisfied with these proofs merely on the ground that I did not know their premisses, have no good reason for their dissatisfaction.

Note

1 B xxxix, note: Immanuel Kant, *Critique of Pure Reason*, trans. Norman Kemp Smith (London: Macmillan and Co., 1950), p. 34. The German words are 'so bleibt es immer ein Skandal der Philosophie . . . , das Dasein der Dinge ausser uns . . . bloss auf *Glauben* annehmen zu müssen, und wenn es jemand einfällt es zu bezweifeln, ihm keinen genugtuenden Beweis entgegenstellen zu können'.

11

J. L. Austin, from *Sense and Sensibilia*

Arguments from illusion often serve to drive a wedge between reality and our perception of it. If what we take to be the case involves a contradiction or differs wildly and strangely from the way things are, perhaps we are unable to detect when our senses accurately inform us about the world and when we fall into error. In the following two lectures, taken from his lectures *Sense and Sensibilia*, J. L. Austin (1911–60) wittily contends that such arguments are misleading. Perhaps the most influential proponent of "ordinary language philosophy," Austin advocated looking with great care at the ways in which we commonly use particular words and how those words have been systematically misused in misleading ways when applied in the service of philosophy.

Below, Austin focuses primarily on the work of A. J. Ayer and H. H. Price, who both argue in one form or another that illusions warrant positing the existence of sense-data, or immediate objects of perception, that are not identical with any external objects perceived. Ayer, to take Austin's primary foil in the pages below, claims that when we place a normally straight stick into water it appears slightly bent. Since the stick only *appears* bent, Ayer concludes that we must be perceiving something that looks like a bent stick. In perception, therefore, we must be directly aware of what he and many others have called sense-data. Further evidence for sense-data can be found in the cases of mirages, where a person may have the experience of a luscious oasis in the middle of a desert. Since she does perceive something, she must be directly perceiving sense-data.

In response, Austin argues at great length that such reasoning rest on a host of confusions and unnecessary assumptions. Illusions are quite common for us, and we have little trouble understanding the examples to which Ayer appeals. We simply see a stick partly submerged in water, confident that though it looks bent we feel quite comfortable in our knowledge as to why it appears that way. Austin further cautions against accepting the second step in the sense-data argument – namely, that we always only perceive sense-data even in normal cases – mainly because it relies upon a specious distinction between veridical (accurate) and delusive experiences, a distinction that remains intelligible only if we pass over the details of ordinary language usage and our everyday experience.

III

The primary purpose of the argument from illusion is to induce people to accept 'sense-data' as the proper and correct answer to the question what they perceive on certain *abnormal, exceptional* occasions; but in fact it is usually followed up with another bit of argument intended to establish that they *always* perceive sense-data. Well, what is the argument?

In Ayer's statement[1] it runs as follows. It is 'based on the fact that material things may present different appearances to different observers, or to the same observer in different conditions, and that the character of these appearances is to some extent causally determined by the state of the conditions and the observer'. As illustrations of this alleged fact, Ayer proceeds to cite perspective ('a coin which looks circular from one point of view may look elliptical from another'); refraction ('a stick which normally appears straight looks bent when it is seen in water'); changes in colour-vision produced by drugs ('such as mescal'); mirror-images; double vision; hallucination; apparent variations in tastes; variations in felt warmth ('according as the hand that is feeling it is itself hot or cold'); variations in felt bulk ('a coin seems larger when it is placed on the tongue than when it is held in the palm of the hand'); and the oft-cited fact that 'people who have had limbs amputated may still continue to feel pain in them'.

He then selects three of these instances for detailed treatment. First, refraction – the stick which normally 'appears straight' but 'looks bent' when seen in water. He makes the 'assumptions' (*a*) that the stick does not *really change its shape* when it is placed in water, and (*b*) that it *cannot be* both crooked and straight.[2] He then concludes ('it follows') that 'at least one of the *visual appearances* of the stick is *delusive*'. Nevertheless, even when 'what we see is not the *real quality* of *a* material thing', it is supposed that we are still seeing something' – and this something is to be called a 'sense-datum'. A sense-datum is to be 'the object of which we are *directly* aware, in perception, if it is not *part* of any *material thing*'. (The italics are mine throughout this and the next two paragraphs.)

Next, mirages. A man who sees a mirage, he says, is 'not perceiving any material thing; for the oasis which he thinks he is perceiving *does not exist*'. But 'his *experience* is not an experience of nothing'; thus 'it is said that he is experiencing sense-data, which are similar in character to what he would be experiencing if he were seeing a real oasis, but are delusive in the sense that *the material thing which they appear to present* is not *really there*'.

Lastly, reflections. When I look at myself in a mirror 'my body *appears to be* some distance behind the glass'; but it cannot actually be in two places at once; thus, my perceptions in this case 'cannot all be *veridical*'. But I do see *something*; and if 'there really is no such material thing as my body in the place where it appears to be, what is it that I am seeing?' Answer – a sense-datum. Ayer adds that 'the same conclusion may be reached by taking any other of my examples'.

Now I want to call attention, first of all, to the name of this argument – the 'argument from *illusion*', and to the fact that it is produced as establishing the conclusion that some at least of our 'perceptions' are *delusive*. For in this there are two clear implications – (*a*) that all the cases cited in the argument are cases of *illusions*; and (*b*) that *illusion* and *delusion* are the same thing. But both of these implications, of course, are quite wrong; and it is by no means unimportant to point this out, for, as we shall see, the argument trades on confusion at just this point.

What, then, would be some genuine examples of illusion? (The fact is that hardly any of the cases cited by Ayer is, at any rate without stretching things, a case of illusion at all.) Well, first, there are some quite clear cases of *optical* illusion – for instance the case we mentioned earlier in which, of two lines of equal length, one is made to look longer than the other. Then again there are illusions produced by professional 'illusionists', conjurors – for instance the Headless Woman on the stage, who is made to look headless, or the ventriloquist's dummy which is made to appear to be talking. Rather different – not (usually) produced on purpose – is the case where wheels rotating rapidly enough in one direction may look as if they were rotating quite slowly in the opposite direction. Delusions, on the other hand, are something altogether different from this. Typical cases would be delusions of persecution, delusions of grandeur. These are primarily a matter of grossly disordered beliefs (and so, probably, behaviour) and may well have nothing in particular to do with perception.[3] But I think we might also say that the patient who sees pink rats has (suffers from) delusions – particularly, no doubt, if, as would probably be the case, he is not clearly aware that his pink rats aren't real rats.[4]

The most important differences here are that the term 'an illusion' (in a perceptual context) does not suggest that something totally unreal is *conjured up* – on the contrary, there just is the arrangement of lines and arrows on the page, the woman on the stage with her head in a black bag, the rotating wheels; whereas the term 'delusion' *does* suggest something totally unreal, not really there at all. (The convictions of the man who has delusions of persecution can be *completely* without foundation.) For this reason delusions are a much more serious matter – something is really wrong, and what's more, wrong *with* the person who has them. But when I see an optical illusion, however well it comes off, there is nothing wrong with me personally, the illusion is not a little (or a large) peculiarity or idiosyncrasy of my own; it is quite public, anyone can see it, and in many cases standard procedures can be laid down for producing it. Furthermore, if we are not actually to be taken in, we need to be *on our guard*; but it is no use to tell the sufferer from delusions to be on his guard. He needs to be cured.

Why is it that we tend – if we do – to confuse illusions with delusions? Well, partly, no doubt the terms are often used loosely. But there is also the point that people may have, without making this explicit, different views or theories about the facts of some cases. Take the case of seeing a ghost, for example. It is not generally known, or agreed, what seeing ghosts *is*. Some people think of seeing ghosts as a case of something being conjured up, perhaps by the disordered nervous system of the victim; so in their view seeing ghosts is a case of delusion. But other people have the idea that what is called seeing ghosts is a case of being taken in by shadows, perhaps, or reflections, or a trick of the light – that is, they assimilate the case in their minds to illusion. In this way, seeing ghosts, for example, may come to be labelled sometimes as 'delusion', sometimes as 'illusion'; and it may not be noticed that it makes a difference which label we use. Rather, similarly, there seem to be different doctrines in the field as to what mirages are. Some seem to take a mirage to be a vision conjured up by the crazed brain of the thirsty and exhausted traveller (delusion), while in other accounts it is a case of atmospheric refraction, whereby something below the horizon is made to appear above it (illusion). (Ayer, you may remember, takes the delusion view, although he cites it along with the rest as a case of illusion. He says not that the oasis appears to be where it is not, but roundly that 'it does not exist'.)

The way in which the 'argument from illusion' positively trades on not distinguishing illusions from delusions is, I think, this. So long as it is being suggested that the cases paraded for our attention are cases of *illusion*, there is the implication (from the ordinary use of the word) that there really is something there that we perceive. But then, when these cases begin to be quietly called delusive, there comes in the very different suggestion of something being conjured up, something unreal or at any rate 'immaterial'. These two implications taken together may then subtly insinuate that in the cases cited there really is something that we are perceiving, but that this is an immaterial something; and this insinuation, even if not conclusive by itself, is certainly well calculated to edge us a little closer towards just the position where the sense-datum theorist wants to have us.

So much, then – though certainly there could be a good deal more – about the differences between illusions and delusions and the reasons for not obscuring them. Now let us look briefly at some of the other cases Ayer lists. Reflections, for instance. No doubt you *can* produce illusions with mirrors, suitably disposed. But is just *any* case of seeing something in a mirror an illusion, as he implies? Quite obviously not. For seeing things in mirrors is a perfectly *normal* occurrence, completely familiar, and there is usually no question of anyone being taken in. No doubt, if you're an infant or an aborigine and have never come across a mirror before, you may be pretty baffled, and even visibly perturbed, when you do. But is that a reason why the rest of us should speak of illusion here? And just the same goes for the phenomena of perspective – again, one *can* play tricks with perspective, but in the ordinary case there is no question of illusion. That a round coin should 'look elliptical' (in one sense) from some points of view is exactly what we expect and what we normally find; indeed, we should be badly put out if we ever found this not to be so. Refraction again – the stick that looks bent in water – is far too familiar a case to be properly called a case of illusion. We may perhaps be prepared to agree that the stick looks bent; but then we can see that it's partly submerged in water, so that is exactly how we should expect it to look.

It is important to realize here how familiarity, so to speak, takes the edge off illusion. Is the cinema a case of illusion? Well, just possibly the first man who ever saw moving pictures may have felt inclined to say that here was a case of illusion. But in fact it's pretty unlikely that even he, even momentarily, was actually taken in; and by now the whole thing is so ordinary a part of our lives that it never occurs to us even to raise the question. One might as well ask whether producing a photograph is producing an illusion – which would plainly be just silly.

Then we must not overlook, in all this talk about illusions and delusions, that there are plenty of more or less unusual cases, not yet mentioned, which certainly aren't either. Suppose that a proof-reader makes a mistake – he fails to notice that what ought to be 'causal' is printed as 'casual'; does he have a delusion? Or is there an illusion before him? Neither, of course; he simply *misreads*. Seeing after-images, too, though not a particularly frequent occurrence and not just an ordinary case of seeing, is neither seeing illusions nor having delusions. And what about dreams? Does the dreamer see illusions? Does he have delusions? Neither; dreams are *dreams*.

Let us turn for a moment to what Price has to say about illusions. He produces,[5] by way of saying 'what the term "illusion" means', the following 'provisional definition': 'An illusory sense-datum of sight or touch is a sense-datum which is such that we tend to take it to be part of the surface of a material object, but if we take it so we are wrong.' It is by no means clear, of course, what this dictum itself means; but still, it seems fairly clear that the definition doesn't actually fit all the cases of illusion. Consider the two lines again. Is there anything here which we tend to take, wrongly, to be part of the surface of a material object? It doesn't seem so. We just see the two lines, we don't think or even tend to think that we see anything else, we aren't even raising the question whether anything is or isn't 'part of the surface' of – what, anyway? the lines? the page? – the trouble is just that one line looks longer than the other, though it isn't. Nor surely, in the case of the Headless Woman, is it a question whether anything is or isn't part of her surface; the trouble is just that she looks as if she had no head.

It is noteworthy, of course, that, before he even begins to consider the 'argument from illusion', Price has already incorporated in this 'definition' the idea that in such cases there is something to be seen *in addition to* the ordinary things – which is part of what the argument is commonly used, and not uncommonly taken, to *prove*. But this idea surely has no place in an attempt to say what 'illusion' *means*. It comes in again, improperly I think, in his account of perspective (which incidentally he also cites as a species of illusion) – 'a distant hillside which is full of protuberances, and slopes upwards at quite a gentle angle, will appear flat and vertical.... This means that the sense-datum, the colour-expanse which we sense, actually *is* flat and vertical.' But why should we accept this account of the matter? Why should we say that there is *anything* we see which *is* flat and vertical, though not 'part of the surface' of any material object? To speak thus is to assimilate all such cases to cases of delusion, where there *is* something not 'part of any material thing'. But we have already discussed the undesirability of this assimilation.

Next, let us have a look at the account Ayer himself gives of some at least of the cases he cites. (In fairness we must remember here that Ayer has a number of quite substantial reservations of his own about the merits and efficacy of the argument from illusion, so that it is not easy to tell just how seriously he intends his exposition of it to be taken; but this is a point we shall come back to.)

First, then, the familiar case of the stick in water. Of this case Ayer says (*a*) that since the stick looks bent but is straight, 'at least one of the visual appearances of the stick is *delusive*'; and (*b*) that 'what we see [directly anyway] is not the real quality of [a few lines later, not part of] a material thing'. Well now: does the stick 'look bent' to begin with? I think we can agree that it does, we have no better way of describing it. But of course it does *not* look *exactly* like a bent stick, a bent stick out of water – at most, it may be said to look rather like a bent stick partly immersed *in* water. After all, we can't help seeing the water the stick is partly immersed in. So exactly what in this case is supposed to be *delusive*? What is wrong, what is even faintly surprising, in the idea of a stick's being straight but looking bent sometimes? Does anyone suppose that if something is straight, then it jolly well has to *look* straight at all times and in all circumstances? Obviously no one seriously supposes this. So what mess are we supposed to get into here, what is the difficulty? For of course it has to be suggested that there *is* a difficulty – a difficulty, furthermore, which calls for a pretty radical solution, the introduction of sense-data. But what is the problem we are invited to solve in this way?

Well, we are told, in this case you are seeing *something*; and what is this something 'if it is not part of any material thing'? But this question is, really, completely mad. The straight part of the stick, the bit not under water, is presumably part of a material thing; don't we see that? And what about the bit *under* water? – we can see that too. We can see, come to that, the water itself. In fact what we see is a *stick partly immersed in water*; and it is particularly extraordinary that this should appear to be called in question – that a question should be raised about *what* we are seeing – since this, after all, is simply the description of the situation with which we started. It was, that is to say, agreed at the start that we were looking at a stick, a 'material thing', part of which was under water. If, to take a rather different case, a church were cunningly camouflaged so that it looked like a barn, how could any serious question be raised about what we see when we look at it? We see, of course, *a church* that now *looks like a barn*. We do *not* see an immaterial barn, an immaterial church, or an immaterial anything else. And what in this case could seriously tempt us to say that we do?

Notice, incidentally, that in Ayer's description of the stick-in-water case, which is supposed to be prior to the drawing of any philosophical conclusions, there has already crept in the unheralded but important expression 'visual appearances' – it is, of course, ultimately to be suggested that all we *ever* get when we see is a visual appearance (whatever that may be).

Consider next the case of my reflection in a mirror. My body, Ayer says, 'appears to be some distance behind the glass'; but as it's in front, it can't really be behind the glass. So what am I seeing? A sense-datum. What about this? Well, once again, although there is no objection to saying that my body 'appears to be some distance behind the glass', in saying this we must remember what sort of situation we are dealing with. It does not 'appear to be' there in a way which might tempt me (though it might tempt a baby or a savage) to go round the back and look for it, and be astonished when this enterprise proved a failure. (To say that A is *in* B doesn't always mean that if you open B you will find A, just as to say that A is *on* B doesn't always mean that you could pick it off – consider 'I saw my face in the mirror', 'There's a pain in my toe', 'I heard him on the radio', 'I saw the image on the screen', etc. Seeing something in a mirror is not like seeing a bun in a shop-window.) But does it follow that, since my body is not actually located behind the mirror, I am not seeing a material thing? Plainly not. For one thing, I can see the mirror (nearly always anyway). I can see my own body 'indirectly', *sc.* in the mirror. I can also see the reflection of my own body or, as some would say, a mirror-image. And a mirror-image (if we choose this answer) is not a 'sense-datum'; it can be photographed, seen by any number of people, and so on. (Of course there is no question here of either illusion or delusion.) And if the question is pressed, what actually *is* some distance, five feet say, behind the mirror, the answer is, not a sense-datum, but some region of the adjoining room.

The mirage case – at least if we take the view, as Ayer does, that the oasis the traveller thinks he can see 'does not exist' – is significantly more amenable to the treatment it is given. For here we are supposing the man to be genuinely deluded, he is *not* 'seeing a material thing'.[6] We don't actually have to say, however, even here that he is 'experiencing sense-data'; for though, as Ayer says above, 'it is convenient to give a name' to what he is experiencing, the fact is that it already has a name – a *mirage*. Again, we should be wise not to accept too readily the statement that what he is experiencing is *'similar in character* to what he would be experiencing if he were seeing a real oasis'. For is it at all likely, really, to be very similar? And, looking ahead, if we were to concede this point we should find the concession being used against us at a later stage – namely, at the stage where we shall be invited to agree that we see sense-data always, in normal cases too.

[. . .]

V

I want now to take up again the philosophical argument as it is set out in the texts we are discussing. As I mentioned earlier, the argument from illusion is intended primarily to persuade us that, in certain exceptional, abnormal situations, what we perceive – directly anyway – is a sense-datum; but then there comes a second stage, in which we are to be brought to agree that what we (directly) perceive is *always* a sense-datum, even in the normal, unexceptional case. It is this second stage of the argument that we must now examine.

Ayer expounds the argument thus.[7] There is, he says, 'no intrinsic difference in kind between those of our perceptions that are veridical in their presentation of material things and those that are delusive. When I look at a straight stick, which is refracted in water and so appears crooked, my experience is qualitatively the same as if I were looking at a stick that really was crooked. . . .' If, however, 'when our perceptions were delusive, we were always perceiving something of a different kind from what we perceived when they were veridical, we should expect our experience to be qualitatively different in the two cases. We should expect to be able to tell from the intrinsic character of a perception whether it was a perception of a sense-datum or of a material thing. But this is not possible. . . .' Price's exposition of this point,[8] to which Ayer refers us, is in fact not perfectly analogous; for Price has already somehow reached the conclusion that we are always aware of sense-data, and here is trying to establish only that we cannot distinguish *normal* sense-data, as 'parts of the surfaces of material things', from *abnormal* ones, not 'parts of the surfaces of material things'. However, the argument used is much the same: 'the abnormal crooked sense-datum of a straight stick standing in water is qualitatively indistinguishable from a normal sense-datum of a crooked stick'; but 'is it not incredible that two entities so similar in all these qualities should really be so utterly different: that the one should be a real constituent of a material object, wholly independent of the observer's mind and organism, while the other is merely the fleeting product of his cerebral processes?'

It is argued further, both by Ayer and Price, that 'even in the case of veridical perceptions we are not directly aware of material things' (or *apud* Price, that our sense-data are not parts of the surfaces of material things) for the reason that 'veridical and delusive perceptions may form a continuous series. Thus, if I gradually approach an object from a distance I may begin by having a series of perceptions which are delusive in the sense that the object appears to be smaller than it really is. Let us assume that this series terminates in a veridical perception.[9] Then the difference in quality between this perception and its immediate predecessor will be of the same order as the difference between any two delusive perceptions that are next to one another in the series....' But 'these are differences of degree and not of kind. But this, it is argued, is not what we should expect if the veridical perception were a perception of an object of a different sort, a material thing as opposed to a sense-datum. Does not the fact that veridical and delusive perceptions shade into one another in the way that is indicated by these examples show that the objects that are perceived in either case are generically the same? And from this it would follow, if it was acknowledged that the delusive perceptions were perceptions of sense-data, that what we directly experienced was always a sense-datum and never a material thing.' As Price puts it, 'it seems most extraordinary that there should be a total difference of nature where there is only an infinitesimal difference of quality'.[10]

Well, what are we to make of the arguments thus set before us?

1. It is pretty obvious, for a start, that the terms in which the argument is stated by Ayer are grossly tendentious. Price, you remember, is not producing the argument as a proof that we are always aware of sense-data; in his view that question has already been settled, and he conceives himself to be faced here only with the question whether any sense-data are 'parts of the surfaces of material objects'. But in Ayer's exposition the argument *is* put forward as a ground for the conclusion that what we are (directly) aware of in perception is always a sense-datum; and if so, it seems a rather serious defect that this conclusion is practically assumed from the very first sentence of the statement of the argument itself. In that sentence Ayer uses, not indeed for the first time, the term 'perceptions' (which incidentally has never been defined or explained), and takes it for granted, here and throughout, that there is at any rate some kind of

entities of which we are aware in absolutely all cases – namely, 'perceptions', delusive or veridical. But of course, if one has already been induced to swallow the idea that every case, whether 'delusive' or 'veridical', supplies us with 'perceptions', one is only too easily going to be made to feel that it would be straining at a gnat not to swallow sense-data in an equally comprehensive style. But in fact one has not even been told what 'perceptions' *are*; and the assumption of their ubiquity has been slipped in without any explanation or argument whatever. But if those to whom the argument is ostensibly addressed were not thus made to concede the essential point from the beginning, would the statement of the argument be quite such plain sailing?

2. Of course we shall also want to enter a protest against the argument's bland assumption of a simple dichotomy between 'veridical and delusive experiences'. There is, as we have already seen, *no* justification at all *either* for lumping all so-called 'delusive' experiences together, *or* for lumping together all so-called 'veridical' experiences. But again, could the argument run quite so smoothly without this assumption? It would certainly – and this, incidentally, would be all to the good – take rather longer to state.

3. But now let us look at what the argument actually says. It begins, you will remember, with an alleged statement of fact – namely, that 'there is no intrinsic difference in kind between those of our perceptions that are veridical in their presentation of material things and those that are delusive' (Ayer), that 'there is no qualitative difference between normal sense-data as such and abnormal sense-data as such' (Price). Now, waiving so far as possible the numerous obscurities in and objections to this manner of speaking, let us ask whether what is being alleged here is actually true. Is it the case that 'delusive and veridical experiences' are not 'qualitatively different'? Well, at least it seems perfectly extraordinary to say so in this sweeping way. Consider a few examples. I may have the experience (dubbed 'delusive' presumably) of dreaming that I am being presented to the Pope. Could it be seriously suggested that having this dream is 'qualitatively indistinguishable' from *actually being* presented to the Pope? Quite obviously not. After all, we have the phrase 'a dream-like quality'; some waking experiences are said to have this dream-like quality, and some artists and writers occasionally try to impart it, usually with scant success, to their works. But of course, if the fact here alleged *were* a fact, the phrase would be perfectly meaningless, because applicable to everything. If dreams were not 'qualitatively' different from waking experiences, then *every* waking experience would be like a dream; the dream-like quality would be, not difficult to capture, but impossible to avoid.[11] It is true, to repeat, that dreams are *narrated* in the same terms as

waking experiences: these terms, after all, are the best terms we have; but it would be wildly wrong to conclude from this that what is narrated in the two cases is *exactly alike*. When we are hit on the head we sometimes say that we 'see stars'; but for all that, seeing stars when you are hit on the head is *not* 'qualitatively' indistinguishable from seeing stars when you look at the sky.

Again, it is simply not true to say that seeing a bright green after-image against a white wall is exactly like seeing a bright green patch actually on the wall; or that seeing a white wall through blue spectacles is exactly like seeing a blue wall; or that seeing pink rats in D.T.s is exactly like really seeing pink rats; or (once again) that seeing a stick refracted in water is exactly like seeing a bent stick. In all these cases we may *say* the same things ('It looks blue', 'It looks bent', etc.), but this is no reason at all for denying the obvious fact that the 'experiences' are *different*.

4. Next, one may well wish at least to ask for the credentials of a curious general principle on which both Ayer and Price seem to rely,[12] to the effect that, if two things are not 'generically the same', the same 'in nature', then they can't be alike, or even very nearly alike. If it were true, Ayer says, that from time to time we perceived things of two different kinds, then 'we should expect' them to be qualitatively different. But why on earth should we? – particularly if, as he suggests would be the case, we never actually found such a thing to be true. It is not at all easy to discuss this point sensibly, because of the initial absurdity in the hypothesis that we perceive just *two* kinds of things. But if, for example, I had never seen a mirror, but were told (*a*) that in mirrors one sees reflections of things, and (*b*) that reflections of things are not 'generically the same' as things, is there any reason why I should forthwith *expect* there to be some whacking big 'qualitative' difference between seeing things and seeing their reflections? Plainly not; if I were prudent, I should simply wait and see what seeing reflections was like. If I am told that a lemon is generically different from a piece of soap, do I 'expect' that no piece of soap could look just like a lemon? Why should I?

(It is worth noting that Price helps the argument along at this point by a bold stroke of rhetoric: how *could* two entities be 'qualitatively indistinguishable', he asks, if one is a 'real constituent of a material object', the other '*a fleeting product of his cerebral processes*'? But how in fact are we supposed to have been persuaded that sense-data are *ever* fleeting products of cerebral processes? Does this colourful description fit, for instance, the reflection of my face in a mirror?)

5. Another erroneous principle which the argument here seems to rely on is this: that it *must* be the case that 'delusive and veridical experiences'

are not (as such) 'qualitatively' or 'intrinsically' distinguishable – for if they were distinguishable, we should never be 'deluded'. But of course this is not so. From the fact that I am sometimes 'deluded', mistaken, taken in through failing to distinguish A from B, it does not follow at all that A and B must be *indistinguishable*. Perhaps I should have noticed the difference if I had been more careful or attentive; perhaps I am just bad at distinguishing things of this sort (e.g. vintages); perhaps, again, I have never learned to discriminate between them, or haven't had much practice at it. As Ayer observes, probably truly, 'a child who had not learned that refraction was a means of distortion would naturally believe that the stick really was crooked as he saw it'; but how is the fact that an uninstructed child probably would not discriminate between *being refracted* and *being crooked* supposed to establish the allegation that there *is* no 'qualitative' difference between the two cases? What sort of reception would I be likely to get from a professional tea-taster, if I were to say to him, 'But there can't be any difference between the flavours of these two brands of tea, for I regularly fail to distinguish between them'? Again, when 'the quickness of the hand deceives the eye', it is not that what the hand is really doing is *exactly like* what we are tricked into thinking it is doing, but simply that it is *impossible to tell* what it is really doing. In this case it may be true that we can't distinguish, and not merely that we don't; but even this doesn't mean that the two cases are exactly alike.

I do not, of course, wish to deny that there may be cases in which 'delusive and veridical experiences' really are 'qualitatively indistinguishable'; but I certainly do wish to deny (*a*) that such cases are anything like as *common* as both Ayer and Price seem to suppose, and (*b*) that there *have* to be such cases to accommodate the undoubted fact that we are sometimes 'deceived by our senses'. We are not, after all, quasi-infallible beings, who can be taken in only where the avoidance of mistake is completely impossible. But if we are prepared to admit that there may be, even that there are, *some* cases in which 'delusive and veridical perceptions' really are indistinguishable, does this admission require us to drag in, or even to let in, sense-data? No. For even if we were to make the prior admission (which we have so far found no reason to make) that in the 'abnormal' cases we perceive sense-data, we should not be obliged to extend this admission to the 'normal' cases too. For why on earth should it *not* be the case that, in some few instances, perceiving one sort of thing is exactly like perceiving another?

6. There is a further quite general difficulty in assessing the force of this argument, which we (in common with the authors of our texts) have slurred over so far. The question which Ayer invites us to consider is

whether two classes of 'perceptions', the veridical and the delusive, are or are not 'qualitatively different', 'intrinsically different in kind'; but how are we supposed to set about even considering this question, when we are not told what 'a perception' *is*? In particular, how many of the circumstances of a situation, as these would ordinarily be stated, are supposed to be included in 'the perception'? For example, to take the stick in water again: it is a feature of this case that part of the stick is under water, and water, of course, is not invisible; is the water, then, part of 'the perception'? It is difficult to conceive of any grounds for denying that it is; but *if* it is, surely this is a perfectly obvious respect in which 'the perception' differs from, is distinguishable from, the 'perception' we have when we look at a bent stick *not* in water. There is a sense, perhaps, in which the presence or absence of water is not the *main thing* in this case – we are supposed to be addressing ourselves primarily to questions about the stick. But in fact, as a great quantity of psychological investigation has shown, discrimination between one thing and another very frequently depends on such more or less extraneous concomitants of the main thing, even when such concomitants are not consciously taken note of. As I said, we are told nothing of what 'a perception' is; but could any defensible account, if such an account were offered, completely exclude all these highly significant attendant circumstances? And if they *were* excluded – in some more or less arbitrary way – how much interest or importance would be left in the contention that 'delusive' and 'veridical' perceptions are indistinguishable? Inevitably, if you rule out the respects in which A and B differ, you may expect to be left with respects in which they are alike.

I conclude, then, that this part of the philosophical argument involves (though not in every case equally essentially) (*a*) acceptance of a quite bogus dichotomy of all 'perceptions' into two groups, the 'delusive' and the 'veridical' – to say nothing of the unexplained introduction of 'perceptions' themselves; (*b*) an implicit but grotesque exaggeration of the *frequency* of 'delusive perceptions'; (*c*) a further grotesque exaggeration of the *similarity* between 'delusive' perceptions and 'veridical' ones; (*d*) the erroneous suggestion that there *must* be such similarity, or even qualitative *identity*; (*e*) the acceptance of the pretty gratuitous idea that things 'generically different' could not be qualitatively alike; and (*f*) – which is really a corollary of (*c*) and (*a*) – the gratuitous neglect of those more or less subsidiary features which often make possible the discrimination of situations which, in other *broad* respects, may be roughly alike. These seem to be rather serious deficiencies.

Notes

1   A. J. Ayer, *The Foundations of Empirical Knowledge* (London: Macmillan, 1969), pp. 3–5.
2   It is not only strange, but also important, that Ayer calls these 'assumptions'. Later on he is going to take seriously the notion of denying at least one of them, which he could hardly do if he had recognized them here as the plain and incontestable facts that they are.
3   The latter point holds, of course, for *some* uses of 'illusion' too; there are the illusions which some people (are said to) lose as they grow older and wiser.
4   Cp. the white rabbit in the play called *Harvey*.
5   H. H. Price, *Perception* (London: Methuen, 1932), p. 27.
6   Not even 'indirectly', no such thing is 'presented'. Doesn't this seem to make the case, though more amenable, a good deal less useful to the philosopher? It's hard to see how normal cases could be said to be *very like* this.
7   Ayer, *The Foundations of Empirical Knowledge*, pp. 5–9.
8   *Perception*, p. 31.
9   But what, we may ask, does this assumption amount to? From what distance *does* an object, a cricket-ball say, 'look the size that it really is'? Six feet? Twenty feet?
10   I omit from consideration a further argument cited by both Price and Ayer, which makes play with the 'causal dependence' of our 'perceptions' upon the conditions of observation and our own 'physiological and psychological states'.
11   This is part, no doubt *only* part, of the absurdity in Descartes' toying with the notion that the whole of our experience might be a dream.
12   Ayer in fact expresses qualms later: see *The Foundations of Empirical Knowledge*, p. 12.

Induction

Hans Reichenbach, from *The Theory of Probability*

This selection is taken from the concluding part of Hans Reichenbach's *The Theory of Probability*. Reichenbach (1891–1953) accepts
Hume's skeptical argument and Hume's major conclusion that
inductive inference cannot yield knowledge of the future. He
agrees with Hume that there is no way to prove the validity of
inductive inference. Attempts to establish a premise such as the
uniformity of nature that could determine the probability of predictions about the future are futile, since such premises are neither
self-evident nor are they provable without circularity.

Despite this agreement with Hume, Reichenbach does think that
induction can be justified. For we can show by a deductive argument that if there is some regular pattern of events (he calls it the
limit of a frequency), the use of inductive methods will reveal it,
provided induction is applied for a long enough time. Induction
will reach the truth if there is a truth to be reached. Particular
predictions should not be classified as beliefs but as provisional
posits that must be adjusted in the light of future experience. Reichenbach describes his justification as "pragmatic" because it shows,
he claims, that induction is useful for action.

The first to criticize the inference of induction by enumeration and to
question its legitimacy was David Hume. Ever since his famous criticism,
philosophers have regarded the problem of induction as an unsolved
riddle precluding the completion of an empiricist theory of knowledge.
In Hume's analysis it does not appear as a problem of probability; he
includes it, rather, in the problem of causality. We observe, Hume

explains, that equal causes are always followed by equal effects. We then infer that the same effects will occur in future. On what grounds do we base this inference? Hume's criticism gave two negative answers to the question:

1. The conclusion of the inductive inference cannot be inferred *a priori*, that is, it does not follow with logical necessity from the premises; or, in modern terminology, it is not tautologically implied by the premises. Hume based this result on the fact that we can at least *imagine* that the same causes will have another effect tomorrow than they had yesterday, though we do not believe it. What is logically impossible cannot be imagined – this psychological criterion was employed by Hume for the establishment of his first thesis.

2. The conclusion of the inductive inference cannot be inferred *a posteriori*, that is, by an argument from experience. Though it is true that the inductive inference has been successful in past experience, we cannot infer that it will be successful in future experience. The very inference would be an inductive inference, and the argument thus would be circular. Its validity presupposes the principle that it claims to prove.

Hume did not see a way out of this dilemma. He regarded the inductive inference as an unjustifiable procedure to which we are conditioned by habit and the apparent cogency of which must be explained as an outcome of habit. The power of habit is so strong that even the clearest insight into the unfounded use of the inductive inference cannot destroy its compelling character. Though this explanation is psychologically true, we cannot admit that it has any bearing on the logical problem. Perhaps the inductive inference is a habit – the logician wants to know whether it is a good habit. The question would call for an answer even if it could be shown that we can never overcome the habit. The logical problem of justification must be carefully distinguished from the question of psychological laws.

Up to our day the problem has subsisted in the skeptical version derived from Hume, in spite of many attempts at its solution. Kant's attempt to solve the problem by regarding the principle of causality as a synthetic judgment *a priori* failed because the concept of the synthetic judgment *a priori* was shown to be untenable. I may add that Kant never attempted to make use of his theory for a detailed analysis of the inductive inference. In the empiricism of our time the problem has come to the fore, overshadowing all other problems of the theory of knowledge. It has held this place persistently without changing the skeptical form that Hume gave it.

A few philosophers tried to escape Hume's skepticism by denying that a problem of the justification of induction exists. Various reasons were given for such a conception. It was said that the rule of induction does not belong to the content of science; that Hume's criticism concerns only a linguistic problem; that the problem of justification is a pseudoproblem; and so on. It is hardly comprehensible that such arguments could ever have been seriously maintained. They misuse an important modern discovery – the distinction between levels of language – for the purpose of contesting the legitimacy of an old problem, upon which, however, this distinction has no bearing.

It is true that the rule of induction belongs, not in the object language of science, but in the metalanguage. It is a *directive* for the construction of sentences, since it tells how to proceed from verified sentences to predictive sentences. I have therefore called it a rule of derivation, the only one that inductive logic requires in addition to the rules of derivation of deductive logic. Such rules, however, are admissible within a scientific language only when they can be justified, that is, when they can be shown to be adequate means for the purpose of derivation. Such a justification is easily given for the rules of derivation of deductive logic: it can be shown that the rules always lead to true sentences if the premises are true. In a systematic exposition of deductive logic this justification of the rules of derivation must be formally given. For the rule of induction such a proof is not possible; that is why the problem of its justification is so involved that it requires a comprehensive analysis.

The frequency theory of probability, with its interpretation of probability statements as posits, makes it possible to give a justification of the rule of induction. The problem will be discussed with respect to the wider form of statistical induction; the results will then include the special case of classical induction. The generalization expressed in the use of statistical induction is relevant because it weakens the inference. Whereas classical induction wishes to establish a rigorous inference that holds for every individual case, statistical induction renounces every assertion about the individual case and makes a prediction only about the whole sequence.

There is another sense in which the statistical version involves a different interpretation of the problem. The classical conception entails the question whether the rule of induction leads to true conclusions, but the statistical version deals only with the question whether the rule of induction leads to a method of approximation, whether it leads to posits that, when repeated, approach the correct result step by step. The answer is that this is so if the sequences under consideration have a limit of the frequency. The inductive posit anticipates the final result and must eventually arrive at the correct value of the limit within an interval of exactness.

The method of anticipation may be illustrated by an example from another field. An airplane flies in the fog to a distant destination. From two ground stations the pilot receives radio messages about his position, ascertained by radio bearings. He then determines the flight direction by means of a map, adjusts the compass to the established course, and flies on, keeping continuously to the direction given by the compass. In the fog he has no other orientation than to follow the adopted course. After a while, however, he inquires again of the ground stations for another determination of his position. It turns out that the airplane was subject to a wind drift that has carried the ship off its course. The pilot, therefore, establishes a new course that he follows thereafter.

This method, repeatedly applied, is a method of approximation. The direction from the position ascertained to the destination is not the most favorable one because of wind currents; but the pilot does not know the changing currents and therefore at first *posits* this direction. He does not believe that he has found the final direction. He knows that only when he is very close to his destination will the straight line be the most favorable flying direction – but he acts as though the coincidence of the most favorable flying direction and a straight-line connection were reached. He thus anticipates the final result. He may do so because he uses this anticipation only in the sense of a posit. By correcting the posit repeatedly, always following the same rule, he must finally come to the correct posit and thus reach his destination.

The analogy with the anticipative method of the rule of induction is obvious. In the analysis of Hume's problem we thus arrive at a preliminary result: if a limit of the frequency exists, positing the persistence of the frequency is justified because this method, applied repeatedly, must finally lead to true statements. We do not maintain the truth of every individual inductive conclusion, but we do not need an assumption of this kind because the application of the rule presupposes only its qualification as a method of approximation.

This consideration bases the justification of induction on the assumption of the existence of a limit of the frequency. It is obvious, however, that for such an assumption no proof can be constructed. When we wish to overcome Hume's skepticism we must eliminate this last assumption from our justification of induction.

The traditional discussion of induction was dominated by the opinion that it is impossible to justify induction without an assumption of this kind, that is, without an assumption stating a general property of the physical world. The supposedly indispensable assumption was formulated as a postulate of the uniformity of nature, expressed, for instance, in the form that similar event patterns repeat themselves. The principle used above, that sequences of events converge toward a limit of the frequency, may be regarded as another and perhaps more precise version of the uniformity postulate. So long as logicians maintained that without a postulate of this kind the inductive inference could not be accounted for, and so long as there was no hope of proving such a postulate true or probable, the theory of induction was condemned to remain an unsolvable puzzle.

The way out of the difficulty is indicated by the following considerations. The insistence on a uniformity postulate derives from an unfortunate attempt to construct the theory of inductive inference by analogy with that of deductive inference – the attempt to supply a premise for the inductive inference that would make the latter deductive. It was known that the inductive conclusion cannot be asserted as true; but it was hoped to give a demonstrative proof, by the addition of such a premise, for the statement that the conclusion is probable to a certain degree. Such a proof is dispensable because we can assert a statement in the sense of a posit even if we do not know a probability, or weight, for it. If the inductive conclusion is recognized as being asserted, not as a statement maintained as true or probable, but as an anticipative posit, it can be shown that a uniformity postulate is not necessary for the derivation of the inductive conclusion.

We used the assumption of the existence of a limit of the frequency in order to prove that, if no probabilities are known, the anticipative posit is the best posit because it leads to success in a finite number of steps. With respect to the individual act of positing, however, the limit assumption does not supply any sort of information. The posit may be wrong, and we can only say that if it turns out to be wrong we are willing to correct it and to try again. But if the limit assumption is dispensable for every individual posit, it can be omitted for the method of positing as a whole. The omission is required because we have no proof for the assumption. But the absence of proof does not mean that *we know that there is no limit*; it means only that *we do not know whether there is a limit*. In that case we have as much reason to try a posit as in the case that the existence of a limit is known; for, if a limit of the frequency exists, we shall find it by the inductive method if only the acts of positing are continued sufficiently. Inductive positing in the sense of a trial-and-error method is justified so long as it is not known that the attempt is hopeless, that there is no limit of the frequency. Should we have no success, the positing was useless; but why not take our chance?

The phrase "take our chance" is not meant here to state that there is a certain probability of success; it means only that there is a possibility of success in the sense that there is no proof that success is excluded. Furthermore, the suggestion to try predictions by means of the inductive method is not an advice of a trial at random, of trying one's luck, so to speak; it is the proposal of a systematic method of trial so devised that if success is attainable the method will find it.

To make the consideration more precise, some auxiliary concepts may be introduced. The distinction between necessary and sufficient conditions is well known in logic. A statement c is a *necessary* condition of a statement a if $a \supset c$ holds, that is, if a cannot be true without c being true. The statement c will be a *sufficient* condition of a if $c \supset a$ holds. For instance, if a physician says that an operation is a necessary condition to save the patient, he does not say that the operation will save the man; he only says that without the operation the patient will die. The operation would be a sufficient condition to save the man if it is certain that it will lead to success; but a statement of this kind would leave open whether there are other means that would also save him.

These concepts can be applied in the discussion of the anticipative posit. If there is a limit of the frequency, the use of the rule of induction will be a sufficient condition to find the limit to a desired degree of approximation. There may be other methods, but this one, at least, is sufficient. Consequently, when we do not know whether there is a limit, we can say, if there is any way to find a limit, the rule of induction will be such a way. It is, therefore, a necessary condition for the existence of a limit, and thus for the existence of a method to find it, that the aim be attainable by means of the rule of induction.

To clarify these logical relations, we shall formulate them in the logical symbolism. We abbreviate by a the statement, "There exists a limit of the frequency"; by b the statement, "I use the rule of induction in a repeated procedure"; by c the statement, "I shall find the limit of the frequency". We then have the relation

$$a \supset (b \supset c) \tag{1}$$

This means, $b \supset c$ is the *necessary* condition of a, or, in other words, the attainability of the aim by the use of the rule of induction is a necessary condition of the existence of a limit. Furthermore, if a is true, b is a *sufficient* condition of c. This means, if there is a limit of the frequency, the use of the rule of induction is a sufficient instrument to find it.

It is in this relation that I find the justification of the rule of induction. Scientific method pursues the aim of predicting the future; in order to construct a precise formulation for this aim we interpret it as meaning that scientific method is intended to find limits of the frequency. Classical induction and predictions of individual events are included in the general formulation as the special case that the relative frequency is $= 1$. It has been shown that if the aim of scientific method is attainable it will be reached by the inductive method. This result eliminates the last assumption we had to use for the justification of induction. The assumption that there is a limit of the frequency must be true if the inductive procedure is to be successful. But we need not know whether it is true when we merely ask whether the inductive procedure is justified. It is justified as an attempt at finding the limit. Since we do not know a sufficient condition to be used for finding a limit, we shall at least make use of a necessary condition. In positing according to the rule of induction, always correcting the posit when additional observation shows different results, we prepare everything so that if there is a limit of the frequency we shall find it. If there is none, we shall certainly not find one – but then all other methods will break down also.

The answer to Hume's question is thus found. Hume was right in asserting that the conclusion of the inductive inference cannot be proved to be true; and we may add that it cannot even be proved to be probable. But Hume was wrong in stating that the inductive procedure is unjustifiable. It can be justified as an instrument that realizes the necessary conditions of prediction, to which we resort because sufficient conditions of prediction are beyond our reach. The justification of induction can be summarized as follows:

> *Thesis θ.* The rule of induction is justified as an instrument of positing because it is a method of which we know that if it is possible to make statements about the future we shall find them by means of this method.

[...]

Some critics have called my justification of induction a weak justification. Such judgments originate from a rationalistic conception of scientific method. In spite of the empiricist trend of modern science, the quest for certainty, a product of the theological orientation of philosophy, still survives in the assertion that some general truths about the future must be known if scientific predictions are to be acceptable. It is hard to see what would be gained by the knowledge of such general truths. As was pointed out earlier, if we knew for certain that sequences of natural events have limits of the frequency, our situation in the face of any individual prediction would not be better than it is without such knowledge, since we would never know whether the observed initial section of the sequence were long enough to supply a satisfactory approximation of the frequency. It is no better with other forms of the uniformity postulate. How does it help to know that similar event patterns repeat themselves, if we do not know whether the pattern under consideration is one of them? In view of our ignorance concerning the individual event expected, all general truths must appear as illusory supports.

The aim of knowing the future is unattainable; there is no demonstrative truth informing us about future happenings. Let us therefore renounce the aim and renounce, too, the critique that measures the attainable in terms of that aim. It is not a weak argument that has been constructed. We can devise a method that will lead to correct predictions if correct predictions can be made – that is ground enough for the application of the method, even if we never know, before the occurrence of the event, whether the prediction is true.

If predictive methods cannot supply a knowledge of the future, they are, nevertheless, sufficient to justify action. In order to analyze the applicability of the inductive method as a basis for action, we must inquire into the presuppositions on which an action depends.

Every action depends on two presuppositions. The first is of a volitional nature: we wish to attain a certain aim. This aim can, at best, be reduced to more general volitional aims, but it cannot be given other than volitional grounds. A man who likes to exercise may justify his volitional aim by stating that he wants to retain a healthy body – but thereby the special volitional aim is only reduced to a more general one. The second presupposition is of a cognitive nature: we must know what will happen under certain conditions in order to be able to judge whether they are adequate for the attainment of the aim. If, for instance, I set up the general volitional aim of a healthy body, I can derive from this aim the usefulness of athletics only when I know that exercise makes the body healthy. Thus for every individual action I must know a statement about the future if the action is intended to contribute to the achievement of a general volitional aim. Only the combination of the two presuppositions, the volitional aim and knowledge about the future, makes purposive action possible. When the physician induces the patient to take an anodyne, he must know, first, whether the patient wants to get rid of his pain, and second, whether the drug will relieve it. When a politician advocates a new law, he wants to reach some goal and assumes that the law will attain it. The two presuppositions for action are of this kind.

The first presupposition, the volitional decision, need not be discussed here. Within the boundaries of a logical analysis we investigate the second presupposition for action, that is, the cognitive presupposition. Now it is clear that, though the inductive rule does not supply knowledge of a future event, it supplies a sufficient reason for action: we are justified in dealing with the anticipative posit as true, not because we can expect success in the individual case, but because if we can ever act successfully we can do so by following the directive of induction.

The justification of induction constructed may, therefore, be called a *pragmatic* justification: it demonstrates the usefulness of the inductive procedure for the purpose of acting. It shows that our actions need not depend on a proof that the sequences under consideration have the limit property. Actions can be made in the sense of trials, and it is sufficient to have a method that will lead to successful trials if success is attainable at all. It is true that this method has no guaranty of success. But who would dare to ask for such a guaranty in the face of the uncertainty of all human planning? The physician who operates on a patient because he knows that the operation will be the only chance to save the patient will be regarded as justified, though he cannot guarantee success. If we cannot base our actions on demonstrative truth, we shall welcome it that we can at least take our chance.

That is a rational argument. But who refers to it when he applies the inductive method in everyday life? If asked why he accepts the inductive rule, he answers that he believes in it, that he is firmly convinced of its validity and simply cannot give up inductive belief. Is there a justification for this belief?

The answer is a definite "No". The belief cannot be justified. As long as such a "No" was averred by a philosophy of skepticism, it constituted a negative judgment on all human planning and acting, which it seemed to prove utterly useless. It is different for the philosophy of logical analysis, which distinguishes between justification of the belief and justification of the action. Actions directed by the rule of induction are legitimate attempts at success; no form of belief is required for the proof. He who wants to act need not believe in success; it is a sufficient reason for action to know how to prepare for success, how to be ready for the case that success is attainable. Belief in success is a personal addition; whoever has it need not give it up. For his actions it is logically irrelevant: whether or not he believes in success, the same actions will follow.

I say "*logically* irrelevant", for I know very well that, psychologically speaking, belief may not be irrelevant. Many a person is not able to act according to his posits unless he believes in their success, since few have the inner strength to take a possible failure into account and yet pursue their aim. Nature seems to have endowed us with the inductive belief as a measure of protection, as it were, facilitating our actions, though without it we would be equally justified, or obliged, to act. It is difficult, indeed, to free oneself from such a belief; and Hume was right when he called the belief in induction an unjustified but ineradicable habit. But since Hume could not show that even without this belief action is justified when it follows the rule of induction, there remained for him only skeptical resignation.

The logician need not share this negative attitude. He can show that we must act according to the rule of induction even if we cannot believe in it. This result may be the reason why it is easier for him to renounce the belief; with the loss of the belief he does not at the same time lose his orientation in the sphere of action. We do not know whether tomorrow the order of the world will not come to an end; tomorrow all known physical laws may be invalidated, the sun may no longer shine, and food no longer nourish us – or at least our own world may come to an end, because we may close our eyes forever. Tomorrow is unknown to us, but this fact need not make any difference in considerations determining our actions. We adjust our actions to the case of a predictable world – if the world is not predictable, very well, then we have acted in vain.

A blind man who has lost his way in the mountains feels a trail with his stick. He does not know where the path will lead him, or whether it may take him so close to the edge of a precipice that he will be plunged into the abyss. Yet he follows the path, groping his way step by step; for if there is any possibility of getting out of the wilderness, it is by feeling his way along the path. As blind men we face the future; but we feel a path. And we know: if we can find a way through the future it is by feeling our way along this path.

13

Michael Levin, "Reliabilism and Induction"

This selection is a paper by Michael Levin (1943–) commissioned for this volume. It presents a view – reliabilism – that aims at showing that Hume's analysis of inductive inference fails to demonstrate that induction does not yield knowledge of future events and scientific laws. According to reliabilism, to know something is to have a true belief caused by a reliable process. In order to have knowledge, it is not necessary to know or to be able to prove that the process is reliable. So even though, as Hume has shown, there is no non-circular argument to prove that inductive inference is reliable, it may be reliable nonetheless; and, if it is, it provides genuine knowledge or, at least, justified belief. Reliabilism is an externalist point of view; it rejects the internalist assumption of Descartes, Hume, and many others that says that we must have access to truths that can be used to establish the reliability of a mode of belief formation in order for the beliefs so caused to be justified. The reliabilist approach can be employed to rebut not only skepticism about induction, but also skepticism about other modes of belief formation such as perception, memory, deduction, and inference to the best explanation.

Because the sun has always risen after periods of darkness, we believe that it will continue to rise, and – ascending to the philosophical level – that we are right to believe this. But, Hume argued, statements about the past and present do not entail statements about the future, so logic plus observation plus memory do not warrant induction. Yet logic, observation, and memory evidently exhaust the possible bases for knowledge.

Hence arises the problem of justifying induction. Solutions have been many, but none has won consensus; indeed, the disarray drives some to deny that people really do generalize from experience, and to seek to reconstruct science without induction.

A Reliabilist Suggestion

Reliabilists have a suggestion (implicit or stated in the works of Dauer, Goldman, Mellor, Nozick, Quine, van Cleve, and Watling). Instead of trying to show that we know or justifiably believe that the sun will rise tomorrow, Hume notwithstanding, they dismiss Humean arguments as irrelevant to whether we know. Knowledge, according to reliabilism, is true belief caused by a reliable process – one that has, does, will, and would produce true belief sufficiently often. (Note the omnitemporality: processes are reliable (or otherwise) *sub specie aeternitatis*.) Since someone may know *p* without knowing or believing that his belief has been caused by a reliable process, he may know *p* without having any idea how or why he does. He need never have considered the reliability of the causes of his belief. There *can* be a reliable process causing him to believe he knows *p*, in which case he knows that he knows. But there doesn't have to be; all that matters for knowledge is that the process causing his belief is reliable, whether he himself realizes it is or not.

So consider your belief that the sun will rise tomorrow, caused by your tendency to project past regularities together with the sun's having risen in the past. Reliabilism says that if the sun *will* rise and if the belief-producing mechanism of inductive inference *is* reliable – if *in fact* inductive extrapolations will continue to be mostly correct – you *know* it will rise. You need not know that induction is reliable to know, or, as we will see, justifiably believe, that the sun will rise tomorrow, or, indeed, for the next billion years. As long as induction *is* reliable, true inductive belief is knowledge. At worst, Humean considerations threaten our knowledge *that induction is reliable, that we possess inductive knowledge*. But one may know or justifiably believe the sun will rise tomorrow without knowing or justifiably believing that one knows it will.

In fact, since reliabilism permits (without requiring) knowledge of knowledge, it allows, even, that induction is known to be reliable by anyone who induces its reliability from its past success, given – the big catch – that induction is in fact reliable. Knowledge that one knows that induction is reliable is likewise available to those who come to believe, presumably in part inductively, that they know that they know induction is reliable – given that induction is reliable The catch is important, because it prohibits any self-contained inductive justification of induction. Inductive justifications of induction are inevitably circular, nor does reliabilism say otherwise.

Although induction raises some distinctive issues, this treatment of inductive skepticism parallels its reply to other skeptical doubts. We know about the external world, the past, etc., so long as our beliefs about them are reliable, whether or not we have any idea why these beliefs are reliable, or even that they are.[1] And, to be sure, this overall reply to skepticism has drawn many rebukes, as has reliabilism as a general analysis of knowledge.[2] Indeed, there are questions about what counts as a "process" and how often is "sufficiently often" in the statement of reliabilism itself. Finally, despite some initial optimism, the Gettier problem has proven intractable. To which I answer: reliabilism can be formulated with tolerable precision, the counterexamples in the literature can be sidestepped or explained away,[3] and Gettier is beginning to emerge as a problem for the very concept of knowledge rather than any particular analysis thereof. At this stage it remains useful to draw the consequences of reliabilism, letting it be known by its fruits, in hope that on the whole it appears to point in the right direction.

Thus heartened, we return to the reliabilist argument, noting that the omnitemporal construction of reliability gives it real bite. Induction *is* not reliable unless it *will* be reliable forever. To strengthen the skeptic's hand, assume contrary to the argument a few paragraphs back that at no time *t* can induction be known to be reliable after *t*, so that induction can never be known to be reliable. Still, so long as induction *is* reliable, we in the early 2000s will have known the conclusions of inductive inferences all along. Perhaps our descendants will have to wait until the end of time to discover whether we knew, but we might nevertheless always have known. Would (will) we in 2010 have been justified? Certainly, assuming that "justified" beliefs are reliabilistically defined as those, whether true or false, produced by reliable processes.[4] If induction *is* reliable, the worst that follows from the impossibility of establishing its reliability now is the impossibility of anyone establishing now that inductive beliefs are justified. They might still *be* justified. Ignorance of the reliability of inductive inference, if such is our burden, does not preclude justified belief in the conclusions of inductive inferences, although we may have to wait forever to discover whether our beliefs were justified. Conceding that we do not know induction to be reliable gives the skeptic nothing.

Well, the reader may think, we were perhaps entitled way back when to draw inductive inferences, but not anymore, not since Hume ended our innocence by showing that we don't know induction to be reliable. It seems irrational to keep using a principle of inference we realize is not known to be reliable. Who would say: "I don't know whether my principle is reliable, but I'm going to use it anyway"?[5] It is *a priori* that no one forms beliefs on what he believes to be an unreliable basis, which makes it *a priori* that no one forms beliefs on a basis he does not believe at least tacitly to be reliable. But all that shows, in light of mankind's continued inductive behavior, is that Hume's arguments do not persuade anyone for more than a few moments that he does not know induction is reliable. As Hume concluded from the impotence of his arguments to convert even himself, a propensity to induce *and* to believe induction reliable are invulnerable to reasoning. Oddly enough, then, given both that Hume is correct and that induction *is* reliable, we cannot help knowing that the sun will rise tomorrow, since we cannot refrain from believing that we are entitled to believe it. As Hume's arguments cannot show that induction is unreliable, only (at most) that we do not know that it is, they can undermine inductive knowledge only by undermining belief. "Human nature" prevents them from doing this.

Hume's inductive psychology also brings out why reliabilism is a more pertinent answer to inductive skepticism than many others currently on offer. To begin with, Hume was clearly right that "infants, nay even brute beasts" induce, and do so without benefit of any "intricate or profound argument." So no intricate argument, however decisively it may warrant induction, mirrors the process by which babies (and animals) actually induce. Further, the inductive processes of babies and animals are plainly continuous with those of human adults, despite nuanced differences that unfold during development. Common to both juvenile and adult inductive "inference" is instinctiveness and unreflectiveness. Consequently, even if *there are* some premises evident to philosophers that entail the reasonableness of induction, nobody comes to his inductive conclusions by them. Now, a belief or inference's being justified is not the same as an individual's being justified in holding that belief or drawing that inference. It is possible, and lamentable, to hold a justifiable belief for the wrong reason. And it is part of epistemic common sense that, not merely are our inductive conclusions justified, but that *we* are justified in drawing them as we do. Hume's psychology challenges this conviction. Even if there is a good argument for induction, inductive practices would remain unjustified because people do not use that (or any other) argument.

Because we expect our inductive conclusions to be warranted by the procedures that actually lead to them, abstruse justifications of induction "give up the question," in Hume's words. This accusation fits four familiar approaches:

1 *Pragmatic vindication.* The idea: projecting the observed ratio of *A*s in ever-larger samples from a possibly infinite population of *B*s eventually converges to the true *A/B* ratio, should it exist. The trouble is, ordinary inducers don't reason about infinite series, and anyway the conclusion: induction works if anything does, is weaker than the conviction of ordinary inducers: induction works, period.
2 *Logical probability.* There are arguments from the probability axioms that in many cases positive instances boost probability. But ordinary inducers know the argument not. Although they behave as if they accepted crude forms of the probability axioms, their thought processes don't mirror deep theorems of the required sort.
3 *Bayesianism.* In addition to probability axioms, Bayesians posit prior distributions of probabilities whose parameters fluctuate during Bernoulli trials. But ordinary inducers do not think about probabilities of probabilities.
4 *Popper.* Popper holds that generalizations are in fact never confirmed. So-called confirmatory observations, e.g. a rising sun, merely fail to disconfirm the generalization being tested, and thereby (merely) "corroborate" it. Allowing that Popper's account is more than wordplay, it fails to explain why anyone would rely on the predictions of undisconfirmed theories, or expect undisconfirmed theories to remain undisconfirmed. That is the inductive expectation in Popperese, and is unquestionably the expectation of scientific theorists and plain practical men.

Reliabilism alone promises to endorse *ordinary* inductive thinking. People do generalize stimuli, a tendency that may be viewed either as a response unmediated by inference caused by psychological mechanisms, or an inference whose leading principle is (deferring projectability issues) the uniformity of nature. Our so generalizing is what must be justified by a justification of induction, and it is justified, according to reliabilism, if it in fact leads to truth. By allowing success to be its own reward, reliabilism sanctions successful inductions however we come by them, without holding the reasonableness of our beliefs hostage to arguments that occur to practically no one. Reliabilism alone permits the inductive inferences we make in the way we make them.

It does justice as well to another tenet of epistemological common sense, that induction works because of the orderly, regular character of the world. Arguments that induction would be rational no matter what–because, for instance, "rationality" means basing expectations about new cases on old–feel unsatisfying, precisely because they demand nothing of reality. Or consider the claim that induction is a metamethod, in that use of any enduringly successful method would ipso facto count as inductively justified, so once again by definition "induction" must succeed. To counter this claim, imagine double-crossing worlds in which *no* first-order method is reliable past the point at which it generated trust. It was such worlds that poor despised Mill rightly warned about when insisting that induction works because "nature is uniform."

Among extant justifications, reliabilism alone recognizes that the world must cooperate if induction is to be warranted. Induction works only if nature is congruent to the way we think. No doubt this congruence is due to more than luck, and there is indeed an evolutionary account of it, assuming it holds. I stress again that the reliabilist does not (or should not) say that induction *is* reliable *since* the world works as we think it does. He does not pretend to know now that this congruence holds omnitemporally. He says that this congruence, if it holds, is enough to justify induction. Reliabilism turns the necessity of the world's cooperation into a virtue, a claim no other theory can make.

Hume's Argument

Conceding that induction might not be or might not be known to be reliable seems like capitulation to the Humean. To help decide whether reliabilism in fact conflicts with interesting Humean conclusions, let us zero in more closely on the central Humean argument. (This focus is meant to be ahistorical.) First, appeals to authority. Here is Wesley Salmon, an author in the pragmatic tradition:

> Given that all of the observed black balls [in an urn] have been licorice-flavored...do the observed facts constitute *evidence* [that the unobserved balls are licorice]? Would we be *justified* in accepting that conclusion on the basis of the facts alleged to be evidence for it?...This is Hume's problem of induction. Can we show that any particular type of ampliative inference can be justified in any way?...Hume's position can be summarized succinctly: We cannot justify any kind of ampliative inference.[6]

Next David Stove, working in the logical probability tradition:

[F]rom premises which prove at most the invalidity of predictive-inductive inferences, along with the unstated premise that any inference is unreasonable if it is invalid, Hume concluded that predictive-inductive inferences are unreasonable.[7]

Israel Scheffler, a Goodmanian, concurs:

If...the truth of our predictions is not guaranteed by deduction from accumulated evidence, what can be their rational justification? This challenge to justify induction (or non-demonstrative inference), arising out of Hume's analysis, has evoked a variety of responses from philosophers.[8]

Knowledgeable representatives of three major schools thus take Hume to argue that all inferences from the observed to the unobserved are unjustified because invalid, hence that knowledge of the unobserved is impossible. This argument can be met by showing the "because" and the "hence" to be non sequiturs, that is, that knowledge of and justified belief about the unobserved are *compatible* with the invalidity of inductive inference. Hume's argument could also be met by showing that we *do* know and hold justified beliefs about the unobserved, despite the invalidity of inductive inference, but such a showing is stronger than needed. Hume's argument fails if we *can* know. Since reliabilism says we can, it contravenes Hume. Remember, Hume did not just *say* induction is unjustified – mere talk is cheap – but offered a reason, the invalidity of inductive inference. The reliabilist says that this is *not* a reason for thinking induction unjustified. That is disagreement.

Suppose I die shortly after predicting the next sunrise, and the sun duly rises. Hume maintains that, because inductive inference is invalid, I did not know and was not entitled to believe that the sun would rise; I just guessed correctly. My belief was not "based on reason." Consequently, an argument meets Hume's if it shows that I might have known, and that my belief might have been more than a lucky guess, even given Hume's premises. Such an argument would not justify my belief that the sun was going to rise, but it would undercut the skeptical basis for calling my belief a lucky guess. This reliabilism does accomplish. It supplies a sense of "based on reason" in which a conclusion not entailed by premises can be "based on reason." More is neither available nor necessary for countering Hume. Nor is it as if reliabilism has found some picky little fault with Hume's reasoning. Reliabilism implies that, if nature is uniform, we do have knowledge, not lucky guesswork. Reliabilism shows just how close we are to inductive knowledge, Hume or no Hume.

Projectability

It is long past time to admit that inducing is not the unrestricted extrapo-lation of observed regularities. All past emeralds have been grue, but the grueness of future emeralds is no part of inductive lore, to be preserved by a justification of induction. Human induction is, rather, a readiness to extrapolate some regularities, involving some predicates only. Goodman calls such predicates "projectible" and their characterization is his "new," i.e. genuine, problem of induction.

To integrate the reliabilist account of induction with Goodman's, let us first recall Goodman's own solution to his riddle. For Goodman, predi-cates become projectible by being projected, by occurring frequently in past inductions. It is no part of Goodman's proposal, but let us reflect anyway that predicates become "entrenched," presumably, through the success of inductions using them – when hypotheses using these predi-cates keep racking up positive instances. "Green" is well-entrenched because inferences from "Past *F*s have been green" to "The next *F* will be green" have been conspicuously sound. That de facto entrenchment, past projections, seems a slender basis for projec*tibility* coheres with Goodman's overall approach to philosophy. He is not out to justify induction in the traditional sense, and indeed regards any quest for philosophical grounding as chimerical. The best a philosophical construc-tion can aim for is harmony with actual practice. In particular, inductive logic can aspire to no more than codification of inductive practice.

Such a limited goal seems to ignore the question of the warrant of ordinary practice itself. Proofs of consistency and completeness are cer-tainly regarded as more germane to warranting formal deductive systems than harmony with informal reasoning. And surely Goodman is acute enough to have noticed this point. It is a virtue of reliabilism that it casts a more favorable light on Goodman's approach to inductive (if not deductive) logic.

To see how, we shift momentarily from an issue of entitlement to an issue of fact. Why do animals and men induce at all? Obviously because so doing has (to date) been adaptive. Successful inducers have been fitter than their non-inducing and less successfully inducing competitors. Good inducers make good reproducers. Moreover, since virtually any fitness-enhancing trait that *can* get selected does get selected, regularity-projecting tendencies must have gotten hard-wired into nervous systems fairly early on, the most successful tendencies the most firmly implanted. The refinement of those tendencies by nature's rough handling has produced our minds. What Goodman's paradox brings out is that there never was any general tendency, innate or acquired, to project regularities. There were and are specific tendencies to notice specific saliencies and project regularities involving those saliencies only. Thinking that the future will be as the past confers no competitive advantage; thinking that future green things will be as inedible as past green things does confer an advantage, and, past a point, thinking that future grellow things will be as inedible as past grellows is disadvantageous. Prewired inductive tendencies thus involve particular properties, namely the entrenched ones, those used in successful next-instance inductions. Entrenched properties are those responsiveness to which has favored survival. Had different, possibly "positional," properties made for successful inductions, different sensitivies would have been selected. So, our tendency to project the predicates we do, while not a consequence of reason, does reflect the nature of the world. How then do we come up with new predicates? My own view is that new properties (indulging in that language) are introduced on the strength of analogies with familiar properties already believed to be projectible. One obvious example is use of wave language to describe changes in the strength of electric and magnetic fields; another is that of nuclear forces defined by their distance-dependent effects on the motion of particles, just as the classical forces of gravity and electromagnetism are. But world enough and time to develop this interesting point has been denied me.

We are thus positioned to give entrenchment its due. The depth of entrenchment of a predicate is part of the case for extrapolating hypotheses in which the predicate occurs.

Reliabilism sanctions a decision to project entrenched predicates if projecting them in fact continues to lead to predictive success. There is no time-independent guarantee that a predicate F well entrenched at time t will still be well entrenched at later time t', since many hypotheses which use F may be falsified in the interim. But this permanent possibility shows only that we cannot know at t whether we are justified at t in projecting entrenched F. For all we know, projecting F might be justified anyway, and will have been justified at t if F is still entrenched at t'. We may not know until the end of time whether we were then justified, but again we must not confuse the impossibility of knowing a projection to be warranted with the projection's being unwarranted. If the world continues the way it has been going, with entrenched predicates staying entrenched and predicates to be entrenched remaining entrenched thereafter, entrenched predicates will be projec*tible*, the right ones to project.

Conclusion

Hume spoke in connection with induction of the "preestablished harmony between the course of nature and the succession of our ideas," which he recommended to devotees of "final causes." Darwinian hindsight enables us to understand this harmony. We anticipate nature because nature shaped us to, genetic extinction the penalty of failure to cut nature at the joints.

Recall the charge that reliabilism endorses conformity to procedures not known to be reliable. Such conformity does indeed seem irrational. Moreover, I've granted that induction may not be known to be reliable, and that sophisticates know that induction may not be known to be reliable. So, it may seem, induction cannot produce knowledge, any more than my accidentally taking a road that actually leads home can produce knowledge of the way to go. I cannot be blamed for plunging ahead if "human nature" compels me, but irrational reliance is not knowledge.

But my urge to take the right road *is* rational if it had the right origin. Suppose a benevolent engineer has laid out the world's roads, and seen to everyone's being prewired to take the right roads to their destinations, having cruelly but elegantly terminated creatures whose wires were crossed. The choices he has induced are reliable, since he would have seen (e.g.) to my (or my replacement's) being prewired to take a different path had that different path led to my door. My safe arrival is part of a plan he has been refining for eons. Given all this, my arrival home can hardly be called an accident. I do not know about the engineer; were I asked why I take this road I would be reduced to unhelpful appeals to "self-evidence;" the efforts of my more philosophical fellow-pilgrims to justify our seemingly inerrant instincts are wholly inconclusive. Still, I *know* the way.

Our tendency to extrapolate certain regularities, to take certain roads into the future, is the residue of a process that famously mimics the work of a planner. Death to those who choose the wrong road, life–and children to transmit their choice–to those who choose rightly. But who knows? Maybe evolution will stop. But *if* reliable belief-forming mechanisms continue to be selected for, our inductions will prove, from the perspective of eternity, to have been correct sufficiently often. Our inductive successes will manifestly have been counterfactually reliable; had the world been different but similar enough to have allowed evolution, our inductive expectations would have been different but still, and therefore non-accidentally, correct. From the perspective of eternity we will not have been just lucky. We will have known.

Notes

1   Arguably, perception and memory can be certified if induction is assumed; from the reliability of memory to date we infer its overall reliability. Induction, on the other hand, cannot be certified even assuming memory and perception. Induction is thus the more challenging problem.

2   For a reply to skepticism independent of reliabilism, see my "Demons, Possibility and Evidence," *Nous* (2000): 408–22.

3   See my "You Can Always Count on Reliabilism," *Philosophy and Phenomenological Research* 57 (1997): 607–17.

4   So reliabilists wishing to recognize justified false belief must not ask reliable processes to produce truth every time.

5   The irrationality of so saying is the point of Laurence Bonjour's counterexamples to reliabilism.

6   *The Foundations of Scientific Inference* (Pittsburgh: University of Pittsburgh Press, 1966), p. 6.

7   *Probability and Hume's Inductive Skepticism* (Oxford: Oxford University Press, 1973), p. 51.

8   *The Anatomy of Inquiry* (New York: Knopf, 1967), p. 228.

Other Minds

14

Thomas Nagel, "Other Minds"

As Thomas Nagel (1937–) describes it in his chapter "Other Minds" from *What Does It All Mean?*, the problem of other minds begins innocently enough. You might wonder whether chocolate ice cream tastes the same to a friend as it does to yourself. She might remark upon its delicious, velvety texture, but how do you know those words are representative of a similar "inner" experience?

Once such doubts take root, Nagel finds them hard to remove. One might think, for example, that a solution lies in a uniform correlation between certain experiences and their behavioral manifestations, but how does one come to know *that*? One might observe such a connection in one's own case, as it were, from the inside, but a single case doesn't seem strong enough to support the generalization from one particular case to all others. Indeed, we might even wonder whether another person has any conscious experience *at all* lying behind her behavior.

Interestingly, Nagel further offers that skepticism about other minds precipitates another worry in the opposite direction: do things quite different in behavior (or lack thereof) nevertheless possess conscious experience? Without any known uniform connection between conscious experience and behavior, it seems possible not only that creatures behaving just like oneself could be automata, but that things sharing no behavioral similarities could have conscious experience. Perhaps trees do feel pain at the loss of a branch.

Nagel leaves us with questions. But perhaps the skeptical picture he describes of a world devoid of conscious experience or thoroughly infused with it proves puzzling only if the initial question about "what it's like" for one to taste chocolate ice cream makes sense. We will avoid weighing in on that issue here, however, leaving the reader to her own thoughts.

There is one special kind of skepticism which continues to be a problem even if you assume that your mind is not the only thing there is – that the physical world you seem to see and feel around you, including your own body, really exists. That is skepticism about the nature or even existence of minds or experiences other than your own.

How much do you really know about what goes on in anyone else's mind? Clearly you observe only the bodies of other creatures, including people. You watch what they do, listen to what they say and to the other sounds they make, and see how they respond to their environment – what things attract them and what things repel them, what they eat, and so forth. You can also cut open other creatures and look at their physical insides, and perhaps compare their anatomy with yours.

But none of this will give you direct access to their experiences, thoughts, and feelings. The only experiences you can actually have are your own: if you believe anything about the mental lives of others, it is on the basis of observing their physical construction and behavior.

To take a simple example, how do you know, when you and a friend are eating chocolate ice cream, whether it tastes the same to him as it tastes to you? You can try a taste of his ice cream, but if it tastes the same as yours, that only means it tastes the same *to you*: you haven't experienced the way it tastes *to him*. There seems to be no way to compare the two flavor experiences directly.

Well, you might say that since you're both human beings, and you can both distinguish among flavors of ice cream – for example you can both tell the difference between chocolate and vanilla with your eyes closed – it's likely that your flavor experiences are similar. But how do you know *that*? The only connection you've ever observed between a type of ice cream and a flavor is in your own case; so what reason do you have to think that similar correlations hold for other human beings? Why isn't it just as consistent with all the evidence that chocolate tastes to him the way vanilla tastes to you, and vice versa?

The same question could be asked about other kinds of experience. How do you know that red things don't look to your friend the way yellow things look to you? Of course if you ask him how a fire engine looks, he'll say it looks red, like blood, and not yellow, like a dandelion;

but that's because he, like you, uses the word "red" for the color that blood and fire engines look to him, *whatever* it is. Maybe it's what you call yellow, or what you call blue, or maybe it's a color experience you've never had, and can't even imagine.

To deny this, you have to appeal to an assumption that flavor and color experiences are uniformly correlated with certain physical stimulations of the sense organs, whoever undergoes them. But the skeptic would say you have no evidence for that assumption, and because of the kind of assumption it is, you *couldn't* have any evidence for it. All you can observe is the correlation in your own case.

Faced with this argument, you might first concede that there is some uncertainty here. The correlation between stimulus and experience may not be exactly the same from one person to another: there may be slight shades of difference between two people's color or flavor experience of the same type of ice cream. In fact, since people are physically different from one another, this wouldn't be surprising. But, you might say, the difference in experience can't be too radical, or else we'd be able to tell. For instance, chocolate ice cream couldn't taste to your friend the way a lemon tastes to you, otherwise his mouth would pucker up when he ate it.

But notice that this claim assumes another correlation from one person to another: a correlation between inner experience and certain kinds of observable reaction. And the same question arises about that. You've observed the connection between puckering of the mouth and the taste you call sour only in your own case: how do you know it exists in other people? Maybe what makes your friend's mouth pucker up is an experience like the one you get from eating oatmeal.

If we go on pressing these kinds of questions relentlessly enough, we will move from a mild and harmless skepticism about whether chocolate ice cream tastes exactly the same to you and to your friend, to a much more radical skepticism about whether there is *any* similarity between your experiences and his. How do you know that when he puts something in his mouth he even has an experience of the kind that you would call a *flavor*? For all you know, it could be something you would call a sound – or maybe it's unlike anything you've ever experienced, or could imagine.

If we continue on this path, it leads finally to the most radical skepticism of all about other minds. How do you even know that your friend is conscious? How do you know that there are *any minds at all* besides your own?

The only example you've ever directly observed of a correlation between mind, behavior, anatomy, and physical circumstances is yourself.

Even if other people and animals had no experiences whatever, no mental inner life of any kind, but were just elaborate biological machines, they would look just the same to you. So how do you know that's not what they are? How do you know that the beings around you aren't all mindless robots? You've never seen into their minds – you couldn't – and their physical behavior could all be produced by purely physical causes. Maybe your relatives, your neighbors, your cat and your dog have *no inner experiences whatever*. If they don't, there is no way you could ever find out.

You can't even appeal to the evidence of their behavior, including what they say – because that assumes that in them outer behavior is connected with inner experience as it is in you; and that's just what you don't know.

To consider the possibility that none of the people around you may be conscious produces an uncanny feeling. On the one hand it seems conceivable, and no evidence you could possibly have can rule it out decisively. On the other hand it is something you can't *really* believe is possible: your conviction that there are minds in those bodies, sight behind those eyes, hearing in those ears, etc., is instinctive. But if its power comes from instinct, is it really knowledge? Once you admit the *possibility* that the belief in other minds is mistaken, don't you need something more reliable to justify holding on to it?

There is another side to this question, which goes completely in the opposite direction.

Ordinarily we believe that other human beings are conscious, and almost everyone believes that other mammals and birds are conscious too. But people differ over whether fish are conscious, or insects, worms, and jellyfish. They are still more doubtful about whether one-celled animals like amoebae and paramecia have conscious experiences, even though such creatures react conspicuously to stimuli of various kinds. Most people believe that plants aren't conscious; and almost no one believes that rocks are conscious, or kleenex, or automobiles, or mountain lakes, or cigarettes. And to take another biological example, most of us would say, if we thought about it, that the individual cells of which our bodies are composed do not have any conscious experiences.

How do we know all these things? How do you know that when you cut a branch off a tree it doesn't hurt the tree – only it can't express its pain because it can't move? (Or maybe it *loves* having its branches pruned.) How do you know that the muscle cells in your heart don't feel pain or excitement when you run up a flight of stairs? How do you know that a kleenex doesn't feel anything when you blow your nose into it?

And what about computers? Suppose computers are developed to the point where they can be used to control robots that look on the outside like dogs, respond in complicated ways to the environment, and behave in many ways just like dogs, though they are just a mass of circuitry and silicon chips on the inside? Would we have any way of knowing whether such machines were conscious?

These cases are different from one another, of course. If a thing is incapable of movement, it can't give any behavioral evidence of feeling or perception. And if it isn't a natural organism, it is radically different from us in internal constitution. But what grounds do we have for thinking that only things that behave like us to some degree and that have an observable physical structure roughly like ours are capable of having experiences of *any* kind? Perhaps trees feel things in a way totally different from us, but we have no way of finding out about it, because we have no way of discovering the correlations between experience and observable manifestations or physical conditions in their case. We could discover such correlations only if we could observe both the experiences and the external manifestations together: but there is no way we can observe the experiences directly, except in our own case. And for the same reason there is no way we could observe the *absence* of any experiences, and consequently the absence of any such correlations, in any other case. You can't tell that a tree has *no* experience, by looking inside it, any more than you can tell a worm *has* experience, by looking inside it.

So the question is: what can you really know about the conscious life in this world beyond the fact that you yourself have a conscious mind? Is it possible that there might be much less conscious life than you assume (none except yours), or much more (even in things you assume to be unconscious)?

15

Bertrand Russell, "Analogy"

Contrary to Nagel's picture of the problem of other minds, Bertrand Russell (1872–1970) believes this brand of skepticism to be, at best, a philosopher's worry. Russell meets this professional burden in the chapter "Analogy," taken from his *Human Knowledge: Its Scope and Limits*, by offering the traditional response to this problem and just what Nagel said was not possible – namely, a postulate linking beliefs with certain forms of behavior.

Russell's postulate begins in an observation of a connection between one's own beliefs and one's behavior. When in pain, for example, I tend to cry out, wince, and tell those around me of my current state. Put generally, from our own case we discover the causal law that when some B (behavior) occurs, I see that it is preceded by some causally antecedent A (belief or experience). We tame the problem of other minds in applying this causal principle (or a series of them) to others exhibiting analogous behavior.

Though the inference from my own case to a host of others may seem originally weak, Russell offers that we can increase the confidence in this inference as the complexity of the case increases. After taking into account all the nuances in another's observable behavior (including utterances), the probability of other causes decreases and the probability of the causal principle increases. Hence, we are justified in inferring that that person has a mental life much like our own.

Many questions can be raised about Russell's proposal. Even if we agree that a fairly weak induction made on the basis of one case is valid, we might wonder about our own case. Do we in fact witness connections between our beliefs and our behaviors in such a way that could support a causal law? I may discover my current anger with my father, for example, only after a trustworthy friend reads my behavior back to me. Examples of this type may ultimately provide evidence for a solution to the problem of other minds, but they do not bode well for an argument from analogy.

The postulates hitherto considered have been such as are required for knowledge of the physical world. Broadly speaking, they have led us to admit a certain degree of knowledge as to the space-time structure of the physical world, while leaving us completely agnostic as regards its qualitative character. But where other human beings are concerned, we feel that we know more than this; we are convinced that other people have thoughts and feelings that are qualitatively fairly similar to our own. We are not content to think that we know only the space-time structure of our friends' minds, or their capacity for initiating causal chains that end in sensations of our own. A philosopher might pretend to think that he knew only this, but let him get cross with his wife and you will see that he does not regard her as a mere spatio-temporal edifice of which he knows the logical properties but not a glimmer of the intrinsic character. We are therefore justified in inferring that his scepticism is professional rather than sincere.

The problem with which we are concerned is the following. We observe in ourselves such occurrences as remembering, reasoning, feeling pleasure and feeling pain. We think that stocks and stones do not have these experiences, but that other people do. Most of us have no doubt that the higher animals feel pleasure and pain, though I was once assured by a fisherman that "fishes have no sense nor feeling". I failed to find out how he had acquired this knowledge. Most people would disagree with him, but would be doubtful about oysters and starfish. However this may be, common sense admits an increasing doubtfulness as we descend in the animal kingdom, but as regards human beings it admits no doubt.

It is clear that belief in the minds of others requires some postulate that is not required in physics, since physics can be content with a knowledge of structure. My present purpose is to suggest what this further postulate may be.

It is clear that we must appeal to something that may be vaguely called "analogy". The behaviour of other people is in many ways analogous to our own, and we suppose that it must have analogous causes. What people say is what we should say if we had certain thoughts, and so we infer that they probably have these thoughts. They give us information which we can sometimes subsequently verify. They behave in ways in which we behave when we are pleased (or displeased) in circumstances in which we should be pleased (or displeased). We may talk over with a friend some incident which we have both experienced, and find that his reminiscences dovetail with our own; this is particularly convincing when he remembers something that we have forgotten but that he recalls to our thoughts. Or again: you set your boy a problem in arithmetic, and with luck he gets the right answer; this persuades you that he is capable of arithmetical reasoning. There are, in short, very many ways in which my responses to stimuli differ from those of "dead" matter, and in all these ways other people resemble me. As it is clear to me that the causal laws governing my behaviour have to do with "thoughts", it is natural to infer that the same is true of the analogous behaviour of my friends.

The inference with which we are at present concerned is not merely that which takes us beyond solipsism, by maintaining that sensations have causes about which *something* can be known. This kind of inference, which suffices for physics, has already been considered. We are concerned now with a much more specific kind of inference, the kind that is involved in our knowledge of the thoughts and feelings of others – assuming that we have such knowledge. It is of course obvious that such knowledge is more or less doubtful. There is not only the general argument that we may be dreaming; there is also the possibility of ingenious automata. There are calculating machines that do sums much better than our schoolboy sons; there are gramophone records that remember impeccably what So-and-so said on such-and-such an occasion; there are people in the cinema who, though copies of real people, are not themselves alive. There is no theoretical limit to what ingenuity could achieve in the way of producing the illusion of life where in fact life is absent.

But, you will say, in all such cases it was the thoughts of human beings that produced the ingenious mechanism. Yes, but how do you know this? And how do you know that the gramophone does *not* "think"?

There is, in the first place, a difference in the causal laws of observable behaviour. If I say to a student "write me a paper on Descartes' reasons for believing in the existence of matter", I shall, if he is industrious, cause a certain response. A gramophone record might be so constructed as to respond to this stimulus, perhaps better than the student, but if so it would be incapable of telling me anything about any other philosopher, even if I threatened to refuse to give it a degree. One of the most notable peculiarities of human behaviour is change of response to a given stimulus. An ingenious person could construct an automaton which would always laugh at his jokes, however often it heard them; but a human being, after laughing a few times, will yawn, and end by saying "how I laughed the first time I heard that joke".

But the differences in observable behaviour between living and dead matter do not suffice to prove that there are "thoughts" connected with living bodies other than my own. It is probably possible theoretically to account for the behaviour of living bodies by purely physical causal laws, and it is probably impossible to refute materialism by external observation alone. If we are to believe that there are thoughts and feelings other than our own, that must be in virtue of some inference in which our own thoughts and feelings are relevant, and such an inference must go beyond what is needed in physics.

I am of course not discussing the history of how we come to believe in other minds. We find ourselves believing in them when we first begin to reflect; the thought that Mother may be angry or pleased is one which arises in early infancy. What I am discussing is the possibility of a postulate which shall establish a rational connection between this belief and data, e.g. between the belief "Mother is angry" and the hearing of a loud voice.

The abstract schema seems to be as follows. We know, from observation of ourselves, a causal law of the form "A causes B", where A is a "thought" and B a physical occurrence. We sometimes observe a B when we cannot observe any A; we then infer an unobserved A. For example: I know that when I say "I'm thirsty", I say so, usually, because I am thirsty, and therefore, when I hear the sentence "I'm thirsty" at a time when I am not thirsty, I assume that some one else is thirsty. I assume this the more readily if I see before me a hot drooping body which goes on to say "I have walked twenty desert miles in this heat with never a drop to drink". It is evident that my confidence in the "inference" is increased by increased complexity in the datum and also by increased certainty of the causal law derived from subjective observation, provided the causal law is such as to account for the complexities of the datum.

It is clear that, in so far as plurality of causes is to be suspected, the kind of inference we have been considering is not valid. We are supposed to know "A causes B", and also to know that B has occurred; if this is to justify us in inferring A, we must know that *only* A causes B. Or, if we are content to infer that A is probable, it will suffice if we can know that in most cases it is A that causes B. If you hear thunder without having seen lightning, you confidently infer that there was lightning, because you are convinced that the sort of noise you heard is seldom caused by anything except lightning. As this example shows, our principle is not only employed to establish the existence of other minds, but is habitually assumed, though in a less concrete form, in physics. I say "a less concrete form" because unseen lightning is only abstractly similar to seen lightning, whereas we suppose the similarity of other minds to our own to be by no means purely abstract.

Complexity in the observed behaviour of another person, when this can all be accounted for by a simple cause such as thirst, increases the probability of the inference by diminishing the probability of some other cause. I think that in ideally favourable circumstances the argument would be formally as follows:

From subjective observation I know that A, which is a thought or feeling, causes B, which is a bodily act, e.g. a statement. I know also that, whenever B is an act of my own body, A is its cause. I now observe an act of the kind B in a body not my own, and I am having no thought or feeling of the kind A. But I still believe, on the basis of self-observation, that only A can cause B; I therefore infer that there was an A which caused B, though it was not an A that I could observe. On this ground I infer that other people's bodies are associated with minds, which resemble mine in proportion as their bodily behaviour resembles my own.

In practice, the exactness and certainty of the above statement must be softened. We cannot be sure that, in our subjective experience, A is the only cause of B. And even if A is the only cause of B in our experience, how can we know that this holds outside our experience? It is not necessary that we should know this with any certainty; it is enough if it is highly probable. It is the assumption of probability in such cases that is our postulate. The postulate may therefore be stated as follows:

If, whenever we can observe whether A and B are present or absent, we find that every case of B has an A as a causal antecedent, then it is probable that most B's have A's as causal antecedents, even in cases where observation does not enable us to know whether A is present or not.

This postulate, if accepted, justifies the inference to other minds, as well as many other inferences that are made unreflectingly by common sense.

16

Norman Malcolm, "Knowledge of Other Minds"

Norman Malcolm (1911–90) finds little to recommend the argument from analogy for the existence of other minds exemplified by the selection from Russell. In his paper "Knowledge of Other Minds," included below, Malcolm offers several arguments against attempts to understand the analogy between oneself and another who behaves similarly. Fundamentally, Malcolm offers the Wittgensteinian critique that the analogy relies upon the faulty assumption that we observe the link between our thoughts, feelings, and sensations, and our behavior.

The first step in the analogy to other minds, as Russell describes it, for example, involves that we observe a connection between our "inner" mental states and our behavior, perhaps the former as the cause of the latter. How do we come to know which "inner" state we are in? We cannot appeal to behavior, for then we would have no need for the analogy in the first place. But if pains are things that are observed, then, Malcolm argues, the criteria for distinguishing pain from, say, a tickle, are "inner" and therefore inapplicable to the states of others. Starting with oneself precludes the possibility of shared criteria, and without shared criteria, self-attributions of pain and attributions to others cannot have the same meaning. Hence, solipsism, or the belief that only oneself and one's experiences are real, is the result. Moreover, Malcolm maintains that purely private observations of inner events can have no conditions for successful identification. For, from the inside, we can't make sense of the distinction between witnessing the same mental state and only thinking that we do. Without a way of determining if the correct identification is made, the notion of a correct identification no longer makes sense.

Lacking both inner and external criteria for the identification of mental states, how are we to address the problem of other minds? Malcolm concludes that in the failure of the argument from analogy we likewise see the dissolution of the problem. An analogy is only necessary if a transition from our own case to others is needed. Instead, we should follow Wittgenstein in viewing first-person self-ascriptions as analogous to non-verbal behavior such as cries and limps.

But Malcolm's proposal seems to come at too high a price. Surely, utterances of "I am in pain" entail "Someone is in pain," yet viewed as equivalent to non-verbal cries of pain, such self-ascriptions can have no logical structure or truth conditions. This seems to replace an epistemological solipsism with a logical one.

I

I believe that the argument from analogy for the existence of other minds still enjoys more credit than it deserves, and my first aim in this paper will be to show that it leads nowhere. J. S. Mill is one of many who have accepted the argument and I take his statement of it as representative. He puts to himself the question, "By what evidence do I know, or by what considerations am I led to believe, that there exist other sentient creatures; that the walking and speaking figures which I see and hear, have sensations and thoughts, or in other words, possess Minds?" His answer is the following:

> I conclude that other human beings have feelings like me, because, first, they have bodies like me, which I know, in my own case, to be the antecedent condition of feelings; and because, secondly, they exhibit the acts, and other outward signs, which in my own case I know by experience to be caused by feelings. I am conscious in myself of a series of facts connected by an uniform sequence, of which the beginning is modifications of my body, the middle is feelings, the end is outward demeanor. In the case of other human beings I have the evidence of my senses for the first and last links of the series, but not for the intermediate link. I find, however, that the sequence between the first and last is as regular and constant in those other cases as it is in mine. In my own case I know that the first link produces the last through the intermediate link, and could not produce it

without. Experience, therefore, obliges me to conclude that there must be an intermediate link; which must either be the same in others as in myself, or a different one: I must either believe them to be alive, or to be automatons: and by believing them to be alive, that is, by supposing the link to be of the same nature as in the case of which I have experience, and which is in all other respects similar, I bring other human beings, as phenomena, under the same generalizations which I know by experience to be the true theory of my own existence.[1]

I shall pass by the possible objection that this would be very *weak* inductive reasoning, based as it is on the observation of a single instance. More interesting is the following point: Suppose this reasoning could yield a conclusion of the sort "It is probable that that human figure" (pointing at some person other than oneself) "has thoughts and feelings." Then there is a question as to whether this conclusion can *mean* anything to the philosopher who draws it, because there is a question as to whether the sentence "That human figure has thoughts and feelings" can mean anything to him. Why should this be a question? Because the assumption from which Mill starts is that he has *no criterion* for determining whether another "walking and speaking figure" does or does not have thoughts and feelings. If he had a criterion he could apply it, establishing with certainty that this or that human figure does or does not have feelings (for the only plausible criterion would lie in behavior and circumstances that are open to view), and there would be no call to resort to tenuous analogical reasoning that yields at best a probability. If Mill has no criterion for the existence of feelings other than his own then in that sense he does not understand the sentence "That human figure has feelings" and therefore does not understand the sentence "It is *probable* that that human figure has feelings."

There is a familiar inclination to make the following reply: "Although I have no criterion of verification still I *understand*, for example, the sentence 'He has a pain.' For I understand the meaning of 'I have a pain,' and 'He has a pain' means that he has the *same* thing I have when I have a pain." But this is a fruitless maneuver. If I do not know how to establish that someone has a pain then I do not know how to establish that he has the *same* as I have when I have a pain.[2] You cannot improve my understanding of "He has a pain" by this recourse to the notion of "the same," unless you give me a criterion for saying that someone *has* the same as I have. If you can do this you will have no use for the argument from analogy: and if you cannot then you do not understand the supposed conclusion of that argument. A philosopher who purports to rely on the analogical argument cannot, I think, escape this dilemma.

There have been various attempts to repair the argument from analogy. Mr Stuart Hampshire has argued[3] that its validity as a method of inference can be established in the following way: Others sometimes infer that I am feeling giddy from my behavior. Now I have direct, non-inferential knowledge, says Hampshire, of my own feelings. So I can check inferences made about me against the facts, checking thereby the accuracy of the "methods" of inference.

> All that is required for testing the validity of any method of factual inference is that each one of us should sometimes be in a position to confront the conclusions of the doubtful method of inference with what is known by him to be true independently of the method of inference in question. Each one of us is certainly in this position in respect of our common methods of inference about the feelings of persons other than ourselves, in virtue of the fact that each one of us is constantly able to compare the results of this type of inference with what he knows to be true directly and non-inferentially; each one of us is in the position to make this testing comparison, whenever he is the designated subject of a statement about feelings and sensations. I, Hampshire, know by what sort of signs I may be misled in inferring Jones' and Smith's feelings, because I have implicitly noticed (though probably not formulated) where Jones, Smith and others generally go wrong in inferring my feelings.[4]

Presumably I can also note when the inferences of others about my feelings do not go wrong. Having ascertained the reliability of some inference-procedures I can use them myself, in a guarded way, to draw conclusions about the feelings of others, with a modest but justified confidence in the truth of those conclusions.

My first comment is that Hampshire has apparently forgotten the purpose of the argument from analogy, which is to provide some probability that "the walking and speaking figures which I see and hear, have sensations and thoughts" (Mill). For the reasoning that he describes involves the assumption that other human figures *do* have thoughts and sensations: for they are assumed to *make inferences* about me from *observations* of my behavior. But the philosophical problem of the existence of other minds *is* the problem of whether human figures other than oneself do, among other things, make observations, inferences, and assertions. Hampshire's supposed defense of the argument from analogy is an *ignoratio elenchi*.

If we struck from the reasoning described by Hampshire all assumption of thoughts and sensations in others we should be left with something roughly like this: "When my behavior is such and such there come from nearby human figures the sounds 'He feels giddy.' And generally I do feel giddy at the time. Therefore when another human figure exhibits the same behavior and I say 'He feels giddy,' it is probable that he does feel giddy." But the reference here to the sentence-like sounds coming from other human bodies is irrelevant, since I must not assume that those sounds express inferences. Thus the reasoning becomes simply the classical argument from analogy: "When my behavior is such and such I feel giddy; so probably when another human figure behaves the same way he feels the same way." This argument, again, is caught in the dilemma about the criterion of the *same*.

The version of analogical reasoning offered by Professor H. H. Price[5] is more interesting. He suggests that "one's evidence for the existence of other minds is derived primarily from the understanding of language" (p. 429). His idea is that if another body gives forth noises one understands, like "There's the bus," and if these noises give one new information, this "provides some evidence that the foreign body which uttered the noises is animated by a mind like one's own.... Suppose I am often in its neighborhood, and it repeatedly produces utterances which I can understand, and which I then proceed to verify for myself. And suppose that this happens in many different kinds of situation. I think that my evidence for believing that this body is animated by a mind like my own would then become very strong" (p. 430). The body from which these informative sounds proceed need not be a human body. "If the rustling of the leaves of an oak formed intelligible words conveying new information to me, and if gorse-bushes made intelligible gestures, I should have evidence that the oak or the gorse-bush was animated by an intelligence like my own" (p. 436). Even if the intelligible and informative sounds did not proceed from a body they would provide evidence for the existence of a (disembodied) mind (p. 435).

Although differing sharply from the classical analogical argument, the reasoning presented by Price is still analogical in form: I know by introspection that when certain combinations of sounds come from me they are "symbols in acts of spontaneous thinking"; therefore similar combinations of sounds, not produced by me, "probably function as instruments to an act of spontaneous thinking, which in this case is not my own" (p. 446). Price says that the reasoning also provides an *explanation* of the otherwise mysterious occurrence of sounds which I understand but did not produce. He anticipates the objection that the hypothesis is nonsensical because unverifiable. "The hypothesis is a perfectly conceivable one," he says, "in the sense that I know very well what the world would have to be like if the hypothesis were true – what sorts of entities there must be in it, and what sorts of events must occur in them. I know from introspection what acts of thinking and perceiving are, and I know what it is for such acts to be combined into the unity of a single mind ..." (pp. 446–7).

I wish to argue against Price that no amount of intelligible sounds coming from an oak tree or a kitchen table could create any probability that it has sensations and thoughts. The question to be asked is: What would show that a tree or table *understands* the sounds that come from it? We can imagine that useful warnings, true descriptions and predictions, even "replies" to questions, should emanate from a tree, so that it came to be of enormous value to its owner. How should we establish that it understood those sentences? Should we "question" it? Suppose that the tree "said" that there was a vixen in the neighborhood, and we "asked" it "What is a vixen?," and it "replied," "A vixen is a female fox." It might go on to do as well for "female" and "fox." This performance might incline us to say that the tree understood the words, in contrast to the possible case in which it answered "I don't know" or did not answer at all. But would it show that the tree understood the words in the same sense that a person could understand them? With a person such a performance would create a presumption that he could make correct *applications* of the word in question: but not so with a tree. To see this point think of the normal teaching of words (e.g., "spoon," "dog," "red") to a child and how one decides whether he understands them. At a primitive stage of teaching one does not require or expect definitions, but rather that the child should *pick out* reds from blues, dogs from cats, spoons from forks. This involves his looking, pointing, reaching for and going to the right things and not the wrong ones. That a child says "red" when a red thing and "blue" when a blue thing is put before him, is indicative of a mastery of those words *only* in conjunction with the other activities of looking, pointing, trying to get, fetching and carrying. Try to suppose that he says the right words but looks at and reaches for the wrong things. Should we be tempted to say that he has mastered the use of those words? No, indeed. The disparity between words and behavior would make us say that he does not understand the words. In the case of a tree there could be no disparity between its words and its "behavior" because it is logically incapable of behavior of the relevant kind.

Since it has nothing like the human face and body it makes no sense to say of a tree, or an electronic computer, that it is looking or pointing at or fetching something. (Of course one can always *invent* a sense for these expressions.) Therefore it would make no sense to say that it did or did not understand the above words. Trees and computers cannot either pass or fail the tests that a child is put through. They cannot even take them. That an object was a source of intelligible sounds or other signs (no matter how sequential) would not be enough by itself to establish that it had thoughts or sensations. How informative sentences and valuable predictions could emanate from a gorse-bush might be a grave scientific problem, but the explanation could never be that the gorse-bush has a mind. Better no explanation than nonsense!

It might be thought that the above difficulty holds only for words whose meaning has a "perceptual content" and that if we imagined, for example, that our gorse-bush produced nothing but pure mathematical propositions we should be justified in attributing thought to it, although not sensation. But suppose there was a remarkable "calculating boy" who could give right answers to arithmetical problems but could not apply numerals to reality in empirical propositions, i.e., he could not *count* any objects. I believe that everyone would be reluctant to say that he *understood* the mathematical signs and truths that he produced. If he could count in the normal way there would not be this reluctance. And "counting in the normal way" involves looking, pointing, reaching, fetching, and so on. That is, it requires the human face and body, and human behavior – or something similar. Things which do not have the human form, or anything like it, not merely do not but *cannot* satisfy the criteria for thinking. I am trying to bring out part of what Wittgenstein meant when he said, "We only say of a human being and what is like one that it thinks" (*Investigations*, §360), and "The human body is the best picture of the human soul" (ibid., p. 178).

I have not yet gone into the most fundamental error of the argument from analogy. It is present whether the argument is the classical one (the analogy between my body and other bodies) or Price's version (the analogy between my language and the noises and signs produced by other things). It is the mistaken assumption that *one learns from one's own case* what thinking, feeling, sensation are. Price gives expression to this assumption when he says: "I know from introspection what acts of thinking and perceiving are...."[6] It is the most natural assumption for a philosopher to make and indeed seems at first to be the only possibility. Yet Wittgenstein has made us see that it leads first to solipsism and then to nonsense. I shall try to state as briefly as possible how it produces those results.

A philosopher who believes that one must learn what thinking, fear, or pain is "from one's own case," does not believe that the thing to be observed is one's behavior, but rather something "inward." He considers behavior to be related to the inward states and occurrences merely as an accompaniment or possibly an effect. He cannot regard behavior as a *criterion* of psychological phenomena: for if he did he would have no use for the analogical argument (as was said before) and also the priority given to "one's own case" would be pointless. He believes that he notes something in himself that he calls "thinking" or "fear" or "pain," and then he tries to infer the presence of the *same* in others. He should then deal with the question of what his criterion of the *same* in others is. This he cannot do because it is of the essence of his viewpoint to reject circumstances and behavior as a criterion of mental phenomena in others. And what else could serve as a criterion? He ought, therefore, to draw the conclusion that the notion of thinking, fear, or pain in others is in an important sense meaningless. He has no idea of what would count for or against it.[7] "That there should be thinking or pain other than my own is unintelligible," he ought to hold. This would be a rigorous solipsism, and a correct outcome of the assumption that one can know only from one's own case what the mental phenomena are. An equivalent way of putting it would be: "When I say 'I am in pain,' by 'pain' I mean a certain inward state. When I say '*He* is in pain,' by 'pain' I mean *behavior*. I cannot attribute pain to others *in the same sense* that I attribute it to myself."

Some philosophers before Wittgenstein may have seen the solipsistic result of starting from "one's own case." But I believe he is the first to have shown how that starting point destroys itself. This may be presented as follows: One supposes that one inwardly picks out something as thinking or pain and thereafter identifies it whenever it presents itself in the soul. But the question to be pressed is, Does one make *correct* identifications? The proponent of these "private" identifications has nothing to say here. He feels sure that he identifies correctly the occurrences in his soul; but feeling sure is no guarantee of being right. Indeed he has no idea of what being *right* could mean. He does not know how to distinguish between actually making correct identifications and being under the impression that he does. (See *Investigations*, §258–9.) Suppose that he identified the emotion of anxiety as the sensation of pain? Neither he nor anyone else could know about this "mistake." Perhaps he makes a mistake *every* time! Perhaps all of us do! We ought to see now that we are talking nonsense. We do not know what a *mistake* would be. We have no standard, no examples, no customary practice, with which to compare our inner recognitions. The inward identification cannot hit the bull's-eye, or miss it either, because there is no bull's-eye. When we see that the ideas of correct and incorrect have no application to the supposed inner identification, the latter notion loses its appearance of sense. Its collapse brings down both solipsism and the argument from analogy.

II

This destruction of the argument from analogy also destroys the *problem* for which it was supposed to provide a solution. A philosopher feels himself in a difficulty about other minds because he assumes that first of all he is acquainted with mental phenomena "from his own case." What troubles him is how to make the transition from his own case to the case of others. When his thinking is freed of the illusion of the priority of his own case, then he is able to look at the familiar facts and to acknowledge that the circumstances, behavior, and utterances of others actually are his *criteria* (not merely his evidence) for the existence of their mental states. Previously this had seemed impossible.

But now he is in danger of flying to the opposite extreme of behaviorism, which errs by believing that through observation of one's own circumstances, behavior, and utterances one can find out that one is thinking or angry. The philosophy of "from one's own case" and behaviorism, though in a sense opposites, make the common assumption that the first-person, present-tense psychological statements are verified by self-observation. According to the "one's own case" philosophy the self-observation cannot be checked by others; according to behaviorism the self-observation would be by means of outward criteria that are available to all. The first position becomes unintelligible; the second is false for at least many kinds of psychological statements. We are forced to conclude that the first-person psychological statements are not (or hardly ever) verified by self-observation. It follows that they have no verification at all; for if they had a verification it would have to be by self-observation.

But if sentences like "My head aches" or "I wonder where she is" do not express observations then what do they do? What is the relation between my declaration that my head aches and the fact that my head aches, if the former is not the report of an observation? The perplexity about the existence of *other* minds has, as the result of criticism, turned into a perplexity about the meaning of one's own psychological sentences about oneself. At our starting point it was the sentence "*His* head aches" that posed a problem; but now it is the sentence "*My* head aches" that puzzles us.

One way in which this problem can be put is by the question, "How does *one know when to say* the words 'My head aches'?" The inclination to ask this question can be made acute by imagining a fantastic but not impossible case of a person who has survived to adult years without ever experiencing pain. He is given various sorts of injections to correct this condition, and on receiving one of these one day, he jumps and exclaims, "Now I feel pain!" One wants to ask, "How did he *recognize* the new sensation as a *pain?*"

Let us note that if the man gives an answer (e.g., "I knew it must be pain because of the way I jumped") then he proves by that very fact that he has not mastered the correct use of the words "I feel pain." They cannot be used to state a *conclusion.* In telling us *how* he did it he will convict himself of a misuse. Therefore the question "How did he recognize his sensation?" requests the impossible. The inclination to ask it is evidence of our inability to grasp the fact that the use of this psychological sentence has nothing to do with recognizing or identifying or observing a state of oneself.

The fact that this imagined case produces an especially strong temptation to ask the "How?" question shows that we have the idea that it must be more difficult to give the right name of one's sensation *the first time.* The implication would be that it is not so difficult *after* the first time. Why should this be? Are we thinking that then the man would have a paradigm of pain with which he could compare his sensations and so be in a position to know right off whether a certain sensation was or was not a pain? But the paradigm would be either something "outer" (behavior) or something "inner" (perhaps a memory impression of the sensation). If the former then he is misusing the first-person sentence. If the latter then the question of whether he compared *correctly* the present sensation with the inner paradigm of pain would be without sense. Thus the idea that the use of the first-person sentences can be governed by paradigms must be abandoned. It is another form of our insistent misconception of the first-person sentence as resting somehow on the identification of a psychological state.

These absurdities prove that we must conceive of the first-person psychological sentences in some entirely different light. Wittgenstein presents us with the suggestion (to which philosophers have not been sufficiently attentive) that the first-person sentences are to be thought of as similar to the natural non-verbal, behavioral expressions of psychological states. "My leg hurts," for example, is to be assimilated to crying, limping, holding one's leg. This is a bewildering comparison and one's first thought is that two sorts of things could not be more unlike. By saying the sentence one can make a *statement*; it has a *contradictory*; it is *true* or *false*; in saying it one *lies* or *tells the truth*; and so on. None of these things, exactly, can be said of crying, limping, holding one's leg. So how can there be any resemblance? But Wittgenstein knew this when he deliberately likened such a sentence to "the primitive, the natural, expressions" of pain, and said that it is "new pain-behavior".[8] Although my limits prevent my attempting it here, I think this analogy ought to be explored. For it has at least two important merits: first, it breaks the hold on us of the question "How does one *know when to say* 'My leg hurts'?" for in the light of the analogy this will be as nonsensical as the question "How does one know when to cry, limp, or hold one's leg?"; second, it explains how the utterance of a first-person psychological sentence by another person can have *importance* for us, although not as an identification – for in the light of the analogy it will have the same importance as the natural behavior which serves as our pre-verbal criterion of the psychological states of others.

Notes

1   J. S. Mill, *An Examination of Sir William Hamilton's Philosophy*, 6th edition (London, 1889), pp. 243–4.
2   "It is no explanation to say: the supposition that he has a pain is simply the supposition that he has the same as I. For *that* part of the grammar is quite clear to me: that is, that one will say that the stove has the same experience as I, *if* one says: it is in pain and I am in pain" (Wittgenstein, *Philosophical Investigations* (New York, 1953), §350).
3   "The Analogy of Feeling," *Mind*, January 1952, pp. 1–12.
4   Ibid., pp. 4–5.
5   "Our Evidence for the Existence of Other Minds," *Philosophy*, vol. 13 (1938), pp. 425–56.
6   Ibid., p. 447.
7   One reason why philosophers have not commonly drawn this conclusion may be, as Wittgenstein acutely suggests, that they assume that they have "an infallible paradigm of identity in the identity of a thing with itself" (*Investigations*, §215).
8   Ibid., §244.

Self-Knowledge

17

René Descartes, "Meditation II"

As the subtitle to his second meditation included here indicates, Descartes argues that the mind is more easily known than the body. This meditation begins with the radical skepticism introduced in the first meditation (see Chapter 5). Though an evil demon may indeed exist who constantly deceives him into believing any number of falsehoods, Descartes reasons that, however potent, this demon could not deceive him into thinking that he does not exist, for the very fact that he entertains this possibility demonstrates his existence. Hence, he draws the famous conclusion "I am, I exist," and in so doing finds the foundational certainty he needs to ground his epistemological project.

However, the *Cogito* (as the argument is sometimes called) serves only to establish *that* he is and not *what* he is. In the past he took himself to be an animal possessing both a body and an immaterial mind, but the evil demon possibility remains even if he is certain that he exists. Since he could be deceived into thinking that he has a body when he does not, Descartes concludes that he is a thing that thinks – a thing that "doubts, understands, affirms, denies, wills, refuses, that imagines also, and perceives."

Still, we commonly believe that we quite easily and extensively know the properties and features of the objects around us. What reason do we have for thinking we know the mind more easily than the body? Descartes answers this question with the famous example of a piece of wax. His senses tell him that the wax has a determinate smell, taste, feel, color, and sound. When the wax is placed before the fire, all these features drastically change. Nevertheless, we presume that it is the same piece of wax. What grounds do we have for such a conclusion? Given that the two states of the wax are so radically different, our senses would tell us that the melted pool of wax before the fire is altogether different from the one with which we began. Therefore, Descartes argues, we must instead perceive its true nature with the mind alone. Indeed, for him, all perception is an act of the mind, and all knowledge results from reason. If objects are in fact perceived by being understood, Descartes offers that he must therefore know his mind more thoroughly and with greater certainty than any body.

Though we might agree with Descartes to some extent – perhaps as a child I knew some of what I believed before I knew that I had a spleen – questions remain as to how much Descartes really knows about himself by the end of this meditation. The eye, for example, cannot see itself unaided, and hence it would be hasty to conclude that any faculty of perception perceives itself clearly and easily.

Of the Nature of the Human Mind; and that it is More Easily Known than the Body

The Meditation of yesterday has filled my mind with so many doubts, that it is no longer in my power to forget them. Nor do I see, meanwhile, any principle on which they can be resolved; and, just as if I had fallen all of a sudden into very deep water, I am so greatly disconcerted as to be made unable either to plant my feet firmly on the bottom or sustain myself by swimming on the surface. I will, nevertheless, make an effort, and try anew the same path on which I had entered yesterday, that is, proceed by casting aside all that admits of the slightest doubt, not less than if I had discovered it to be absolutely false; and I will continue always in this track until I shall find something that is certain, or at least, if I can do nothing more, until I shall know with certainty that there is nothing certain. Archimedes, that he might transport the entire globe from the place it occupied to another, demanded only a point that was firm and immovable; so also, I shall be entitled to entertain the highest expectations, if I am fortunate enough to discover only one thing that is certain and indubitable.

I suppose, accordingly, that all the things which I see are false (fictitious); I believe that none of those objects which my fallacious memory represents ever existed; I suppose that I possess no senses; I believe that body, figure, extension, motion, and place are merely fictions of my mind. What is there, then, that can be esteemed true? Perhaps this only, that there is absolutely nothing certain.

But how do I know that there is not something different altogether from the objects I have now enumerated, of which it is impossible to entertain the slightest doubt? Is there not a God, or some being, by whatever name I may designate him, who causes these thoughts to arise in my mind? But why suppose such a being, for it may be I myself am capable of producing them? Am I, then, at least not something? But I before denied that I possessed senses or a body; I hesitate, however, for what follows from that? Am I so dependent on the body and the senses that without these I cannot exist? But I had the persuasion that there was absolutely nothing in the world, that there was no sky and no earth, neither minds nor bodies; was I not, therefore, at the same time, persuaded that I did not exist? Far from it; I assuredly existed, since I was persuaded. But there is I know not what being, who is possessed at once of the highest power and the deepest cunning, who is constantly employing all his ingenuity in deceiving me. Doubtless, then, I exist, since I am deceived; and, let him deceive me as he may, he can never bring it about that I am nothing, so long as I shall be conscious that I am something. So that it must, in fine, be maintained, all things being maturely and carefully considered, that this proposition (*pronunciatum*) I am, I exist, is necessarily true each time it is expressed by me, or conceived in my mind.

But I do not yet know with sufficient clearness what I am, though assured that I am; and hence, in the next place, I must take care, lest perchance I inconsiderately substitute some other object in room of what is properly myself, and thus wander from truth, even in that knowledge (cognition) which I hold to be of all others the most certain and evident. For this reason, I will now consider anew what I formerly believed myself to be, before I entered on the present train of thought; and of my previous opinion I will retrench all that can in the least be invalidated by the grounds of doubt I have adduced, in order that there may at length remain nothing but what is certain and indubitable. What then did I formerly think I was? Undoubtedly I judged that I was a man. But what is a man? Shall I say a rational animal? Assuredly not; for it would be necessary forthwith to inquire into what is meant by animal, and what by rational, and thus, from a single question, I should insensibly glide into others, and these more difficult than the first; nor do I now possess enough of leisure to warrant me in wasting my time amid subtleties of this sort. I prefer here to attend to the thoughts that sprung up of themselves in my mind, and were inspired by my own nature alone, when I applied myself to the consideration of what I was. In the first place, then, I thought that I possessed a countenance, hands, arms, and all the fabric of members that appears in a corpse, and which I called by the name of body. It further occurred to me that I was nourished, that I walked, perceived, and thought, and all those actions I referred to the soul; but what the soul itself was I either did not stay to consider, or, if I did, I imagined that it was something extremely rare and subtile, like wind, or flame, or ether, spread through my grosser parts. As regarded the body, I did not even doubt of its nature, but thought I distinctly knew it, and if I had wished to describe it according to the notions I then entertained, I should have explained myself in this manner: By body I understand all that can be terminated by a certain figure; that can be comprised in a certain place, and so fill a certain space as therefrom to exclude every other body; that can be perceived either by touch, sight, hearing, taste, or smell; that can be moved in different ways, not indeed of itself, but by something foreign to it by which it is touched [and from which it receives the impression];[1] for the power of self-motion, as likewise that of perceiving and thinking, I held as by no means pertaining to the nature of body; on the contrary, I was somewhat astonished to find such faculties existing in some bodies.

But [as to myself, what can I now say that I am], since I suppose there exists an extremely powerful, and, if I may so speak, malignant being, whose whole endeavours are directed towards deceiving me? Can I affirm that I possess any one of all those attributes of which I have lately spoken as belonging to the nature of body? After attentively considering them in my own mind, I find none of them that can properly be said to belong to myself. To recount them were idle and tedious. Let us pass, then, to the attributes of the soul. The first mentioned were the powers of nutrition and walking; but, if it be true that I have no body, it is true likewise that I am capable neither of walking nor of being nourished. Perception is another attribute of the soul; but perception too is impossible without the body: besides, I have frequently, during sleep, believed that I perceived objects which I afterwards observed I did not in reality perceive. Thinking is another attribute of the soul; and here I discover what properly belongs to myself. This alone is inseparable from me. I am – I exist: this is certain; but how often? As often as I think; for perhaps it would even happen, if I should wholly cease to think, that I should at the same time altogether cease to be. I now admit nothing that is not necessarily true: I am therefore, precisely speaking, only a thinking thing, that is, a mind (*mens sive animus*), understanding, or reason – terms whose signification was before unknown to me. I am, however, a real thing, and really existent; but what thing? The answer was, a thinking thing. The question now arises, am I aught besides? I will stimulate my imagination with a view to discover whether I am not still something more than a thinking being. Now it is plain I am not the assemblage of members called the human body; I am not a thin and penetrating air diffused through all these members, or wind, or flame, or vapour, or breath, or any of all the things I can imagine; for I supposed that all these were not, and, without changing the supposition, I find that I still feel assured of my existence.

But it is true, perhaps, that those very things which I suppose to be non-existent, because they are unknown to me, are not in truth different from myself whom I know. This is a point I cannot determine, and do not now enter into any dispute regarding it. I can only judge of things that are known to me: I am conscious that I exist, and I who know that I exist inquire into what I am. It is, however, perfectly certain that the knowledge of my existence, thus precisely taken, is not dependent on things, the existence of which is as yet unknown to me: and consequently it is not dependent on any of the things I can feign in imagination. Moreover, the phrase itself, I frame an image (*effingo*), reminds me of my error; for I should in truth frame one if I were to imagine myself to be anything, since to imagine is nothing more than to contemplate the figure or image of a corporeal thing; but I already know that I exist, and that it is possible at the same time that all those images, and in general all that relates to the nature of body, are merely dreams [or chimeras]. From this I discover that it is not more reasonable to say, I will excite my imagination that I may know more distinctly what I am, than to express myself as follows: I am now awake, and perceive something real; but because my perception is not sufficiently clear, I will of express purpose go to sleep that my dreams may represent to me the object of my perception with more truth and clearness. And, therefore, I know that nothing of all that I can embrace in imagination belongs to the knowledge which I have of myself, and that there is need to recall with the utmost care the mind from this mode of thinking, that it may be able to know its own nature with perfect distinctness.

But what, then, am I? A thinking thing, it has been said. But what is a thinking thing? It is a thing that doubts, understands [conceives], affirms, denies, wills, refuses, that imagines also, and perceives. Assuredly it is not little, if all these properties belong to my nature. But why should they not belong to it? Am I not that very being who now doubts of almost everything; who, for all that, understands and conceives certain things, who affirms one alone as true, and denies the others; who desires to know more of them, and does not wish to be deceived; who imagines many things, sometimes even despite his will; and is likewise percipient of many, as if through the medium of the senses. Is there nothing of all this as true as that I am, even although I should be always dreaming, and although he who gave me being employed all his ingenuity to deceive me? Is there also any one of these attributes that can be properly distinguished from my thought, or that can be said to be separate from myself? For it is of itself so evident that it is I who doubt, I who understand, and I who desire, that it is here unnecessary to add anything by way of rendering it more clear. And I am as certainly the same being who imagines; for, although it may be (as I before supposed) that nothing I imagine is true, still the power of imagination does not cease really to exist in me and to form part of my thoughts. In fine, I am the same being who perceives, that is, who apprehends certain objects as by the organs of sense, since, in truth, I see light, hear a noise, and feel heat. But it will be said that these presentations are false, and that I am dreaming. Let it be so. At all events it is certain that I seem to see light, hear a noise, and feel heat; this cannot be false, and this is what in me is properly called perceiving (*sentire*), which is nothing else than thinking. From this I begin to know what I am with somewhat greater clearness and distinctness than heretofore.

But, nevertheless, it still seems to me, and I cannot help believing, that corporeal things, whose images are formed by thought [which fall under the senses], and are examined by the same, are known with much greater distinctness than that I know not what part of myself which is not imaginable; although, in truth, it may seem strange to say that I know and comprehend with greater distinctness things whose existence appears to me doubtful, that are unknown, and do not belong to me, than others of whose reality I am persuaded, that are known to me, and appertain to my proper nature; in a word, than myself. But I see clearly what is the state of the case. My mind is apt to wander, and will not yet submit to be restrained within the limits of truth. Let us therefore leave the mind to itself once more, and, according to it every kind of liberty [permit it to consider the objects that appear to it from without], in order that, having afterwards withdrawn it from these gently and opportunely [and fixed it on the consideration of its being and the properties it finds in itself], it may then be the more easily controlled.

Let us now accordingly consider the objects that are commonly thought to be [the most easily, and likewise] the most distinctly known, viz., the bodies we touch and see; not, indeed, bodies in general, for these general notions are usually somewhat more confused, but one body in particular. Take, for example, this piece of wax; it is quite fresh, having been but recently taken from the beehive; it has not yet lost the sweetness of the honey it contained; it still retains somewhat of the odour of the flowers from which it was gathered; its colour, figure, size, are apparent (to the sight); it is hard, cold, easily handled; and sounds when struck upon with the finger. In fine, all that contributes to make a body as distinctly known as possible, is found in the one before us. But, while I am speaking, let it be placed near the fire – what remained of the taste exhales, the smell evaporates, the colour changes, its figure is destroyed, its size increases, it becomes liquid, it grows hot, it can hardly be handled, and, although struck upon, it emits no sound. Does the same wax still remain after this change? It must be admitted that it does remain; no one doubts it, or judges otherwise. What, then, was it I knew with so much distinctness in the piece of wax? Assuredly, it could be nothing of all that I observed by means of the senses, since all the things that fell under taste, smell, sight, touch, and hearing are changed, and yet the same wax remains. It was perhaps what I now think, viz., that this wax was neither the sweetness of honey, the pleasant odour of flowers, the whiteness, the figure, nor the sound, but only a body that a little before appeared to me conspicuous under these forms, and which is now perceived under others. But, to speak precisely, what is it that I imagine when I think of it in this way? Let it be attentively considered, and, retrenching all that does not belong to the wax, let us see what remains. There certainly remains nothing, except something extended, flexible, and movable. But what is meant by flexible and movable? Is it not that I imagine that the piece of wax, being round, is capable of becoming square, or of passing from a square into a triangular figure? Assuredly such is not the case, because I conceive that it admits of an infinity of similar changes; and I am, moreover, unable to compass this infinity by imagination, and consequently this conception which I have of the wax is not the product of the faculty of imagination. But what now is this extension? Is it not also unknown? for it becomes greater when the wax is melted, greater when it is boiled, and greater still when the heat increases; and I should not conceive [clearly and] according to truth, the wax as it is, if I did not suppose that the piece we are considering admitted even of a wider variety of extension than I ever imagined. I must, therefore, admit that I cannot even comprehend by imagination what the piece of wax is, and that it is the mind alone (*mens*, Lat.; *entendement*, F.) which perceives it. I speak of one piece in particular; for, as to wax in general, this is still more evident. But what is the piece of wax that can be perceived only by the [understanding of] mind? It is certainly the same which I see, touch, imagine; and, in fine, it is the same which, from the beginning, I believed it to be. But (and this it is of moment to observe) the perception of it is neither an act of sight, of touch, nor of imagination, and never was either of these, though it might formerly seem so, but is simply an intuition (*inspectio*) of the mind, which may be imperfect and confused, as it formerly was, or very clear and distinct, as it is at present, according as the attention is more or less directed to the elements which it contains, and of which it is composed.

But, meanwhile, I feel greatly astonished when I observe [the weakness of my mind, and] its proneness to error. For although, without at all giving expression to what I think, I consider all this in my own mind, words yet occasionally impede my progress, and I am almost led into error by the terms of ordinary language. We say, for example, that we see the same wax when it is before us, and not that we judge it to be the same from its retaining the same colour and figure: whence I should forthwith be disposed to conclude that the wax is known by the act of sight, and not by the intuition of the mind alone, were it not for the analogous instance of human beings passing on in the street below, as observed from a window. In this case I do not fail to say that I see the men themselves, just as I say that I see the wax; and yet what do I see from the window beyond hats and cloaks that might cover artificial machines, whose motions might be determined by springs? But I judge that there are human beings from these appearances, and thus I comprehend, by the faculty of judgment alone which is in the mind, what I believed I saw with my eyes.

The man who makes it his aim to rise to knowledge superior to the common, ought to be ashamed to seek occasions of doubting from the vulgar forms of speech: instead, therefore, of doing this, I shall proceed with the matter in hand, and inquire whether I had a clearer and more perfect perception of the piece of wax when I first saw it, and when I thought I knew it by means of the external sense itself, or, at all events, by the common sense (*sensus communis*), as it is called, that is, by the imaginative faculty; or whether I rather apprehend it more clearly at present, after having examined with greater care, both what it is, and in what way it can be known. It would certainly be ridiculous to entertain any doubt on this point. For what, in that first perception, was there distinct? What did I perceive which any animal might not have perceived? But when I distinguish the wax from its exterior forms, and when, as if I had stripped it of its vestments, I consider it quite naked, it is certain, although some error may still be found in my judgment, that I cannot, nevertheless, thus apprehend it without possessing a human mind.

But, finally, what shall I say of the mind itself, that is, of myself? for as yet I do not admit that I am anything but mind. What, then! I who seem to possess so distinct an apprehension of the piece of wax – do I not know myself, both with greater truth and certitude, and also much more distinctly and clearly? For if I judge that the wax exists because I see it, it assuredly follows, much more evidently, that I myself am or exist, for the same reason: for it is possible that what I see may not in truth be wax, and that I do not even possess eyes with which to see anything; but it cannot be that when I see, or, which comes to the same thing, when I think I see, I myself who think am nothing. So likewise, if I judge that the wax exists because I touch it, it will still also follow that I am; and if I determine that my imagination, or any other cause, whatever it be, persuades me of the existence of the wax, I will still draw the same conclusion. And what is here remarked of the piece of wax is applicable to all the other things that are external to me. And further, if the [notion or] perception of wax appeared to me more precise and distinct, after that not only sight and touch, but many other causes besides, rendered it manifest to my apprehension, with how much greater distinctness must I now know myself, since all the reasons that contribute to the knowledge of the nature of wax, or of any body whatever, manifest still better the nature of my mind? And there are besides so many other things in the mind itself that contribute to the illustration of its nature, that those dependent on the body, to which I have here referred, scarcely merit to be taken into account.

But, in conclusion, I find I have insensibly reverted to the point I desired; for, since it is now manifest to me that bodies themselves are not properly perceived by the senses nor by the faculty of imagination, but by the intellect alone; and since they are not perceived because they are seen and touched, but only because they are understood [or rightly comprehended by thought], I readily discover that there is nothing more easily or clearly apprehended than my own mind. But because it is difficult to rid one's self so promptly of an opinion to which one has been long accustomed, it will be desirable to tarry for some time at this stage, that, by long continued meditation, I may more deeply impress upon my memory this new knowledge.

Note

1   The square brackets in this chapter mark Descartes' own additions to the revised French translation (Eds).

18

David Hume, "Of Personal Identity"

Descartes argues that self-knowledge of a sort forms the foundation upon which to build the remainder of our beliefs. In contrast, Hume, in *A Treatise concerning Human Nature*, offers that "gazing inward" through introspection does not reveal a simple "I" or self as Descartes thought. Instead, we merely encounter a parade of impressions without a perceiver. We mistake ourselves as having an idea of a simple self distinct from this experiential flux, Hume offers, because of our conflation of a series of similar ideas with an identity, or an idea of a simple and persisting object. Continuing to employ the idea of a simple self is, then, unintelligible, since it is empirically groundless, but here again we engage in the folly as a result of a feeling arising from custom or habit.

However, in inveighing against the existence of a Cartesian self, Hume argues that our perceptions are each conceivably distinguishable – and hence distinct – existences. But if each perception is a distinct existence, we then require an explanation as to why just these perceptions occur in this succession. From his radical empiricist standpoint, Hume does not quite possess the philosophical resources to explain our apparent mental unity. He admits as much in the Appendix to the *Treatise*, which is also included here, confessing that the problem proves too much for him, that he must "plead the privilege of a skeptic" and leave it unanswered. Hume apparently never satisfied himself on this point, and the topic of personal identity is noticeably absent from his later work.

There are some philosophers, who imagine we are every moment intimately conscious of what we call our Self; that we feel its existence and its continuance in existence; and are certain, beyond the evidence of a demonstration, both of its perfect identity and simplicity. The strongest sensation, the most violent passion, say they, instead of distracting us from this view, only fix it the more intensely, and make us consider their influence on *self* either by their pain or pleasure. To attempt a farther proof of this were to weaken its evidence; since no proof can be deriv'd from any fact, of which we are so intimately conscious; nor is there any thing, of which we can be certain, if we doubt of this.

Unluckily all these positive assertions are contrary to that very experience, which is pleaded for them, nor have we any idea of *self*, after the manner it is here explain'd. For from what impression could this idea be deriv'd? This question 'tis impossible to answer without a manifest contradiction and absurdity; and yet 'tis a question, which must necessarily be answer'd, if we would have the idea of self pass for clear and intelligible. It must be some one impression, that gives rise to every real idea. But self or person is not any one impression, but that to which our several impressions and ideas are suppos'd to have a reference. If any impression gives rise to the idea of self, that impression must continue invariably the same, thro' the whole course of our lives; since self is suppos'd to exist after that manner. But there is no impression constant and invariable. Pain and pleasure, grief and joy, passions and sensations succeed each other, and never all exist at the same time. It cannot, therefore, be from any of these impressions, or from any other, that the idea of self is deriv'd; and consequently there is no such idea.

But farther, what must become of all our particular perceptions upon this hypothesis? All these are different, and distinguishable, and separable from each other, and may be separately consider'd, and may exist separately, and have no need of any thing to support their existence. After what manner, therefore, do they belong to self; and how are they connected with it? For my part, when I enter most intimately into what I call *myself*, I always stumble on some particular perception or other, of heat or cold, light or shade, love or hatred, pain or pleasure. I never can catch *myself* at any time without a perception, and never can observe any thing but the perception. When my perceptions are remov'd for any time, as by sound sleep; so long am I insensible of *myself*, and may truly be said not to exist. And were all my perceptions remov'd by death, and could I neither think, nor feel, nor see, nor love, nor hate after the dissolution of my body, I should be entirely annihilated, nor do I conceive what is farther requisite to make me a perfect non-entity. If any one upon serious and unprejudic'd reflexion, thinks he has a different notion of *himself*, I must confess I can reason no longer with him. All I can allow him is, that he may be in the right as well as I, and that we are essentially different in this particular. He may, perhaps, perceive something simple and continu'd, which he calls *himself*; tho' I am certain there is no such principle in me.

But setting aside some metaphysicians of this kind, I may venture to affirm of the rest of mankind, that they are nothing but a bundle or collection of different perceptions, which succeed each other with an inconceivable rapidity, and are in a perpetual flux and movement. Our eyes cannot turn in their sockets without varying our perceptions. Our thought is still more variable than our sight; and all our other senses and faculties contribute to this change; nor is there any single power of the soul, which remains unalterably the same, perhaps for one moment. The mind is a kind of theatre, where several perceptions successively make their appearance; pass, re-pass, glide away, and mingle in an infinite variety of postures and situations. There is properly no *simplicity* in it at one time, nor *identity* in different; whatever natural propension we may have to imagine that simplicity and identity. The comparison of the theatre must not mislead us. They are the successive perceptions only, that constitute the mind; nor have we the most distant notion of the place, where these scenes are represented, or of the materials, of which it is compos'd.

What then gives us so great a propension to ascribe an identity to these successive perceptions, and to suppose ourselves possest of an invariable and uninterrupted existence thro' the whole course of our lives? In order to answer this question, we must distinguish betwixt personal identity, as it regards our thought or imagination, and as it regards our passions or the concern we take in ourselves. The first is our present subject; and to explain it perfectly we must take the matter pretty deep, and account for that identity, which we attribute to plants and animals; there being a great analogy betwixt it, and the identity of a self or person.

We have a distinct idea of an object, that remains invariable and uninterrupted thro' a suppos'd variation of time; and this idea we call that of *identity* or *sameness*. We have also a distinct idea of several different objects existing in succession, and connected together by a close relation; and this to an accurate view affords as perfect a notion of *diversity*, as if there was no manner of relation among the objects. But tho' these two ideas of identity, and a succession of related objects be in themselves perfectly distinct, and even contrary, yet 'tis certain, that in our common way of thinking they are generally confounded with each other. That action of the imagination, by which we consider the uninterrupted and invariable object, and that by which we reflect on the

204 Skeptical Topics: Self-Knowledge

succession of related objects, are almost the same to the feeling, nor is there much more effort of thought requir'd in the latter case than in the former. The relation facilitates the transition of the mind from one object to another, and renders its passage as smooth as if it contemplated one continu'd object. This resemblance is the cause of the confusion and mistake, and makes us substitute the notion of identity, instead of that of related objects. However at one instant we may consider the related succession as variable or interrupted, we are sure the next to ascribe to it a perfect identity, and regard it as invariable and uninterrupted. Our propensity to this mistake is so great from the resemblance above-mention'd, that we fall into it before we are aware; and tho' we incessantly correct ourselves by reflexion, and return to a more accurate method of thinking, yet we cannot long sustain our philosophy, or take off this biass from the imagination. Our last resource is to yield to it, and boldly assert that these different related objects are in effect the same, however interrupted and variable. In order to justify to ourselves this absurdity, we often feign some new and unintelligible principle, that connects the objects together, and prevents their interruption or variation. Thus we feign the continu'd existence of the perceptions of our senses, to remove the interruption; and run into the notion of a *soul*, and *self*, and *substance*, to disguise the variation. But we may farther observe, that where we do not give rise to such a fiction, our propension to confound identity with relation is so great, that we are apt to imagine[1] something unknown and mysterious, connecting the parts, beside their relation; and this I take to be the case with regard to the identity we ascribe to plants and vegetables. And even when this does not take place, we still feel a propensity to confound these ideas, tho' we are not able fully to satisfy ourselves in that particular, nor find any thing invariable and uninterrupted to justify our notion of identity.

Thus the controversy concerning identity is not merely a dispute of words. For when we attribute identity, in an improper sense, to variable or interrupted objects, our mistake is not confin'd to the expression, but is commonly attended with a fiction, either of something invariable and uninterrupted, or of something mysterious and inexplicable, or at least with a propensity to such fictions. What will suffice to prove this hypothesis to the satisfaction of every fair enquirer, is to shew from daily experience and observation, that the objects, which are variable or interrupted, and yet are suppos'd to continue the same, are such only as consist of a succession of parts, connected together by resemblance, contiguity, or causation. For as such a succession answers evidently to our notion of diversity, it can only be by mistake we ascribe to it an identity; and as the relation of parts, which leads us into this mistake, is really nothing but a quality, which produces an association of ideas, and an easy transition of the imagination from one to another, it can only be from the resemblance, which this act of the mind bears to that, by which we contemplate one continu'd object, that the error arises. Our chief business, then, must be to prove, that all objects, to which we ascribe identity, without observing their invariableness and uninterruptedness, are such as consist of a succession of related objects.

In order to this, suppose any mass of matter, of which the parts are contiguous and connected, to be plac'd before us; 'tis plain we must attribute a perfect identity to this mass, provided all the parts continue uninterruptedly and invariably the same, whatever motion or change of place we may observe either in the whole or in any of the parts. But supposing some very *small* or *inconsiderable* part to be added to the mass, or substracted from it; tho' this absolutely destroys the identity of the whole, strictly speaking; yet as we seldom think so accurately, we scruple not to pronounce a mass of matter the same, where we find so trivial an alteration. The passage of the thought from the object before the change to the object after it, is so smooth and easy, that we scarce perceive the transition, and are apt to imagine, that 'tis nothing but a continu'd survey of the same object.

There is a very remarkable circumstance, that attends this experiment; which is, that tho' the change of any considerable part in a mass of matter destroys the identity of the whole, yet we must measure the greatness of the part, not absolutely, but by its *proportion* to the whole. The addition or diminution of a mountain would not be sufficient to produce a diversity in a planet; tho' the change of a very few inches would be able to destroy the identity of some bodies. 'Twill be impossible to account for this, but by reflecting that objects operate upon the mind, and break or interrupt the continuity of its actions not according to their real greatness, but according to their proportion to each other: And therefore, since this interruption makes an object cease to appear the same, it must be the uninterrupted progress of the thought, which constitutes the imperfect identity.

This may be confirm'd by another phenomenon. A change in any considerable part of a body destroys its identity; but 'tis remarkable, that where the change is produc'd *gradually* and *insensibly* we are less apt to ascribe to it the same effect. The reason can plainly be no other, than that the mind, in following the successive changes of the body, feels an easy passage from the surveying its condition in one moment to the viewing of it in another, and at no particular time perceives any interruption in its actions. From which continu'd perception, it ascribes a continu'd existence and identity to the object.

But whatever precaution we may use in introducing the changes gradually, and making them proportionable to the whole, 'tis certain, that where the changes are at last observ'd to become considerable, we make a scruple of ascribing identity to such different objects. There is, however, another artifice, by which we may induce the imagination to advance a step farther; and that is, by producing a reference of the parts to each other, and a combination to some *common end* or purpose. A ship, of which a considerable part has been chang'd by frequent reparations, is still consider'd as the same; nor does the difference of the materials hinder us from ascribing an identity to it. The common end, in which the parts conspire, is the same under all their variations, and affords an easy transition of the imagination from one situation of the body to another.

But this is still more remarkable, when we add a *sympathy* of parts to their *common end*, and suppose that they bear to each other, the reciprocal relation of cause and effect in all their actions and operations. This is the case with all animals and vegetables; where not only the several parts have a reference to some general purpose, but also a mutual dependance on, and connexion with each other. The effect of so strong a relation is, that tho' every one must allow, that in a very few years both vegetables and animals endure a *total* change, yet we still attribute identity to them, while their form, size, and substance are entirely alter'd. An oak, that grows from a small plant to a large tree, is still the same oak; tho' there be not one particle of matter, or figure of its parts the same. An infant becomes a man, and is sometimes fat, sometimes lean, without any change in his identity.

We may also consider the two following phenomena, which are remarkable in their kind. The first is, that tho' we commonly be able to distinguish pretty exactly betwixt numerical and specific identity, yet it sometimes happens, that we confound them, and in our thinking and reasoning employ the one for the other. Thus a man, who hears a noise, that is frequently interrupted and renew'd, says, it is still the same noise; tho' 'tis evident the sounds have only a specific identity or resemblance, and there is nothing numerically the same, but the cause, which produc'd them. In like manner it may be said without breach of the propriety of language, that such a church, which was formerly of brick, fell to ruin, and that the parish rebuilt the same church of free-stone, and according to modern architecture. Here neither the form nor materials are the same, nor is there any thing common to the two objects, but their relation to the inhabitants of the parish; and yet this alone is sufficient to make us denominate them the same. But we must observe, that in these cases the first object is in a manner annihilated before the second comes into existence; by which means, we are never presented in any one point of time with the idea of difference and multiplicity; and for that reason are less scrupulous in calling them the same.

Secondly, we may remark, that tho' in a succession of related objects, it be in a manner requisite, that the change of parts be not sudden nor entire, in order to preserve the identity, yet where the objects are in their nature changeable and inconstant, we admit of a more sudden transition, than would otherwise be consistent with that relation. Thus as the nature of a river consists in the motion and change of parts; tho' in less than four and twenty hours these be totally alter'd; this hinders not the river from continuing the same during several ages. What is natural and essential to any thing is, in a manner, expected; and what is expected makes less impression, and appears of less moment, than what is unusual and extraordinary. A considerable change of the former kind seems really less to the imagination, than the most trivial alteration of the latter; and by breaking less the continuity of the thought, has less influence in destroying the identity.

We now proceed to explain the nature of *personal identity*, which has become so great a question in philosophy, especially of late years in *England*, where all the abstruser sciences are study'd with a peculiar ardour and application. And here 'tis evident, the same method of reasoning must be continu'd, which has so successfully explain'd the identity of plants, and animals, and ships, and houses, and of all the compounded and changeable productions either of art or nature. The identity, which we ascribe to the mind of man, is only a fictitious one, and of a like kind with that which we ascribe to vegetables and animal bodies. It cannot, therefore, have a different origin, but must proceed from a like operation of the imagination upon like objects.

But lest this argument should not convince the reader; tho' in my opinion perfectly decisive; let him weigh the following reasoning, which is still closer and more immediate. 'Tis evident, that the identity, which we attribute to the human mind, however perfect we may imagine it to be, is not able to run the several different perceptions into one, and make them lose their characters of distinction and difference, which are essential to them. 'Tis still true, that every distinct perception, which enters into the composition of the mind, is a distinct existence, and is different, and distinguishable, and separable from every other perception, either contemporary or successive. But, as, notwithstanding this distinction and separability, we suppose the whole train of perceptions to be united by identity, a question naturally arises concerning this relation of identity; whether it be something that really binds our several perceptions together, or only associates their ideas in the imagination. That is, in other words, whether in pronouncing concerning the identity of a person, we observe some real bond among his perceptions, or only feel one among the ideas we form of them. This question we might easily decide, if we would recollect what has been already prov'd at large, that the understanding never observes any real connexion among objects, and that even the union of cause and effect, when strictly examin'd, resolves itself into a customary association of ideas. For from thence it evidently follows, that identity is nothing really belonging to these different perceptions, and uniting them together; but is merely a quality, which we attribute to them, because of the union of their ideas in the imagination, when we reflect upon them. Now the only qualities, which can give ideas an union in the imagination, are these three relations above-mention'd. These are the uniting principles in the ideal world, and without them every distinct object is separable by the mind, and may be separately consider'd, and appears not to have any more connexion with any other object, than if disjoin'd by the greatest difference and remoteness. 'Tis, therefore, on some of these three relations of resemblance, contiguity and causation, that identity depends; and as the very essence of these relations consists in their producing an easy transition of ideas; it follows, that our notions of personal identity, proceed entirely from the smooth and uninterrupted progress of the thought along a train of connected ideas, according to the principles above-explain'd.

The only question, therefore, which remains, is, by what relations this uninterrupted progress of our thought is produc'd, when we consider the successive existence of a mind or thinking person. And here 'tis evident we must confine ourselves to resemblance and causation, and must drop contiguity, which has little or no influence in the present case.

To begin with *resemblance*; suppose we could see clearly into the breast of another, and observe that succession of perceptions, which constitutes his mind or thinking principle, and suppose that he always preserves the memory of a considerable part of past perceptions; 'tis evident that nothing could more contribute to the bestowing a relation on this succession amidst all its variations. For what is the memory but a faculty, by which we raise up the images of past perceptions? And as an image necessarily resembles its object, must not the frequent placing of these resembling perceptions in the chain of thought, convey the imagination more easily from one link to another, and make the whole seem like the continuance of one object? In this particular, then, the memory not only discovers the identity, but also contributes to its production, by producing the relation of resemblance among the perceptions. The case is the same whether we consider ourselves or others.

As to *causation*; we may observe, that the true idea of the human mind, is to consider it as a system of different perceptions or different existences, which are link'd together by the relation of cause and effect, and mutually produce, destroy, influence, and modify each other. Our impressions give rise to their correspondent ideas; and these ideas in their turn produce other impressions. One thought chases another, and draws after it a third, by which it is expell'd in its turn. In this respect, I cannot compare the soul more properly to any thing than to a republic or commonwealth, in which the several members are united by the reciprocal ties of government and subordination, and give rise to other persons, who propagate the same republic in the incessant changes of its parts. And as the same individual republic may not only change its members, but also its laws and constitutions; in like manner the same person may vary his character and disposition, as well as his impressions and ideas, without losing his identity. Whatever changes he endures, his several parts are still connected by the relation of causation. And in this view our identity with regard to the passions serves to corroborate that with regard to the imagination, by the making our distant perceptions influence each other, and by giving us a present concern for our past or future pains or pleasures.

As memory alone acquaints us with the continuance and extent of this succession of perceptions, 'tis to be consider'd, upon that account chiefly, as the source of personal identity. Had we no memory, we never should have any notion of causation, nor consequently of that chain of causes and effects, which constitute our self or person. But having once acquir'd this notion of causation from the memory, we can extend the same chain of causes, and consequently the identity of our persons beyond our memory, and can comprehend times, and circumstances, and actions, which we have entirely forgot, but suppose in general to have existed. For how few of our past actions are there, of which we have any memory? Who can tell me, for instance, what were his thoughts and actions on the first of January 1715, the 11th of March 1719, and the 3rd of August 1733? Or will he affirm, because he has entirely forgot the incidents of these days, that the present self is not the same person with the self of that time; and by that means overturn all the most establish'd notions of personal identity? In this view, therefore, memory does not so much *produce* as *discover* personal identity, by shewing us the relation of cause and effect among our different perceptions. 'Twill be incumbent on those, who affirm that memory produces entirely our personal identity, to give a reason why we can thus extend our identity beyond our memory.

The whole of this doctrine leads us to a conclusion, which is of great importance in the present affair, *viz.* that all the nice and subtile questions concerning personal identity can never possibly be decided, and are to be regarded rather as grammatical than as philosophical difficulties. Identity depends on the relations of ideas; and these relations produce identity, by means of that easy transition they occasion. But as the relations, and the easiness of the transition may diminish by insensible degrees, we have no just standard, by which we can decide any dispute concerning the time, when they acquire or lose a title to the name of identity. All the disputes concerning the identity of connected objects are merely verbal, except so far as the relation of parts gives rise to some fiction or imaginary principle of union, as we have already observ'd.

What I have said concerning the first origin and uncertainty of our notion of identity, as apply'd to the human mind, may be extended with little or no variation to that of *simplicity*. An object, whose different co-existent parts are bound together by a close relation, operates upon the imagination after much the same manner as one perfectly simple and indivisible, and requires not a much greater stretch of thought in order to its conception. From this similarity of operation we attribute a simplicity to it, and feign a principle of union as the support of this simplicity, and the center of all the different parts and qualities of the object. [...]

Appendix

I had entertain'd some hopes, that however deficient our theory of the intellectual world might be, it would be free from those contradictions, and absurdities, which seem to attend every explication, that human reason can give of the material world. But upon a more strict review of the section concerning *personal identity*, I find myself involv'd in such a labyrinth, that, I must confess, I neither know how to correct my former opinions, nor how to render them consistent. If this be not a good *general* reason for scepticism, 'tis at least a sufficient one (if I were not already abundantly supplied) for me to entertain a diffidence and modesty in all my decisions. I shall propose the arguments on both sides, beginning with those that induc'd me to deny the strict and proper identity and simplicity of a self or thinking being.

When we talk of *self* or *substance*, we must have an idea annex'd to these terms, otherwise they are altogether unintelligible. Every idea is deriv'd from preceding impressions; and we have no impression of self or substance, as something simple and individual. We have, therefore, no idea of them in that sense.

Whatever is distinct, is distinguishable; and whatever is distinguishable, is separable by the thought or imagination. All perceptions are distinct. They are, therefore, distinguishable, and separable, and may be conceiv'd as separately existent, and may exist separately, without any contradiction or absurdity.

When I view this table and that chimney, nothing is present to me but particular perceptions, which are of a like nature with all the other perceptions. This is the doctrine of philosophers. But this table, which is present to me, and that chimney, may and do exist separately. This is the doctrine of the vulgar, and implies no contradiction. There is no contradiction, therefore, in extending the same doctrine to all the perceptions.

In general, the following reasoning seems satisfactory. All ideas are borrow'd from preceding perceptions. Our ideas of objects, therefore, are deriv'd from that source. Consequently no proposition can be intelligible or consistent with regard to objects, which is not so with regard to perceptions. But 'tis intelligible and consistent to say, that objects exist distinct and independent, without any common *simple* substance or subject of inhesion. This proposition, therefore, can never be absurd with regard to perceptions.

When I turn my reflexion on *myself*, I never can perceive this *self* without some one or more perceptions; nor can I ever perceive any thing but the perceptions. 'Tis the composition of these, therefore, which forms the self.

We can conceive a thinking being to have either many or few perceptions. Suppose the mind to be reduc'd even below the life of an oyster. Suppose it to have only one perception, as of thirst or hunger. Consider it in that situation. Do you conceive any thing but merely that perception? Have you any notion of *self* or *substance*? If not, the addition of other perceptions can never give you that notion.

The annihilation, which some people suppose to follow upon death, and which entirely destroys this self, is nothing but an extinction of all particular perceptions; love and hatred, pain and pleasure, thought and sensation. These therefore must be the same with self; since the one cannot survive the other.

Is *self* the same with *substance*? If it be, how can that question have place, concerning the subsistence of self, under a change of substance? If they be distinct, what is the difference betwixt them? For my part, I have a notion of neither, when conceiv'd distinct from particular perceptions.

Philosophers begin to be reconcil'd to the principle, *that we have no idea of external substance, distinct from the ideas of particular qualities.* This must pave the way for a like principle with regard to the mind, *that we have no notion of it, distinct from the particular perceptions.*

So far I seem to be attended with sufficient evidence. But having thus loosen'd all our particular perceptions, when I proceed to explain the principle of connexion, which binds them together, and makes us attribute to them a real simplicity and identity; I am sensible, that my account is very defective, and that nothing but the seeming evidence of the precedent reasonings could have induc'd me to receive it. If perceptions are distinct existences, they form a whole only by being connected together. But no connexions among distinct existences are ever discoverable by human understanding. We only *feel* a connexion or determination of the thought, to pass from one object to another. It follows, therefore, that the thought alone finds personal identity, when reflecting on the train of past perceptions, that compose a mind, the ideas of them are felt to be connected together, and naturally introduce each other. However extraordinary this conclusion may seem, it need not surprise us. Most philosophers seem inclin'd to think, that personal identity *arises* from consciousness; and consciousness is nothing but a reflected thought or perception. The present philosophy, therefore, has so far a promising aspect. But all my hopes vanish, when I come to explain the principles, that unite our successive perceptions in our thought or consciousness. I cannot discover any theory, which gives me satisfaction on this head.

In short there are two principles, which I cannot render consistent; nor is it in my power to renounce either of them, viz. *that all our distinct perceptions are distinct existences*, and *that the mind never perceives any real connexion among distinct existences*. Did our perceptions either inhere in something simple and individual, or did the mind perceive some real connexion among them, there would be no difficulty in the case. For my part, I must plead the privilege of a sceptic, and confess, that this difficulty is too hard for my understanding. I pretend not, however, to pronounce it absolutely insuperable. Others, perhaps, or myself, upon more mature reflexions, may discover some hypothesis, that will reconcile those contradictions.

Note

1 If the reader is desirous to see how a great genius may be influenc'd by these seemingly trivial principles of the imagination, as well as the mere vulgar, let him read my Lord *Shaftsbury*'s reasonings concerning the uniting principle of the universe, and the identity of plants and animals. See his *Moralists*: or, *Philosophical rhapsody*.

19

Immanuel Kant, from ''The Paralogisms of Pure Reason''

The passages below, from Immanuel Kant's (1724–1804) *Critique of Pure Reason* (1781), are taken from a section entitled ''The Paralogisms of Pure Reason.'' Although Kant's technical terminology causes his writing to be obscure, the basic idea he is trying to get across is not difficult to formulate. Descartes claimed that the mind or self is more easily known than the body and that from the *Cogito, ergo sum* one can prove that the self is an immaterial, permanent, simple, self-identical, and potentially immortal substance. Hume raised doubts about Descartes' argument by simply pointing out that when one tries to observe oneself amidst the flux of experience, one finds nothing that exemplifies these attributes. ''I can never catch *myself* at any time without a perception, and can never observe anything but the perception,'' writes Hume. But Hume's observation makes us wonder about the ''I'' that is not able to catch itself. After all, we use the first person singular pronoun quite frequently, and in our usage we seem to be referring to something or other. What can this object of reference be? What can we know about it? These are the questions Kant considers in the Paralogisms.

The Paralogisms take the form of a series of searching criticisms directed against rational psychology, the effort exemplified by Descartes' *Cogito* to grasp the essence of the self *a priori*. Descartes, Hume, and Kant all agree that when we look into ourselves we do not become acquainted directly with the self whose nature we are attempting to apprehend. Descartes made use of metaphysical reasoning to determine the nature of the self, but Hume rejected this approach because it failed to be supported by experience. Kant argues instead that there is an important function for the "I," namely to express the fact of self-consciousness but that the self that underlies our inner experience can never become known. We cannot eliminate the "I" in favor of the bundle of perceptions as Hume thought, because the pronoun represents the indispensable fact of self-consciousness and corresponds to some real though unknown thing in itself.

We can, however, use as the foundation of such a science nothing but the single, and in itself perfectly empty, representation of the *I*, of which we cannot even say that it is a concept, but merely a consciousness that accompanies all concepts. By this *I*, or *he*, or *it* (the thing), which thinks, nothing is represented beyond a transcendental subject of thoughts = *x*, which is known only through the thoughts that are its predicates, and of which, apart from them, we can never have the slightest concept, so that we are really turning round it in a perpetual circle, having already to use its representation, before we can form any judgment about it. And this inconvenience is really inevitable, because consciousness in itself is not so much a representation, distinguishing a particular object, but really a form of representation in general, in so far as it is to be called knowledge, of which alone I can say that I think something by it.

It must seem strange, however, from the very beginning, that the condition under which I think, and which therefore is a property of my own subject only, should be valid at the same time for everything which thinks, and that, depending on a proposition which seems to be empirical, we should venture to found the apodictical and general judgment, namely, that everything which thinks is such as the voice of my own consciousness declares it to be within me. The reason of it is, that we are constrained to attribute *a priori* to things all the qualities which form the conditions, under which alone we are able to think them. Now it is impossible for me to form the smallest representation of a thinking being by any external experience, but I can do it through self-consciousness only. Such objects therefore are nothing but a transference of my own consciousness to other things, which thus, and thus only, can be represented as thinking beings. The proposition *I think* is used in this case, however, as problematical only; not so far as it may contain the perception of an existence (the Cartesian, *cogito, ergo sum*), but with regard to its mere possibility, in order to see what properties may be deduced from such a simple proposition with regard to its subject, whether such subject exists or not. [...]

I may say of everything, that it is a substance, so far as I distinguish it from what are mere predicates and determinations. Now in all our thinking the I is the subject, in which thoughts are inherent as determinations only; nor can that I ever be used as a determination of any other thing. Thus everybody is constrained to look upon himself as the substance, and on thinking as the accidents only of his being, and determinations of his state.

But what use are we to make of such a concept of a substance? That I, as a thinking being, *continue* for myself, and naturally neither *arise* nor *perish*, is no legitimate deduction from it; and yet this conclusion would be the only advantage that could be gained from the concept of the substantiality of my own thinking subject, and, but for that, I could do very well without it.

So far from being able to deduce these properties from the pure category of substance, we have on the contrary to observe the permanency of an object in our experience and then lay hold of this permanency, if we wish to apply to it the empirically useful concept of substance. In this case, however, we had no experience to lay hold of, but have only formed a deduction from the concept of the relation which all thinking has to the I, as the common subject to which it belongs. Nor should we, whatever we did, succeed by any certain observation in proving such permanency. For though the I exists in all thoughts, not the slightest intuition is connected with that representation, by which it might be distinguished from other objects of intuition. We may very well perceive therefore that this representation appears again and again in every act of thought, but not that it is a constant and permanent intuition, in which thoughts, as being changeable, come and go.

Hence it follows that in the first syllogism of transcendental psychology reason imposes upon us an apparent knowledge only, by representing the constant logical subject of thought as the knowledge of the real subject in which that knowledge inheres. Of that subject, however, we have not and cannot have the slightest knowledge, because consciousness is that which alone changes representations into thoughts, and in which therefore, as the transcendental subject, all our perceptions must be found. Beside this logical meaning of the I, we have no knowledge of the subject in itself, which forms the substratum and foundation of it and of all our thoughts. In spite of this, the proposition that the soul is a substance may well be allowed to stand, if only we see that this concept cannot help us on in the least or teach us any of the ordinary conclusions of rationalising psychology, as, for instance, the everlasting continuance of the soul amid all changes and even in death, and that it therefore signifies a substance in idea only, and not in reality. [...]

It is clear that the subject of inherence is designated transcendentally only by the I, which accompanies the thought, without our perceiving the smallest quality of it, in fact, without our knowing anything about it. It signifies a something in general (a transcendental subject) the representation of which must no doubt be simple, because nothing is determined in it, and nothing can be represented more simple than by the concept of a mere something. The simplicity however of the representation of a subject is not therefore a knowledge of the simplicity of the subject, because no account whatever is taken of its qualities when it is designated by the entirely empty expression I, an expression that can be applied to every thinking subject. [...]

The identity of my consciousness at different times is therefore a formal condition only of my thoughts and their coherence, and proves in no way the numerical identity of my subject, in which, in spite of the logical identity of the I, such a change may have passed as to make it impossible to retain its identity, though we may still attribute to it the same name of I, which in every other state, and even in the change of the subject, might yet retain the thought of the preceding and hand it over to the subsequent subject.

Although the teaching of some old schools that everything is in a flux, and nothing in the world permanent, cannot be admitted, if we admit substances, yet it must not be supposed that it can be refuted by the unity of self-consciousness. For we ourselves cannot judge from our own consciousness whether, as souls, we are permanent or not, because we reckon as belonging to our own identical self that only of which we are conscious, and therefore are constrained to admit that, during the whole time of which we are conscious, we are one and the same. From the point of view of a stranger, however, such a judgment would not be valid, because, perceiving in the soul no permanent phenomena, except the representation of the I, which accompanies and connects them all, we cannot determine whether that I (being a mere thought) be not in the same state of flux as the other thoughts which are chained together by the I. [...]

We thus see that all the wrangling about the nature of a thinking being, and its association with the material world, arises simply from our filling the gap, due to our ignorance, with paralogisms of reason, and by changing thoughts into things and hypostatizing them. On this an imaginary science is built up, both by those who assert and by those who deny, some pretending to know about objects of which no human being has any conception, while others make their own representations to be objects, all turning round in a constant circle of ambiguities and contradictions. Nothing but a sober, strict, and just criticism can free us of this dogmatical illusion, which, through theories and systems, deceives so many by an imaginary happiness. It alone can limit our speculative pretensions to the sphere of possible experience, and this not by a shallow scoffing at repeated failures or by pious sighs over the limits of our reason, but by a demarcation made according to well-established principles, writing the *nihil ulterius* with perfect assurance on those Herculean columns which Nature herself has erected, in order that the voyage of our reason should be continued so far only as the continuous shores of experience extend – shores which we can never forsake without being driven upon a boundless ocean, which, after deceiving us again and again, makes us in the end cease all our laborious and tedious endeavours as perfectly hopeless. [...]

We see from all this, that rational psychology owes its origin to a mere misunderstanding. The unity of consciousness, on which the categories are founded, is mistaken for an intuition of the subject as object, and the category of substance applied to it. But that unity is only the unity in *thought*, by which alone no object is given, and to which, therefore, the category of substance, which always presupposes a given *intuition*, cannot be applied, and therefore the subject cannot be known. The subject of the categories, therefore, cannot, by thinking them, receive a concept of itself, as an object of the categories; for in order to think the categories, it must presuppose its pure self-consciousness, the very thing that had to be explained. In like manner the subject, in which the representation of time has its original source, cannot determine by it its own existence in time; and if the latter is impossible, the former, as a determination of oneself (as of a thinking being in general) by means of the categories, is equally so. [...]

The dialectical illusion in rational psychology arises from our confounding an idea of reason (that of a pure intelligence) with the altogether indefinite concept of a thinking being in general. What we are doing is, that we conceive ourselves for the sake of a possible experience, taking no account, as yet, of any real experience, and thence conclude that we are able to become conscious of our existence, independently of experience and of its empirical conditions. We are, therefore, confounding the possible abstraction of our own empirically determined existence with the imagined consciousness of a possible separate existence of our thinking self, and we bring ourselves to believe that we know the substantial within us as the transcendental subject, while what we have in our thoughts is only the unity of consciousness, on which, as on the mere form of knowledge, all determination is based.

20

Friedrich Nietzsche, from *Beyond Good and Evil*

This selection is from *Beyond Good and Evil* by Friedrich Nietzsche (1844–1900). Nietzsche attacks the main lines of thought in the Western philosophical tradition; the systems of the great philosophers are simply dogmatic expressions of their underlying prejudices. The core of the selection is a criticism of Descartes' use of *Cogito, ergo sum* to bring his skepticism to a halt. The "I" in Descartes' "I think" is simply a grammatical illusion, a false and dubious interpretation of a complex fact that unjustifiably makes us think that we are acquainted with a self separate from the body.

To speak seriously, there are good grounds for hoping that all dogmatizing in philosophy, the solemn air of finality it has given itself notwithstanding, may none the less have been no more than a noble childishness and tyronism; and the time is perhaps very close at hand when it will be grasped in case after case *what* has been sufficient to furnish the foundation-stone for such sublime and unconditional philosophers' edifices as the dogmatics have hitherto been constructing – some popular superstition or other from time immemorial (such as the soul superstition which, as the subject-and-ego superstition, has not yet ceased to do mischief even today), perhaps some play on words, a grammatical seduction, or an audacious generalization on the basis of very narrow, very personal, very human, all too human facts. [...]

What makes one regard philosophers half mistrustfully and half mockingly is not that one again and again detects how innocent they are – how often and how easily they fall into error and go astray, in short their childishness and childlikeness – but that they display altogether insufficient honesty, while making a mighty and virtuous noise as soon as the problem of truthfulness is even remotely touched on. They pose as having discovered and attained their real opinions through the self-evolution of a cold, pure, divinely unperturbed dialectic (in contrast to the mystics of every rank, who are more honest and more stupid than they – these speak of 'inspiration'): while what happens at bottom is that a prejudice, a notion, an 'inspiration', generally a desire of the heart sifted and made abstract, is defended by them with reasons sought after the event – they are one and all advocates who do not want to be regarded as such, and for the most part no better than cunning pleaders for their prejudices, which they baptize 'truths' – and *very* far from possessing the courage of the conscience which admits this fact to itself, very far from possessing the good taste of the courage which publishes this fact, whether to warn a foe or a friend or out of high spirits and in order to mock itself. The tartuffery, as stiff as it is virtuous, of old Kant as he lures us along the dialectical bypaths which lead, more correctly, mislead, to his 'categorical imperative' – this spectacle makes us smile, we who are fastidious and find no little amusement in observing the subtle tricks of old moralists and moral-preachers. Not to speak of that hocus-pocus of mathematical form in which, as if in iron, Spinoza encased and masked his philosophy – 'the love of *his* wisdom', to render that word fairly and squarely – so as to strike terror into the heart of any assailant who should dare to glance at that invincible maiden and Pallas Athene – how much personal timidity and vulnerability this masquerade of a sick recluse betrays!

It has gradually become clear to me what every great philosophy has hitherto been: a confession on the part of its author and a kind of involuntary and unconscious memoir; moreover, that the moral (or immoral) intentions in every philosophy have every time constituted the real germ of life out of which the entire plant has grown. . . .

There are still harmless self-observers who believe 'immediate certainties' exist, for example 'I think' or, as was Schopenhauer's superstition, 'I will': as though knowledge here got hold of its object pure and naked, as 'thing in itself', and no falsification occurred either on the side of the subject or on that of the object. But I shall reiterate a hundred times that 'immediate certainty', like 'absolute knowledge' and 'thing in itself', contains a *contradictio in adjecto*: we really ought to get free from the seduction of words! Let the people believe that knowledge is total knowledge, but the philosopher must say to himself: when I analyse the event expressed in the sentence 'I think', I acquire a series of rash assertions which are difficult, perhaps impossible, to prove – for example, that it is *I* who think, that it has to be something at all which thinks, that thinking is an activity and operation on the part of an entity thought of as a cause, that an 'I' exists, finally that what is designated by 'thinking' has already been determined – that I *know* what thinking is. For if I had not already decided that matter within myself, by what standard could I determine that what is happening is not perhaps 'willing' or 'feeling'? Enough: this 'I think' presupposes that I *compare* my present state with other known states of myself in order to determine what it is: on account of this retrospective connection with other 'knowledge' at any rate it possesses no immediate certainty for me. In place of that 'immediate certainty' in which the people may believe in the present case, the philosopher acquires in this way a series of metaphysical questions, true questions of conscience for the intellect, namely: 'Whence do I take the concept thinking? Why do I believe in cause and effect? What gives me the right to speak of an "I", and even of an "I" as cause, and finally of an "I" as cause of thought?' Whoever feels able to answer these metaphysical questions straight away with an appeal to a sort of *intuitive* knowledge, as he does who says: 'I think, and know that this at least is true, actual and certain' – will find a philosopher today ready with a smile and two question-marks. 'My dear sir,' the philosopher will perhaps give him to understand, 'it is improbable you are not mistaken: but why do you want the truth at all?'

As for the superstitions of the logicians, I shall never tire of underlining a concise little fact which these superstitious people are loath to admit – namely, that a thought comes when 'it' wants, not when 'I' want; so that it is a *falsification* of the facts to say: the subject 'I' is the condition of the predicate 'think'. *It* thinks: but that this 'it' is precisely that famous old 'I' is, to put it mildly, only an assumption, an assertion, above all not an 'immediate certainty'. For even with this 'it thinks' one has already gone too far: this 'it' already contains an *interpretation* of the event and does not belong to the event itself. The inference here is in accordance with the habit of grammar: 'thinking is an activity, to every activity pertains one who acts, consequently –'. It was more or less in accordance with the same scheme that the older atomism sought, in addition to the 'force' which acts, that little lump of matter in which it resides, out of which it acts, the atom; more rigorous minds at last learned to get along without this 'residuum of earth', and perhaps we and the logicians as well will one day accustom ourselves to getting along without that little 'it' (which is what the honest old 'I' has evaporated into).

21

Ludwig Wittgenstein, from
Tractatus Logico-Philosophicus

The Viennese philosopher Ludwig Wittgenstein (1889–1951) was
perhaps one of the most influential thinkers of the twentieth century, especially in the areas of philosophy of language, philosophy
of mind, and philosophy of mathematics. He is also known for his
enigmatic style. The short passage included below, taken from his
book *Tractatus Logico-Philosophicus*, provides evidence for this reputation.

At the heart of the passage lies an analogy between the "metaphysical" or "philosophical" subject and the eye. Just as the eye
does not fall within the visual field but instead determines its
bounds, Wittgenstein offers that the metaphysical subject cannot
be found within the world but serves to limit it. Moreover, nothing
that falls within the scope of the metaphysical subject implies that it
is within those bounds, just as no object falling within the visual
field by itself indicates that it is seen by someone. The "truth" in
solipsism, or the view that oneself is the only existing thing, therefore amounts to the way in which I (the metaphysical subject) am
the world that I perceive, the world constituted by what I touch,
taste, smell, hear, and see.

What can we say about this metaphysical subject? Wittgenstein's
picture of the self or subject shares similarities with Hume's in that
he claims that the metaphysical subject exists apart from the world
and cannot be found within it. While it's true, for example, that I
often see my own limbs and nose as I go about my daily business,
I need not; I could imagine myself lost in a dark room where I
literally couldn't see my hand in front of my face, yet in such a

situation I as a subject would not disappear. Wittgenstein's account also sounds similar to Kant in that the philosophical subject serves as the limit or form of my experience and, accordingly, my world. Wittgenstein also seems to suggest, much like Kant, that this subject resists our attempts to acquire knowledge of it, since it does not fall within our world as a possible object of knowledge. Hence, Wittgenstein offers little as to the nature of the metaphysical subject, and the compelling analogy he gives of the eye and the visual field holds little promise of our discovering it.

5.6   *The limits of my language* mean the limits of my world.

5.61   Logic pervades the world: the limits of the world are also its limits.

So we cannot say in logic, 'The world has this in it, and this, but not that.'

For that would appear to presuppose that we were excluding certain possibilities, and this cannot be the case, since it would require that logic should go beyond the limits of the world; for only in that way could it view those limits from the other side as well.

We cannot think what we cannot think; so what we cannot think we cannot *say* either.

5.62   This remark provides the key to the problem, how much truth there is in solipsism.

For what the solipsist *means* is quite correct; only it cannot be *said*, but makes itself manifest.

The world is *my* world: this is manifest in the fact that the limits of *language* (of that language which alone I understand) mean the limits of *my* world.

5.621   The world and life are one.

5.63   I am my world. (The microcosm.)

5.631   There is no such thing as the subject that thinks or entertains ideas.

If I wrote a book called *The World as I found it*, I should have to include a report on my body, and should have to say which parts were subordinate to my will, and which were not, etc., this being a method of isolating the subject, or rather of showing that in an important sense there is no subject; for it alone could *not* be mentioned in that book.

5.632   The subject does not belong to the world: rather, it is a limit of the world.

5.633   Where *in* the world is a metaphysical subject to be found?

You will say that this is exactly like the case of the eye and the visual field. But really you do *not* see the eye.

And nothing *in the visual field* allows you to infer that it is seen by an eye.

5.6331   For the form of the visual field is surely not like this

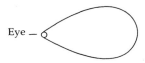

5.634   This is connected with the fact that no part of our experience is at the same time a priori.

Whatever we see could be other than it is.

Whatever we can describe at all could be other than it is.

There is no a priori order of things.

5.64   Here it can be seen that solipsism, when its implications are followed out strictly, coincides with pure realism. The self of solipsism shrinks to a point without extension, and there remains the reality co-ordinated with it.

5.641   Thus there really is a sense in which philosophy can talk about the self in a non-psychological way.

What brings the self into philosophy is the fact that 'the world is my world'.

The philosophical self is not the human being, not the human body, or the human soul, with which psychology deals, but rather the metaphysical subject, the limit of the world – not a part of it.

Religious Belief

22

Michel de Montaigne, from "Apology for Raymond Sebond"

Michel de Montaigne (1533–92) is known as a writer of essays; in fact, he created that literary form. His collection of more than 100 essays takes up a wide variety of topics; the longest, "Apology for Raymond Sebond", from which the text below is extracted, is a sympathetic presentation of skepticism, which he knew about from the classical texts that had recently become available in Europe. He lived in France during a time of religious conflict between Catholics and Protestants. He used skeptical arguments to defend, rather than undermine, religious faith.

In the "Apology" he asks "What can I know?" to which he answers: very little. In this unsystematic and diffuse discussion, he tries to undermine human pretensions to superiority, and to show that human reason is a rather weak reed and incapable, by itself, of founding religion or any other intellectual structure. The senses are deceptive, and, therefore, human knowledge lacks any reliable foundation. He anticipates Descartes in his skeptical employment of dreams and in his query about the interaction between mind and body. There is no criterion of truth. Man must put himself in God's hands if any understanding of the world is to be possible. Montaigne is a fideist who uses skeptical arguments to undermine reason and make way for faith.

The man who is presumptuous of his knowledge does not yet know what knowledge is. [...] Is it possible to imagine anything so ridiculous as that this miserable and puny creature, who is not even master of himself, exposed to the attacks of all things, should call himself master and emperor of the universe, the least part of which it is not in his power to know, much less to command? [...] Presumption is our natural and original malady. The most vulnerable and frail of all creatures is man, and at the same time the most arrogant. [...] Humility and submissiveness alone can make a good man. The knowledge of his duty should not be left to each man's judgment; it should be prescribed to him, not left to the choice of his reason. Otherwise, judging by the imbecility and infinite variety of our reasons and opinions, we would finally forge for ourselves duties that would set us to eating one another, as Epicurus says. [...] It is not by reasoning or by our understanding that we have received our religion; it is by external authority and command. [...]

The Pyrrhonians have kept themselves a wonderful advantage in combat, having rid themselves of the need to cover up. It does not matter to them that they are struck, provided they strike; and they do their work with everything. If they win, your proposition is lame; if you win, theirs is. If they lose, they confirm ignorance; if you lose, you confirm it. If they prove that nothing is known, well and good; if they do not know how to prove it, just as good. *So that, since equal reasons are found on both sides of the same subject, it may be the easier to suspend judgment on each side* [Cicero].

And they set store by the fact that they can find much more easily why a thing is false than that it is true; and what is not than what is; and what they do not believe than what they believe.

Their expressions are: "I establish nothing; it is no more thus than thus, or than neither way; I do not understand it; the appearances are equal on all sides; it is equally legitimate to speak for and against. "Nothing seems true, which may not seem false." Their sacramental word is ἐπέχω, that is to say, "I hold back, I do not budge." Those are their refrains, and others of similar substance. Their effect is a pure, complete, and very perfect postponement and suspension of judgment. They use their reason to inquire and debate, but not to conclude and choose. Whoever will imagine a perpetual confession of ignorance, a judgment without leaning or inclination, on any occasion whatever, he has a conception of Pyrrhonism.

I express this point of view as well as I can, because many find it difficult to conceive; and its authors themselves represent it rather obscurely and diversely.

As for the actions of life, they are of the common fashion in that. They lend and accommodate themselves to natural inclinations, to the impulsion and constraint of passions, to the constitutions of laws and customs, and to the tradition of the arts. *For God wished us not to know, but only to use, those things* [Cicero]. They let their common actions be guided by those things, without any taking sides or judgment. Which is why I cannot very well reconcile with this principle what they say of Pyrrho. They portray him as stupid and immobile, adopting a wild and unsociable way of life, waiting for carts to hit him, risking himself on precipices, refusing to conform to the laws. That is outdoing his doctrine. He did not want to make himself a stump or a stone; he wanted to make himself a living, thinking, reasoning man, enjoying all natural pleasures and comforts, employing and using all his bodily and spiritual faculties in regular and upright fashion. The fantastic, imaginary, false privileges that man has arrogated to himself, of regimenting, arranging, and fixing truth, he honestly renounced and gave up.

Moreover, there is no sect that is not constrained to permit its sage to conform in a number of things that are not understood, or perceived, or accepted, if he wants to live. And when he goes to sea, he follows this course, not knowing if it will be useful to him, and relies on the vessel being good, the pilot experienced, the season suitable – merely probable circumstances. He is bound to follow them and to let himself be swayed by appearances, provided that they show no express contrariness. He has a body, he has a soul; his senses impel him, his mind stirs him. Even though he does not discover in himself that peculiar and singular mark of the right to judge, and perceives that he must not pledge his consent, since there may be some falsehood resembling this truth, he does not fail to carry on the functions of his life fully and comfortably.

How many arts there are that profess to consist of conjecture more than of knowledge, that do not decide on the true and the false and merely follow what seems to be! There are, they say, both a true and a false, and there is in us the means to seek it, but not to test it by a touchstone. We are much better if we let ourselves be led without inquisitiveness in the way of the world. A soul guaranteed against prejudice is marvelously advanced toward tranquillity. People who judge and check their judges never submit to them as they ought. How much more docile and easily led, both by the laws of religion and by political laws, are the simple and incurious minds, than those minds that survey divine and human causes like pedagogues!

There is nothing in man's invention that has so much verisimilitude and usefulness. It presents man naked and empty, acknowledging his natural weakness, fit to receive from above some outside power; stripped of human knowledge, and all the more apt to lodge divine knowledge in himself, annihilating his judgment to make more room for faith; neither disbelieving nor setting up any doctrine against the common observances; humble, obedient, teachable, zealous; a sworn enemy of heresy, and consequently free from the vain and irreligious opinions introduced by the false sects. He is a blank tablet prepared to take from the finger of God such forms as he shall be pleased to engrave on it. The more we cast ourselves back on God and commit ourselves to him, and renounce ourselves, the better we are. "Receive things thankfully," says the Preacher, "in the aspect and taste that they are offered to thee, from day to day; the rest is beyond thy knowledge." *The Lord knoweth the thoughts of man, that they are vanity* [Psalms].

We see indeed that the finger moves, and that the foot moves; that some parts stir of themselves without our leave, and that others we move by our command; that a certain apprehension engenders a blush, a certain other, pallor. One imagination acts only on the spleen, another on the brain; one makes us laugh, another weep. Another paralyzes and stuns all our senses, and arrests the movement of our limbs. At one object the stomach rises; at another, a certain part lower down.

But how a spiritual impression can cut such a swath in a massive and solid object, and the nature of the relation and connection between these wonderful springs of action, no man has ever known. [...]

The first consideration that I offer on the subject of the senses is that I have my doubts whether man is provided with all the senses of nature. I see many animals that live a complete and perfect life, some without sight, others without hearing; who knows whether we too do not still lack one, two, three, or many other senses? For if any one is lacking, our reason cannot discover its absence. It is the privilege of the senses to be the extreme limit of our perception. [...]

Those who have compared our life to a dream were perhaps more right than they thought. When we dream, our soul lives, acts, exercises all her faculties, neither more nor less than when she is awake; but if more loosely and obscurely, still surely not so much so that the difference is as between night and bright daylight; rather as between night and shade. There she sleeps, here she slumbers: more and less. It is always darkness, and Cimmerian darkness.

Sleeping we are awake, and waking asleep. I do not see so clearly in sleep; but my wakefulness I never find pure and cloudless enough. Moreover sleep in its depth sometimes puts dreams to sleep. But our wakefulness is never so awake as to purge and properly dissipate reveries, which are the dreams of the waking, and worse than dreams.

Since our reason and our soul accept the fancies and opinions which arise in it while sleeping, and authorize the actions of our dreams with the same approbation as they do those of the day, why do we not consider the possibility that our thinking, our acting, may be another sort of dreaming, and our waking another kind of sleep? [...]

These humors which thus change the operations of our sight, how do we know but that they predominate in animals and are the ordinary thing with them? For we see some that have yellow eyes like our sufferers from jaundice, others that have them red and bloodshot. It is probable that to them the color of objects appears different than to us. Which of the two is the true judgment? For it is not said that the essence of things is referred to man alone. Hardness, whiteness, depth, and bitterness concern the service and knowledge of the animals as well as ours; nature has given to them the use of these as well as to us. [...]

To judge the action of the senses, then, we should first of all be in agreement with the animals, and second, among ourselves. Which we are not in the least; and we get into disputes at every turn because one man hears, sees, or tastes something differently from someone else; and we dispute about the diversity of the images that the senses bring us as much as about anything else. By the ordinary rule of nature, a child hears, sees, and tastes otherwise than a man of thirty, and he otherwise than a sexagenarian.

The senses are in some people more obscure and dim, in others more open and acute. We receive things in one way and another, according to what we are and what they seem to us. Now since our seeming is so uncertain and controversial, it is no longer a miracle if we are told that we can admit that snow appears white to us, but that we cannot be responsible for proving that it is so of its essence and in truth; and, with this starting point shaken, all the knowledge in the world necessarily goes by the board. [...]

Now, since our condition accommodates things to itself and transforms them according to itself, we no longer know what things are in truth; for nothing comes to us except falsified and altered by our senses. When the compass, the square, and the ruler are off, all the proportions drawn from them, all the buildings erected by their measure, are also necessarily imperfect and defective. The uncertainty of our senses makes everything they produce uncertain.[...]

To judge the appearances that we receive of objects, we would need a judicatory instrument; to verify this instrument, we need a demonstration; to verify the demonstration, an instrument: there we are in a circle.

Since the senses cannot decide our dispute, being themselves full of uncertainty, it must be reason that does so. No reason can be established without another reason: there we go retreating back to infinity.

Our conception is not itself applied to foreign objects, but is conceived through the mediation of the senses; and the senses do not comprehend the foreign object, but only their own impressions. And thus the conception and semblance we form is not of the object, but only of the impression and effect made on the sense; which impression and the object are different things. Wherefore whoever judges by appearances judges by something other than the object.

And as for saying that the impressions of the senses convey to the soul the quality of the foreign objects by resemblance, how can the soul and understanding make sure of this resemblance, having of itself no communication with foreign objects? Just as a man who does not know Socrates, seeing his portrait, cannot say that it resembles him.

Now if anyone should want to judge by appearances anyway, to judge by all appearances is impossible, for they clash with one another by their contradictions and discrepancies, as we see by experience. Shall some selected appearances rule the others? We shall have to verify this selection by another selection, the second by a third; and thus it will never be finished.

Finally, there is no existence that is constant, either of our being or of that of objects. And we, and our judgment, and all mortal things go on flowing and rolling unceasingly. Thus nothing certain can be established about one thing by another, both the judging and the judged being in continual change and motion.[...]

Nor can man raise himself above himself and humanity; for he can see only with his own eyes, and seize only with his own grasp.

He will rise, if God by exception lends him a hand; he will rise by abandoning and renouncing his own means, and letting himself be raised and uplifted by purely celestial means.

23

Blaise Pascal, from *Pensées*

The great French mathematician Blaise Pascal (1623–62) argues in the selection below that skepticism regarding our nature as created by God is unavoidable if reason is to be our guide. Skeptics can too easily engender uncertainty even as to whether we are awake or asleep and, accordingly, whether we are actually experiencing a world or merely dreaming. Conceding any certainty in matters of our true nature, Pascal asserts that we must silence reason and look to faith in order to know ourselves as we actually are.

Lacking any rational grounds for belief in Christianity, however, why should one accept it? How are we to know that God even exists? Pascal's answer to this question is that each of us is already involved in a wager as to the existence of God. We can place one of two bets: either we bet that God doesn't exist or we bet that he does. The prudent bet, Pascal offers, is to believe that God exists, for if he does, the reward is a life of eternal happiness; if he does not, the loss is but believing one falsehood. In contrast, wagering that he does not exist carries the possibility of losing an infinite amount of happiness and promises, at most, a reward of believing one truth. When facing a choice between an infinite and a finite result, the rational wager is clear: the infinite must be chosen, and hence, one must believe in God.

Even if it is the more prudent wager, how can I make myself believe in God in the face of doubt? Pascal suggests that we are creatures of habit, and as one follows the rituals of Christianity, eventually one cannot help but believe in its teachings. Moreover, followers of these teachings will embody a set of virtues such as honesty, humility, and sincerity – characteristics beneficial to others as well as themselves. Given all these benefits, the wager is clear and becomes even more so over time.

But perhaps the wager is not so clear, for Pascal is likewise betting on the truth of a number of crucial assumptions. He assumes that God rewards believers and punishes disbelievers, though the supreme being may in fact respect conviction to beliefs that risk the greatest loss. Indeed, perhaps a second assumption of Pascal's is false, and the divine judge we will face at the end of life is not a Christian God.

The strongest of the sceptics' arguments, to say nothing of minor points, is that we cannot be sure that these principles are true (faith and revelation apart) except through some natural intuition. Now this natural intuition affords no convincing proof that they are true. There is no certainty, apart from faith, as to whether man was created by a good God, an evil demon, or just by chance, and so it is a matter of doubt, depending on our origin, whether these innate principles are true, false or uncertain.

Moreover, no one can be sure, apart from faith, whether he is sleeping or waking, because when we are asleep we are just as firmly convinced that we are awake as we are now. As we often dream we are dreaming, piling up one dream on another, is it not possible that this half of our life is itself just a dream, on to which the others are grafted, and from which we shall awake when we die? That while it lasts we are as little in possession of the principles of truth and goodness as during normal sleep? All this passage of time, of life, all these different bodies which we feel, the different thoughts which stir us, may be no more than illusions like the passage of time and vain phantoms of our dreams. We think we are seeing space, shape, movement, we feel time pass, we measure it, in fact we behave just as we do when we are awake. As a result, since half our life is spent in sleep, on our own admission and despite appearances we have no idea of the truth because all our intuitions are simply illusions during that time. Who knows whether the other half of our lives, when we think we are awake, is not another sleep slightly different from the first, on to which our dreams are grafted as our sleep appears, and from which we awake when we think we are sleeping? And who can doubt that, if we dreamed in the company of others and our dreams happened to agree, which is common enough, and if we were alone when awake, we should think things had been turned upside-down?

These are the main points on each side, to say nothing of minor arguments, like those the sceptics direct against the influences of habit, education, local customs, and so on, which the slightest puff of scepticism overturns, though they convince the majority of ordinary people, who have only this vain basis for their dogmas. You have only to look at their books; if you are not sufficiently persuaded you soon will be, perhaps too much so.

I pause at the dogmatists' only strong point, which is that we cannot doubt natural principles if we speak sincerely and in all good faith.

To which the sceptics reply, in a word, that uncertainty as to our origin entails uncertainty as to our nature. The dogmatists have been trying to answer that ever since the world began.

(Anyone wanting ampler information about scepticism should look at their books; he will soon be persuaded, perhaps too much so.)

This means open war between men, in which everyone is obliged to take sides, either with the dogmatists or with the sceptics, because anyone who imagines he can stay neutral is a sceptic *par excellence*. This neutrality is the essence of their clique. Anyone who is not against them is their staunch supporter, and that is where their advantage appears. They are not even for themselves; they are neutral, indifferent, suspending judgment on everything, including themselves.

What then is man to do in this state of affairs? Is he to doubt everything, to doubt whether he is awake, whether he is being pinched or burned? Is he to doubt whether he is doubting, to doubt whether he exists?

No one can go that far, and I maintain that a perfectly genuine sceptic has never existed. Nature backs up helpless reason and stops it going so wildly astray.

Is he, on the other hand, to say that he is the certain possessor of truth, when at the slightest pressure he fails to prove his claim and is compelled to loose his grasp?

What sort of freak then is man! How novel, how monstrous, how chaotic, how paradoxical, how prodigious! Judge of all things, feeble earthworm, repository of truth, sink of doubt and error, glory and refuse of the universe!

Who will unravel such a tangle? This is certainly beyond dogmatism and scepticism, beyond all human philosophy. Man transcends man. Let us then concede to the sceptics what they have so often proclaimed, that truth lies beyond our scope and is an unattainable quarry, that it is no earthly denizen, but at home in heaven, lying in the lap of God, to be known only in so far as it pleases him to reveal it. Let us learn our true nature from the uncreated and incarnate truth.

If we seek truth through reason we cannot avoid one of these three sects. You cannot be a sceptic or a Platonist without stifling nature, you cannot be a dogmatist without turning your back on reason.

Nature confounds the sceptics and Platonists, and reason confounds the dogmatists. What then will become of you, man, seeking to discover your true condition through natural reason? You cannot avoid one of these three sects nor survive in any of them.

Know then, proud man, what a paradox you are to yourself. Be humble, impotent reason! Be silent, feeble nature! Learn that man infinitely transcends man, hear from your master your true condition, which is unknown to you.

Listen to God.

Is it not as clear as day that man's condition is dual? The point is that if man had never been corrupted, he would, in his innocence, confidently enjoy both truth and felicity, and, if man had never been anything but corrupt, he would have no idea either of truth or bliss. But unhappy as we are (and we should be less so if there were no element of greatness in our condition) we have an idea of happiness but we cannot attain it. We perceive an image of the truth and possess nothing but falsehood, being equally incapable of absolute ignorance and certain knowledge; so obvious is it that we once enjoyed a degree of perfection from which we have unhappily fallen.

Let us then conceive that man's condition is dual. Let us conceive that man infinitely transcends man, and that without the aid of faith he would remain inconceivable to himself, for who cannot see that unless we realize the duality of human nature we remain invincibly ignorant of the truth about ourselves?

It is, however, an astounding thing that the mystery furthest from our ken, that of the transmission of sin, should be something without which we can have no knowledge of ourselves.

Without doubt nothing is more shocking to our reason than to say that the sin of the first man has implicated in its guilt men so far from the original sin that they seem incapable of sharing it. This flow of guilt does not seem merely impossible to us, but indeed most unjust. What could be more contrary to the rules of our miserable justice than the eternal damnation of a child, incapable of will, for an act in which he seems to have so little part that it was actually committed 6,000 years before he existed? Certainly nothing jolts us more rudely than this doctrine, and yet, but for this mystery, the most incomprehensible of all, we remain incomprehensible to ourselves. The knot of our condition was twisted and turned in that abyss, so that it is harder to conceive of man without this mystery than for man to conceive of it himself.

This shows that God, in his desire to make the difficulties of our existence unintelligible to us, hid the knot so high, or more precisely, so low, that we were quite unable to reach it. Consequently it is not through the proud activity of our reason but through its simple submission that we can really know ourselves.

These fundamental facts, solidly established on the inviolable authority of religion, teach us that there are in faith two equally constant truths. One is that man in the state of his creation, or in the state of grace, is exalted above the whole of nature, made like unto God and sharing in his divinity. The other is that in the state of corruption and sin he has fallen from that first state and has become like the beasts. These two propositions are equally firm and certain.

Scripture openly declares this when it says in certain places: *My delights were with the sons of men – I will pour out my spirit upon all flesh – Ye are gods,* while saying in others: *All flesh is grass – Man is like the beasts that perish – I said in my heart concerning the estate of the sons of men.*

Whence it is clearly evident that man through grace is made like unto God and shares his divinity, and without grace he is treated like the beasts of the field. [...]   (434)

The Wager

Infinity – nothing. Our soul is cast into the body where it finds number, time, dimensions; it reasons about these things and calls them natural, or necessary, and can believe nothing else.

Unity added to infinity does not increase it at all, any more than a foot added to an infinite measurement: the finite is annihilated in the presence of the infinite and becomes pure nothingness. So it is with our mind before God, with our justice before divine justice. There is not so great a disproportion between our justice and God's as between unity and infinity.

God's justice must be as vast as his mercy. Now his justice towards the damned is less vast and ought to be less startling to us than his mercy towards the elect.

We know that the infinite exists without knowing its nature, just as we know that it is untrue that numbers are finite. Thus it is true that there is an infinite number, but we do not know what it is. It is untrue that it is even, untrue that it is odd, for by adding a unit it does not change its nature. Yet it is a number, and every number is even or odd. (It is true that this applies to every finite number.)

Therefore we may well know that God exists without knowing what he is.

Is there no substantial truth, seeing that there are so many true things which are not truth itself?

Thus we know the existence and nature of the finite because we too are finite and extended in space.

We know the existence of the infinite without knowing its nature, because it too has extension but unlike us no limits.

But we do not know either the existence or the nature of God, because he has neither extension nor limits.

But by faith we know his existence, through glory we shall know his nature.

Now I have already proved that it is quite possible to know that something exists without knowing its nature.

Let us now speak according to our natural lights.

If there is a God, he is infinitely beyond our comprehension, since, being indivisible and without limits, he bears no relation to us. We are therefore incapable of knowing either what he is or whether he is. That being so, who would dare to attempt an answer to the question? Certainly not we, who bear no relation to him.

Who then will condemn Christians for being unable to give rational grounds for their belief, professing as they do a religion for which they cannot give rational grounds? They declare that it is a folly, *stultitiam*, in expounding it to the world, and then you complain that they do not prove it. If they did prove it they would not be keeping their word. It is by being without proof that they show they are not without sense. 'Yes, but although that excuses those who offer their religion as such, and absolves them from the criticism of producing it without rational grounds, it does not absolve those who accept it.' Let us then examine this point, and let us say: 'Either God is or he is not.' But to which view shall we be inclined? Reason cannot decide this question. Infinite chaos separates us. At the far end of this infinite distance a coin is being spun which will come down heads or tails. How will you wager? Reason cannot make you choose either, reason cannot prove either wrong.

Do not then condemn as wrong those who have made a choice, for you know nothing about it. 'No, but I will condemn them not for having made this particular choice, but any choice, for, although the one who calls heads and the other one are equally at fault, the fact is that they are both at fault: the right thing is not to wager at all.'

Yes, but you must wager. There is no choice, you are already committed. Which will you choose then? Let us see: since a choice must be made, let us see which offers you the least interest. You have two things to lose: the true and the good; and two things to stake: your reason and your will, your knowledge and your happiness; and your nature has two things to avoid: error and wretchedness. Since you must necessarily choose, your reason is no more affronted by choosing one rather than the other. That is one point cleared up. But your happiness? Let us weigh up the gain and the loss involved in calling heads that God exists. Let us assess the two cases: if you win you win everything, if you lose you lose nothing. Do not hesitate then; wager that he does exist. 'That is wonderful. Yes, I must wager, but perhaps I am wagering too much.' Let us see: since there is an equal chance of gain and loss, if you stood to win only two lives for one you could still wager, but supposing you stood to win three?

You would have to play (since you must necessarily play) and it would be unwise of you, once you are obliged to play, not to risk your life in order to win three lives at a game in which there is an equal chance of losing and winning. But there is an eternity of life and happiness. That being so, even though there were an infinite number of chances, of which only one were in your favour, you would still be right to wager one in order to win two; and you would be acting wrongly, being obliged to play, in refusing to stake one life against three in a game, where out of an infinite number of chances there is one in your favour, if there were an infinity of infinitely happy life to be won. But here there is an infinity of infinitely happy life to be won, one chance of winning against a finite number of chances of losing, and what you are staking is finite. That leaves no choice; wherever there is infinity, and where there are not infinite chances of losing against that of winning, there is no room for hesitation, you must give everything. And thus, since you are obliged to play, you must be renouncing reason if you hoard your life rather than risk it for an infinite gain, just as likely to occur as a loss amounting to nothing.

For it is no good saying that it is uncertain whether you will win, that it is certain that you are taking a risk, and that the infinite distance between the certainty of what you are risking and the uncertainty of what you may gain makes the finite good you are certainly risking equal to the infinite good that you are not certain to gain. This is not the case. Every gambler takes a certain risk for an uncertain gain, and yet he is taking a certain finite risk for an uncertain finite gain without sinning against reason. Here there is no infinite distance between the certain risk and the uncertain gain: that is not true. There is, indeed, an infinite distance between the certainty of winning and the certainty of losing, but the proportion between the uncertainty of winning and the certainty of what is being risked is in proportion to the chances of winning or losing. And hence if there are as many chances on one side as on the other you are playing for even odds. And in that case the certainty of what you are risking is equal to the uncertainty of what you may win; it is by no means infinitely distant from it. Thus our argument carries infinite weight, when the stakes are finite in a game where there are even chances of winning and losing and an infinite prize to be won.

This is conclusive and if men are capable of any truth this is it.

'I confess, I admit it, but is there really no way of seeing what the cards are?' – 'Yes. Scripture and the rest, etc.' – 'Yes, but my hands are tied and my lips are sealed; I am being forced to wager and I am not free; I am being held fast and I am so made that I cannot believe. What do you want me to do then?' – 'That is true, but at least get it into your head that, if you are unable to believe, it is because of your passions, since reason impels you to believe and yet you cannot do so. Concentrate then not on convincing yourself by multiplying proofs of God's existence but by diminishing your passions. You want to find faith and you do not know the road. You want to be cured of unbelief and you ask for the remedy: learn from those who were once bound like you and who now wager all they have. These are people who know the road you wish to follow, who have been cured of the affliction of which you wish to be cured: follow the way by which they began. They behaved just as if they did believe, taking holy water, having masses said, and so on. That will make you believe quite naturally, and will make you more docile.'[1] – 'But that is what I am afraid of.' – 'But why? What have you to lose? But to show you that this is the way, the fact is that this diminishes the passions which are your great obstacles....'

End of this address.

'Now what harm will come to you from choosing this course? You will be faithful, honest, humble, grateful, full of good works, a sincere, true friend.... It is true you will not enjoy noxious pleasures, glory and good living, but will you not have others?

'I tell you that you will gain even in this life, and that at every step you take along this road you will see that your gain is so certain and your risk so negligible that in the end you will realize that you have wagered on something certain and infinite for which you have paid nothing.'

'How these words fill me with rapture and delight!'

'If my words please you and seem cogent, you must know that they come from a man who went down upon his knees before and after to pray this infinite and indivisible being, to whom he submits his own, that he might bring your being also to submit to him for your own good and for his glory: and that strength might thus be reconciled with lowliness.'

(233)

Custom is our nature. Anyone who grows accustomed to faith believes it, and can no longer help fearing hell, and believes nothing else.

Anyone accustomed to believe that the king is to be feared....

Who then can doubt that our soul, being accustomed to see number, space, movement, believes in this and nothing else? (419)

'Do you believe that it is impossible for God to be infinite and indivisible?' – 'Yes.' – 'Very well, I will show you something infinite and indivisible: it is a point moving everywhere at an infinite speed.

'For it is one and the same everywhere and wholly present in every place. From this natural phenomenon which previously seemed impossible to you you should realize that there may be others which you do not yet know. Do not conclude from your apprenticeship that there is nothing left for you to learn, but that you still have an infinite amount to learn.'

(231)

It is untrue that we are worthy to be loved by others. It is unfair that we should want such a thing. If we were born reasonable and impartial, with a knowledge of ourselves and others, we should not give our wills this bias. However, we are born with it, and so we are born unfair.

For everything tends towards itself: this is contrary to all order.

The tendency should be towards the general, and the bias towards self is the beginning of all disorder, in war, politics, economics, in man's individual body.

The will is therefore depraved. If the members of natural and civil communities tend to the good of the whole body, the communities themselves should tend towards another more general body of which they are members. We should therefore tend towards the general. Thus we are born unfair and depraved. (477)

No religion except our own has taught that man is born sinful, no philosophical sect has said so, so none has told the truth.

No sect and no religion has always existed on earth except Christianity.

(606)

We are greatly indebted to those who point out our faults, for they mortify us, they teach us that we have incurred contempt, but they do not prevent us incurring it in the future, for we have plenty of other faults to deserve it. They prepare us for the exercise of correcting and eradicating a given fault.

(535)

The heart has its reasons of which reason knows nothing: we know this in countless ways.

I say that it is natural for the heart to love the universal being or itself, according to its allegiance, and it hardens itself against either as it chooses. You have rejected one and kept the other. Is it reason that makes you love yourself?

(277)

It is the heart which perceives God and not the reason. That is what faith is: God perceived by the heart, not by the reason.

(278)

The only knowledge which is contrary alike to common sense and human nature is the only one always to have existed among men. (604)

Only Christianity makes men both happy and lovable: the code of the gentleman does not allow you to be both happy and lovable.

(542)

Note

1   *abêtira*. That is, the unbeliever will act unthinkingly and mechanically, and in this become more like the beasts, from whom man was differentiated, according to contemporary philosophy, by his faculty of reason.

24

David Hume, from "Of Miracles"

In the chapter "Of Miracles" from his *Enquiry*, David Hume (1711–76), perhaps one of religion's most staunch critics, attempts to undermine the foundation of Christianity by calling into question its evidence. Hume's strategy is to show that we will always have reason to believe that reports of miraculous events are false.

Hume begins by locating Christianity's authority in the recorded testimony of its apostles who served as witnesses to a set of miracles. If these miracles turned out not to have happened, Christianity loses any claim to authority, becoming mere delusion and superstition. Are we to believe these witnesses? Miracles are defined as events that violate the laws of nature. Given that testimony is reliable only to the degree to which what it reports is probable, any report of a violation of a natural law will be considerably less probable than competing explanations that square with common regularities. The wise person, Hume offers, proportions her belief to the evidence, and even the authority of a person known to be trustworthy does not suffice to counterbalance the great improbability of the miraculous. Hence, we have no reason to believe that these miracles took place – indeed, we should believe the opposite.

Hume does concede that his argument leaves room for testimony of miracles to amount to a proof of their happening, if, for example, a quite large number of reliable witnesses were to report similarly on an event thereby making it more probable than the expected constant conjunction between events captured in natural laws. This possibility, Hume argues, is nevertheless itself highly improbable, for there has never been a sufficient number of witnesses to a particular miracle to warrant believing it as probably true.

Moreover, Hume offers that the reports of supernatural occurrences issue most frequently from lesser developed cultures or from a lesser developed time of one's own culture, and we are left wondering why we are not fortunate to witness miracles in our own time. Should any doubt remain, Hume asserts that the world's many religions offer competing and contradictory accounts of miracles that likewise claim to prove each as the true and authoritative faith. They cannot all be accurate; however, we have no way of adjudicating between them beyond the tendentious testimony of their scriptures.

Although Hume's arguments are not decisive against Christianity – and indeed any religion that places stock in the miracles recorded in its scriptures – he has certainly issued a challenge that will not be so easily met.

Part I

[...] I flatter myself, that I have discovered an argument of a like nature, which, if just, will, with the wise and learned, be an everlasting check to all kinds of superstitious delusion, and consequently, will be useful as long as the world endures. For so long, I presume, will the accounts of miracles and prodigies be found in all history, sacred and profane.

Though experience be our only guide in reasoning concerning matters of fact; it must be acknowledged, that this guide is not altogether infallible, but in some cases is apt to lead us into errors. One, who in our climate, should expect better weather in any week of June than in one of December, would reason justly, and conformably to experience; but it is certain, that he may happen, in the event, to find himself mistaken. However, we may observe, that, in such a case, he would have no cause to complain of experience; because it commonly informs us beforehand of the uncertainty, by that contrariety of events, which we may learn from a diligent observation. All effects follow not with like certainty from their supposed causes. Some events are found, in all countries and all ages, to have been constantly conjoined together: Others are found to have been more variable, and sometimes to disappoint our expectations; so that, in our reasonings concerning matter of fact, there are all imaginable degrees of assurance, from the highest certainty to the lowest species of moral evidence.

A wise man, therefore, proportions his belief to the evidence. In such conclusions as are founded on an infallible experience, he expects the event with the last degree of assurance, and regards his past experience as a full *proof* of the future existence of that event. In other cases, he proceeds with more caution: He weighs the opposite experiments: He considers which side is supported by the greater number of experiments: to that side he inclines, with doubt and hesitation; and when at last he fixes his judgement, the evidence exceeds not what we properly call *probability*. All probability, then, supposes an opposition of experiments and observations, where the one side is found to overbalance the other, and to produce a degree of evidence, proportioned to the superiority. A hundred instances or experiments on one side, and fifty on another, afford a doubtful expectation of any event; though a hundred uniform experiments, with only one that is contradictory, reasonably beget a pretty strong degree of assurance. In all cases, we must balance the opposite experiments, where they are opposite, and deduct the smaller number from the greater, in order to know the exact force of the superior evidence.

To apply these principles to a particular instance; we may observe, that there is no species of reasoning more common, more useful, and even necessary to human life, than that which is derived from the testimony of men, and the reports of eye-witnesses and spectators. This species of reasoning, perhaps, one may deny to be founded on the relation of cause and effect. I shall not dispute about a word. It will be sufficient to observe that our assurance in any argument of this kind is derived from no other principle than our observation of the veracity of human testimony, and of the usual conformity of facts to the reports of witnesses. It being a general maxim, that no objects have any discoverable connexion together, and that all the inferences, which we can draw from one to another, are founded merely on our experience of their constant and regular conjunction; it is evident, that we ought not to make an exception to this maxim in favour of human testimony, whose connexion with any event seems, in itself, as little necessary as any other. Were not the memory tenacious to a certain degree; had not men commonly an inclination to truth and a principle of probity; were they not sensible to shame, when detected in a falsehood: Were not these, I say, discovered by *experience* to be qualities, inherent in human nature, we should never repose the least confidence in human testimony. A man delirious, or noted for falsehood and villany, has no manner of authority with us.

And as the evidence, derived from witnesses and human testimony, is founded on past experience, so it varies with the experience, and is regarded either as a *proof* or a *probability*, according as the conjunction between any particular kind of report and any kind of object has been found to be constant or variable. There are a number of circumstances to be taken into consideration in all judgements of this kind; and the ultimate standard, by which we determine all disputes, that may arise concerning them, is always derived from experience and observation. Where this experience is not entirely uniform on any side, it is attended with an unavoidable contrariety in our judgements, and with the same opposition and mutual destruction of argument as in every other kind of evidence. We frequently hesitate concerning the reports of others. We balance the opposite circumstances, which cause any doubt or uncertainty; and when we discover a superiority on any side, we incline to it; but still with a diminution of assurance, in proportion to the force of its antagonist.

This contrariety of evidence, in the present case, may be derived from several different causes; from the opposition of contrary testimony; from the character or number of the witnesses; from the manner of their delivering their testimony; or from the union of all these circumstances. We entertain a suspicion concerning any matter of fact, when the witnesses contradict each other; when they are but few, or of a doubtful character; when they have an interest in what they affirm; when they deliver their testimony with hesitation, or on the contrary, with too violent asseverations. There are many other particulars of the same kind, which may diminish or destroy the force of any argument, derived from human testimony.

Suppose, for instance, that the fact, which the testimony endeavours to establish, partakes of the extraordinary and the marvellous; in that case, the evidence, resulting from the testimony, admits of a diminution, greater or less, in proportion as the fact is more or less unusual. The reason why we place any credit in witnesses and historians, is not derived from any *connexion*, which we perceive *a priori*, between testimony and reality, but because we are accustomed to find a conformity between them. But when the fact attested is such a one as has seldom fallen under our observation, here is a contest of two opposite experiences; of which the one destroys the other, as far as its force goes, and the superior can only operate on the mind by the force, which remains. The very same principle of experience, which gives us a certain degree of assurance in the testimony of witnesses, gives us also, in this case, another degree of assurance against the fact, which they endeavour to establish; from which contradiction there necessarily arises a counterpoize, and mutual destruction of belief and authority.

I should not believe such a story were it told me by Cato, was a proverbial saying in Rome, even during the lifetime of that philosophical patriot.[1] The incredibility of a fact, it was allowed, might invalidate so great an authority.

The Indian prince, who refused to believe the first relations concerning the effects of frost, reasoned justly; and it naturally required very strong testimony to engage his assent to facts, that arose from a state of nature, with which he was unacquainted, and which bore so little analogy to those events, of which he had had constant and uniform experience. Though they were not contrary to his experience, they were not conformable to it.[2]

But in order to encrease the probability against the testimony of witnesses, let us suppose, that the fact, which they affirm, instead of being only marvellous, is really miraculous; and suppose also, that the testimony considered apart and in itself, amounts to an entire proof; in that case, there is proof against proof, of which the strongest must prevail, but still with a diminution of its force, in proportion to that of its antagonist.

A miracle is a violation of the laws of nature; and as a firm and unalterable experience has established these laws, the proof against a miracle, from the very nature of the fact, is as entire as any argument from experience can possibly be imagined. Why is it more than probable, that all men must die; that lead cannot, of itself, remain suspended in the air; that fire consumes wood, and is extinguished by water; unless it be, that these events are found agreeable to the laws of nature, and there is required a violation of these laws, or in other words, a miracle to prevent them? Nothing is esteemed a miracle, if it ever happen in the common course of nature. It is no miracle that a man, seemingly in good health, should die on a sudden: because such a kind of death, though more unusual than any other, has yet been frequently observed to happen. But it is a miracle, that a dead man should come to life; because that has never been observed in any age or country. There must, therefore, be a uniform experience against every miraculous event, otherwise the event would not merit that appellation. And as a uniform experience amounts to a proof, there is here a direct and full *proof*, from the nature of the fact, against the existence of any miracle; nor can such a proof be destroyed, or the miracle rendered credible, but by an opposite proof, which is superior.[3]

The plain consequence is (and it is a general maxim worthy of our attention), 'That no testimony is sufficient to establish a miracle, unless the testimony be of such a kind, that its falsehood would be more miraculous, than the fact, which it endeavours to establish; and even in that case there is a mutual destruction of arguments, and the superior only gives us an assurance suitable to that degree of force, which remains, after deducting the inferior.' When anyone tells me, that he saw a dead man restored to life, I immediately consider with myself, whether it be more probable, that this person should either deceive or be deceived, or that the fact, which he relates, should really have happened. I weigh the one miracle against the other; and according to the superiority, which I discover, I pronounce my decision, and always reject the greater miracle. If the falsehood of his testimony would be more miraculous, than the event which he relates; then, and not till then, can he pretend to command my belief or opinion.

Part II

In the foregoing reasoning we have supposed, that the testimony, upon which a miracle is founded, may possibly amount to an entire proof, and that the falsehood of that testimony would be a real prodigy: But it is easy to shew, that we have been a great deal too liberal in our concession, and that there never was a miraculous event established on so full an evidence.

For *first*, there is not to be found, in all history, any miracle attested by a sufficient number of men, of such unquestioned good-sense, education, and learning, as to secure us against all delusion in themselves; of such undoubted integrity, as to place them beyond all suspicion of any design to deceive others; of such credit and reputation in the eyes of mankind, as to have a great deal to lose in case of their being detected in any falsehood; and at the same time, attesting facts performed in such a public manner and in so celebrated a part of the world, as to render the detection unavoidable: All which circumstances are requisite to give us a full assurance in the testimony of men.

Secondly. We may observe in human nature a principle which, if strictly examined, will be found to diminish extremely the assurance, which we might, from human testimony, have, in any kind of prodigy. The maxim, by which we commonly conduct ourselves in our reasonings, is, that the objects, of which we have no experience, resemble those, of which we have; that what we have found to be most usual is always most probable; and that where there is an opposition of arguments, we ought to give the preference to such as are founded on the greatest number of past observations. But though, in proceeding by this rule, we readily reject any fact which is unusual and incredible in an ordinary degree; yet in advancing farther, the mind observes not always the same rule; but when anything is affirmed utterly absurd and miraculous, it rather the more readily admits of such a fact, upon account of that very circumstance, which ought to destroy all its authority. The passion of *surprise* and *wonder*, arising from miracles, being an agreeable emotion, gives a sensible tendency towards the belief of those events, from which it is derived. And this goes so far, that even those who cannot enjoy this pleasure immediately, nor can believe those miraculous events, of which they are informed, yet love to partake of the satisfaction at second-hand or by rebound, and place a pride and delight in exciting the admiration of others.

With what greediness are the miraculous accounts of travellers received, their descriptions of sea and land monsters, their relations of wonderful adventures, strange men, and uncouth manners? But if the spirit of religion join itself to the love of wonder, there is an end of common sense; and human testimony, in these circumstances, loses all pretensions to authority. A religionist may be an enthusiast, and imagine he sees what has no reality: he may know his narrative to be false, and yet persevere in it, with the best intentions in the world, for the sake of promoting so holy a cause: or even where this delusion has not place, vanity, excited by so strong a temptation, operates on him more powerfully than on the rest of mankind in any other circumstances; and self-interest with equal force. His auditors may not have, and commonly have not, sufficient judgement to canvass his evidence: what judgement they have, they renounce by principle, in these sublime and mysterious subjects: or if they were ever so willing to employ it, passion and a heated imagination disturb the regularity of its operations. Their credulity increases his impudence: and his impudence overpowers their credulity.

Eloquence, when at its highest pitch, leaves little room for reason or reflection; but addressing itself entirely to the fancy or the affections, captivates the willing hearers, and subdues their understanding. Happily, this pitch it seldom attains. But what a Tully or a Demosthenes could scarcely effect over a Roman or Athenian audience, every *Capuchin*, every itinerant or stationary teacher can perform over the generality of mankind, and in a higher degree, by touching such gross and vulgar passions.

The many instances of forged miracles, and prophecies, and supernatural events, which, in all ages, have either been detected by contrary evidence, or which detect themselves by their absurdity, prove sufficiently the strong propensity of mankind to the extraordinary and the marvellous, and ought reasonably to beget a suspicion against all relations of this kind. This is our natural way of thinking, even with regard to the most common and most credible events. For instance: There is no kind of report which rises so easily, and spreads so quickly, especially in country places and provincial towns, as those concerning marriages; insomuch that two young persons of equal condition never see each other twice, but the whole neighbourhood immediately join them together. The pleasure of telling a piece of news so interesting, of propagating it, and of being the first reporters of it, spreads the intelligence. And this is so well known, that no man of sense gives attention to these reports, till he find them confirmed by some greater evidence. Do not the same passions, and others still stronger, incline the generality of mankind to believe and report, with the greatest vehemence and assurance, all religious miracles?

Thirdly. It forms a strong presumption against all supernatural and miraculous relations, that they are observed chiefly to abound among ignorant and barbarous nations; or if a civilized people has ever given admission to any of them, that people will be found to have received them from ignorant and barbarous ancestors, who transmitted them with that inviolable sanction and authority, which always attend received opinions. When we peruse the first histories of all nations, we are apt to imagine ourselves transported into some new world; where the whole frame of nature is disjointed, and every element performs its operations in a different manner, from what it does at present. Battles, revolutions, pestilence, famine and death, are never the effect of those natural causes, which we experience. Prodigies, omens, oracles, judgements, quite obscure the few natural events, that are intermingled with them. But as the former grow thinner every page, in proportion as we advance nearer the enlightened ages, we soon learn, that there is nothing mysterious or supernatural in the case, but that all proceeds from the usual propensity of mankind towards the marvellous, and that, though this inclination may at intervals receive a check from sense and learning, it can never be thoroughly extirpated from human nature.

It is strange, a judicious reader is apt to say, upon the perusal of these wonderful historians, *that such prodigious events never happen in our days.* But it is nothing strange, I hope, that men should lie in all ages. You must surely have seen instances enough of that frailty. You have yourself heard many such marvellous relations started, which, being treated with scorn by all the wise and judicious, have at last been abandoned even by the vulgar. Be assured, that those renowned lies, which have spread and flourished to such a monstrous height, arose from like beginnings; but being sown in a more proper soil, shot up at last into prodigies almost equal to those which they relate. [...]

I may add as a *fourth* reason, which diminishes the authority of prodigies, that there is no testimony for any, even those which have not been expressly detected, that is not opposed by an infinite number of witnesses; so that not only the miracle destroys the credit of testimony, but the testimony destroys itself. To make this the better understood, let us consider, that, in matters of religion, whatever is different is contrary; and that it is impossible the religions of ancient Rome, of Turkey, of Siam, and of China should, all of them, be established on any solid foundation. Every miracle, therefore, pretended to have been wrought in any of these religions (and all of them abound in miracles), as its direct scope is to establish the particular system to which it is attributed; so has it the same force, though more indirectly, to overthrow every other system. In destroying a rival system, it likewise destroys the credit of those miracles, on which that system was established; so that all the prodigies of different religions are to be regarded as contrary facts, and the evidences of these prodigies, whether weak or strong, as opposite to each other. According to this method of reasoning, when we believe any miracle of Mahomet or his successors, we have for our warrant the testimony of a few barbarous Arabians: And on the other hand, we are to regard the authority of Titus Livius, Plutarch, Tacitus, and, in short, of all the authors and witnesses, Grecian, Chinese, and Roman Catholic, who have related any miracle in their particular religion; I say, we are to regard their testimony in the same light as if they had mentioned that Mahometan miracle, and had in express terms contradicted it, with the same certainty as they have for the miracle they relate. This argument may appear over subtile and refined; but is not in reality different from the reasoning of a judge, who supposes, that the credit of two witnesses, maintaining a crime against any one, is destroyed by the testimony of two others, who affirm him to have been two hundred leagues distant, at the same instant when the crime is said to have been committed.

One of the best attested miracles in all profane history, is that which Tacitus reports of Vespasian, who cured a blind man in Alexandria, by means of his spittle, and a lame man by the mere touch of his foot; in obedience to a vision of the god Serapis, who had enjoined them to have recourse to the Emperor, for these miraculous cures. The story may be seen in that fine historian;[4] where every circumstance seems to add weight to the testimony, and might be displayed at large with all the force of argument and eloquence, if any one were now concerned to enforce the evidence of that exploded and idolatrous superstition. The gravity, solidity, age, and probity of so great an emperor, who, through the whole course of his life, conversed in a familiar manner with his friends and courtiers, and never affected those extraordinary airs of divinity assumed by Alexander and Demetrius. The historian, a contemporary writer, noted for candour and veracity, and withal, the greatest and most penetrating genius, perhaps, of all antiquity; and so free from any tendency to credulity, that he even lies under the contrary imputation, of atheism and profaneness: The persons, from whose authority he related the miracle, of established character for judgement and veracity, as we may well presume; eye-witnesses of the fact, and confirming their testimony, after the Flavian family was despoiled of the empire, and could no longer give any reward, as the price of a lie. *Utrumque, qui interfuere, nunc quoque memorant, postquam nullum mendacio pretium.* To which if we add the public nature of the facts, as related, it will appear, that no evidence can well be supposed stronger for so gross and so palpable a falsehood. [...]

The wise lend a very academic faith to every report which favours the passion of the reporter; whether it magnifies his country, his family, or himself, or in any other way strikes in with his natural inclinations and propensities. But what greater temptation than to appear a missionary, a prophet, an ambassador from heaven? Who would not encounter many dangers and difficulties, in order to attain so sublime a character? Or if, by the help of vanity and a heated imagination, a man has first made a convert of himself, and entered seriously into the delusion; who ever scruples to make use of pious frauds, in support of so holy and meritorious a cause? [...]

How many stories of this nature have, in all ages, been detected and exploded in their infancy? How many more have been celebrated for a time, and have afterwards sunk into neglect and oblivion? Where such reports, therefore, fly about, the solution of the phenomenon is obvious; and we judge in conformity to regular experience and observation, when we account for it by the known and natural principles of credulity and delusion. And shall we, rather than have a recourse to so natural a solution, allow of a miraculous violation of the most established laws of nature?

I need not mention the difficulty of detecting a falsehood in any private or even public history, at the place, where it is said to happen; much more when the scene is removed to ever so small a distance. Even a court of judicature, with all the authority, accuracy, and judgement, which they can employ, find themselves often at a loss to distinguish between truth and falsehood in the most recent actions. But the matter never comes to any issue, if trusted to the common method of altercation and debate and flying rumours; especially when men's passions have taken part on either side.

In the infancy of new religions, the wise and learned commonly esteem the matter too inconsiderable to deserve their attention or regard. And when afterwards they would willingly detect the cheat, in order to undeceive the deluded multitude, the season is now past, and the records and witnesses, which might clear up the matter, have perished beyond recovery.

No means of detection remain, but those which must be drawn from the very testimony itself of the reporters: and these, though always sufficient with the judicious and knowing, are commonly too fine to fall under the comprehension of the vulgar.

Upon the whole, then, it appears, that no testimony for any kind of miracle has ever amounted to a probability, much less to a proof; and that, even supposing it amounted to a proof, it would be opposed by another proof; derived from the very nature of the fact, which it would endeavour to establish. It is experience only, which gives authority to human testimony; and it is the same experience, which assures us of the laws of nature. When, therefore, these two kinds of experience are contrary, we have nothing to do but substract the one from the other, and embrace an opinion, either on one side or the other, with that assurance which arises from the remainder. But according to the principle here explained, this substraction, with regard to all popular religions, amounts to an entire annihilation; and therefore we may establish it as a maxim, that no human testimony can have such force as to prove a miracle, and make it a just foundation for any such system of religion.

I beg the limitations here made may be remarked, when I say, that a miracle can never be proved, so as to be the foundation of a system of religion. For I own, that otherwise, there may possibly be miracles, or violations of the usual course of nature, of such a kind as to admit of proof from human testimony; though, perhaps, it will be impossible to find any such in all the records of history. Thus, suppose, all authors, in all languages, agree, that, from the first of January 1600, there was a total darkness over the whole earth for eight days: suppose that the tradition of this extraordinary event is still strong and lively among the people: that all travellers, who return from foreign countries, bring us accounts of the same tradition, without the least variation or contradiction: it is evident, that our present philosophers, instead of doubting the fact, ought to receive it as certain, and ought to search for the causes whence it might be derived. The decay, corruption, and dissolution of nature, is an event rendered probable by so many analogies, that any phenomenon, which seems to have a tendency towards that catastrophe, comes within the reach of human testimony, if that testimony be very extensive and uniform.

But suppose, that all the historians who treat of England, should agree, that, on the first of January 1600, Queen Elizabeth died; that both before and after her death she was seen by her physicians and the whole court, as is usual with persons of her rank; that her successor was acknowledged and proclaimed by the parliament; and that, after being interred a month, she again appeared, resumed the throne, and governed England for three years: I must confess that I should be surprised at the concurrence of so many odd circumstances, but should not have the least inclination to believe so miraculous an event. I should not doubt of her pretended death, and of those other public circumstances that followed it: I should only assert it to have been pretended, and that it neither was, nor possibly could be real. You would in vain object to me the difficulty, and almost impossibility of deceiving the world in an affair of such consequence; the wisdom and solid judgement of that renowned queen; with the little or no advantage which she could reap from so poor an artifice: All this might astonish me; but I would still reply, that the knavery and folly of men are such common phenomena, that I should rather believe the most extraordinary events to arise from their concurrence, than admit of so signal a violation of the laws of nature.

But should this miracle be ascribed to any new system of religion; men, in all ages, have been so much imposed on by ridiculous stories of that kind, that this very circumstance would be a full proof of a cheat, and sufficient, with all men of sense, not only to make them reject the fact, but even reject it without farther examination. Though the Being to whom the miracle is ascribed, be, in this case, Almighty, it does not, upon that account, become a whit more probable; since it is impossible for us to know the attributes or actions of such a Being, otherwise than from the experience which we have of his productions, in the usual course of nature. This still reduces us to past observation, and obliges us to compare the instances of the violation of truth in the testimony of men, with those of the violation of the laws of nature by miracles, in order to judge which of them is most likely and probable. As the violations of truth are more common in the testimony concerning religious miracles, than in that concerning any other matter of fact; this must diminish very much the authority of the former testimony, and make us form a general resolution, never to lend any attention to it, with whatever specious pretence it may be covered. [...]

I am the better pleased with the method of reasoning here delivered, as I think it may serve to confound those dangerous friends or disguised enemies to the *Christian Religion*, who have undertaken to defend it by the principles of human reason. Our most holy religion is founded on *Faith*, not on reason; and it is a sure method of exposing it to put it to such a trial as it is, by no means, fitted to endure. To make this more evident, let us examine those miracles, related in scripture; and not to lose ourselves in too wide a field, let us confine ourselves to such as we find in the *Pentateuch*, which we shall examine, according to the principles of these pretended Christians, not as the word or testimony of God himself, but as the production of a mere human writer and historian. Here then we are first to consider a book, presented to us by a barbarous and ignorant people, written in an age when they were still more barbarous, and in all probability long after the facts which it relates, corroborated by no concurring testimony, and resembling those fabulous accounts, which every nation gives of its origin. Upon reading this book, we find it full of prodigies and miracles. It gives an account of a state of the world and of human nature entirely different from the present: Of our fall from that state: Of the age of man, extended to near a thousand years: Of the destruction of the world by a deluge: Of the arbitrary choice of one people, as the favourites of heaven; and that people the countrymen of the author: Of their deliverance from bondage by prodigies the most astonishing imaginable: I desire any one to lay his hand upon his heart, and after a serious consideration declare, whether he thinks that the falsehood of such a book, supported by such a testimony, would be more extraordinary and miraculous than all the miracles it relates; which is, however, necessary to make it be received, according to the measures of probability above established.

What we have said of miracles may be applied, without any variation, to prophecies; and indeed, all prophecies are real miracles, and as such only, can be admitted as proofs of any revelation. If it did not exceed the capacity of human nature to foretell future events, it would be absurd to employ any prophecy as an argument for a divine mission or authority from heaven. So that, upon the whole, we may conclude, that the *Christian Religion* not only was at first attended with miracles, but even at this day cannot be believed by any reasonable person without one. Mere reason is insufficient to convince us of its veracity: And whoever is moved by *Faith* to assent to it, is conscious of a continued miracle in his own person, which subverts all the principles of his understanding, and gives him a determination to believe what is most contrary to custom and experience.

Notes

1   Plutarch, in vita Catonis.

2   No Indian, it is evident, could have experience that water did not freeze in cold climates. This is placing nature in a situation quite unknown to him; and it is impossible for him to tell *a priori* what will result from it. It is making a new experiment, the consequence of which is always uncertain. One may sometimes conjecture from analogy what will follow; but still this is but conjecture. And it must be confessed, that, in the present case of freezing, the event follows contrary to the rules of analogy, and is such as a rational Indian would not look for. The operations of cold upon water are not gradual, according to the degrees of cold; but whenever it comes to the freezing point, the water passes in a moment, from the utmost liquidity to perfect hardness. Such an event, therefore, may be denominated *extra-ordinary*, and requires a pretty strong testimony, to render it credible to people in a warm climate: But still it is not *miraculous*, nor contrary to uniform experience of the course of nature in cases where all the circumstances are the same. The inhabitants of Sumatra have always seen water fluid in their own climate, and the freezing of their rivers ought to be deemed a prodigy: But they never saw water in Muscovy during the winter; and therefore they cannot reasonably be positive what would there be the consequence.

3   Sometimes an event may not, *in itself, seem* to be contrary to the laws of nature, and yet, if it were real, it might, by reason of some circumstances, be denominated a miracle; because, in *fact*, it is contrary to these laws. Thus if a person, claiming a divine authority, should command a sick person to be well, a healthful man to fall down dead, the clouds to pour rain, the winds to blow, in short, should order many natural events, which immediately follow upon his command; these might justly be esteemed miracles, because they are really, in this case, contrary to the laws of nature. For if any suspicion remain, that the event and command concurred by accident, there is no miracle and no transgression of the laws of nature. If this suspicion be removed, there is evidently a miracle, and a transgression of these laws; because nothing can be more contrary to nature than that the voice or command of a man should have such an influence. A miracle may be accurately defined, *a transgression of a law of nature by a particular volition of the Deity, or by the interposition of some invisible agent.* A miracle may either be discoverable by men or not. This alters not its nature and essence. The raising of a house or ship into the air is a visible miracle. The raising of a feather, when the wind wants ever so little of a force requisite for that purpose, is as real a miracle, though not so sensible with regard to us.

4   Hist. lib. iv. cap. 81. Suetonius gives nearly the same account *in vita* Vesp.

25

Søren Kierkegaard, from
Concluding Unscientific Postscript

Søren Kierkegaard (1813–55), much like Descartes, finds skepticism regarding the limits of human understanding to be useful. To deflect the attacks upon Christianity by those who claim that it is beyond rational justification, Kierkegaard emphasizes the objective absurdity inherent in its central teachings, the "absolute paradox" that one would have to accept should one elect to become a Christian. This central truth – that an eternal god entered time and became human – is a paradox so absurd that it proves repellent to reason. In accepting and indeed promoting the rational groundlessness of Christian faith, Kierkegaard intends to make room for what he calls the truth of subjectivity, or knowledge based upon a leap of faith.

Skeptical doubt used in this way is a prime example of fideism, or the view that some or all knowledge is tied to faith at the expense of reason. In Kierkegaard's case, one becomes a Christian not through persuasive argument or by locating rational justification for the religion's fundamental principles. Rather, one must abandon the understanding's common standards of justification, reason, and coherence. The absolute paradox of Christianity throws one into doubt about its veracity and even the possibility of settling the question of its truth. From this position of profound doubt, one then makes an unmediated leap of faith, what Kierkegaard sometimes refers to as the inwardness of subjectivity, one that cannot be recommended "from the outside."

Although eloquently and quite humorously argued, profound problems plague Kierkegaard's proposal. What Kierkegaard labels the "objective" nature of human understanding seems to capture an important fact about the way in which we form beliefs – namely, that we generally rely upon justification to anchor, to amend, or to persevere in our beliefs. This is to say that it remains a valid question whether one can maintain belief in the absence of *any* rational justification, and an even more difficult one to explain how belief can be sustained as the understanding reels from the absurdity of what seems to be an outright contradiction.

But perhaps this reaction in the end provides mounting evidence for Kierkegaard's thesis. Pointing out such "objective" difficulties may merely mire us in the negative, skeptical dimension of his project, leaving us poised to risk the leap of faith that we can only know as individuals.

The objective problem is: Is Christianity true? The subjective problem is: What is the individual's relationship to Christianity? Quite simply, how may I, Johannes Climacus, participate in the happiness promised by Christianity? The problem concerns myself alone; partly because, if it is properly set forth, it will concern everyone in exactly the same way; and partly because all the other points of view take faith for granted, as trivial.

In order to make my problem clear, I shall first describe the objective problem and show how it should be treated. In this way the historical aspect will be given its due. After this I shall describe the subjective problem.

The Objective Problem of the Truth of Christianity

From an objective point of view Christianity is a historical fact whose truth must be considered in a purely objective manner, for the modest scholar is far too objective not to leave himself outside – though as a matter of fact, he may count himself as a believer. "Truth" in this objective sense may mean either (1) historical truth or (2) philosophical truth. As historical truth, the truth claims must be decided by a critical examination of the various sources in the same way we determine other historical claims. Considered philosophically, the doctrine that has been historically verified must be related to the eternal truth.

The inquiring, philosophical, and learned researcher raises the question of the truth, but not the subjective truth, that is, the truth as appropriated. The inquiring researcher is interested, but he is not infinitely, personally, and passionately interested in a way that relates his own eternal happiness to this truth. Far be it for the objective person to be so immodest, so presumptuous as that!

Such an inquirer must be in one of two states. Either he is already in faith convinced of the truth of Christianity – and in such a relationship he cannot be infinitely interested in the objective inquiry, since faith itself consists in being infinitely concerned with Christianity and regards every competing interest as a temptation; or he is not in faith but objectively considering the subject matter, and as such not in a condition of being infinitely interested in the question.

I mention this in order to draw your attention to what will be developed in the second part of this work, namely, that the problem of the truth of Christianity is never appropriately set forth in this objective manner, that is, it does not arise at all, since Christianity lies in decision. Let the scholarly researcher work with indefatigable zeal even to the point of shortening his life in devoted service to scholarship. Let the speculative philosopher spare neither time nor effort. They are nevertheless not personally and passionately concerned. On the contrary, they wouldn't want to be but will want to develop an objective and disinterested stance. They are only concerned about objective truth, so that the question of personal appropriation is relatively unimportant, something that will follow their findings as a matter of course. In the last analysis what matters to the individual is of minor significance. Herein precisely lies the scholar's exalted equanimity as well as the comedy of his parrot-like pedantry.

The Historical Point of View

When Christianity is considered through its historical documents, it becomes vital to get a trustworthy account of what Christian doctrine really is. If the researcher is infinitely concerned with his relationship to this truth, he will immediately despair, because it is patently clear that in historical matters the greatest certainty is still only an approximation, and an approximation is too weak for one to build his eternal happiness upon, since its incommensurability with eternal happiness prevents it from obtaining. So the scholar, having only a historical interest in the truth of Christianity, begins his work with tremendous zeal and contributes important research until his seventieth year. Then just fourteen days before his death he comes upon a new document that casts fresh light over one whole side of his inquiry. Such an objective personality is the antithesis of the restless concern of the subject who is infinitely interested in eternal happiness and who surely deserves to have a decisive answer to the question concerning that happiness.

When one raises the historical question of the truth of Christianity or of what is and what is not Christian truth, we come directly to the Holy Scriptures as the central document. The historical investigation focuses first on the Bible.

The Holy Scriptures

It is very important that the scholar secure the highest possible reliability in his work. In this regard it is important for me not to pretend that I have learning or show that I have none, for my purpose here is more important. And that is to have it understood and remembered that even with the most impressive scholarly credentials and persistence, even if all the intelligence of all the critics met in one single head, still one would get no further than an approximation. We could never show more than that there is an incommensurability between the infinite personal concern for one's eternal happiness and the reliability of the documents.

When the Scriptures are considered as the ultimate arbiter, which determines what is and what is not Christian, it becomes imperative to secure their reliability through a critical historical investigation. So we must deal here with several issues: the canonicity of each book of the Bible, their authenticity, their integrity, the trustworthiness of the authors, and finally, we must assume a dogmatic guarantee: inspiration. When one thinks of the prodigious labors that the English are devoting to digging the tunnel under the Thames, the incredible expenditure of time and effort, and how a little accident can upset the whole project for a long time, one may be able to get some idea of what is involved in the undertaking that we are describing. How much time, what diligence, what glorious acumen, what remarkable scholarship from generation to generation have been requisitioned to accomplish this work of supreme wonder! And yet a single little dialectical doubt can suddenly touch the foundations and for a long time disturb the whole project, closing the underground way to Christianity, which one has tried to establish objectively and scientifically, instead of approaching the problem as it would be approached, above ground – subjectively.

But let us assume first that the critics have established everything that scholarly theologians in their happiest moments ever dreamed to prove about the Bible. These books and no others belong to the canon. They are authentic, complete, their authors are trustworthy – it is as though every letter were divinely inspired (one cannot say more than this, for inspiration is an object of faith and is qualitatively dialectical. It cannot be reached by a quantitative increment.) Furthermore, there is not the slightest contradiction in these holy writings. For let us be careful in formulating our hypothesis. If there is even a word that is problematic, the parenthesis of uncertainty begins again, and the critical philological enterprise will lead one astray. In general, all that is needed to cause us to question our findings is a little circumspection, the renunciation of every learned middle-term, which could in a twinkle of the eye degenerate into a hundred-year parenthesis.

And so it comes to pass that everything we hoped for with respect to the Scriptures has been firmly established. What follows from this? Has anyone who didn't previously have faith come a single step closer to faith? Of course not, not a single step closer. For faith isn't produced through academic investigations. It doesn't come directly at all, but, on the contrary, it is precisely in objective analysis that one loses the infinite personal and passionate concern that is the requisite condition for faith, its ubiquitous ingredient, wherein faith comes into existence.

Has anyone who had faith gained anything in terms of faith's strength and power? No, not the least. Rather, his prodigious learning which lies like a dragon at faith's door, threatening to devour it, will become a handicap, forcing him to put forth an even greater prodigious effort in fear and trembling in order not to fall into temptation and confuse knowledge with faith. Whereas faith had uncertainty as a useful teacher, it now finds that certainty is its most dangerous enemy. Take passion away and faith disappears, for certainty and passion are incompatible. Let an analogy throw light on this point. He who believes that God exists and providentially rules the world finds it easier to preserve his faith (and not a fantasy) in an imperfect world where passion is kept awake, than in an absolutely perfect world; for in such an ideal world faith is unthinkable. This is the reason that we are taught that in eternity faith will be annulled.

Now let us assume the opposite, that the opponents have succeeded in proving what they desired to establish regarding the Bible and did so with a certainty that transcended their wildest hopes. What then? Has the enemy abolished Christianity? Not a whit. Has he harmed the believer? Not at all. Has he won the right of being free from the responsibility of becoming a believer? By no means. Simply because these books are not by these authors, are not authentic, lack integrity, do not seem to be inspired (though this cannot be demonstrated since it is a matter of faith), it in no way follows that these authors have not existed, and above all it does not follow that Christ never existed. In so far as faith perdures, the believer is at liberty to assume it, just as free (mark well!); for if he accepted the content of faith on the basis of evidence, he would now be on the verge of giving up faith. If things ever came this far, the believer is somewhat to blame, for he invited the procedure and began to play into the hands of unbelief by attempting to prove the content of faith.

Here is the heart of the matter, and I come back to learned theology. For whose sake is the proof sought? Faith does not need it. Yes, it must regard it as an enemy. But when faith begins to feel ashamed, when like a young woman for whom love ceases to suffice, who secretly feels ashamed of her lover and must therefore have it confirmed by others that he really is quite remarkable, so likewise when faith falters and begins to lose its passion, when it begins to cease to be faith, then proof becomes necessary in order to command respect from the side of unbelief.

So when the subject of faith is treated objectively, it becomes impossible for a person to relate himself to the decision of faith with passion, let alone with infinitely concerned passion. It is a self-contradiction and as such comical to be infinitely concerned about what at best can only be an approximation. If in spite of this, we still preserve passion, we obtain fanaticism. For the person with infinite passionate concern, every relevant detail becomes something of infinite value. The error lies not in the infinite passion but in the fact that its object has become an approximation.

As soon as one takes subjectivity away – and with it subjectivity's passion – and with passion the infinite concern – it becomes impossible to make a decision – either with regard to this problem or any other; for every decision, every genuine decision, is a subjective action. A contemplator (i.e., an objective subject) experiences no infinite urge to make a decision and sees no need for a commitment anywhere. This is the falsity of objectivity and this is the problem with the Hegelian notion of mediation as the mode of transition in the continuous process, where nothing endures and where nothing is infinitely decided because the movement turns back on itself and again turns back; but the movement itself is a chimera and philosophy becomes wise afterwards. Objectively speaking, this method produces results in great supply, but it does not produce a single decisive result. This is as is expected, since decisiveness inheres in subjectivity, essentially in passion and maximally in the personal passion that is infinitely concerned about one's eternal happiness.

Christianity is spirit, spirit is inwardness, inwardness is subjectivity, subjectivity is essentially passion and at its maximum infinite personal and passionate concern about one's eternal happiness.

Becoming Subjective

Objectively we only consider the subject matter, subjectively we consider the subject and his subjectivity, and behold, subjectivity is precisely our subject matter. It must constantly be kept in mind that the subjective problem is not about some other subject matter but simply about subjectivity itself. Since the problem is about a decision, and all decisions lie in subjectivity, it follows that not a trace of objectivity remains, for at the moment that subjectivity slinks away from the pain and crisis of decision, the problem becomes to a degree objective. If the Introduction still awaits another work before a judgment can be made on the subject matter, if the philosophical system still lacks a paragraph, if the speaker still has a final argument, the decision is postponed. We do not raise the question of the truth of Christianity in the sense that when it has been decided, subjectivity is ready and willing to accept it. No, the question is about the subject's acceptance of it, and it must be regarded as an infernal illusion or a deceitful evasion which seeks to avoid the decision by taking an objective treatment of the subject matter and assumes that a subjective commitment will follow from the objective deliberation as a matter of course. On the contrary, the decision lies in subjectivity and an objective acceptance is either a pagan concept or one devoid of all meaning.

Christianity will give the single individual eternal happiness, a good that cannot be divided into parts but can only be given to one person at a time. Although we presuppose that subjectivity is available to be appropriated, a possibility that involves accepting this good, it is not a subjectivity without qualification, without a genuine understanding of the meaning of this good. Subjectivity's development or transformation, its infinite concentration in itself with regard to an eternal happiness – this highest good of Infinity, an eternal happiness – this is subjectivity's developed possibility. As such, Christianity protests against all objectivity and will infinitely concern itself only with subjectivity. If there is any Christian truth, it first arises in subjectivity. Objectively it does not arise at all. If its truth is only in a single person, then Christianity exists in him alone, and there is greater joy in heaven over this one than over all world history and philosophical systems which, as objective forces, are incommensurable with the Christian idea.

Philosophy teaches that the way to truth is to become objective, but Christianity teaches that the way is to become subjective, that is, to become a subject in truth. Lest we seem to be trading on ambiguities, let it be said clearly that Christianity aims at intensifying passion to its highest pitch but passion is subjectivity and does not exist objectively at all.

Subjective Truth, Inwardness; Truth is Subjectivity

For an objective reflection the truth becomes an object, something object-ive, and thought points away from the subject. For subjective reflection the truth becomes a matter of appropriation, of inwardness, of subjectiv-ity, and thought must penetrate deeper and still deeper into the subject and his subjectivity. Just as in objective reflection, when objectivity had come into being, subjectivity disappeared, so here the subjectivity of the subject becomes the final stage, and objectivity disappears. It is not for an instant forgotten that the subject is an existing individual, and that existence is a process of becoming, and that therefore the idea of truth being an identity of thought and being is a chimera of abstraction; this is not because the truth is not such an identity but because the believer is an existing individual for whom the truth cannot be such an identity as long as he exists as a temporal being.

If an existing subject really could transcend himself, the truth would be something complete for him, but where is this point outside of himself? The $1 = 1$ is a mathematical point that does not exist, and insofar as one would take this standpoint, he will not stand in another's way. It is only momentarily that the existential subject experiences the unity of the infinite and the finite, which transcends existence, and that moment is the moment of passion. While scribbling modern philosophy is contemp-tuous of passion, passion remains the highest point of existence for the individual who exists in time. In passion the existential subject is made infinite in imagination's eternity, and at the same time he is himself.

All essential knowledge concerns existence, or only that knowledge that relates to existence is essential, is essential knowledge. All know-ledge that is not existential, that does not involve inward reflection, is really accidental knowledge, its degree and compass are essentially a matter of no importance. This essential knowledge that relates itself essentially to the existing individual is not to be equated with the above-mentioned abstract identity between thought and being. But it means that knowledge must relate itself to the knower, who is essentially an existing individual, and therefore all essential knowledge essentially relates itself to existence, to that which exists. But all ethical and all ethical-religious knowledge has this essential relationship to the exist-ence of the knower.

In order to elucidate the difference between the objective way of reflection and the subjective way, I shall now show how subjective reflection makes its way back into inwardness. The highest point of inwardness in an existing person is passion, for passion corresponds to truth as a paradox, and the fact that the truth becomes a paradox is grounded in its relation to an existing individual. The one corresponds to the other. By forgetting that we are existing subjects, we lose passion and truth ceases to be a paradox, but the knowing subject begins to lose his humanity and becomes fantastic and the truth likewise becomes a fantastic object for this kind of knowledge.

When the question of truth is put forward in an objective manner, reflection is directed objectively to the truth as an object to which the knower is related. The reflection is not on the relationship but on whether he is related to the truth. If that which he is related to is the truth, the subject is in the truth. When the question of truth is put forward in a subjective manner, reflection is directed subjectively to the individual's relationship. If the relation's HOW is in truth, the individual is in truth, even if the WHAT to which he is related is not true.

We may illustrate this by examining the knowledge of God. Objectively the reflection is on whether the object is the true God; subjectively reflection is on whether the individual is related to a what in such a way that his relationship in truth is a God-relationship. On which side does the truth lie? Ah, let us not lean towards mediation and say, it is on neither side but in the mediation of both of them.

The existing individual who chooses the objective way enters upon the entire approximation process that is supposed to bring God into the picture. But this in all eternity cannot be done because God is Subject and therefore exists only for the subjective individual in inwardness. The existing individual who chooses the subjective way comprehends instantly the entire dialectical difficulty involved in having to use some time, perhaps a long time, in order to find God objectively. He comprehends this dialectical difficulty in all its pain because every moment without God is a moment lost – so important is the matter of being related to God. In this way God certainly becomes a postulate but not in the useless sense in which it is often taken. It becomes the only way in which an existing individual comes into a relation with God – when the dialectical contradiction brings passion to the point of despair and helps him embrace God with the category of despair (faith). Now the postulate is far from being arbitrary or optional. It becomes a life-saving necessity, so that it is no longer simply a postulate, but rather the individual's postulation of the existence of God is a necessity.

Now the problem is to calculate on which side there is the most truth: *either* the side of one who seeks the true God objectively and pursues the approximate truth of the God-idea *or* the side of one who is driven by infinite concern for his relationship to God. No one who has not been corrupted by science can have any doubt in the matter.

If one who lives in a Christian culture goes up to God's house, the house of the true God, with a true conception of God, with knowledge of God and prays–but prays in a false spirit; and one who lives in an idolatrous land prays with the total passion of the infinite, although his eyes rest on the image of an idol; where is there most truth? The one prays in truth to God, although he worships an idol. The other prays in untruth to the true God and therefore really worships an idol.

When a person objectively inquires about the problem of immortality and another person embraces it as an uncertainty with infinite passion, where is there most truth, and who really has the greater certainty? The one has entered into an inexhaustible approximation, for certainty of immortality lies precisely in the subjectivity of the individual. The other is immortal and fights against his uncertainty.

Let us consider Socrates. Today everyone is playing with some proof or other. Some have many, some fewer. But Socrates! He put the question objectively in a hypothetical manner: "*if* there is immortality." Compared to the modern philosopher with three proofs for immortality, should we consider Socrates a doubter? Not at all. On this little *if* he risks his entire life, he dares to face death, and he has directed his life with infinite passion so that the *if* is confirmed – *if* there is immortality. Is there any better proof for life after death? But those who have the three proofs do not at all pattern their lives in conformity with the idea. If there is an immortality, it must feel disgust over their lackadaisical manner of life. Can any better refutation be given of the three proofs? These crumbs of uncertainty helped Socrates because they hastened the process along, inciting the passions. The three proofs that others have are of no help at all because they are dead to the spirit, and the fact that they need three proofs proves that they are spiritually dead. The Socratic ignorance that Socrates held fast with the entire passion of his inwardness was an expression of the idea that eternal truth is related to an existing individual, and that this will be in the form of a paradox as long as he exists; and yet it is just possible that there is more truth in Socratic ignorance than is contained in the "objective truth" of the philosophical systems, which flirts with the spirit of the times and cuddles up to associate professors.

The objective accent falls on *what* is said; the subjective accent falls on *how* it is said. This distinction is valid even for aesthetics and shows itself in the notion that what may be objectively true may in the mouth of certain people become false. This distinction is illustrated by the saying that the difference between the older days and our day is that in the old days only a few knew the truth while in ours all know it, except that the inwardness towards it is in inverse proportion to the scope of its possession. Aesthetically the contradiction that the truth becomes error in certain mouths is best understood comically. In the ethical-religious domain the accent is again on the *how*. But this is not to be understood as referring to decorum, modulation, delivery, and so on, but to the individual's relationship to the proposition, the way he relates himself to it. Objectively it is a question simply about the content of the proposition, but subjectively it is a question of inwardness. At its maximum this inward *how* is the passion of infinity and the passion of the infinite is itself the truth. But since the passion of the infinite is exactly subjectivity, subjectivity is the truth. Objectively there is no infinite decision or commitment, and so it is objectively correct to annul the difference between good and evil as well as the law of noncontradiction and the difference between truth and untruth. Only in subjectivity is there decision and commitment, so that to seek this in objectivity is to be in error. It is the passion of infinity that brings forth decisiveness, not its content, for its content is precisely itself. In this manner the subjective *how* and subjectivity are the truth.

But the *how* that is subjectively emphasized because the subject is an existing individual is also subject to a temporal dialectic. In passion's decisive moment, where the road swings off from the way to objective knowledge, it appears that the infinite decision is ready to be made. But in that moment the existing individual finds himself in time, and the subjective *how* becomes transformed into a striving, a striving that is motivated by and is repeatedly experienced in the decisive passion of the infinite. But this is still a striving.

When subjectivity is truth, subjectivity's definition must include an expression for an opposition to objectivity, a reminder of the fork in the road, and this expression must also convey the tension of inwardness. Here is such a definition of truth: *the objective uncertainty, held fast in an appropriation process of the most passionate inwardness, is the truth*, the highest truth available for an *existing* person. There where the way swings off (and where that is cannot be discovered objectively but only subjectively), at that place objective knowledge is annulled. Objectively speaking he has only uncertainty, but precisely there the infinite passion of inwardness is intensified, and truth is precisely the adventure to choose objective uncertainty with the passion of inwardness.

When I consider nature in order to discover God, I do indeed see his omnipotence and wisdom, but I see much more that disturbs me. The result of all this is objective uncertainty, but precisely here is the place for inwardness because inwardness apprehends the objective uncertainty with the entire passion of infinity. In the case of mathematical statements objectivity is already given, but because of the nature of mathematics, the truth is existentially indifferent.

Now the above definition of truth is an equivalent description of faith. Without risk there is no faith. Faith is precisely the contradiction between the infinite passion of inwardness and objective uncertainty. If I can grasp God objectively, I do not believe, but because I cannot know God objectively, I must have faith, and if I will preserve myself in faith, I must constantly be determined to hold fast to the objective uncertainty, so as to remain out upon the ocean's deep, over seventy thousand fathoms of water, and still believe.

In the sentence "subjectivity, inwardness is truth," we see the essence of Socratic wisdom, whose immortal service is exactly to have recognized the essential meaning of existence, that the knower is an *existing* subject, and for this reason in his ignorance Socrates enjoyed the highest relationship to truth within the paganism. This is a truth that speculative philosophy unhappily again and again forgets: that the knower is an existing subject. It is difficult enough to recognize this fact in our objective age, long after the genius of Socrates.

When subjectivity, inwardness, is the truth, the truth becomes objectively determined as a paradox, and that it is paradoxical is made clear by the fact that subjectivity is truth, for it repels objectivity, and the expression for the objective repulsion is the intensity and measure of inwardness. The paradox is the objective uncertainty, which is the expression for the passion of inwardness, which is precisely the truth. This is the Socratic principle. The eternal, essential truth, that is, that which relates itself essentially to the individual because it concerns his existence (all other knowledge is, Socratically speaking, accidental, its degree and scope being indifferent), is a paradox. Nevertheless, the eternal truth is not essentially in itself paradoxical, but it becomes so by relating itself to an existing individual. Socratic ignorance is the expression of this objective uncertainty, the inwardness of the existential subject is the truth. To anticipate what I will develop later, Socratic ignorance is an analogy to the category of the absurd, only that there is still less objective certainty in the absurd, and therefore infinitely greater tension in its inwardness. The Socratic inwardness that involves existence is an analogy to faith, except that this inwardness is repulsed not by ignorance but by the absurd, which is infinitely deeper. Socratically the eternal, essential truth is by no means paradoxical in itself, but only by virtue of its relation to an existing individual.

Subjectivity, inwardness, is the truth. Is there a still more inward expression for this? Yes, there is. If subjectivity is seen as the truth, we may posit the opposite principle: that subjectivity is untruth, error. Socratically speaking, subjectivity is untruth if it fails to understand that subjectivity is truth and desires to understand itself objectively. But now we are presupposing that subjectivity in becoming the truth has a difficulty to overcome in as much as it is in untruth. So we must work backwards, back to inwardness. Socratically, the way back to the truth takes place through recollection, supposing that we have memories of that truth deep within us.

Let us call this untruth of the individual "sin." Seen from eternity the individual cannot be in sin, nor can he be eternally presupposed as having been in sin. So it must be that he becomes a sinner by coming into existence (for the beginning point is that subjectivity is untruth). He is not born as a sinner in the sense that he is sinful before he is born, but he is born in sin and as a sinner. We shall call this state *original sin*. But if existence has acquired such power over him, he is impotent to make his way back to eternity through the use of his memory (supposing that there is truth in the Platonic idea that we may discover truth through recollection). If it was already paradoxical that the eternal truth related itself to an existing individual, now it is absolutely paradoxical that it relates itself to such an individual. But the more difficult it is for him through memory to transcend existence, the more inwardness must increase in intense passion, and when it is made impossible for him, when he is held so fast in existence that the back door of recollection is forever closed to him through sin, then his inwardness will be the deepest possible.

Subjectivity is truth. Through this relationship between the eternal truth and the existing individual the paradox comes into existence. Let us now go further and suppose that the eternal truth is essentially a paradox. How does this paradox come into existence? By juxtaposing the eternal, essential truth with temporal existence. When we set them together within the truth itself, the truth becomes paradoxical. The eternal truth has come into time. This is the paradox. If the subject is hindered by sin from making his way back to eternity by looking inward through recollection, he need not trouble himself about this, for now the eternal essential truth is no longer behind him, but it is in front of him, through its being in existence or having existed, so that if the individual does not *existentially* get hold of the truth, he will never get hold of it.

It is impossible to accentuate existence more than this. When the eternal truth is related to an existing individual, truth becomes a paradox. The paradox repels the individual because of the objective uncertainty and ignorance towards inwardness. But since this paradox in itself is not paradoxical, it does not push the spirit far enough. For without risk there is no faith, and the greater the risk the greater the faith, and the more objective reliability, the less inwardness (for inwardness is precisely subjectivity). Indeed, the less objective reliability, the deeper becomes the possible inwardness. When the paradox is in itself paradoxical, it repels the individual by the power of the absurd, and the corresponding passion, which is produced in the process, is faith. But subjectivity, inwardness, is truth, for otherwise we have forgotten the Socratic contribution; but there is no more striking expression for inwardness than when the retreat from existence through recollection back to eternity is made impossible; and when the truth as paradox encounters the individual who is caught in the vice-grip of sin's anxiety and suffering, but who is also aware of the tremendous risk involved in faith – when he nevertheless makes the leap of faith – this is subjectivity at its height.

When Socrates believed in the existence of God, he held fast to an objective uncertainty in passionate inwardness, and in that contradiction, in that risk faith came into being. Now it is different. Instead of the objective uncertainty, there is objective certainty about the object – certainty that it is absurd, and it is, again, faith that holds fast to that object in passionate inwardness. Compared with the gravity of the absurd, Socratic ignorance is a joke, and compared with the strenuosity of faith in believing the paradox, Socratic existential inwardness is a Greek life of leisure.

What is the absurd? The absurd is that the eternal truth has entered time, that God has entered existence, has been born, has grown, and so on, has become precisely like any other human being, quite indistinguishable from other humans. The absurd is precisely by its objective repulsion the measure of the inwardness of faith. Suppose there is a man who desires to have faith. Let the comedy begin. He desires to obtain faith with the help of objective investigation and what the approximation process of evidential inquiry yields. What happens? With the help of the increment of evidence the absurd is transformed to something else; it becomes probable, it becomes more probable still, it becomes perhaps highly and overwhelmingly probable. Now that there is respectable evidence for the content of his faith, he is ready to believe it, and he prides himself that his faith is not like that of the shoemaker, the tailor, and the simple folk, but comes after a long investigation. Now he prepares himself to believe it. Any proposition that is almost probable, reasonably probable, highly and overwhelmingly probable, is something that is almost known and as good as known, highly and overwhelmingly known – but it is not believed, not through faith; for the absurd is precisely faith's object and the only positive attitude possible in relation to it is faith and not knowledge.

Christianity has declared itself to be the eternal that has entered time, that has proclaimed itself as the *paradox* and demands faith's inwardness in relation to that which is a scandal to the Jews and folly to the Greeks – and as absurd to the understanding. It is impossible to say this more strongly than by saying: subjectivity is truth, and objectivity is repelled by it – by virtue of the absurd.

Subjectivity culminates in passion. Christianity is the paradox; paradox and passion belong together as a perfect match, and the paradox is perfectly suited to one whose situation is to be in the extremity of existence. Indeed, there never has been found in all the world two lovers more suited to each other than passion and paradox, and the strife between them is a lover's quarrel, when they argue about which one first aroused the other's passion. And so it is here. The existing individual by means of the paradox has come to the extremity of existence. And what is more wonderful for lovers than to be granted a long time together with each other without anything disturbing their relation except that which makes it more inwardly passionate? And this is what is granted to the unspeculative understanding between the passion and paradox, for they will dwell harmoniously together in time and be changed first in eternity.

But the speculative philosopher views things altogether differently. He believes but only to a certain degree. He puts his hand to the plow but quickly looks about for something to know. From a Christian perspective it is hard to see how he could reach the highest good in this manner.

Part III

Responses and Reactions

26

René Descartes, from "Meditation VI"

In the sixth and final meditation, excerpted below, Descartes attempts to dispel the radical doubt with which he began (see chapter 5, "Meditation I"). To remove the possibility of false beliefs, Descartes considered the possibility that he might be dreaming the sensory experience that he takes to be about an external world, and he then further imagines an evil demon who constantly deceives him into believing (falsely) that $2 + 2 = 4$, or that he has a material body. Once such profound skepticism has been raised, how can it be put to rest?

Descartes' answer involves a reliance upon God. In "Meditation II" (see chapter 17), Descartes concluded that he clearly and distinctly perceived that he was a thinking thing, incapable of being deceived into believing that he did not exist, however powerful the evil demon. Building outward from that base of certainty, Descartes argues that since God exists and is no deceiver, what he perceives clearly and distinctly must be true. Accordingly, though he realizes that his senses can at times deceive him, he concludes that corporeal objects do indeed exist, though not in the form immediately reported by his senses. His move back to certainty also entails, he believes, that he is fundamentally an immaterial, thinking thing separable from his material body. He clearly and distinctly perceives the differences in the essential properties of his mind and body; hence, they must be metaphysically separable.

Broadly speaking, then, Descartes dispels his radical skepticism through an epistemological vigilance: he may be tempted to believe the compelling falsehoods that his senses report about the way the world is, for example, but he can remain confident that his beliefs are indeed true so long as he respects his criterion of certainty – that whatever he perceives clearly and distinctly is guaranteed by God to be true.

Of the Existence of Material Things, and of the Real Distinction between the Mind and Body of Man

[…] [I]n the first place, I will recall to my mind the things I have hitherto held as true, because perceived by the senses, and the foundations upon which my belief in their truth rested; I will, in the second place, examine the reasons that afterwards constrained me to doubt of them; and, finally, I will consider what of them I ought now to believe.

Firstly, then, I perceived that I had a head, hands, feet and other members composing that body which I considered as part, or perhaps even as the whole, of myself. I perceived further, that that body was placed among many others, by which it was capable of being affected in diverse ways, both beneficial and hurtful; and what was beneficial I remarked by a certain sensation of pleasure, and what was hurtful by a sensation of pain. And, besides this pleasure and pain, I was likewise conscious of hunger, thirst, and other appetites, as well as certain corporeal inclinations towards joy, sadness, anger, and similar passions. And, out of myself, besides the extension, figure, and motions of bodies, I likewise perceived in them hardness, heat, and the other tactile qualities, and, in addition, light, colours, odours, tastes, and sounds, the variety of which gave me the means of distinguishing the sky, the earth, the sea, and generally all the other bodies, from one another. And certainly, considering the ideas of all these qualities, which were presented to my mind, and which alone I properly and immediately perceived, it was not without reason that I thought I perceived certain objects wholly different from my thought, namely, bodies from which those ideas proceeded; for I was conscious that the ideas were presented to me without my consent being required, so that I could not perceive any object, however desirous I might be, unless it were present to the organ of sense; and it was wholly out of my power not to perceive it when it was thus present. And because the ideas I perceived by the senses were much more lively and clear, and even, in their own way, more distinct than any of those I could of myself frame by meditation, or which I found impressed on my memory, it seemed that they could not have proceeded from myself, and must therefore have been caused in me by some other objects: and as of those objects I had no knowledge beyond what the ideas themselves gave me, nothing was so likely to occur to my mind as the supposition that the objects were similar to the ideas which they caused. And because I recollected also that I had formerly trusted to the senses, rather than to reason, and that the ideas which I myself formed were not so clear as those I perceived by sense, and that they were even for the most part composed of parts of the latter, I was readily persuaded that I had no idea in my intellect which had not formerly passed through the senses. Nor was I altogether wrong in likewise believing that that body which, by a special right, I called my own, pertained to me more properly and strictly than any of the others; for in truth, I could never be separated from it as from other bodies: I felt in it and on account of it all my appetites and affections, and in fine I was affected in its parts by pain and the titillation of pleasure, and not in the parts of the other bodies that were separated from it. But when I inquired into the reason why, from this I know not what sensation of pain, sadness of mind should follow, and why from the sensation of pleasure joy should arise, or why this indescribable twitching of the stomach, which I call hunger, should put me in mind of taking food, and the parchedness of the throat of drink, and so in other cases, I was unable to give any explanation, unless that I was so taught by nature; for there is assuredly no affinity, at least none that I am able to comprehend, between this irritation of the stomach and the desire of food, any more than between the perception of an object that causes pain and the consciousness of sadness which springs from the perception. And in the same way it seemed to me that all the other judgments I had formed regarding the objects of sense, were dictates of nature; because I remarked that those judgments were formed in me, before I had leisure to weigh and consider the reasons that might constrain me to form them.

But, afterwards, a wide experience by degrees sapped the faith I had reposed in my senses; for I frequently observed that towers, which at a distance seemed round, appeared square when more closely viewed, and that colossal figures, raised on the summits of these towers, looked like small statues, when viewed from the bottom of them; and, in other instances without number, I also discovered error in judgments founded on the external senses; and not only in those founded on the external, but even in those that rested on the internal senses; for is there aught more internal than pain? and yet I have sometimes been informed by parties whose arm or leg had been amputated, that they still occasionally seemed to feel pain in that part of the body which they had lost – a circumstance that led me to think that I could not be quite certain even that any one of my members was affected when I felt pain in it. And to these grounds of doubt I shortly afterwards also added two others of very wide generality: the first of them was that I believed I never perceived anything when awake which I could not occasionally think I also perceived when asleep, and as I do not believe that the ideas I seem to perceive in my sleep proceed from objects external to me, I did not any more observe any ground for believing this of such as I seem to perceive when awake; the second was that since I was as yet ignorant of the author of my being, or at least supposed myself to be so, I saw nothing to prevent my having been so constituted by nature as that I should be deceived even in matters that appeared to me to possess the greatest truth. And, with respect to the grounds on which I had before been persuaded of the existence of sensible objects, I had no great difficulty in finding suitable answers to them; for as nature seemed to incline me to many things from which reason made me averse, I thought that I ought not to confide much in its teachings. And although the perceptions of the senses were not dependent on my will, I did not think that I ought on that ground to conclude that they proceeded from things different from myself, since perhaps there might be found in me some faculty, though hitherto unknown to me, which produced them.

But now that I begin to know myself better, and to discover more clearly the author of my being, I do not, indeed, think that I ought rashly to admit all which the senses seem to teach, nor, on the other hand, is it my conviction that I ought to doubt in general of their teachings.

And, firstly, because I know that all which I clearly and distinctly conceive can be produced by God exactly as I conceive it, it is sufficient that I am able clearly and distinctly to conceive one thing apart from another, in order to be certain that the one is different from the other, seeing they may at least be made to exist separately, by the omnipotence of God; and it matters not by what power this separation is made, in order to be compelled to judge them different; and, therefore, merely because I know with certitude that I exist, and because, in the meantime, I do not observe that aught necessarily belongs to my nature or essence beyond my being a thinking thing, I rightly conclude that my essence consists only in my being a thinking thing [or a substance whose whole essence or nature is merely thinking].[1] And although I may, or rather, as I will shortly say, although I certainly do possess a body with which I am very closely conjoined; nevertheless, because, on the one hand, I have a clear and distinct idea of myself, in as far as I am only a thinking and unextended thing, and as, on the other hand, I possess a distinct idea of body, in as far as it is only an extended and unthinking thing, it is certain that I [that is, my mind, by which I am what I am] is entirely and truly distinct from my body, and may exist without it.

Moreover, I find in myself diverse faculties of thinking that have each their special mode: for example, I find I possess the faculties of imagining and perceiving, without which I can indeed clearly and distinctly conceive myself as entire, but I cannot reciprocally conceive them without conceiving myself, that is to say, without an intelligent substance in which they reside, for [in the notion we have of them, or to use the terms of the schools] in their formal concept, they comprise some sort of intellection; whence I perceive that they are distinct from myself as modes are from things. I remark likewise certain other faculties, as the power of changing place, of assuming diverse figures, and the like, that cannot be conceived and cannot therefore exist, any more than the preceding, apart from a substance in which they inhere. It is very evident, however, that these faculties, if they really exist, must belong to some corporeal or extended substance, since in their clear and distinct concept there is contained some sort of extension, but no intellection at all. Farther, I cannot doubt but that there is in me a certain passive faculty of perception, that is, of receiving and taking knowledge of the ideas of sensible things; but this would be useless to me, if there did not also exist in me, or in some other thing, another active faculty capable of forming and producing those ideas. But this active faculty cannot be in me [in as far as I am but a thinking thing], seeing that it does not presuppose thought, and also that those ideas are frequently produced in my mind without my contributing to it in any way, and even frequently contrary to my will. This faculty must therefore exist in some substance different from me, in which all the objective reality of the ideas that are produced by this faculty is contained formally or eminently, as I before remarked: and this substance is either a body, that is to say, a corporeal nature in which is contained formally [and in effect] all that is objectively [and by representation] in those ideas; or it is God himself, or some other creature, of a rank superior to body, in which the same is contained eminently. But as God is no deceiver, it is manifest that he does not of himself and immediately communicate those ideas to me, nor even by the intervention of any creature in which their objective reality is not formally, but only eminently, contained. For as he has given me no faculty whereby I can discover this to be the case, but, on the contrary, a very strong inclination to believe that those ideas arise from corporeal objects, I do not see how he could be vindicated from the charge of deceit, if in truth they proceeded from any other source, or were produced by other causes than corporeal things: and accordingly it must be concluded, that corporeal objects exist. Nevertheless they are not perhaps exactly such as we perceive by the senses, for their comprehension by the senses is, in many instances, very obscure and confused; but it is at least necessary to admit that all which I clearly and distinctly conceive as in them, that is, generally speaking, all that is comprehended in the object of speculative geometry, really exists external to me.

But with respect to other things which are either only particular, as, for example, that the sun is of such a size and figure, etc., or are conceived with less clearness and distinctness, as light, sound, pain, and the like, although they are highly dubious and uncertain, nevertheless on the ground alone that God is no deceiver, and that consequently he has permitted no falsity in my opinions which he has not likewise given me a faculty of correcting, I think I may with safety conclude that I possess in myself the means of arriving at the truth. And, in the first place, it cannot be doubted that in each of the dictates of nature there is some truth: for by nature, considered in general, I now understand nothing more than God himself, or the order and disposition established by God in created things; and by my nature in particular I understand the assemblage of all that God has given me.

But there is nothing which that nature teaches me more expressly [or more sensibly] than that I have a body which is ill affected when I feel pain, and stands in need of food and drink when I experience the sensations of hunger and thirst, etc. And therefore I ought not to doubt but that there is some truth in these informations.

Nature likewise teaches me by these sensations of pain, hunger, thirst, etc., that I am not only lodged in my body as a pilot in a vessel, but that I am besides so intimately conjoined, and as it were intermixed with it, that my mind and body compose a certain unity. For if this were not the case, I should not feel pain when my body is hurt, seeing I am merely a thinking thing, but should perceive the wound by the understanding alone, just as a pilot perceives by sight when any part of his vessel is damaged; and when my body has need of food or drink, I should have a clear knowledge of this, and not be made aware of it by the confused sensations of hunger and thirst: for, in truth, all these sensations of hunger, thirst, pain, etc., are nothing more than certain confused modes of thinking, arising from the union and apparent fusion of mind and body.

Besides this, nature teaches me that my own body is surrounded by many other bodies, some of which I have to seek after, and others to shun. And indeed, as I perceive different sorts of colours, sounds, odours, tastes, heat, hardness, etc., I safely conclude that there are in the bodies from which the diverse perceptions of the senses proceed, certain varieties corresponding to them, although, perhaps, not in reality like them; and since, among these diverse perceptions of the senses, some are agreeable, and others disagreeable, there can be no doubt that my body, or rather my entire self, in as far as I am composed of body and mind, may be variously affected, both beneficially and hurtfully, by surrounding bodies.

But there are many other beliefs which, though seemingly the teaching of nature, are not in reality so, but which obtained a place in my mind through a habit of judging inconsiderately of things. It may thus easily happen that such judgments shall contain error: thus, for example, the opinion I have that all space in which there is nothing to affect [or make an impression on] my senses is void; that in a hot body there is something in every respect similar to the idea of heat in my mind; that in a white or green body there is the same whiteness or greenness which I perceive; that in a bitter or sweet body there is the same taste, and so in other instances; that the stars, towers, and all distant bodies, are of the same size and figure as they appear to our eyes, etc. But that I may avoid everything like indistinctness of conception, I must accurately define what I properly understand by being taught by nature. For nature is here taken in a narrower sense than when it signifies the sum of all the things which God has given me; seeing that in that meaning the notion comprehends much that belongs only to the mind [to which I am not here to be understood as referring when I use the term nature]; as, for example, the notion I have of the truth, that what is done cannot be undone, and all the other truths I discern by the natural light [without the aid of the body]; and seeing that it comprehends likewise much besides that belongs only to body, and is not here any more contained under the name nature, as the quality of heaviness, and the like, of which I do not speak – the term being reserved exclusively to designate the things which God has given to me as a being composed of mind and body. But nature, taking the term in the sense explained, teaches me to shun what causes in me the sensation of pain, and to pursue what affords me the sensation of pleasure, and other things of this sort; but I do not discover that it teaches me, in addition to this, from these diverse perceptions of the senses, to draw any conclusions respecting external objects without a previous [careful and mature] consideration of them by the mind: for it is, as appears to me, the office of the mind alone, and not of the composite whole of mind and body, to discern the truth in those matters. Thus, although the impression a star makes on my eye is not larger than that from the flame of a candle, I do not, nevertheless, experience any real or positive impulse determining me to believe that the star is not greater than the flame; the true account of the matter being merely that I have so judged from my youth without any rational ground. And, though on approaching the fire I feel heat, and even pain on approaching it too closely, I have, however, from this no ground for holding that something resembling the heat I feel is in the fire, any more than that there is something similar to the pain; all that I have ground for believing is, that there is something in it, whatever it may be, which excites in me those sensations of heat or pain. So also, although there are spaces in which I find nothing to excite and affect my senses, I must not therefore conclude that those spaces contain in them no body; for I see that in this, as in many other similar matters, I have been accustomed to pervert the order of nature, because these perceptions of the senses, although given me by nature merely to signify to my mind what things are beneficial and hurtful to the composite whole of which it is a part, and being sufficiently clear and distinct for that purpose, are nevertheless used by me as infallible rules by which to determine immediately the essence of the bodies that exist out of me, of which they can of course afford me only the most obscure and confused knowledge. [...]

To commence this examination accordingly, I here remark, in the first place, that there is a vast difference between mind and body, in respect that body, from its nature, is always divisible, and that mind is entirely indivisible. For in truth, when I consider the mind, that is, when I consider myself in so far only as I am a thinking thing, I can distinguish in myself no parts, but I very clearly discern that I am somewhat absolutely one and entire: and although the whole mind seems to be united to the whole body, yet, when a foot, an arm, or any other part is cut off, I am conscious that nothing has been taken from my mind; nor can the faculties of willing, perceiving, conceiving, etc., properly be called its parts, for it is the same mind that is exercised [all entire] in willing, in perceiving, and in conceiving, etc. But quite the opposite holds in corporeal or extended things; for I cannot imagine any one of them [how small soever it may be], which I cannot easily sunder in thought, and which, therefore, I do not know to be divisible. This would be sufficient to teach me that the mind or soul of man is entirely different from the body, if I had not already been apprised of it on other grounds.

I remark, in the next place, that the mind does not immediately receive the impression from all the parts of the body, but only from the brain, or perhaps even from one small part of it, viz., that in which the common sense (*sensus communis*) is said to be, which as often as it is affected in the same way, gives rise to the same perception in the mind, although meanwhile the other parts of the body may be diversely disposed, as is proved by innumerable experiments, which it is unnecessary here to enumerate.

I remark, besides, that the nature of body is such that none of its parts can be moved by another part a little removed from the other, which cannot likewise be moved in the same way by any one of the parts that lie between those two, although the most remote part does not act at all. As, for example, in the cord A, B, C, D [which is in tension], if its last part D be pulled, the first part A will not be moved in a different way than it would be were one of the intermediate parts B or C to be pulled, and the last part D meanwhile to remain fixed. And in the same way, when I feel pain in the foot, the science of physics teaches me that this sensation is experienced by means of the nerves dispersed over the foot, which, extending like cords from it to the brain, when they are contracted in the foot, contract at the same time the inmost parts of the brain in which they have their origin, and excite in these parts a certain motion appointed by nature to cause in the mind a sensation of pain, as if existing in the foot: but as these nerves must pass through the tibia, the leg, the loins, the back, and neck, in order to reach the brain, it may happen that although their extremities in the foot are not affected, but only certain of their parts that pass through the loins or neck, the same movements, nevertheless, are excited in the brain by this motion as would have been caused there by a hurt received in the foot, and hence the mind will necessarily feel pain in the foot, just as if it had been hurt; and the same is true of all the other perceptions of our senses.

I remark, finally, that as each of the movements that are made in the part of the brain by which the mind is immediately affected, impresses it with but a single sensation, the most likely supposition in the circumstances is, that this movement causes the mind to experience, among all the sensations which it is capable of impressing upon it, that one which is the best fitted, and generally the most useful for the preservation of the human body when it is in full health. But experience shows us that all the perceptions which nature has given us are of such a kind as I have mentioned; and accordingly, there is nothing found in them that does not manifest the power and goodness of God. Thus, for example, when the nerves of the foot are violently or more than usually shaken, the motion passing through the medulla of the spine to then innermost parts of the brain affords a sign to the mind on which it experiences a sensation, viz., of pain, as if it were in the foot, by which the mind is admonished and excited to do its utmost to remove the cause of it as dangerous and hurtful to the foot. It is true that God could have so constituted the nature of man as that the same motion in the brain would have informed the mind of something altogether different: the motion might, for example, have been the occasion on which the mind became conscious of itself, in so far as it is in the brain, or in so far as it is in some place intermediate between the foot and the brain, or, finally, the occasion on which it perceived some other object quite different, whatever that might be; but nothing of all this would have so well contributed to the preservation of the body as that which the mind actually feels. In the same way, when we stand in need of drink, there arises from this want a certain parchedness in the throat that moves its nerves, and by means of them the internal parts of the brain, and this movement affects the mind with the sensation of thirst, because there is nothing on that occasion which is more useful for us than to be made aware that we have need of drink for the preservation of our health; and so in other instances.

Whence it is quite manifest, that notwithstanding the sovereign goodness of God, the nature of man, in so far as it is composed of mind and body, cannot but be sometimes fallacious. For, if there is any cause which excites, not in the foot, but in some one of the parts of the nerves that stretch from the foot to the brain, or even in the brain itself, the same movement that is ordinarily created when the foot is ill affected, pain will be felt, as it were, in the foot, and the sense will thus be naturally deceived; for as the same movement in the brain can but impress the mind with the same sensation, and as this sensation is much more frequently excited by a cause which hurts the foot than by one acting in a different quarter, it is reasonable that it should lead the mind to feel pain in the foot rather than in any other part of the body. And if it sometimes happens that the parchedness of the throat does not arise, as is usual, from drink being necessary for the health of the body, but from quite the opposite cause, as is the case with the dropsical; yet it is much better that it should be deceitful in that instance, than if, on the contrary, it were continually fallacious when the body is well-disposed; and the same holds true in other cases.

And certainly this consideration is of great service, not only in enabling me to recognise the errors to which my nature is liable, but likewise in rendering it more easy to avoid or correct them: for, knowing that all my senses more usually indicate to me what is true than what is false, in matters relating to the advantage of the body, and being able almost always to make use of more than a single sense in examining the same object, and besides this, being able to use my memory in connecting present with past knowledge, and my understanding which has already discovered all the causes of my errors, I ought no longer to fear that falsity may be met with in what is daily presented to me by the senses. And I ought to reject all the doubts of those bygone days as hyperbolical and ridiculous, especially the general uncertainty respecting sleep, which I could not distinguish from the waking state: for I now find a very marked difference between the two states, in respect that our memory can never connect our dreams with each other and with the course of life, in the way it is in the habit of doing with events that occur when we are awake. And, in truth, if some one, when I am awake, appeared to me all of a sudden and as suddenly disappeared, as do the images I see in sleep, so that I could not observe either whence he came or whither he went, I should not without reason esteem it either a spectre or phantom formed in my brain, rather than a real man. But when I perceive objects with regard to which I can distinctly determine both the place whence they come, and that in which they are, and the time at which they appear to me, and when, without interruption, I can connect the perception I have of them with the whole of the other parts of my life, I am perfectly sure that what I thus perceive occurs while I am awake and not during sleep. And I ought not in the least degree to doubt of the truth of those presentations, if, after having called together all my senses, my memory, and my understanding for the purpose of examining them, no deliverance is given by any one of these faculties which is repugnant to that of any other: for since God is no deceiver, it necessarily follows that I am not herein deceived. But because the necessities of action frequently oblige us to come to a determination before we have had leisure for so careful an examination, it must be confessed that the life of man is frequently obnoxious to error with respect to individual objects; and we must, in conclusion, acknowledge the weakness of our nature.

Note

1 The square brackets in this chapter mark Descartes' own additions to the revised French translation (Eds).

27

Jean-Baptiste Molière, from *The Forced Marriage*

Molière (1622–73) was a French dramatist known for his comedies, many of which are still performed today. The following selection is a scene from his play *The Forced Marriage*. The main character, Sganarelle, is engaged to be married to a much younger, pleasure-loving woman, Dorimena. He worries about her fidelity, and seeks the advice of various philosophers. He consults a verbose Aristotelian who does not allow him an opportunity to say anything. He moves on to speak with Marphurius, a Pyrrhonian scholar. In this scene, skepticism is presented as an absurdity when applied to the affairs of ordinary life.

MARPHURIUS: What can I do for you Sganarelle?

SGANARELLE: I need your advice on a small matter, Doctor. That's why I'm here. [*aside*] This one is better. At least, he pays attention to you.

MARPHURIUS: [*after a pause*] Sganarelle, I have thought about what you said, and you will have to change your way of speaking. Our philosophy enjoins us never to enunciate a decisive proposition, but to speak of everything with modest uncertainty, suspending our judgment. For this reason, you must not say, "I am here," but "I think I am here."

SGANARELLE: I think?

MARPHURIUS: Precisely.

SGANARELLE: But I think it because I am here.

MARPHURIUS: One thing does not necessarily follow from the other. You can think so without its being true.

SGANARELLE: What? Isn't it true that I'm here?

MARPHURIUS: It may or may not be so. We must doubt everything.

SGANARELLE: If I'm not here, who is this talking to you?

MARPHURIUS: I think that you are here, and it seems to me that I am speaking to you, but we cannot be sure.

SGANARELLE: What the devil is this? You're making fun of me. Here I am and there you are and thinking or seeming has nothing to do with it. Let's drop these subtleties, if you don't mind, and continue with my business. I want to get married.

MARPHURIUS: I know nothing about that.

SGANARELLE: I'm telling you about it.

MARPHURIUS: That may be.

SGANARELLE: The girl is very young and very beautiful.

MARPHURIUS: That is not impossible.

SGANARELLE: Does it make sense or not for me to marry her?

MARPHURIUS: Either one or the other.

SGANARELLE: That's what I want to know. Marry her or not marry her?

MARPHURIUS: It depends.

SGANARELLE: Am I getting into trouble?

MARPHURIUS: You could be.

SGANARELLE: Please, a straightforward answer.

MARPHURIUS: I am trying to give you one.

SGANARELLE: I'm very attached to her.

MARPHURIUS: That might be understandable.

SGANARELLE: Her father has agreed.

MARPHURIUS: That is not unlikely.

SGANARELLE: But I'm afraid of becoming a – a cuckold.

MARPHURIUS: It could happen.

SGANARELLE: What do you think?

MARPHURIUS: Nothing is beyond belief.

SGANARELLE: What would you do, in my place?

MARPHURIUS: I do not know.

SGANARELLE: What do you suggest I do?

MARPHURIUS: Whatever you think best.

SGANARELLE: I'm losing my temper.

MARPHURIUS: I wash my hands of it.

SGANARELLE: You old fool! You thinker! You *seemer*!

MARPHURIUS: What will be will be.

SGANARELLE: I'll soon make you change your tune, you numskull.

[*He seizes Marphurius' stick and beats him all around the stage with it. Marphurius squeals and cringes.*]

There's the fee for your useless advice. And now I'm satisfied.

MARPHURIUS: [*recovering*] You dare to attack me, to lay my own stick about my back, to beat me, a philosopher!

SGANARELLE: Marphurius, you'll have to change your way of speaking. We must doubt everything. You must not say I've beaten you but only it seems as if I've beaten you.

MARPHURIUS: I am going off immediately to complain to the police.

SGANARELLE: I wash my hands of it.

MARPHURIUS: I have wounds on my body.

SGANARELLE: Nothing is beyond belief.

MARPHURIUS: And you are responsible for them.

SGANARELLE: It's not impossible.

MARPHURIUS: I'll have a warrant made out for your arrest.

SGANARELLE: I know nothing about that.

MARPHURIUS: You will go straight to prison.

SGANARELLE: What will be will be.

MARPHURIUS: I'll show you–

[*He stamps off, waving his stick.*]

SGANARELLE: Impossible to get a straight word out of him. You know as much when you finish as when you began. Where can I turn for advice? The wedding's coming nearer and nearer. Was there ever a man in such a plight before?

28

David Hume, from *A Treatise of Human Nature*

In his compelling and quite moving conclusion to Book I of *A Treatise of Human Nature*, included below, we find Hume who, in pausing to reflect on the philosophical waters he has just navigated, appears profoundly unsettled with his skeptical conclusions. It's no wonder, for over the course of the pages that precede this chapter he has systematically investigated and dislodged many beliefs that are fundamental to our existence in the world: the objective necessity of causality, the existence and persistence of external bodies, the power and reliability of our senses and our faculty of reason, our reliance upon induction and the uniformity of nature, and even our deeply held notions of personal identity. We can certainly understand, then, why Hume finds himself mired in a philosophical malaise to the point of momentary paralysis, admitting that following his conclusions he stands "ready to reject all belief and reasoning, and can look upon no opinion even as more probably or likely than another."

The cure for his "philosophical melancholy," Hume suggests, ultimately comes from "nature herself." A good meal, a solitary walk, a conversation with friends, and a game of backgammon all serve to dispel the despair felt so vividly in the midst of skeptical reflection. Indeed, when we leave the study, common sense reasserts itself upon us with such force that our original conclusions seem almost ridiculous. Hume even goes so far as to consider burning all his books so as never to abandon common beliefs in favor of philosophy and its extreme skepticism.

In the end, however, philosophy cannot be rejected altogether. Hume realizes that in some cases the most fundamental beliefs we

share prove illusory, and he understandably finds himself compelled to discard them. Moreover, we cannot simply abandon
reasoning, for we then forfeit all philosophy and science, leaving
only the imagination and superstition to guide us. Given the short-
comings of both common sense and philosophical reasoning,
Hume humbly offers toward the end of the chapter that he will
attempt to strike a serviceable balance between the two. At the very
least, he admits that he will be satisfied if he can bring the subject of
human nature and the mind "a little more into fashion."

Conclusion of this Book

But before I launch out into those immense depths of philosophy, which
lie before me, I find myself inclin'd to stop a moment in my present
station, and to ponder that voyage, which I have undertaken, and which
undoubtedly requires the utmost art and industry to be brought to a
happy conclusion. Methinks I am like a man, who having struck on many
shoals, and having narrowly escap'd shipwreck in passing a small frith,
has yet the temerity to put out to sea in the same leaky weather-beaten
vessel, and even carries his ambition so far as to think of compassing the
globe under these disadvantageous circumstances. My memory of past
errors and perplexities, makes me diffident for the future. The wretched
condition, weakness, and disorder of the faculties, I must employ in my
enquiries, increase my apprehensions. And the impossibility of
amending or correcting these faculties, reduces me almost to despair,
and makes me resolve to perish on the barren rock, on which I am at
present, rather than venture myself upon that boundless ocean, which
runs out into immensity. This sudden view of my danger strikes me
with melancholy; and as 'tis usual for that passion, above all others, to
indulge itself; I cannot forbear feeding my despair, with all those
desponding reflections, which the present subject furnishes me with in
such abundance.

I am first affrighted and confounded with that forelorn solitude, in
which I am plac'd in my philosophy, and fancy myself some strange
uncouth monster, who not being able to mingle and unite in society, has
been expell'd all human commerce, and left utterly abandon'd and dis-
consolate. Fain would I run into the crowd for shelter and warmth; but
cannot prevail with myself to mix with such deformity. I call upon others

to join me, in order to make a company apart; but no one will hearken to me. Every one keeps at a distance, and dreads that storm, which beats upon me from every side. I have expos'd myself to the enmity of all metaphysicians, logicians, mathematicians, and even theologians; and can I wonder at the insults I must suffer? I have declar'd my disapprobation of their systems; and can I be surpris'd, if they should express a hatred of mine and of my person? When I look abroad, I foresee on every side, dispute, contradiction, anger, calumny and detraction. When I turn my eye inward, I find nothing but doubt and ignorance. All the world conspires to oppose and contradict me; tho' such is my weakness, that I feel all my opinions loosen and fall of themselves, when unsupported by the approbation of others. Every step I take is with hesitation, and every new reflection makes me dread an error and absurdity in my reasoning.

For with what confidence can I venture upon such bold enterprises, when beside those numberless infirmities peculiar to myself, I find so many which are common to human nature? Can I be sure, that in leaving all establish'd opinions I am following truth; and by what criterion shall I distinguish her, even if fortune should at last guide me on her foot-steps? After the most accurate and exact of my reasonings, I can give no reason why I should assent to it; and feel nothing but a *strong* propensity to consider objects *strongly* in that view, under which they appear to me. Experience is a principle, which instructs me in the several conjunctions of objects for the past. Habit is another principle, which determines me to expect the same for the future; and both of them conspiring to operate upon the imagination, make me form certain ideas in a more intense and lively manner, than others, which are not attended with the same advantages. Without this quality, by which the mind enlivens some ideas beyond others (which seemingly is so trivial, and so little founded on reason) we could never assent to any argument, nor carry our view beyond those few objects, which are present to our senses. Nay, even to these objects we could never attribute any existence, but what was dependent on the senses; and must comprehend them entirely in that succession of perceptions, which constitutes our self or person. Nay farther, even with relation to that succession, we could only admit of those perceptions, which are immediately present to our consciousness, nor could those lively images, with which the memory presents us, be ever receiv'd as true pictures of past perceptions. The memory, senses, and understanding are, therefore, all of them founded on the imagination, or the vivacity of our ideas.

No wonder a principle so inconstant and fallacious should lead us into errors, when implicitely follow'd (as it must be) in all its variations. 'Tis this principle, which makes us reason from causes and effects; and 'tis the same principle, which convinces us of the continu'd existence of external objects, when absent from the senses. But tho' these two operations be equally natural and necessary in the human mind, yet in some circumstances they are directly contrary, nor is it possible for us to reason justly and regularly from causes and effects, and at the same time believe the continu'd existence of matter. How then shall we adjust those principles together? Which of them shall we prefer? Or in case we prefer neither of them, but successively assent to both, as is usual among philosophers, with what confidence can we afterwards usurp that glorious title, when we thus knowingly embrace a manifest contradiction?

This contradiction would be more excusable, were it compensated by any degree of solidity and satisfaction in the other parts of our reasoning. But the case is quite contrary. When we trace up the human understanding to its first principles, we find it to lead us into such sentiments, as seem to turn into ridicule all our past pains and industry, and to discourage us from future enquiries. Nothing is more curiously enquir'd after by the mind of man, than the causes of every phenomenon; nor are we content with knowing the immediate causes, but push on our enquiries, till we arrive at the original and ultimate principle. We would not willingly stop before we are acquainted with that energy in the cause, by which it operates on its effect; that tie, which connects them together; and that efficacious quality, on which the tie depends. This is our aim in all our studies and reflections: And how must we be disappointed, when we learn, that this connexion, tie, or energy lies merely in ourselves, and is nothing but that determination of the mind, which is acquir'd by custom, and causes us to make a transition from an object to its usual attendant, and from the impression of one to the lively idea of the other? Such a discovery not only cuts off all hope of ever attaining satisfaction, but even prevents our very wishes; since it appears, that when we say we desire to know the ultimate and operating principle, as something, which resides in the external object, we either contradict ourselves, or talk without a meaning.

This deficiency in our ideas is not, indeed, perceiv'd in common life, nor are we sensible, that in the most usual conjunctions of cause and effect we are as ignorant of the ultimate principle, which binds them together, as in the most unusual and extraordinary. But this proceeds merely from an illusion of the imagination; and the question is, how far we ought to yield to these illusions. This question is very difficult, and reduces us to a very dangerous dilemma, whichever way we answer it. For if we assent to every trivial suggestion of the fancy; beside that these suggestions are often contrary to each other; they lead us into such errors, absurdities, and obscurities, that we must at last become asham'd of our credulity. Nothing is more dangerous to reason than the flights of the imagination, and nothing has been the occasion of more mistakes among philosophers. Men of bright fancies may in this respect be compar'd to those angels, whom the scripture represents as covering their eyes with their wings. This has already appear'd in so many instances, that we may spare ourselves the trouble of enlarging upon it any farther.

But on the other hand, if the consideration of these instances makes us take a resolution to reject all the trivial suggestions of the fancy, and adhere to the understanding, that is, to the general and more establish'd properties of the imagination; even this resolution, if steadily executed, would be dangerous, and attended with the most fatal consequences. For I have already shewn, that the understanding, when it acts alone, and according to its most general principles, entirely subverts itself, and leaves not the lowest degree of evidence in any proposition, either in philosophy or common life. We save ourselves from this total scepticism only by means of that singular and seemingly trivial property of the fancy, by which we enter with difficulty into remote views of things, and are not able to accompany them with so sensible an impression, as we do those, which are more easy and natural. Shall we, then, establish it for a general maxim, that no refin'd or elaborate reasoning is ever to be receiv'd? Consider well the consequences of such a principle. By this means you cut off entirely all science and philosophy: You proceed upon one singular quality of the imagination, and by a parity of reason must embrace all of them: And you expressly contradict yourself; since this maxim must be built on the preceding reasoning, which will be allow'd to be sufficiently refin'd and metaphysical. What party, then, shall we choose among these difficulties? If we embrace this principle, and condemn all refin'd reasoning, we run into the most manifest absurdities. If we reject it in favour of these reasonings, we subvert entirely the human understanding. We have, therefore, no choice left but betwixt a false reason and none at all. For my part, I know not what ought to be done in the present case. I can only observe what is commonly done; which is, that this difficulty is seldom or never thought of; and even where it has once been present to the mind, is quickly forgot, and leaves but a small impression behind it. Very refin'd reflections have little or no influence upon us; and yet we do not, and cannot establish it for a rule, that they ought not to have any influence; which implies a manifest contradiction.

But what have I here said, that reflections very refin'd and metaphysical have little or no influence upon us? This opinion I can scarce forbear retracting, and condemning from my present feeling and experience. The *intense* view of these manifold contradictions and imperfections in human reason has so wrought upon me, and heated my brain, that I am ready to reject all belief and reasoning, and can look upon no opinion even as more probable or likely than another. Where am I, or what? From what causes do I derive my existence, and to what condition shall I return? Whose favour shall I court, and whose anger must I dread? What beings surround me? and on whom have I any influence, or who have any influence on me? I am confounded with all these questions, and begin to fancy myself in the most deplorable condition imaginable, inviron'd with the deepest darkness, and utterly depriv'd of the use of every member and faculty.

Most fortunately it happens, that since reason is incapable of dispelling these clouds, nature herself suffices to that purpose, and cures me of this philosophical melancholy and delirium, either by relaxing this bent of mind, or by some avocation, and lively impression of my senses, which obliterate all these chimeras. I dine, I play a game of backgammon. I converse, and am merry with my friends; and when after three or four hour's amusement, I would return to these speculations, they appear so cold, and strain'd, and ridiculous, that I cannot find in my heart to enter into them any farther.

Here then I find myself absolutely and necessarily determin'd to live, and talk, and act like other people in the common affairs of life. But notwithstanding that my natural propensity, and the course of my animal spirits and passions reduce me to this indolent belief in the general maxims of the world, I still feel such remains of my former disposition, that I am ready to throw all my books and papers into the fire, and resolve never more to renounce the pleasures of life for the sake of reasoning and philosophy. For these are my sentiments in that splenetic humour, which governs me at present. I may, nay I must yield to the current of nature, in submitting to my senses and understanding; and in this blind submission I shew most perfectly my sceptical disposition and principles. But does it follow, that I must strive against the current of nature, which leads me to indolence and pleasure; that I must seclude myself, in some measure, from the commerce and society of men, which is so agreeable; and that I must torture my brain with subtilities and sophistries, at the very time that I cannot satisfy myself concerning the reasonableness of so painful an application, nor have any tolerable prospect of arriving by its means at truth and certainty. Under what obligation do I lie of making such an abuse of time? And to what end can it serve either for the service of mankind, or for my own private interest?

No: If I must be a fool, as all those who reason or believe any thing *certainly* are, my follies shall at least be natural and agreeable. Where I strive against my inclination, I shall have a good reason for my resistance; and will no more be led a wandering into such dreary solitudes, and rough passages, as I have hitherto met with.

These are the sentiments of my spleen and indolence; and indeed I must confess, that philosophy has nothing to oppose to them, and expects a victory more from the returns of a serious good-humour'd disposition, than from the force of reason and conviction. In all the incidents of life we ought still to preserve our scepticism. If we believe, that fire warms, or water refreshes, 'tis only because it costs us too much pain to think otherwise. Nay if we are philosophers, it ought only to be upon sceptical principles, and from an inclination, which we feel to the employing ourselves after that manner. Where reason is lively, and mixes itself with some propensity, it ought to be assented to. Where it does not, it never can have any title to operate upon us.

At the time, therefore, that I am tir'd with amusement and company, and have indulg'd a *reverie* in my chamber, or in a solitary walk by a river-side, I feel my mind all collected within itself, and am naturally *inclin'd* to carry my view into all those subjects, about which I have met with so many disputes in the course of my reading and conversation. I cannot forbear having a curiosity to be acquainted with the principles of moral good and evil, the nature and foundation of government, and the cause of those several passions and inclinations, which actuate and govern me. I am uneasy to think I approve of one object, and disapprove of another; call one thing beautiful, and another deform'd; decide concerning truth and falshood, reason and folly, without knowing upon what principles I proceed. I am concern'd for the condition of the learned world, which lies under such a deplorable ignorance in all these particulars. I feel an ambition to arise in me of contributing to the instruction of mankind, and of acquiring a name by my inventions and discoveries. These sentiments spring up naturally in my present disposition; and should I endeavour to banish them, by attaching myself to any other business or diversion, I *feel* I should be a loser in point of pleasure; and this is the origin of my philosophy.

But even suppose this curiosity and ambition should not transport me into speculations without the sphere of common life, it would necessarily happen, that from my very weakness I must be led into such enquiries. 'Tis certain, that superstition is much more bold in its systems and hypotheses than philosophy; and while the latter contents itself with assigning new causes and principles to the phenomena, which appear in the visible world, the former opens a world of its own, and presents us with scenes, and beings, and objects, which are altogether new. Since therefore 'tis almost impossible for the mind of man to rest, like those of beasts, in that narrow circle of objects, which are the subject of daily conversation and action, we ought only to deliberate concerning the choice of our guide, and ought to prefer that which is safest and most agreeable. And in this respect I make bold to recommend philosophy, and shall not scruple to give it the preference to superstition of every kind or denomination. For as superstition arises naturally and easily from the popular opinions of mankind, it seizes more strongly on the mind, and is often able to disturb us in the conduct of our lives and actions. Philosophy on the contrary, if just, can present us only with mild and moderate sentiments; and if false and extravagant, its opinions are merely the objects of a cold and general speculation, and seldom go so far as to interrupt the course of our natural propensities. The Cynics are an extraordinary instance of philosophers, who from reasonings purely philosophical ran into as great extravagancies of conduct as any *Monk* or *Dervise* that ever was in the world. Generally speaking, the errors in religion are dangerous; those in philosophy only ridiculous.

I am sensible, that these two cases of the strength and weakness of the mind will not comprehend all mankind, and that there are in *England*, in particular, many honest gentlemen, who being always employ'd in their domestic affairs, or amusing themselves in common recreations, have carried their thoughts very little beyond those objects, which are every day expos'd to their senses. And indeed, of such as these I pretend not to make philosophers, nor do I expect them either to be associates in these researches or auditors of these discoveries. They do well to keep themselves in their present situation; and instead of refining them into philosophers, I wish we could communicate to our founders of systems, a share of this gross earthy mixture, as an ingredient, which they commonly stand much in need of, and which would serve to temper those fiery particles, of which they are compos'd. While a warm imagination is allow'd to enter into philosophy, and hypotheses embrac'd merely for being specious and agreeable, we can never have any steady principles, nor any sentiments, which will suit with common practice and experience. But were these hypotheses once remov'd, we might hope to establish a system or set of opinions, which if not true (for that, perhaps, is too much to be hop'd for) might at least be satisfactory to the human mind, and might stand the test of the most critical examination. Nor should we despair of attaining this end, because of the many chimerical systems, which have successively arisen and decay'd away among men, would we consider the shortness of that period, wherein these questions have been the subjects of enquiry and reasoning. Two thousand years with such long interruptions, and under such mighty discouragements are a small space of time to give any tolerable perfection to the sciences; and perhaps we are still in too early an age of the world to discover any principles, which will bear the examination of the latest posterity. For my part, my only hope is, that I may contribute a little to the advancement of knowledge, by giving in some particulars a different turn to the speculations of philosophers, and pointing out to them more distinctly those subjects, where alone they can expect assurance and conviction. Human Nature is the only science of man; and yet has been hitherto the most neglected. 'Twill be sufficient for me, if I can bring it a little more into fashion; and the hope of this serves to compose my temper from that spleen, and invigorate it from that indolence, which sometimes prevail upon me. If the reader finds himself in the same easy disposition, let him follow me in my future speculations. If not, let him follow his inclination, and wait the returns of application and good humour. The conduct of a man, who studies philosophy in this careless manner, is more truly sceptical than that of one, who feeling in himself an inclination to it, is yet so overwhelm'd with doubts and scruples, as totally to reject it. A true sceptic will be diffident of his philosophical doubts, as well as of his philosophical conviction; and will never refuse any innocent satisfaction, which offers itself, upon account of either of them.

Nor is it only proper we should in general indulge our inclination in the most elaborate philosophical researches, notwithstanding our sceptical principles, but also that we should yield to that propensity, which inclines us to be positive and certain in *particular points*, according to the light, in which we survey them in any *particular instant*. 'Tis easier to forbear all examination and enquiry, than to check ourselves in so natural a propensity, and guard against that assurance, which always arises from an exact and full survey of an object. On such an occasion we are apt not only to forget our scepticism, but even our modesty too; and make use of such terms as these, *'tis evident, 'tis certain, 'tis undeniable*; which a due deference to the public ought, perhaps, to prevent. I may have fallen into this fault after the example of others; but I here enter a *caveat* against any objections, which may be offer'd on that head; and declare that such expressions were extorted from me by the present view of the object, and imply no dogmatical spirit, nor conceited idea of my own judgment, which are sentiments that I am sensible can become no body, and a sceptic still less than any other.

29

Thomas Reid, from *Essays on the Intellectual Powers of Man*

Thomas Reid (1710–96) was a Scottish philosopher, a contemporary of David Hume, and a professor of philosophy at Aberdeen and later at Glasgow. He is best known for his efforts to refute Hume's skepticism, but, in his major works, *Inquiry into the Human Mind*, *Essays on the Intellectual Powers of Man*, and *Essays on the Active Powers of Man*, he developed a systematic approach to the philosophical problems of knowledge, action, and morals. He defended common sense, by which he meant various principles inherent in the constitution of the human mind that regulates judgments and actions. Because these principles are first principles, they are not in need of proof, but they are not vulnerable to skeptical arguments because it is unreasonable, he argues, to demand a proof. His defense of common sense against skepticism has often been compared to Moore's defense, an example of which is included earlier in this volume (see chapter 10).

The selection below is an excerpt from Reid's chapter 14, "Reflections on the Common Theory of Ideas," from the second essay of the *Essays on the Intellectual Powers of Man*. In it, he argues that the skepticism of Hume is one of the consequences of the theory of ideas (or the representative theory of knowledge) that can be found in various versions throughout the whole history of Western philosophy. This theory is epitomized in this remark of Locke's from his *An Essay concerning Human Understanding*: "For since the Things, the Mind contemplates, are none of them, besides it self, present to the Understanding, 'tis necessary that something else, as a Sign or Representation of the thing it considers, should be present to it: And these are *Ideas"* (Book IV, xxi, 4). According to most accounts of the theory of ideas, our knowledge of the external world is based upon inferences from inner ideas to the things that the ideas are taken to represent. Reid, like Berkeley before him, points out that such inferences cannot be shown to be valid. In this selection, Reid denies the very existence of ideas and attempts to refute the arguments used to support the theory. On his view, there is no intermediary between the mind and its objects; we perceive the external world directly; no shaky inference is necessary.

To prevent mistakes, the reader must again be reminded, that if by ideas are meant only the acts or operations of our minds in perceiving, remembering, or imagining objects, I am far from calling in question the existence of those acts; we are conscious of them every day and every hour of life; and I believe no man of a sound mind ever doubted of the real existence of the operations of mind, of which he is conscious. Nor is it to be doubted that, by the faculties which God has given us, we can conceive things that are absent, as well as perceive those that are within the reach of our senses; and that such conceptions may be more or less distinct, and more or less lively and strong. We have reason to ascribe to the all-knowing and all-perfect Being distinct conceptions of all things existent and possible, and of all their relations; and if these conceptions are called his eternal ideas, there ought to be no dispute among philosophers about a word. The ideas, of whose existence I require the proof, are not the operations of any mind, but supposed objects of those operations. They are not perception, remembrance, or conception, but things that are said to be perceived, or remembered, *or* imagined.

Nor do I dispute the existence of what the vulgar call the objects of perception. These, by all who acknowledge their existence, are called real things, not ideas. But philosophers maintain that, besides these, there are immediate objects of perception in the mind itself: that, for instance, we do not see the sun immediately, but an idea; or, as Mr Hume calls it, an impression in our own minds. This idea is said to be the image, the resemblance, the representative of the sun, if there be a sun. It is from the existence of the idea that we must infer the existence of the sun. But the idea, being immediately perceived, there can be no doubt, as philosophers think, of its existence.

In like manner, when I remember, or when I imagine anything, all men acknowledge that there must be something that is remembered, or that is imagined; that is, some object of those operations. The object remembered must be something that did exist in time past: the object imagined may be something that never existed. But, say the philosophers, besides these objects which all men acknowledge, there is a more immediate object which really exists in the mind at the same time we remember or imagine. This object is an idea or image of the thing remembered or imagined.

The *first* reflection I would make on this philosophical opinion is, that it is directly contrary to the universal sense of men who have not been instructed in philosophy. When we see the sun or moon, we have no doubt that the very objects which we immediately see are very far distant from us, and from one another. We have not the least doubt that this is the sun and moon which God created some thousands of years ago, and which have continued to perform their revolutions in the heavens ever since. But how are we astonished when the philosopher informs us that we are mistaken in all this; that the sun and moon which we see are not, as we imagine, many miles distant from us, and from each other, but that they are in our own mind; that they had no existence before we saw them, and will have none when we cease to perceive and to think of them; because the objects we perceive are only ideas in our own minds, which can have no existence a moment longer than we think of them!

If a plain man, uninstructed in philosophy, has faith to receive these mysteries, how great must be his astonishment! He is brought into a new world, where everything he sees, tastes, or touches, is an idea – a fleeting kind of being which he can conjure into existence, or can annihilate in the twinkling of an eye.

After his mind is somewhat composed, it will be natural for him to ask his philosophical instructor, Pray, sir, are there then no substantial and permanent beings called the sun and moon, which continue to exist whether we think of them or not?

Here the philosophers differ. Mr Locke, and those that were before him, will answer to this question, that it is very true there are substantial and permanent beings called the sun and moon; but they never appear to us in their own person, but by their representatives, the ideas in our own minds, and we know nothing of them but what we can gather from those ideas.

Bishop Berkeley and Mr Hume would give a different answer to the question proposed. They would assure the querist that it is a vulgar error, a mere prejudice of the ignorant and unlearned, to think that there are any permanent and substantial beings called the sun and moon; that the heavenly bodies, our own bodies, and all bodies whatsoever, are nothing but ideas in our minds; and that there can be nothing like the ideas of one mind, but the ideas of another mind. There is nothing in nature but minds and ideas, says the Bishop; nay, says Mr Hume, there is nothing in nature but ideas only; for what we call a mind is nothing but a train of ideas connected by certain relations between themselves.

In this representation of the theory of ideas, there is nothing exaggerated or misrepresented, as far as I am able to judge; and surely nothing farther is necessary to shew that, to the uninstructed in philosophy, it must appear extravagant and visionary, and most contrary to the dictates of common understanding.

There is the less need of any farther proof of this, that it is very amply acknowledged by Mr Hume in his Essay on the Academical or Sceptical Philosophy. "It seems evident," says he, "that men are carried, by a natural instinct or prepossession, to repose faith in their senses; and that, without any reasoning, or even almost before the use of reason, we always suppose an external universe, which depends not on our perception, but would exist though we and every sensible creature were absent or annihilated. Even the animal creation are governed by a like opinion, and preserve this belief of external objects in all their thoughts, designs, and actions."

"It seems also evident that, when men follow this blind and powerful instinct of nature, they always suppose the very images presented by the senses to be the external objects, and never entertain any suspicion that the one are nothing but representations of the other. This very table which we see white, and feel hard, is believed to exist independent of our perception, and to be something external to the mind which perceives it; our presence bestows not being upon it; our absence annihilates it not: it preserves its existence uniform and entire, independent of the situation of intelligent beings who perceive or contemplate it.

"But this universal and primary notion of all men is soon destroyed by the slightest philosophy, which teaches us that nothing can ever be present to the mind, but an image or perception; and that the senses are only the inlets through which these images are received, without being ever able to produce any immediate intercourse between the mind and the object."

It is therefore acknowledged by this philosopher, to be a natural instinct or prepossession, an universal and primary opinion of all men, a primary instinct of nature, that the objects which we immediately perceive by our senses, are not images in our minds, but external objects, and that their existence is independent of us and our perception. [...]

A *second* reflection upon this subject is – that the authors who have treated of ideas, have generally taken their existence for granted, as a thing that could not be called in question; and such arguments as they have mentioned incidentally, in order to prove it, seem too weak to support the conclusion.

Mr Locke, in the introduction to his Essay, tells us, that he uses the word idea to signify whatever is the immediate object of thought; and then adds, "I presume it will be easily granted me that there are such ideas in men's minds; every one is conscious of them in himself; and men's words and actions will satisfy him that they are in others." I am indeed conscious of perceiving, remembering, imagining; but that the objects of these operations are images in my mind, I am not conscious. I am satisfied, by men's words and actions, that they often perceive the same objects which I perceive, which could not be, if those objects were ideas in their own minds.

There is an argument which is hinted at by Malebranche, and by several other authors, which deserves to be more seriously considered. As I find it most clearly expressed and most fully urged by Dr Samuel Clarke, I shall give it in his words, in his second reply to Leibnitz, §4. "The soul, without being present to the images of the things perceived, could not possibly perceive them. A living substance can only there perceive, where it is present, either to the things themselves (as the omnipresent God is to the whole universe) or to the images of things, as the soul is in its proper *sensorium*."

Sir Isaac Newton expresses the same sentiment, but with his usual reserve, in a query only.

The ingenious Dr Porterfield, in his Essay concerning the motions of our eyes, adopts this opinion with more confidence. His words are: "How body acts upon mind, or mind upon body, I know not; but this I am very certain of, that nothing can act, or be acted upon, where it is not; and therefore our mind can never perceive anything but its own proper modifications, and the various states of the sensorium, to which it is present: so that it is not the external sun and moon which are in the heavens, which our mind perceives, but only their image or representation impressed upon the sensorium. How the soul of a seeing man sees these images, or how it receives those ideas, from such agitations in the sensorium, I know not; but I am sure it can never perceive the external bodies themselves, to which it is not present."

These, indeed, are great authorities: but, in matters of philosophy, we must not be guided by authority, but by reason. Dr Clarke, in the place cited, mentions slightly, as the reason of his opinion, that "nothing can any more act, or be acted upon when it is not present, than it can be where it is not." And again, in his third reply to Leibnitz, §11 – "We are sure the soul cannot perceive what it is not present to, because nothing can act, or be acted upon, where it is not." The same reason we see is urged by Dr Porterfield.

That nothing can act immediately where it is not, I think must be admitted: for I agree with Sir Isaac Newton, that power without substance is inconceivable. It is a consequence of this, that nothing can be acted upon immediately where the agent is not present: let this, therefore be granted. To make the reasoning conclusive, it is farther necessary, that, when we perceive objects, either they act upon us, or we act upon them. This does not appear self-evident, nor have I ever met with any proof of it. I shall briefly offer the reasons why I think it ought not to be admitted.

When we say that one being acts upon another, we mean that some power or force is exerted by the agent, which produces, or has a tendency to produce, a change in the thing acted upon. If this be the meaning of the phrase, as I conceive it is, there appears no reason for asserting that, in perception, either the object acts upon the mind, or the mind upon the object.

An object, in being perceived, does not act at all. I perceive the walls of the room where I sit; but they are perfectly inactive, and therefore act not upon the mind. To be perceived, is what logicians call an external denomination, which implies neither action nor quality in the object perceived. Nor could men ever have gone into this notion, that perception is owing to some action of the object upon the mind, were it not that we are so prone to form our notions of the mind from some similitude we conceive between it and body. Thought in the mind is conceived to have some analogy to motion in a body: and, as a body is put in motion, by being acted upon by some other body; so we are apt to think the mind is made to perceive, by some impulse it receives from the object. But reasonings, drawn from such analogies, ought never to be trusted. They are, indeed, the cause of most of our errors with regard to the mind. And we might as well conclude, that minds may be measured by feet and inches, or weighed by ounces and drachms, because bodies have those properties.

I see as little reason, in the second place, to believe that in perception the mind acts upon the object. To perceive an object is one thing, to act upon it is another; nor is the last at all included in the first. To say that I act upon the wall by looking at it, is an abuse of language, and has no meaning. Logicians distinguish two kinds of operations of mind: the first kind produces no effect without the mind; the last does. The first they call *immanent acts*, the second *transitive*. All intellectual operations belong to the first class; they produce no effect upon any external object. But, without having recourse to logical distinctions, every man of common sense knows, that to think of an object, and to act upon it, are very different things.

As we have, therefore, no evidence that, in perception, the mind acts upon the object, or the object upon the mind, but strong reasons to the contrary, Dr Clarke's argument against our perceiving external objects immediately falls to the ground.

This notion, that, in perception, the object must be contiguous to the percipient, seems, with many other prejudices, to be borrowed from analogy. In all the external senses, there must, as has been before observed, be some impression made upon the organ of sense by the object, or by something coming from the object. An impression supposes contiguity. Hence we are led by analogy to conceive something similar in the operations of the mind. Many philosophers resolve almost every operation of mind into impressions and feelings, words manifestly borrowed from the sense of touch. And it is very natural to conceive contiguity necessary between that which makes the impression, and that which receives it; between that which feels, and that which is felt. And though no philosopher will now pretend to justify such analogical reasoning as this, yet it has a powerful influence upon the judgment, while we contemplate the operations of our minds, only as they appear through the deceitful medium of such analogical notions and expressions.

When we lay aside those analogies, and reflect attentively upon our perception of the objects of sense, we must acknowledge that, though we are conscious of perceiving objects, we are altogether ignorant how it is brought about; and know as little how we perceive objects as how we were made. And, if we should admit an image in the mind, or contiguous to it, we know as little how perception may be produced by this image as by the most distant object. Why, therefore, should we be led, by a theory which is neither grounded on evidence, nor, if admitted, can explain any one phenomenon of perception, to reject the natural and immediate dictates of those perceptive powers, to which, in the conduct of life, we find a necessity of yielding implicit submission?

There remains only one other argument that I have been able to find urged against our perceiving external objects immediately. It is proposed by Mr Hume, who, in the essay already quoted, after acknowledging that it is an universal and primary opinion of all men, that we perceive external objects immediately, subjoins what follows:–

"But this universal and primary opinion of all men is soon destroyed by the slightest philosophy, which teaches us that nothing can ever be present to the mind but an image or perception; and that the senses are only the inlets through which these images are received, without being ever able to produce any immediate intercourse between the mind and the object. The table, which we see, seems to diminish as we remove farther from it: but the real table, which exists independent of us, suffers no alteration. It was, therefore, nothing but its image which was present to the mind. These are the obvious dictates of reason; and no man who reflects ever doubted that the existences which we consider, when we say *this house*, and *that tree*, are nothing but perceptions in the mind, and fleeting copies and representations of other existences, which remain uniform and independent. So far, then, we are necessitated, by reasoning, to depart from the primary instincts of nature, and to embrace a new system with regard to the evidence of our senses.''

We have here a remarkable conflict between two contradictory opinions, wherein all mankind are engaged. On the one side stand all the vulgar, who are unpractised in philosophical researches, and guided by the uncorrupted primary instincts of nature. On the other side stand all the philosophers, ancient and modern; every man, without exception, who reflects. In this division, to my great humiliation, I find myself classed with the vulgar.

The passage now quoted is all I have found in Mr Hume's writings upon this point: and, indeed, there is more reasoning in it than I have found in any other author; I shall, therefore, examine it minutely.

First, he tells us, that "this universal and primary opinion of all men is soon destroyed by the slightest philosophy, which teaches us that nothing can ever be present to the mind but an image or perception."

The phrase of being present to the mind has some obscurity; but I conceive he means being an immediate object of thought; an immediate object, for instance, of perception, of memory, or of imagination. If this be the meaning (and it is the only pertinent one I can think of) there is no more in this passage but an assertion of the proposition to be proved, and an assertion that philosophy teaches it. If this be so, I beg leave to dissent from philosophy till she gives me reason for what she teaches. For, though common sense and my external senses demand my assent to their dictates upon their own authority, yet philosophy is not entitled to this privilege. But, that I may not dissent from so grave a personage without giving a reason, I give this as the reason of my dissent:– I see the sun when he shines; I remember the battle of Culloden; and neither of these objects is an image or perception.

He tells us, in the next place, "That the senses are only the inlets through which these images are received."

I know that Aristotle and the schoolmen taught that images or species flow from objects, and are let in by the senses, and strike upon the mind;

but this has been so effectually refuted by Des Cartes, by Malebranche, and many others, that nobody now pretends to defend it. Reasonable men consider it as one of the most unintelligible and unmeaning parts of the ancient system. To what cause is it owing that modern philosophers are so prone to fall back into this hypothesis, as if they really believed it? For, of this proneness I could give many instances besides this of Mr Hume; and I take the cause to be, that images in the mind, and images let in by the senses, are so nearly allied, and so strictly connected, that they must stand or fall together. The old system consistently maintained both: but the new system has rejected the doctrine of images let in by the senses, holding, nevertheless, that there are images in the mind; and, having made this unnatural divorce of two doctrines which ought not to be put asunder, that which they have retained often leads them back involuntarily to that which they have rejected.

Mr Hume surely did not seriously believe that an image of sound is let in by the ear, an image of smell by the nose, an image of hardness and softness, of solidity and resistance, by the touch. For, besides the absurdity of the thing, which has often been shewn, Mr Hume, and all modern philosophers, maintain that the images which are the immediate objects of perception have no existence when they are not perceived; whereas, if they were let in by the senses, they must be, before they are perceived, and have a separate existence.

He tell us, farther, that philosophy teaches that the senses are unable to produce any immediate intercourse between the mind and the object. Here, I still require the reasons that philosophy gives for this; for, to my apprehension, I immediately perceive external objects, and this, I conceive is the immediate intercourse here meant.

Hitherto I see nothing that can be called an argument. Perhaps it was intended only for illustration. The argument, the only argument, follows:–

The table which we see seems to diminish as we remove farther from it; but the real table, which exists independent of us, suffers no alteration. It was, therefore, nothing but its image which was presented to the mind. These are the obvious dictates of reason.

To judge of the strength of this argument, it is necessary to attend to a distinction which is familiar to those who are conversant in the mathematical sciences – I mean the distinction between real and apparent magnitude. The real magnitude of a line is measured by some known measure of length – as inches, feet, or miles: the real magnitude of a surface or solid, by known measures of surface or of capacity. This magnitude is an object of touch only, and not of sight; nor could we even have had any conception of it, without the sense of touch; and Bishop Berkeley, on that account, calls it *tangible magnitude*.

Apparent magnitude is measured by the angle which an object subtends at the eye. Supposing two right lines drawn from the eye to the extremities of the object making an angle, of which the object is the subtense, the apparent magnitude is measured by this angle. This apparent magnitude is an object of sight, and not of touch. Bishop Berkeley calls it *visible magnitude*.

If it is asked what is the apparent magnitude of the sun's diameter, the answer is, that it is about thirty-one minutes of a degree. But, if it is asked what is the real magnitude of the sun's diameter, the answer must be, so many thousand miles, or so many diameters of the earth. From which it is evident that real magnitude, and apparent magnitude, are things of a different nature, though the name of magnitude is given to both. The first has three dimensions, the last only two; the first is measured by a line, the last by an angle.

From what has been said, it is evident that the real magnitude of a body must continue unchanged, while the body is unchanged. This we grant. But is it likewise evident, that the apparent magnitude must continue the same while the body is unchanged? So far otherwise, that every man who knows anything of mathematics can easily demonstrate, that the same individual object, remaining in the same place, and unchanged, must necessarily vary in its apparent magnitude, according as the point from which it is seen is more or less distant; and that its apparent length or breadth will be nearly in a reciprocal proportion to the distance of the spectator. This is as certain as the principles of geometry.

We must likewise attend to this – that, though the real magnitude of a body is not originally an object of sight, but of touch, yet we learn by experience to judge of the real magnitude in many cases by sight. We learn by experience to judge of the distance of a body from the eye within certain limits; and, from its distance and apparent magnitude taken together, we learn to judge of its real magnitude.

And this kind of judgment, by being repeated every hour and almost every minute of our lives, becomes, when we are grown up, so ready and so habitual, that it very much resembles the original perceptions of our senses, and may not improperly be called *acquired perception*.

Whether we call it judgment or acquired perception is a verbal difference. But it is evident that, by means of it, we often discover by one sense things which are properly and naturally the objects of another. Thus I can say, without impropriety, I hear a drum, I hear a great bell, or I hear a small bell; though it is certain that the figure or size of the sounding body is not originally an object of hearing. In like manner, we learn by experience how a body of such a real magnitude and at such a distance appears to the eye. But neither its real magnitude, nor its distance from the eye, are properly objects of sight, any more than the form of a drum or the size of a bell, are properly objects of hearing.

If these things be considered, it will appear that Mr Hume's argument hath no force to support his conclusion – nay, that it leads to a contrary conclusion. The argument is this: the table we see seems to diminish as we remove farther from it; that is, its apparent magnitude is diminished; but the real table suffers no alteration – to wit, in its real magnitude; therefore, it is not the real table we see. I admit both the premises in this syllogism, but I deny the conclusion. The syllogism has what the logicians call two middle terms: apparent magnitude is the middle term in the first premise; real magnitude in the second. Therefore, according to the rules of logic, the conclusion is not justly drawn from the premises; but, laying aside the rules of logic, let us examine it by the light of common sense.

Let us suppose, for a moment, that it is the real table we see: Must not this real table seem to diminish as we remove farther from it? It is demonstrable that it must. How then can this apparent diminution be an argument that it is not the real table? When that which must happen to the real table, as we remove farther from it, does actually happen to the table we see, it is absurd to conclude from this, that it is not the real table we see. It is evident, therefore, that this ingenious author has imposed upon himself by confounding real magnitude with apparent magnitude, and that his argument is a mere sophism.

I observed that Mr Hume's argument not only has no strength to support his conclusion, but that it leads to the contrary conclusion – to wit, that it is the real table we see; for this plain reason, that the table we see has precisely that apparent magnitude which it is demonstrable the real table must have when placed at that distance.

This argument is made much stronger by considering that the real table may be placed successively at a thousand different distances, and, in every distance, in a thousand different positions; and it can be determined demonstratively, by the rules of geometry and perspective, what must be its apparent magnitude and apparent figure, in each of those distances and positions. Let the table be placed successively in as many of those different distances and different positions as you will, or in them all; open your eyes and you shall see a table precisely of that apparent magnitude, and that apparent figure, which the real table must have in that distance and in that position. Is not this a strong argument that it is the real table you see?

In a word, the appearance of a visible object is infinitely diversified, according to its distance and position. The visible appearances are innumerable, when we confine ourselves to one object, and they are multiplied according to the variety of objects. Those appearances have been matter of speculation to ingenious men, at least since the time of Euclid. They have accounted for all this variety, on the supposition that the objects we see are external, and not in the mind itself. The rules they have demonstrated about the various projections of the sphere, about the appearances of the planets in their progressions, stations, and retrogradations, and all the rules of perspective, are built on the supposition that the objects of sight are external. They can each of them be tried in thousands of instances. In many arts and professions, innumerable trials are daily made; nor were they ever found to fail in a single instance. Shall we say that a false supposition, invented by the rude vulgar, has been so lucky in solving an infinite number of phenomena of nature? This, surely, would be a greater prodigy than philosophy ever exhibited: add to this, that, upon the contrary hypothesis – to wit, that the objects of sight are internal – no account can be given of any one of those appearances, nor any physical cause assigned why a visible object should, in any one case, have one apparent figure and magnitude rather than another.

Thus, I have considered every argument I have found advanced to prove the existence of ideas, or images of external things, in the mind; and, if no better arguments can be found, I cannot help thinking that the whole history of philosophy has never furnished an instance of an opinion so unanimously entertained by philosophers upon so slight grounds. [...]

A *fourth* reflection is, that ideas do not make any of the operations of the mind to be better understood, although it was probably with that view that they have been first invented, and afterwards so generally received.

We are at a loss to know how we perceive distant objects; how we remember things past; how we imagine things that have no existence. Ideas in the mind seem to account for all these operations: they are all by the means of ideas reduced to one operation – to a kind of feeling, or immediate perception of things present and in contact with the percipient; and feeling is an operation so familiar that we think it needs no explication, but may serve to explain other operations.

But this feeling, or immediate perception, is as difficult to be comprehended as the things which we pretend to explain by it. Two things may be in contact without any feeling or perception; there must therefore be in the percipient a power to feel or to perceive. How this power is produced, and how it operates, is quite beyond the reach of our knowledge. As little can we know whether this power must be limited to things present, and in contact with us. Nor can any man pretend to prove that the Being who gave us the power to perceive things present, may not give us the power to perceive things that are distant, to remember things past, and to conceive things that never existed.

Some philosophers have endeavoured to make all our senses to be only different modifications of touch; a theory which serves only to confound things that are different, and to perplex and darken things that are clear. The theory of ideas resembles this, by reducing all the operations of the human understanding to the perception of ideas in our own minds. This power of perceiving ideas is as inexplicable as any of the powers explained by it: and the contiguity of the object contributes nothing at all to make it better understood; because there appears no connection between contiguity and perception, but what is grounded on prejudices drawn from some imagined similitude between mind and body, and from the supposition that, in perception, the object acts upon the mind, or the mind upon the object. We have seen how this theory has led philosophers to confound those operations of mind, which experience teaches all men to be different, and teaches them to distinguish in common language; and that it has led them to invent a language inconsistent with the principles upon which all language is grounded.

The *last* reflection I shall make upon this theory, is – that the natural and necessary consequences of it furnish a just prejudice against it to every man who pays a due regard to the common sense of mankind.

Not to mention that it led the Pythagoreans and Plato to imagine that we see only the shadows of external things, and not the things themselves, and that it gave rise to the Peripatetic doctrine of sensible *species*, one of the greatest absurdities of that ancient system, let us only consider the fruits it has produced since it was new-modelled by Des Cartes. That great reformer in philosophy saw the absurdity of the doctrine of ideas coming from external objects, and refuted it effectually, after it had been received by philosophers for thousands of years; but he still retained ideas in the brain and in the mind. Upon this foundation all our modern systems of the powers of the mind are built. And the tottering state of those fabrics, though built by skilful hands, may give a strong suspicion of the unsoundness of the foundation.

It was this theory of ideas that led Des Cartes, and those that followed him, to think it necessary to prove, by philosophical arguments, the existence of material objects. And who does not see that philosophy must make a very ridiculous figure in the eyes of sensible men, while it is employed in mustering up metaphysical arguments, to prove that there is a sun and a moon, an earth and a sea? Yet we find these truly great men, Des Cartes, Malebranche, Arnauld, and Locke, seriously employing themselves in this argument.

Surely their principles led them to think that all men, from the beginning of the world, believed the existence of these things upon insufficient grounds, and to think that they would be able to place upon a more rational foundation this universal belief of mankind. But the misfortune is, that all the laboured arguments they have advanced, to prove the existence of those things we see and feel, are mere sophisms: Not one of them will bear examination.

I might mention several paradoxes, which Mr Locke, though by no means fond of paradoxes, was led into by this theory of ideas. Such as, that the secondary qualities of body are no qualities of body at all, but sensations of the mind: That the primary qualities of body are resemblances of our sensations: That we have no notion of duration, but from the succession of ideas in our minds: That personal identity consists in consciousness; so that the same individual thinking being may make two or three different persons, and several different thinking beings make one person: That judgment is nothing but a perception or the agreement or disagreement of our ideas. Most of these paradoxes I shall have occasion to examine.

However, all these consequences of the doctrine of ideas were tolerable, compared with those which came afterwards to be discovered by Berkeley and Hume:– That there is no material world: No abstract ideas or notions: That the mind is only a train of related impressions and ideas, without any subject on which they may be impressed: That there is neither space nor time, body nor mind, but impressions and ideas only: And, to sum up all, That there is no probability, even in demonstration itself, nor any one proposition more probable than its contrary.

These are the noble fruits which have grown upon this theory of ideas, since it began to be cultivated by skilful hands. It is no wonder that sensible men should be disgusted at philosophy, when such wild and shocking paradoxes pass under its name. However, as these paradoxes have, with great acuteness and ingenuity, been deduced by just reasoning from the theory of ideas, they must at last bring this advantage, that positions so shocking to the common sense of mankind, and so contrary to the decisions of all our intellectual powers, will open men's eyes, and break the force of the prejudice which hath held them entangled in that theory.

30

Immanuel Kant, from *Prolegomena* and *Critique of Pure Reason*

Immanuel Kant (1724–1804) asserted that Hume's skepticism awoke him from his dogmatic slumber. Traditional views of objective knowledge claimed that the human mind is capable of knowing the existence and attributes of things as they are in themselves, that the mind is able to adapt to the reality of things. That view, Kant believes, leads to skepticism, for there is no way to establish that the way things appear conform to the way things are in themselves. Kant's transcendental idealism represents a new way of thinking about human knowledge according to which the human understanding organizes sensory input in accordance with its own categories and principles.

In the first selection below from Kant's *Prolegomena to Any Future Metaphysics*, he avows his debt to Hume. The second set of selections consists of some passages from the *Critique of Pure Reason* in which he explains his new orientation in philosophy by analogy with Copernicus' new orientation in astronomy. Also included are passages ("Refutation of Idealism") in which he offers his proof of the existence of an external world and other passages about Hume and skepticism in which he characterizes skepticism as "a resting-place of reason" but not a "permanent dwelling-place."

Since the Essays of Locke and Leibnitz, or rather since the origin of metaphysics so far as we know its history, nothing has ever happened which was more decisive to its fate than the attack made upon it by David Hume. He threw no light on this species of knowledge, but he certainly struck a spark from which light might have been obtained, had it caught some inflammable substance and had its smouldering fire been carefully nursed and developed.

Hume started from a single but important concept in Metaphysics, viz., that of Cause and Effect (including its derivatives force and action, etc.). He challenges reason, which pretends to have given birth to this idea from herself, to answer him by what right she thinks anything to be so constituted, that if that thing be posited, something else also must necessarily be posited; for this is the meaning of the concept of cause. He demonstrated irrefutably that it was perfectly impossible for reason to think *a priori* and by means of concepts a combination involving necessity. We cannot at all see why, in consequence of the existence of one thing, another must necessarily exist, or how the concept of such a combination can arise *a priori*. Hence he inferred, that reason was altogether deluded with reference to this concept, which she erroneously considered as one of her children, whereas in reality it was nothing but a bastard of imagination, impregnated by experience, which subsumed certain representations under the Law of Association, and mistook the subjective necessity of habit for an objective necessity arising from insight. Hence he inferred that reason had no power to think such combinations, even generally, because her concepts would then be purely fictitious, and all her pretended *a priori* cognitions nothing but common experiences marked with a false stamp. In plain language there is not, and cannot be, any such thing as metaphysics at all.

However hasty and mistaken Hume's conclusion may appear, it was at least founded upon investigation, and this investigation deserved the concentrated attention of the brighter spirits of his day as well as determined efforts on their part to discover, if possible, a happier solution of the problem in the sense proposed by him, all of which would have speedily resulted in a complete reform of the science.

But Hume suffered the usual misfortune of metaphysicians, of not being understood. It is positively painful to see how utterly his opponents, Reid, Oswald, Beattie, and lastly Priestley, missed the point of the problem; for while they were ever taking for granted that which he doubted, and demonstrating with zeal and often with impudence that which he never thought of doubting, they so misconstrued his valuable suggestion that everything remained in its old condition, as if nothing had happened.

The question was not whether the concept of cause was right, useful, and even indispensable for our knowledge of nature, for this Hume had never doubted; but whether that concept could be thought by reason *a priori*, and consequently whether it possessed an inner truth, independent of all experience, implying a wider application than merely to the objects of experience. This was Hume's problem. It was a question concerning the *origin*, not concerning the *indispensable need* of the concept. Were the former decided, the conditions of the use and the sphere of its valid application would have been determined as a matter of course.

But to satisfy the conditions of the problem, the opponents of the great thinker should have penetrated very deeply into the nature of reason, so far as it is concerned with pure thinking – a task which did not suit them. They found a more convenient method of being defiant without any insight, viz., the appeal to *common sense*. It is indeed a great gift of God, to possess right, or (as they now call it) plain common sense. But this common sense must be shown practically, by well-considered and reasonable thoughts and words, not by appealing to it as an oracle, when no rational justification can be advanced. To appeal to common sense, when insight and science fail, and no sooner – this is one of the subtle discoveries of modern times, by means of which the most superficial ranter can safely enter the lists with the most thorough thinker, and hold his own. But as long as a particle of insight remains, no one would think of having recourse to this subterfuge. For what is it but an appeal to the opinion of the multitude, of whose applause the philosopher is ashamed, while the popular charlatan glories and confides in it? I should think that Hume might fairly have laid as much claim to common sense as Beattie, and in addition to a critical reason (such as the latter did not possess), which keeps common sense in check and prevents it from speculating, or, if speculations are under discussion, restrains the desire to decide because it cannot satisfy itself concerning its own arguments. By this means alone can common sense remain sound. Chisels and hammers may suffice to work a piece of wood, but for steel-engraving we require an engraver's needle. Thus common sense and speculative understanding are each serviceable in their own way, the former in judgments which apply immediately to experience, the latter when we judge universally from mere concepts, as in metaphysics, where sound common sense, so called in spite of the inapplicability of the word, has no right to judge at all.

I openly confess, the suggestion of David Hume was the very thing, which many years ago first interrupted my dogmatic slumber, and gave my investigations in the field of speculative philosophy quite a new direction. I was far from following him in the conclusions at which he arrived by regarding, not the whole of his problem, but a part, which by itself can give us no information. If we start from a well-founded, but undeveloped, thought, which another has bequeathed to us, we may well hope by continued reflection to advance farther than the acute man, to whom we owe the first spark of light.

I therefore first tried whether Hume's objection could not be put into a general form, and soon found that the concept of the connexion of cause and effect was by no means the only idea by which the understanding thinks the connexion of things *a priori*, but rather that metaphysics consists altogether of such connexions. I sought to ascertain their number, and when I had satisfactorily succeeded in this by starting from a single principle, I proceeded to the deduction of these concepts, which I was now certain were not deduced from experience, as Hume had apprehended, but sprang from the pure understanding. This deduction (which seemed impossible to my acute predecessor, which had never even occurred to any one else, though no one had hesitated to use the concepts without investigating the basis of their objective validity) was the most difficult task ever undertaken in the service of metaphysics; and the worst was that metaphysics, such as it then existed, could not assist me in the least, because this deduction alone can render metaphysics possible. But as soon as I had succeeded in solving Hume's problem not merely in a particular case, but with respect to the whole faculty of pure reason, I could proceed safely, though slowly, to determine the whole sphere of pure reason completely and from general principles, in its circumference as well as in its contents. This was required for metaphysics in order to construct its system according to a reliable method. [...]

We have been long accustomed to seeing antiquated knowledge produced as new by taking it out of its former context, and reducing it to system in a new suit of any fancy pattern under new titles. Most readers will set out by expecting nothing else from the Critique; but these Prolegomena may persuade him that it is a perfectly new science, of which no one has ever even thought, the very idea of which was unknown, and for which nothing hitherto accomplished can be of the smallest use, except it be the suggestion of Hume's doubts. Yet even he did not suspect such a formal science, but ran his ship ashore, for safety's sake, landing on scepticism, there to let it lie and rot; whereas my object is rather to give it a pilot, who, by means of safe astronomical principles drawn from a knowledge of the globe, and provided with a complete chart and compass, may steer the ship safely, whither he listeth.

* * *

Metaphysic, a completely isolated and speculative science of reason, which declines all teaching of experience, and rests on concepts only (not on their application to intuition, as mathematics), in which reason therefore is meant to be her own pupil, has hitherto not been so fortunate as to enter on the secure path of a science, although it is older than all other sciences, and would remain, even if all the rest were swallowed up in the abyss of an all-destroying barbarism. In metaphysic, reason, even if it tries only to understand *a priori* (as it pretends to do) those laws which are confirmed by the commonest experience, is constantly brought to a standstill, and we are obliged again and again to retrace our steps, because they do not lead us where we want to go; while as to any unanimity among those who are engaged in the same work, there is so little of it in metaphysic, that it has rather become an arena, specially destined, it would seem, for those who wish to exercise themselves in mock fights, and where no combatant has, as yet, succeeded in gaining an inch of ground that he could call permanently his own. It cannot be denied, therefore, that the method of metaphysic has hitherto consisted in groping only, and, what is the worst, in groping among mere concepts.

What then can be the cause that hitherto no secure method of science has been discovered? Shall we say that it is impossible? Then why should nature have visited our reason with restless aspiration to look for it, as if it were its most important concern? Nay more, how little should we be justified in trusting our reason if, with regard to one of the most important objects we wish to know, it not only abandons us, but lures us on by vain hopes, and in the end betrays us! Or, if hitherto we have only failed to meet with the right path, what indications are there to make us hope that, if we renew our researches, we shall be more successful than others before us?

The examples of mathematics and natural science, which by one revolution have become what they now are, seem to me sufficiently remarkable to induce us to consider, what may have been the essential element in that intellectual revolution which has proved so beneficial to them, and to make the experiment, at least, so far as the analogy between them, as sciences of reason, which metaphysic allows it, of imitating them. Hitherto it has been supposed that all our knowledge must conform to the objects: but, under that supposition, all attempts to establish anything about them *a priori*, by means of concepts, and thus to enlarge our knowledge, have come to nothing. The experiment therefore ought to be made, whether we should not succeed better with the problems of metaphysic, by assuming that the objects must conform to our mode of cognition, for this would better agree with the demanded possibility of an *a priori* knowledge of them, which is to settle something about objects, before they are given us. We have here the same case as with the first thought of Copernicus, who, not being able to get on in the explanation of the movements of the heavenly bodies, as long as he assumed that all the stars turned round the spectator, tried, whether he could not succeed better, by assuming the spectator to be turning round, and the stars to be at rest. A similar experiment may be tried in metaphysic, so far as the *intuition* of objects is concerned. If the intuition had to conform to the constitution of objects, I do not see how we could know anything of it *a priori*; but if the object (as an object of the senses) conforms to the constitution of our faculty of intuition, I can very well conceive such a possibility. As, however, I cannot rest in these intuitions, if they are to become knowledge, but have to refer them, as representations, to something as their object, and must determine that object by them, I have the choice of admitting, either that the *concepts*, by which I carry out that determination, conform to the object, being then again in the same perplexity on account of the manner how I can know anything about it *a priori*; or that the objects, or what is the same, the experience in which alone they are known (as given objects), must conform to those concepts. In the latter case, the solution becomes more easy, because experience, as a kind of knowledge, requires understanding, and I must therefore, even before objects are given to me, presuppose the rules of the understanding as existing within me *a priori*, these rules being expressed in concepts *a priori*, to which all objects of experience must necessarily conform, and with which they must agree. With regard to objects, so far as they are conceived by reason only, and conceived as necessary, and which can never be given in experience, at least in that form in which they are conceived by reason, we shall find that the attempts at conceiving them (for they must admit of being conceived) will furnish afterwards an excellent test of our new method of thought, according to which we do not know of things anything *a priori* except what we ourselves put into them.

* * *

Refutation of Idealism

Idealism (I mean *material* idealism) is the theory which declares the existence of objects in space, without us, as either doubtful only and not demonstrable, or as false and impossible. The *former* is the *problematical* idealism of Descartes, who declares one empirical assertion only to be undoubted, namely, that of *I am*; the *latter* is the *dogmatical* idealism of

Berkeley, who declares space and all things to which it belongs as an inseparable condition, as something impossible in itself, and, therefore, the things in space as mere imaginations. Dogmatic idealism is inevitable, if we look upon space as a property belonging to things by themselves, for in that case space and all of which it is a condition, would be a non-entity. The ground on which that idealism rests has been removed by us in the transcendental Aesthetic. Problematical idealism, which asserts nothing, but only pleads our inability of proving any existence except our own by means of immediate experience, is reasonable and in accordance with a sound philosophical mode of thought, which allows of no decisive judgment, before a sufficient proof has been found. The required proof will have to demonstrate that we may have not only an imagination, but also an experience of external things, and this it seems can hardly be effected in any other way except by proving that even our internal experience, which Descartes considers as undoubted, is possible only under the supposition of external experience.

Theorem

The simple, but empirically determined Consciousness of my own existence, proves the Existence of objects in space outside myself.

Proof

I am conscious of my own existence as determined in time, and all determination in time presupposes something permanent in the perception. That *permanent*, however, cannot be an intuition within me, because all the causes which determine my existence, so far as they can be found within me, are representations, and as such require themselves something permanent, different from them, in reference to which their change, and therefore my existence in time in which they change, may be determined. The perception of this permanent, therefore, is possible only through a thing *outside* me, and not through the mere *representation* of a thing outside me, and the determination of my existence in time is, consequently, possible only by the existence of real things, which I perceive outside me. Now, as the consciousness in time is necessarily connected with the consciousness of the possibility of that determination of time, it is also necessarily connected with the existence of things outside me, as the condition of the determination of time. In other words, the consciousness of my own existence is, at the same time, an immediate consciousness of the existence of other things.

Note 1 It will have been perceived that in the foregoing proof the trick played by idealism has been turned against it, and with greater justice. Idealism assumed that the only immediate experience is the internal, and that from it we can no more than *infer* external things, though in an untrustworthy manner only, as always happens if from given effects we infer *definite* causes: it being quite possible that the cause of the representations, which are ascribed by us, it may be wrongly, to external things, may lie within ourselves. We, however, have proved that external experience is really immediate, and that only by means of it, though not the consciousness of our own existence, yet its determination in time, that is, internal experience, becomes possible. No doubt the representation of *I am*, which expresses the consciousness that can accompany all thought, is that which immediately includes the existence of a subject: but it does not yet include a *knowledge* of it, and therefore no empirical knowledge, that is, experience. For that we require, besides the thought of something existing, intuition also, and in this case internal intuition in respect to which, that is, to time, the subject must be determined. For that purpose external objects are absolutely necessary, so that internal experience itself is possible, mediately only, and through external experience.

Note 2 This view is fully confirmed by the empirical use of our faculty of knowledge, as applied to the determination of time. Not only are we unable to perceive any determination of time, except through a change in external relations (motion) with reference to what is permanent in space (for instance, the movement of the sun with respect to terrestrial objects), but we really have nothing permanent to which we could refer the concept of a substance, as an intuition, except *matter* only: and even its permanence is not derived from external experience, but presupposed *a priori* as a necessary condition of all determination of time, and therefore also of the determination of the internal sense with respect to our own existence through the existence of external things. The consciousness of myself, in the representation of the ego, is not an intuition, but a merely *intellectual* representation of the spontaneity of a thinking subject. Hence that ego has not the slightest predicate derived from intuition, which predicate, as *permanent*, might serve as the correlate of the determination of time in the internal sense: such as is, for instance, *impermeability* in matter, as an *empirical* intuition.

Note 3 Because the existence of external objects is required for the possibility of a definite consciousness of ourselves, it does not follow that every intuitional representation of external things involves, at the same time, their existence; for such a representation may well be the mere effect of the faculty of imagination (in dreams as well as in madness); but it can be such an effect only through the reproduction of former external perceptions, which, as we have shown, is impossible without the reality of *external* objects. What we wanted to prove here was only that internal experience in general is possible only through external experience in general. Whether this or that supposed experience be purely imaginary, must be settled according to its own particular determinations, and through a comparison with the criteria of all real experience.

* * *

The celebrated David Hume was one of those geographers of human reason who supposed that all those questions were sufficiently disposed of by being relegated outside that horizon, which, however, he was not able to determine. He was chiefly occupied with the principle of causality, and remarked quite rightly, that the truth of this principle (and even the objective validity of the concept of an efficient cause in general) was based on no knowledge, i.e. on no cognition *a priori*, and that its authority rested by no means on the necessity of such a law, but merely on its general usefulness in experience, and on a kind of subjective necessity arising from thence, which he called *habit*. From the inability of reason to employ this principle beyond the limits of experience he inferred the nullity of all the pretensions of reason in her attempts to pass beyond what is empirical.

This procedure of subjecting the *facts* of reason to examination, and, if necessary, to blame, may be termed the *censorship* of reason. There can be no doubt that such a censorship must inevitably lead to *doubts* against all the transcendental employment of such principles. But this is only the second and by no means the last step in our enquiry. The first step in matters of pure reason, which marks its infancy, is *dogmatism*. The second, which we have just described, is *scepticism*, and marks the stage of caution on the part of reason, when rendered wiser by experience. But a third step is necessary, that of the maturity and manhood of judgment, based on firm and universally applicable maxims, when not the facts of reason, but reason itself in its whole power and fitness for pure knowledge *a priori* comes to be examined. This is not the *censura* merely, but the true *criticism* of reason, by which not the *barrier* only, but the fixed *frontiers* of reason, not ignorance only on this or that point, but ignorance with reference to all possible questions of a certain kind, must be proved from principles, instead of being merely guessed at. Thus *scepticism* is a resting-place of reason, where it may reflect for a time on its dogmatical wanderings and gain a survey of the region where it happens to be, in order to choose its way with greater certainty for the future: but it can never be its permanent dwelling-place. That can only be found in perfect certainty, whether of our knowledge of the objects themselves or of the limits within which all our knowledge of objects is enclosed.

Hume is, perhaps, the most ingenious of all sceptics, and without doubt the most important with regard to the influence which the sceptical method may exercise in awakening reason to a thorough examination of its rights. It will therefore be worth our while to make clear to ourselves the course of his reasoning and the errors of an intelligent and estimable man, who at the outset of his enquiries was certainly on the right track of truth.

Hume was probably aware, though he never made it quite clear to himself, that in judgments of a certain kind we pass beyond our concept of the object. I have called this class of judgments *synthetical*. There is no difficulty as to how I may, by means of experience, pass beyond the concept which I have hitherto had. Experience is itself such a synthesis of perceptions through which a concept, which I have by means of one perception, is increased by means of other perceptions. But we imagine that we are able also *a priori* to pass beyond our concept and thus to enlarge our knowledge. This we attempt to do either by the pure understanding, in relation to that which can at least be an *object of experience*, or even by means of pure reason, in relation to such qualities of things, or even the existence of such things, as can never occur in experience. Hume in his scepticism did not distinguish between these two kinds of judgments as he ought to have done, but regarded this augmentation of concepts by themselves, and, so to say, the spontaneous generation of our understanding (and of our reason), without being impregnated by experience, as perfectly impossible. Considering all principles *a priori* as imaginary, he arrived at the conclusion that they were nothing but a habit arising from experience and its laws; that they were therefore merely empirical, that is, in themselves, contingent rules to which we wrongly ascribe necessity and universality. In order to establish this strange proposition, he appealed to the generally admitted principle of the relation between cause and effect. For as no faculty of the understanding could lead us from the concept of a thing to the existence of something else that should follow from it universally and necessarily, he thought himself justified in concluding that, without experience, we have nothing that could augment our concept and give us a right to form a judgment that extends itself *a priori*. That the light of the sun which shines on the wax should melt the wax and at the same time harden the clay, no understanding, he maintained, could guess from the concepts which we had before of these things, much less infer, according to a law, experience only being able to teach us such a law. We have seen, on the contrary, in the transcendental logic that, though we can never pass *immediately* beyond the content of a concept that is given us, we are nevertheless able, entirely *a priori*, but yet in reference to something else, namely, possible experience, to know the law of its connection with other things. If, therefore, wax, which was formerly hard, melts, I can know *a priori* that *something* else must have preceded (for instance the heat of the sun) upon which this melting has followed according to a permanent law, although without experience I could never know *a priori* definitely either from the effect the cause, or from the cause the effect. Hume was therefore wrong in inferring from the mere contingency of our being determined according to the law of causality, the contingency of that law itself, and he mistook our passing beyond the concept of a thing to some possible experience (which is entirely *a priori* and constitutes the objective reality of it) for the synthesis of the objects of real experience which, no doubt, is always empirical. He thus changed a principle of affinity which resides in the understanding and predicates necessary connection, into a rule of association residing in the imitative faculty of imagination, which can only represent contingent, but never objective connections.

The sceptical errors of that otherwise singularly acute thinker arose chiefly from a defect, which he shared, however, in common with all dogmatists, namely, of not having surveyed systematically all kinds of synthesis *a priori* of the understanding. For in doing this he would, without mentioning others, have discovered, for instance, the *principle of permanency* as one which, like causality, anticipates experience. He would thus have been able also to fix definite limits to the understanding in its attempts at expansion *a priori* and to pure reason. He only *narrows* the sphere of our understanding, without definitely *limiting* it, and produces a general mistrust, but no definite knowledge of that ignorance which to us is inevitable. He only subjects certain principles of the understanding to his *censura*, but does not place the understanding, with reference to all its faculties, on the balance of criticism. He is not satisfied with denying to the understanding what in reality it does not possess, but goes on to deny to it all power of expanding *a priori*, though he has never really tested all its powers. For this reason, what always defeats scepticism has happened to Hume also, namely, that he himself becomes subject to scepticism, because his objections rest on facts only which are contingent, and not on principles which alone can force a surrender of the right of dogmatical assertion.

As, besides this, he does not sufficiently distinguish between the well-grounded claims of the understanding and the dialectical pretensions of reason, against which, however, his attacks are chiefly directed, it so happens that reason, the peculiar tendency of which has not in the least been destroyed, but only checked, does not at all consider itself shut out from its attempts at expansion, and can never be entirely turned away from them, although it may be punished now and then. Mere attacks only provoke counter attacks, and make us more obstinate in enforcing our own views. But a complete survey of all that is really our own, and the conviction of a certain though a small possession, make us perceive the vanity of higher claims, and induce us, after surrendering all disputes, to live contentedly and peacefully within our own limited, but undisputed domain.

These sceptical attacks are not only dangerous, but even destructive to the uncritical dogmatist who has not measured the sphere of his understanding, and has not, therefore, determined, according to principles, the limits of his own possible knowledge, and does not know beforehand how much he is really able to achieve, but thinks that he is able to find all this out by a purely tentative method. For if he has been found out in one single assertion of his, which he cannot justify, or the fallacy of which he cannot evolve according to principles, suspicion falls on all his assertions, however plausible they may appear.

And thus the sceptic is the true schoolmaster to lead the dogmatic speculator towards a sound criticism of the understanding and of reason. When he has once been brought there, he need fear no further attacks, for he has learnt to distinguish his own possession from that which lies completely beyond it, and on which he can lay no claim, nor become involved in any disputes regarding it. Thus the sceptical method, though it *cannot* in itself *satisfy* with regard to the problems of reason, is nevertheless an excellent preparation in order to awaken its circumspection, and to indicate the true means whereby the legitimate possessions of reason may be secured against all attacks.

31

Martin Heidegger, from *Being and Time*

This brief selection is from *Being and Time* by Martin Heidegger (1889–1976). In this influential work, Heidegger undertakes to provide a philosophical account of the human person or *Dasein*, as he calls it in German. "Dasein is an entity which does not just occur among other entities. Rather it is ontically distinguished by the fact that, in its very Being, that Being is an *issue* for it." Heidegger claims that there is no intelligible problem of our knowledge of the external world, because we are beings who are in the world; our knowledge of the world is made possible by various non-cognitive relations between Dasein and things in the world. We do not have to infer the existence of the world from data contained in consciousness; there is no private sphere or " 'cabinet' of consciousness" as Descartes thought, so, according to Heidegger, the question the skeptics raise cannot be intelligibly asked.

Perception is consummated when one *addresses* oneself to something as something and *discusses* it as such. This amounts to *interpretation* in the broadest sense; and on the basis of such interpretation, perception becomes an act of *making determinate*. What is thus perceived and made determinate can be expressed in propositions, and can be retained and preserved as what has thus been asserted. This perceptive retention of an assertion about something is itself a way of Being-in-the-world; it is not to be Interpreted as a 'procedure' by which a subject provides itself with representations (*Vorstellungen*) of something which remain stored up 'inside' as having been thus appropriated, and with regard to which the question of how they 'agree' with actuality can occasionally arise.

When Dasein directs itself towards something and grasps it, it does not somehow first get out of an inner sphere in which it has been proximally encapsulated, but its primary kind of Being is such that it is always 'outside' alongside entities which it encounters and which belong to a world already discovered. Nor is any inner sphere abandoned when Dasein dwells alongside the entity to be known, and determines its character; but even in this 'Being-outside' alongside the object, Dasein is still 'inside', if we understand this in the correct sense; that is to say, it is itself 'inside' as a Being-in-the-world which knows. And furthermore, the perceiving of what is known is not a process of returning with one's booty to the 'cabinet' of consciousness after one has gone out and grasped it; even in perceiving, retaining, and preserving, the Dasein which knows *remains outside*, and it does so *as Dasein*. If I 'merely' know (*Wissen*) about some way in which the Being of entities is interconnected, if I 'only' represent them, if I 'do no more' than 'think' about them, I am no less alongside the entities outside in the world than when I *originally* grasp them. Even the forgetting of something, in which every relationship of Being towards what one formerly knew has seemingly been obliterated, must be conceived *as a modification of the primordial Being-in*; and this holds for every delusion and for every error.

We have now pointed out how those modes of Being-in-the-world which are constitutive for knowing the world are interconnected in their foundations; this makes it plain that in knowing, Dasein achieves a new *status of Being (Scinsstand)* towards a world which has already been discovered in Dasein itself. This new possibility of Being can develop itself autonomously; it can become a task to be accomplished, and as scientific knowledge it can take over the guidance for Being-in-the-world. But a '*commercium*' of the subject with a world does not get *created* for the first time by knowing, nor does it *arise* from some way in which the world acts upon a subject. Knowing is a mode of Dasein founded upon Being-in-the-world. Thus Being-in-the-world, as a basic state, must be Interpreted *beforehand*. [...]

The question of whether there is a world at all and whether its Being can be proved, makes no sense if it is raised by Dasein as Being-in-the-world; and who else would raise it? [...]

But the world is disclosed essentially *along with the* Being of Dasein; with the disclosedness of the world, the 'world' has in each case been discovered too. Of course entities within-the-world in the sense of the Real as merely present-at-hand, are the very things that can remain concealed. But even the Real can be discovered only on the basis of a world which has already been disclosed. And only on this basis can anything Real still remain *hidden*.

32

W. V. Quine, from "Two Dogmas of Empiricism" and "Epistemology Naturalized"

The two selections from Quine that follow consist of Part VI of his article "Two Dogmas of Empiricism" and the whole of "Epistemology Naturalized." Quine (1908–2000) accepts the main outcome of Hume's skepticism: "I do not see that we are farther along today than where Hume left us. The Humean predicament is the human predicament." Descartes quest for certainty is "a lost cause." Traditional efforts to anchor human knowledge in unshakable foundations cannot achieve their goal; it is futile to think "of grounding natural science upon immediate experience in a firmly logical way." We should stop "dreaming of deducing science from observations." Quine attempts to reconcile skepticism with empiricism: "Whatever evidence there *is* for science *is* sensory evidence. . . . The stimulation of his sensory receptors is all the evidence anybody has to go on, ultimately, in arriving at his picture of the world."

Instead of attempting to search for the ultimate foundations of knowledge, Quine suggests that epistemology should be concerned with how science actually proceeds. "Why not settle for psychology? . . . Better to discover how science is in fact developed and learned than to fabricate a fictitious structure to similar effect." This is what he means by naturalizing epistemology. Epistemology, for Quine, becomes an empirical and psychological account of how experience causes us to modify our beliefs and theories. So even though skepticism has required us to surrender the goals of traditional epistemology, the new naturalized epistemology has significant tasks ahead of it in understanding the actual workings of science rather than the idealized model that has been overthrown by skeptical arguments.

Empiricism without the Dogmas

The totality of our so-called knowledge or beliefs, from the most casual matters of geography and history to the profoundest laws of atomic physics or even of pure mathematics and logic, is a man-made fabric which impinges on experience only along the edges. Or, to change the figure, total science is like a field of force whose boundary conditions are experience. A conflict with experience at the periphery occasions re-adjustments in the interior of the field. Truth values have to be redistributed over some of our statements. Re-evaluation of some statements entails re-evaluation of others, because of their logical interconnections—the logical laws being in turn simply certain further statements of the system, certain further elements of the field. Having re-evaluated one statement we must re-evaluate some others, which may be statements logically connected with the first or may be the statements of logical connections themselves. But the total field is so underdetermined by its boundary conditions, experience, that there is much latitude of choice as to what statements to re-evaluate in the light of any single contrary experience. No particular experiences are linked with any particular statements in the interior of the field, except indirectly through considerations of equilibrium affecting the field as a whole.

If this view is right, it is misleading to speak of the empirical content of an individual statement – especially if it is a statement at all remote from the experiential periphery of the field. Furthermore it becomes folly to seek a boundary between synthetic statements, which hold contingently on experience, and analytic statements, which hold come what may. Any statement can be held true come what may, if we make drastic enough adjustments elsewhere in the system. Even a statement very close to the periphery can be held true in the face of recalcitrant experience by pleading hallucination or by amending certain statements of the kind called logical laws. Conversely, by the same token, no statement is immune to revision. Revision even of the logical law of the excluded middle has been proposed as a means of simplifying quantum mechanics; and what difference is there in principle between such a shift and the shift whereby Kepler superseded Ptolemy, or Einstein Newton, or Darwin Aristotle?

For vividness I have been speaking in terms of varying distances from a sensory periphery. Let me try now to clarify this notion without metaphor. Certain statements, though *about* physical objects and not sense experience, seem peculiarly germane to sense experience – and in a selective way: some statements to some experiences, others to others. Such statements, especially germane to particular experiences, I picture as near the periphery. But in this relation of "germaneness" I envisage nothing more than a loose association reflecting the relative likelihood, in practice, of our choosing one statement rather than another for revision in the event of recalcitrant experience. For example, we can imagine recalcitrant experiences to which we would surely be inclined to accommodate our system by re-evaluating just the statement that there are brick houses on Elm Street, together with related statements on the same topic. We can imagine other recalcitrant experiences to which we would be inclined to accommodate our system by re-evaluating just the statement that there are no centaurs, along with kindred statements. A recalcitrant experience can, I have urged, be accommodated by any of various alternative re-evaluations in various alternative quarters of the total system; but, in the cases which we are now imagining, our natural tendency to disturb the total system as little as possible would lead us to focus our revisions upon these specific statements concerning brick houses or centaurs. These statements are felt, therefore, to have a sharper empirical reference than highly theoretical statements of physics or logic or ontology. The latter statements may be thought of as relatively centrally located within the total network, meaning merely that little preferential connection with any particular sense data obtrudes itself.

As an empiricist I continue to think of the conceptual scheme of science as a tool, ultimately, for predicting future experience in the light of past experience. Physical objects are conceptually imported into the situation as convenient intermediaries – not by definition in terms of experience, but simply as irreducible posits comparable, epistemologically, to the gods of Homer. For my part I do, qua lay physicist, believe in physical objects and not in Homer's gods; and I consider it a scientific error to believe otherwise. But in point of epistemological footing the physical objects and the gods differ only in degree and not in kind. Both sorts of entities enter our conception only as cultural posits. The myth of physical objects is epistemologically superior to most in that it has proved more efficacious than other myths as a device for working a manageable structure into the flux of experience.

Positing does not stop with macroscopic physical objects. Objects at the atomic level are posited to make the laws of macroscopic objects, and ultimately the laws of experience, simpler and more manageable; and we need not expect or demand full definition of atomic and subatomic entities in terms of macroscopic ones, any more than definition of macroscopic things in terms of sense data. Science is a continuation of common sense, and it continues the common-sense expedient of swelling ontology to simplify theory.

Physical objects, small and large, are not the only posits. Forces are another example; and indeed we are told nowadays that the boundary between energy and matter is obsolete. Moreover, the abstract entities which are the substance of mathematics – ultimately classes and classes of classes and so on up – are another posit in the same spirit. Epistemologically these are myths on the same footing with physical objects and gods, neither better nor worse except for differences in the degree to which they expedite our dealings with sense experiences.

The overall algebra of rational and irrational numbers is underdetermined by the algebra of rational numbers, but is smoother and more convenient; and it includes the algebra of rational numbers as a jagged or gerrymandered part. Total science, mathematical and natural and human, is similarly but more extremely underdetermined by experience. The edge of the system must be kept squared with experience; the rest, with all its elaborate myths or fictions, has as its objective the simplicity of laws.

Ontological questions, under this view, are on a par with questions of natural science. Consider the question whether to countenance classes as entities. This, as I have argued elsewhere, is the question whether to quantify with respect to variables which take classes as values. Now Carnap has maintained that this is a question not of matters of fact but of choosing a convenient language form, a convenient conceptual scheme or framework for science. With this I agree, but only on the proviso that the same be conceded regarding scientific hypotheses generally. Carnap has recognized that he is able to preserve a double standard for ontological questions and scientific hypotheses only by assuming an absolute distinction between the analytic and the synthetic; and I need not say again that this is a distinction which I reject.

The issue over there being classes seems more a question of convenient conceptual scheme; the issue over there being centaurs, or brick houses on Elm Street, seems more a question of fact. But I have been urging that this difference is only one of degree, and that it turns upon our vaguely pragmatic inclination to adjust one strand of the fabric of science rather than another in accommodating some particular recalcitrant experience. Conservatism figures in such choices, and so does the quest for simplicity.

Carnap, Lewis, and others take a pragmatic stand on the question of choosing between language forms, scientific frameworks; but their pragmatism leaves off at the imagined boundary between the analytic and the synthetic. In repudiating such a boundary I espouse a more thorough pragmatism. Each man is given a scientific heritage plus a continuing barrage of sensory stimulation; and the considerations which guide him in warping his scientific heritage to fit his continuing sensory promptings are, where rational, pragmatic.

Epistemology Naturalized

Epistemology is concerned with the foundations of science. Conceived thus broadly, epistemology includes the study of the foundations of mathematics as one of its departments. Specialists at the turn of the century thought that their efforts in this particular department were achieving notable success: mathematics seemed to reduce altogether to logic. In a more recent perspective this reduction is seen to be better describable as a reduction to logic and set theory. This correction is a disappointment epistemologically, since the firmness and obviousness that we associate with logic cannot be claimed for set theory. But still the success achieved in the foundations of mathematics remains exemplary by comparative standards, and we can illuminate the rest of epistemology somewhat by drawing parallels to this department.

Studies in the foundations of mathematics divide symmetrically into two sorts, conceptual and doctrinal. The conceptual studies are concerned with meaning, the doctrinal with truth. The conceptual studies are concerned with clarifying concepts by defining them, some in terms of others. The doctrinal studies are concerned with establishing laws by proving them, some on the basis of others. Ideally the obscurer concepts would be defined in terms of the clearer ones so as to maximize clarity, and the less obvious laws would be proved from the more obvious ones so as to maximize certainty. Ideally the definitions would generate all the concepts from clear and distinct ideas, and the proofs would generate all the theorems from self-evident truths.

The two ideals are linked. For, if you define all the concepts by use of some favored subset of them, you thereby show how to translate all theorems into these favored terms. The clearer these terms are, the likelier it is that the truths couched in them will be obviously true, or derivable from obvious truths. If in particular the concepts of mathematics were all reducible to the clear terms of logic, then all the truths of mathematics would go over into truths of logic; and surely the truths of logic are all obvious or at least potentially obvious, i.e., derivable from obvious truths by individually obvious steps.

This particular outcome is in fact denied us, however, since mathematics reduces only to set theory and not to logic proper. Such reduction still enhances clarity, but only because of the interrelations that emerge and not because the end terms of the analysis are clearer than others. As for the end truths, the axioms of set theory, these have less obviousness and certainty to recommend them than do most of the mathematical theorems that we would derive from them. Moreover, we know from Gödel's work that no consistent axiom system can cover mathematics even when we renounce self-evidence. Reduction in the foundations of mathematics remains mathematically and philosophically fascinating, but it does not do what the epistemologist would like of it: it does not reveal the ground of mathematical knowledge, it does not show how mathematical certainty is possible.

Still there remains a helpful thought, regarding epistemology generally, in that duality of structure which was especially conspicuous in the foundations of mathematics. I refer to the bifurcation into a theory of concepts, or meaning, and a theory of doctrine, or truth; for this applies to the epistemology of natural knowledge no less than to the foundations of mathematics. The parallel is as follows. Just as mathematics is to be reduced to logic, or logic and set theory, so natural knowledge is to be based somehow on sense experience. This means explaining the notion of body in sensory terms; here is the conceptual side. And it means justifying our knowledge of truths of nature in sensory terms; here is the doctrinal side of the bifurcation.

Hume pondered the epistemology of natural knowledge on both sides of the bifurcation, the conceptual and the doctrinal. His handling of the conceptual side of the problem, the explanation of body in sensory terms, was bold and simple: he identified bodies outright with the sense impressions. If common sense distinguishes between the material apple and our sense impressions of it on the ground that the apple is one and enduring while the impressions are many and fleeting, then, Hume held, so much the worse for common sense; the notion of its being the same apple on one occasion and another is a vulgar confusion.

Nearly a century after Hume's *Treatise*, the same view of bodies was espoused by the early American philosopher Alexander Bryan Johnson.[1] "The word iron names an associated sight and feel," Johnson wrote.

What then of the doctrinal side, the justification of our knowledge of truths about nature? Here, Hume despaired. By his identification of bodies with impressions he did succeed in construing some singular statements about bodies as indubitable truths, yes; as truths about impressions, directly known. But general statements, also singular statements about the future, gained no increment of certainty by being construed as about impressions.

On the doctrinal side, I do not see that we are farther along today than where Hume left us. The Humean predicament is the human predicament. But on the conceptual side there has been progress. There the crucial step forward was made already before Alexander Bryan Johnson's day, although Johnson did not emulate it. It was made by Bentham in his theory of fictions. Bentham's step was the recognition of contextual definition, or what he called paraphrasis. He recognized that to explain a term we do not need to specify an object for it to refer to, nor even specify a synonymous word or phrase; we need only show, by whatever means, how to translate all the whole sentences in which the term is to be used. Hume's and Johnson's desperate measure of identifying bodies with impressions ceased to be the only conceivable way of making sense of talk of bodies, even granted that impressions were the only reality. One could undertake to explain talk of bodies in terms of talk of impressions by translating one's whole sentences about bodies into whole sentences about impressions, without equating the bodies themselves to anything at all.

This idea of contextual definition, or recognition of the sentence as the primary vehicle of meaning, was indispensable to the ensuing developments in the foundations of mathematics. It was explicit in Frege, and it attained its full flower in Russell's doctrine of singular descriptions as incomplete symbols.

Contextual definition was one of two resorts that could be expected to have a liberating effect upon the conceptual side of the epistemology of natural knowledge. The other is resort to the resources of set theory as auxiliary concepts. The epistemologist who is willing to eke out his austere ontology of sense impressions with these set-theoretic auxiliaries is suddenly rich: he has not just his impressions to play with, but sets of them, and sets of sets, and so on up. Constructions in the foundations of mathematics have shown that such set-theoretic aids are a powerful addition; after all, the entire glossary of concepts of classical mathematics is constructible from them. Thus equipped, our epistemologist may not need either to identify bodies with impressions or to settle for contextual definition; he may hope to find in some subtle construction of sets upon sets of sense impressions a category of objects enjoying just the formula properties that he wants for bodies.

The two resorts are very unequal in epistemological status. Contextual definition is unassailable. Sentences that have been given meaning as wholes are undeniably meaningful, and the use they make of their component terms is therefore meaningful, regardless of whether any translations are offered for those terms in isolation. Surely Hume and A. B. Johnson would have used contextual definition with pleasure if they had thought of it. Recourse to sets, on the other hand, is a drastic ontological move, a retreat from the austere ontology of impressions. There are philosophers who would rather settle for bodies outright than accept all these sets, which amount, after all, to the whole abstract ontology of mathematics.

This issue has not always been clear, however, owing to deceptive hints of continuity between elementary logic and set theory. This is why mathematics was once believed to reduce to logic, that is, to an innocent and unquestionable logic, and to inherit these qualities. And this is probably why Russell was content to resort to sets as well as to contextual definition when in *Our Knowledge of the External World* and elsewhere he addressed himself to the epistemology of natural knowledge, on its conceptual side.

To account for the external world as a logical construct of sense data – such, in Russell's terms, was the program. It was Carnap, in his *Der logische Aufbau der Welt* of 1928, who came nearest to executing it.

This was the conceptual side of epistemology; what of the doctrinal? There the Humean predicament remained unaltered. Carnap's constructions, if carried successfully to completion, would have enabled us to translate all sentences about the world into terms of sense data, or observation, plus logic and set theory. But the mere fact that a sentence is *couched* in terms of observation, logic, and set theory does not mean that it can be *proved* from observation sentences by logic and set theory. The most modest of generalizations about observable traits will cover more cases than its utterer can have had occasion actually to observe. The hopelessness of grounding natural science upon immediate experience in a firmly logical way was acknowledged. The Cartesian quest for certainty had been the remote motivation of epistemology, both on its conceptual and its doctrinal side; but that quest was seen as a lost cause. To endow the truths of nature with the full authority of immediate experience was as forlorn a hope as hoping to endow the truths of mathematics with the potential obviousness of elementary logic.

What then could have motivated Carnap's heroic efforts on the conceptual side of epistemology, when hope of certainty on the doctrinal side was abandoned? There were two good reasons still. One was that such constructions could be expected to elicit and clarify the sensory evidence for science, even if the inferential steps between sensory evidence and scientific doctrine must fall short of certainty. The other reason was that such constructions would deepen our understanding of our discourse about the world, even apart from questions of evidence; it would make all cognitive discourse as clear as observation terms and logic and, I must regretfully add, set theory.

It was sad for epistemologists, Hume and others, to have to acquiesce in the impossibility of strictly deriving the science of the external world from sensory evidence. Two cardinal tenets of empiricism remained unassailable, however, and so remain to this day. One is that whatever evidence there *is* for science *is* sensory evidence. The other, to which I shall recur, is that all inculcation of meanings of words must rest ultimately on sensory evidence. Hence the continuing attractiveness of the idea of a *logischer Aufbau* in which the sensory content of discourse would stand forth explicitly.

If Carnap had successfully carried such a construction through, how could he have told whether it was the right one? The question would have had no point. He was seeking what he called a *rational reconstruction*. Any construction of physicalistic discourse in terms of sense experience, logic, and set theory would have been seen as satisfactory if it made the physicalistic discourse come out right. If there is one way there are many, but any would be a great achievement.

But why all this creative reconstruction, all this make-believe? The stimulation of his sensory receptors is all the evidence anybody has had to go on, ultimately, in arriving at his picture of the world. Why not just see how this construction really proceeds? Why not settle for psychology? Such a surrender of the epistemological burden to psychology is a move that was disallowed in earlier times as circular reasoning. If the epistemologist's goal is validation of the grounds of empirical science, he defeats his purpose by using psychology or other empirical science in the validation. However, such scruples against circularity have little point once we have stopped dreaming of deducing science from observations. If we are out simply to understand the link between observation and science, we are well advised to use any available information, including that provided by the very science whose link with observation we are seeking to understand.

But there remains a different reason, unconnected with fears of circularity, for still favoring creative reconstruction. We should like to be able to *translate* science into logic and observation terms and set theory. This would be a great epistemological achievement, for it would show all the rest of the concepts of science to be theoretically superfluous. It would legitimize them – to whatever degree the concepts of set theory, logic, and observation are themselves legitimate – by showing that everything done with the one apparatus could in principle be done with the other. If psychology itself could deliver a truly translational reduction of this kind, we should welcome it; but certainly it cannot, for certainly we did not grow up learning definitions of physicalistic language in terms of a prior language of set theory, logic, and observation. Here, then, would be good reason for persisting in a rational reconstruction: we want to establish the essential innocence of physical concepts, by showing them to be theoretically dispensable.

The fact is, though, that the construction which Carnap outlined in *Der logische Aufbau der Welt* does not give translational reduction either. It would not even if the outline were filled in. The crucial point comes where Carnap is explaining how to assign sense qualities to positions in physical space and time. These assignments are to be made in such a way as to fulfill, as well as possible, certain desiderata which he states, and with growth of experience the assignments are to be revised to suit. This plan, however illuminating, does not offer any key to *translating* the sentences of science into terms of observation, logic, and set theory.

We must despair of any such reduction. Carnap had despaired of it by 1936, when, in "Testability and meaning,"[2] he introduced so-called *reduction forms* of a type weaker than definition. Definitions had shown always how to translate sentences into equivalent sentences. Contextual definition of a term showed how to translate sentences containing the term into equivalent sentences lacking the term. Reduction forms of Carnap's liberalized kind, on the other hand, do not in general give equivalences; they give implications. They explain a new term, if only partially, by specifying some sentences which are implied by sentences containing the term, and other sentences which imply sentences containing the term.

It is tempting to suppose that the countenancing of reduction forms in this liberal sense is just one further step of liberalization comparable to the earlier one, taken by Bentham, of countenancing contextual definition. The former and sterner kind of rational reconstruction might have been represented as a fictitious history in which we imagined our ancestors introducing the terms of physicalistic discourse on a phenomenalistic and set-theoretic basis by a succession of contextual definitions. The new and more liberal kind of rational reconstruction is a fictitious history in which we imagine our ancestors introducing those terms by a succession rather of reduction forms of the weaker sort.

This, however, is a wrong comparison. The fact is rather that the former and sterner kind of rational reconstruction, where definition reigned, embodied no fictitious history at all. It was nothing more nor less than a set of directions – or would have been, if successful – for accomplishing everything in terms of phenomena and set theory that we now accomplish in terms of bodies. It would have been a true reduction by translation, a legitimation by elimination. *Definire est eliminare.* Rational reconstruction by Carnap's later and looser reduction forms does none of this.

To relax the demand for definition, and settle for a kind of reduction that does not eliminate, is to renounce the last remaining advantage that we supposed rational reconstruction to have over straight psychology; namely, the advantage of translational reduction. If all we hope for is a reconstruction that links science to experience in explicit ways short of translation, then it would seem more sensible to settle for psychology. Better to discover how science is in fact developed and learned than to fabricate a fictitious structure to a similar effect.

The empiricist made one major concession when he despaired of deducing the truths of nature from sensory evidence. In despairing now even of translating those truths into terms of observation and logico-mathematical auxiliaries, he makes another major concession. For suppose we hold, with the old empiricist Peirce, that the very meaning of a statement consists in the difference its truth would make to possible experience. Might we not formulate, in a chapter-length sentence in observational language, all the difference that the truth of a given statement might make to experience, and might we not then take all this as the translation? Even if the difference that the truth of the statement would make to experience ramifies indefinitely, we might still hope to embrace it all in the logical implications of our chapter-length formulation, just as we can axiomatize an infinity of theorems. In giving up hope of such translation, then, the empiricist is conceding that the empirical meanings of typical statements about the external world are inaccessible and ineffable.

How is this inaccessibility to be explained? Simply on the ground that the experiential implications of a typical statement about bodies are too complex for finite axiomatization, however lengthy? No; I have a different explanation. It is that the typical statement about bodies has no fund of experiential implications it can call its own. A substantial mass of theory, taken together, will commonly have experiential implications; this is how we make verifiable predictions. We may not be able to explain why we arrive at theories which make successful predictions, but we do arrive at such theories.

Sometimes also an experience implied by a theory fails to come off; and then, ideally, we declare the theory false. But the failure falsifies only a block of theory as a whole, a conjunction of many statements. The failure shows that one or more of those statements is false, but it does not show which. The predicted experiences, true and false, are not implied by any one of the component statements of the theory rather than another. The component statements simply do not have empirical meanings, by Peirce's standard; but a sufficiently inclusive portion of theory does. If we can aspire to a sort of *logischer Aufbau der Welt* at all, it must be to one in which the texts slated for translation into observational and logico-mathematical terms are mostly broad theories taken as wholes, rather than just terms or short sentences. The translation of a theory would be a ponderous axiomatization of all the experiential difference that the truth of the theory would make. It would be a queer translation, for it would translate the whole but none of the parts. We might better speak in such a case not of translation but simply of observational evidence for theories; and we may, following Peirce, still fairly call this the empirical meaning of the theories.

These considerations raise a philosophical question even about ordinary unphilosophical translation, such as from English into Arunta or Chinese. For, if the English sentences of a theory have their meaning only together as a body, then we can justify their translation into Arunta only together as a body. There will be no justification for pairing off the component English sentences with component Arunta sentences, except as these correlations make the translation of the theory as a whole come out right. Any translations of the English sentences into Arunta sentences will be as correct as any other, so long as the net empirical implications of the theory as a whole are preserved in translation. But it is to be expected that many different ways of translating the component sentences, essentially different individually, would deliver the same empirical implications for the theory as a whole; deviations in the translation of one component sentence could be compensated for in the translation of another component sentence. Insofar, there can be no ground for saying which of two glaringly unlike translations of individual sentences is right.

For an uncritical mentalist, no such indeterminacy threatens. Every term and every sentence is a label attached to an idea, simple or complex, which is stored in the mind. When on the other hand we take a verification theory of meaning seriously, the indeterminacy would appear to be inescapable. The Vienna Circle espoused a verification theory of meaning but did not take it seriously enough. If we recognize with Peirce that the meaning of a sentence turns purely on what would count as evidence for its truth, and if we recognize with Duhem that theoretical sentences have their evidence not as single sentences but only as larger blocks of theory, then the indeterminacy of translation of theoretical sentences is the natural conclusion. And most sentences, apart from observation sentences, are theoretical. This conclusion, conversely, once it is embraced, seals the fate of any general notion of propositional meaning or, for that matter, state of affairs.

Should the unwelcomeness of the conclusion persuade us to abandon the verification theory of meaning? Certainly not. The sort of meaning that is basic to translation, and to the learning of one's own language, is necessarily empirical meaning and nothing more. A child learns his first words and sentences by hearing and using them in the presence of appropriate stimuli. These must be external stimuli, for they must act both on the child and on the speaker from whom he is learning. Language is socially inculcated and controlled; the inculcation and control turn strictly on the keying of sentences to shared stimulation. Internal factors may vary *ad libitum* without prejudice to communication as long as the keying of language to external stimuli is undisturbed. Surely one has no choice but to be an empiricist so far as one's theory of linguistic meaning is concerned.

What I have said of infant learning applies equally to the linguist's learning of a new language in the field. If the linguist does not lean on related languages for which there are previously accepted translation practices, then obviously he has no data but the concomitances of native utterance and observable stimulus situation. No wonder there is indeterminacy of translation – for of course only a small fraction of our utterances report concurrent external stimulation. Granted, the linguist will end up with unequivocal translations of everything; but only by making many arbitrary choices – arbitrary even though unconscious – along the way. Arbitrary? By this I mean that different choices could still have made everything come out right that is susceptible in principle to any kind of check.

Let me link up, in a different order, some of the points I have made. The crucial consideration behind my argument for the indeterminacy of translation was that a statement about the world does not always or usually have a separable fund of empirical consequences that it can call its own. That consideration served also to account for the impossibility of an epistemological reduction of the sort where every sentence is equated to a sentence in observational and logico-mathematical terms. And the impossibility of that sort of epistemological reduction dissipated the last advantage that rational reconstruction seemed to have over psychology.

Philosophers have rightly despaired of translating everything into observational and logico-mathematical terms. They have despaired of this even when they have not recognized, as the reason for this irreducibility, that the statements largely do not have their private bundles of empirical consequences. And some philosophers have seen in this irreducibility the bankruptcy of epistemology. Carnap and the other logical positivists of the Vienna Circle had already pressed the term "metaphysics" into pejorative use, as connoting meaninglessness; and the term "epistemology" was next. Wittgenstein and his followers, mainly at Oxford, found a residual philosophical vocation in therapy: in curing philosophers of the delusion that there were epistemological problems.

But I think that at this point it may be more useful to say rather that epistemology still goes on, though in a new setting and a clarified status. Epistemology, or something like it, simply falls into place as a chapter of psychology and hence of natural science. It studies a natural phenomenon, viz., a physical human subject. This human subject is accorded a certain experimentally controlled input – certain patterns of irradiation in assorted frequencies, for instance – and in the fullness of time the subject delivers as output a description of the three-dimensional external world and its history. The relation between the meager input and the torrential output is a relation that we are prompted to study for somewhat the same reasons that always prompted epistemology; namely, in order to see how evidence relates to theory, and in what ways one's theory of nature transcends any available evidence.

Such a study could still include, even, something like the old rational reconstruction, to whatever degree such reconstruction is practicable; for imaginative constructions can afford hints of actual psychological processes, in much the way that mechanical simulations can. But a conspicuous difference between old epistemology and the epistemological enterprise in this new psychological setting is that we can now make free use of empirical psychology.

The old epistemology aspired to contain, in a sense, natural science; it would construct it somehow from sense data. Epistemology in its new setting, conversely, is contained in natural science, as a chapter of psychology. But the old containment remains valid too, in its way. We are studying how the human subject of our study posits bodies and projects his physics from his data, and we appreciate that our position in the world is just like his. Our very epistemological enterprise, therefore, and the psychology wherein it is a component chapter, and the whole of natural science wherein psychology is a component book – all this is our own construction or projection from stimulations like those we were meting out to our epistemological subject. There is thus reciprocal containment, though containment in different senses: epistemology in natural science and natural science in epistemology.

This interplay is reminiscent again of the old threat of circularity, but it is all right now that we have stopped dreaming of deducing science from sense data. We are after an understanding of science as an institution or process in the world, and we do not intend that understanding to be any better than the science which is its object. This attitude is indeed one that Neurath was already urging in Vienna Circle days, with his parable of the mariner who has to rebuild his boat while staying afloat in it.

One effect of seeing epistemology in a psychological setting is that it resolves a stubborn old enigma of epistemological priority. Our retinas are irradiated in two dimensions, yet we see things as three-dimensional without conscious inference. Which is to count as observation – the unconscious two-dimensional reception or the conscious three-dimensional apprehension? In the old epistemological context the conscious form had priority, for we were out to justify our knowledge of the external world by rational reconstruction, and that demands awareness. Awareness ceased to be demanded when we gave up trying to justify our knowledge of the external world by rational reconstruction. What to count as observation now can be settled in terms of the stimulation of sensory receptors, let consciousness fall where it may.

The Gestalt psychologists' challenge to sensory atomism, which seemed so relevant to epistemology forty years ago, is likewise deactivated. Regardless of whether sensory atoms or Gestalten are what favor the forefront of our consciousness, it is simply the stimulations of our sensory receptors that are best looked upon as the input to our cognitive mechanism. Old paradoxes about unconscious data and inference, old problems about chains of inference that would have to be completed too quickly – these no longer matter.

In the old anti-psychologistic days the question of epistemological priority was moot. What is epistemologically prior to what? Are Gestalten prior to sensory atoms because they are noticed, or should we favor sensory atoms on some more subtle ground? Now that we are permitted to appeal to physical stimulation, the problem dissolves; *A* is epistemologically prior to *B* if *A* is causally nearer than *B* to the sensory receptors.

Or, what is in some ways better, just talk explicitly in terms of causal proximity to sensory receptors and drop the talk of epistemological priority.

Around 1932 there was debate in the Vienna Circle over what to count as observation sentences, or *Protokollsätze*.[3] One position was that they had the form of reports of sense impressions. Another was that they were statements of an elementary sort about the external world, e.g., "A red cube is standing on the table." Another, Neurath's, was that they had the form of reports of relations between percipients and external things: "Otto now sees a red cube on the table." The worst of it was that there seemed to be no objective way of settling the matter: no way of making real sense of the question.

Let us now try to view the matter unreservedly in the context of the external world. Vaguely speaking, what we want of observation sentences is that they be the ones in closest causal proximity to the sensory receptors. But how is such proximity to be gauged? The idea may be rephrased this way: observation sentences are sentences which, as we learn language, are most strongly conditioned to concurrent sensory stimulation rather than to stored collateral information. Thus let us imagine a sentence queried for our verdict as to whether it is true or false; queried for our assent or dissent. Then the sentence is an observation sentence if our verdict depends only on the sensory stimulation present at the time.

But a verdict cannot depend on present stimulation to the exclusion of stored information. The very fact of our having learned the language evinces much storing of information, and of information without which we should be in no position to give verdicts on sentences however observational. Evidently then we must relax our definition of observation sentence to read thus: a sentence is an observation sentence if all verdicts on it depend on present sensory stimulation and on no stored information beyond what goes into understanding the sentence.

This formulation raises another problem: how are we to distinguish between information that goes into understanding a sentence and information that goes beyond? This is the problem of distinguishing between analytic truth, which issues from the mere meanings of words, and synthetic truth, which depends on more than meanings. Now I have long maintained that this distinction is illusory. There is one step toward such a distinction, however, which does make sense: a sentence that is true by mere meanings of words should be expected, at least if it is simple, to be subscribed to by all fluent speakers in the community. Perhaps the controversial notion of analyticity can be dispensed with, in our definition of observation sentence, in favor of this straightforward attribute of community-wide acceptance.

This attribute is of course no explication of analyticity. The community would agree that there have been black dogs, yet none who talk of analyticity would call this analytic. My rejection of the analyticity notion just means drawing no line between what goes into the mere understanding of the sentences of a language and what else the community sees eye-to-eye on. I doubt that an objective distinction can be made between meaning and such collateral information as is community-wide.

Turning back then to our task of defining observation sentences, we get this: an observation sentence is one on which all speakers of the language give the same verdict when given the same concurrent stimulation. To put the point negatively, an observation sentence is one that is not sensitive to differences in past experience within the speech community.

This formulation accords perfectly with the traditional role of the observation sentence as the court of appeal of scientific theories. For by our definition the observation sentences are the sentences on which all members of the community will agree under uniform stimulation. And what is the criterion of membership in the same community? Simply general fluency of dialogue. This criterion admits of degrees, and indeed we may usefully take the community more narrowly for some studies than for others. What count as observation sentences for a community of specialists would not always so count for a larger community.

There is generally no subjectivity in the phrasing of observation sentences, as we are now conceiving them; they will usually be about bodies. Since the distinguishing trait of an observation sentence is intersubjective agreement under agreeing stimulation, a corporeal subject matter is likelier than not.

The old tendency to associate observation sentences with a subjective sensory subject matter is rather an irony when we reflect that observation sentences are also meant to be the intersubjective tribunal of scientific hypotheses. The old tendency was due to the drive to base science on something firmer and prior in the subject's experience; but we dropped that project.

The dislodging of epistemology from its old status of first philosophy loosed a wave, we saw, of epistemological nihilism. This mood is reflected somewhat in the tendency of Polányi, Kuhn, and the late Russell Hanson to belittle the role of evidence and to accentuate cultural relativism. Hanson ventured even to discredit the idea of observation, arguing that so-called observations vary from observer to observer with the amount of knowledge that the observers bring with them. The veteran physicist looks at some apparatus and sees an x-ray tube. The neophyte, looking at the same place, observes rather "a glass and metal instrument replete with wires, reflectors, screws, lamps, and pushbuttons."[4] One man's observation is another man's closed book or flight of fancy. The notion of observation as the impartial and objective source of evidence for science is bankrupt. Now my answer to the x-ray example was already hinted a little while back: what counts as an observation sentence varies with the width of community considered. But we can also always get an absolute standard by taking in all speakers of the language, or most.[5] It is ironical that philosophers, finding the old epistemology untenable as a whole, should react by repudiating a part which has only now moved into clear focus.

Clarification of the notion of observation sentence is a good thing, for the notion is fundamental in two connections. These two correspond to the duality that I remarked upon early in this lecture: the duality between concept and doctrine, between knowing what a sentence means and knowing whether it is true. The observation sentence is basic to both enterprises. Its relation to doctrine, to our knowledge of what is true, is very much the traditional one: observation sentences are the repository of evidence for scientific hypotheses. Its relation to meaning is fundamental too, since observation sentences are the ones we are in a position to learn to understand first, both as children and as field linguists. For observation sentences are precisely the ones that we can correlate with observable circumstances of the occasion of utterance or assent, independently of variations in the past histories of individual informants. They afford the only entry to a language.

The observation sentence is the cornerstone of semantics. For it is, as we just saw, fundamental to the learning of meaning. Also, it is where meaning is firmest. Sentences higher up in theories have no empirical consequences they can call their own; they confront the tribunal of sensory evidence only in more or less inclusive aggregates. The observation sentence, situated at the sensory periphery of the body scientific, is the minimal verifiable aggregate; it has an empirical content all its own and wears it on its sleeve.

The predicament of the indeterminacy of translation has little bearing on observation sentences. The equating of an observation sentence of our language to an observation sentence of another language is mostly a matter of empirical generalization; it is a matter of identity between the range of stimulations that would prompt assent to the one sentence and the range of stimulations that would prompt assent to the other.[6]

It is no shock to the preconceptions of old Vienna to say that epistemology now becomes semantics. For epistemology remains centered as always on evidence, and meaning remains centered as always on verification; and evidence is verification. What is likelier to shock preconceptions is that meaning, once we get beyond observation sentences, ceases in general to have any clear applicability to single sentences; also that epistemology merges with psychology, as well as with linguistics.

This rubbing out of boundaries could contribute to progress, it seems to me, in philosophically interesting inquiries of a scientific nature. One possible area is perceptual norms. Consider, to begin with, the linguistic phenomenon of phonemes. We form the habit, in hearing the myriad variations of spoken sounds, of treating each as an approximation to one or another of a limited number of norms – around thirty altogether – constituting so to speak a spoken alphabet. All speech in our language can be treated in practice as sequences of just those thirty elements, thus rectifying small deviations. Now outside the realm of language also there is probably only a rather limited alphabet of perceptual norms altogether, toward which we tend unconsciously to rectify all perceptions. These, if experimentally identified, could be taken as epistemological building blocks, the working elements of experience. They might prove in part to be culturally variable, as phonemes are, and in part universal.

Again there is the area that the psychologist Donald T. Campbell calls evolutionary epistemology.[7] In this area there is work by Hüseyin Yilmaz, who shows how some structural traits of color perception could have been predicted from survival value.[8] And a more emphatically epistemological topic that evolution helps to clarify is induction, now that we are allowing epistemology the resources of natural science.

Notes

1   A. B. Johnson, *A Treatise on Language* (New York, 1836; Berkeley, 1947).
2   *Philosophy of Science* 3 (1936), 419–71; 4 (1937), 1–40.
3   Carnap and Neurath in *Erkenntnis* 3 (1932), 204–28.
4   N. R. Hanson, "Observation and interpretation," in S. Morgenbesser, ed., *Philosophy of Science Today* (New York: Basic Books, 1966).
5   This qualification allows for occasional deviants such as the insane or the blind. Alternatively, such cases might be excluded by adjusting the level of fluency of dialogue whereby we define sameness of language. (For prompting this note and influencing the development of this paper also in more substantial ways I am indebted to Burton Dreben.)

6 Cf. Quine, *Word and Object* (Cambridge, Mass.: MIT Press, 1960), pp. 31–46, 68.

7 D. T. Campbell, "Methodological suggestions from a comparative psychology of knowledge processes," *Inquiry* 2 (1959), 152–82.

8 Hüseyin Yilmaz, "On color vision and a new approach to general perception," in E. E. Bernard and M. R. Kare, eds., *Biological Prototypes and Synthetic Systems* (New York: Plenum, 1962); "Perceptual invariance and the psychophysical law," *Perception and Psychophysics* 2 (1967), 533–8.

Richard Rorty, "Solidarity or Objectivity?"

In the selection below, "Solidarity or Objectivity?" Richard Rorty (1931–) develops a version of pragmatism built upon an acceptance of traditional skeptical argumentation. The Pyrrhonist tradition has frequently pointed out that there can be no non-circular justification for our methods of justification. We cannot establish by non-fallacious arguments a criterion of truth, if by a criterion we mean something that we can prove to be a reliable indicator of truth. The best we can do, for Rorty, is to appeal to the most successful methods of justification that our community has developed (ethnocentrism), where success is measured by the production of beliefs that the members of the community find good to believe (pragmatism). We are forced to abandon the quest for objectivity if that means establishing a system of belief that corresponds to an independent reality. Skeptics have argued that we have no way of ascertaining that our beliefs do correspond to independent facts, that there is no neutral point of view or perspective from which such correspondence can be established. Rorty's view is one of the best examples of a philosophical position that has thoroughly absorbed and incorporated the insights of skepticism. Pragmatism in general counts as a skeptical position because, in the light of skeptical arguments, it surrenders the realism and the correspondence view of truth implicit in the quest for objectivity.

Solidarity or Objectivity?

There are two principal ways in which reflective human beings try, by placing their lives in a larger context, to give sense to those lives. The first is by telling the story of their contribution to a community. This community may be the actual historical one in which they live, or another actual one, distant in time or place, or a quite imaginary one, consisting perhaps of a dozen heroes and heroines selected from history or fiction or both. The second way is to describe themselves as standing in immediate relation to a nonhuman reality. This relation is immediate in the sense that it does not derive from a relation between such a reality and their tribe, or their nation, or their imagined band of comrades. I shall say that stories of the former kind exemplify the desire for solidarity, and that stories of the latter kind exemplify the desire for objectivity. Insofar as a person is seeking solidarity, she does not ask about the relation between the practices of the chosen community and something outside that community. Insofar as she seeks objectivity, she distances herself from the actual persons around her not by thinking of herself as a member of some other real or imaginary group, but rather by attaching herself to something which can be described without reference to any particular human beings.

The tradition in Western culture which centers around the notion of the search for Truth, a tradition which runs from the Greek philosophers through the Enlightenment, is the clearest example of the attempt to find a sense in one's existence by turning away from solidarity to objectivity. The idea of Truth as something to be pursued for its own sake, not because it will be good for oneself, or for one's real or imaginary community, is the central theme of this tradition. It was perhaps the growing awareness by the Greeks of the sheer diversity of human communities which stimulated the emergence of this ideal. A fear of parochialism, of being confined within the horizons of the group into which one happens to be born, a need to see it with the eyes of a stranger, helps produce the skeptical and ironic tone characteristic of Euripides and Socrates. Herodotus' willingness to take the barbarians seriously enough to describe their customs in detail may have been a necessary prelude to Plato's claim that the way to transcend skepticism is to envisage a common goal of humanity – a goal set by human nature rather than by Greek culture. The combination of Socratic alienation and Platonic hope gives rise to the idea of the intellectual as someone who is in touch with the nature of things, not by way of the opinions of his community, but in a more immediate way.

Plato developed the idea of such an intellectual by means of distinctions between knowledge and opinion, and between appearance and reality. Such distinctions conspire to produce the idea that rational inquiry should make visible a realm to which nonintellectuals have little access, and of whose very existence they may be doubtful. In the Enlightenment, this notion became concrete in the adoption of the Newtonian physical scientist as a model of the intellectual. To most thinkers of the eighteenth century, it seemed clear that the access to Nature which physical science had provided should now be followed by the establishment of social, political, and economic institutions which were in accordance with Nature. Ever since, liberal social thought has centered around social reform as made possible by objective knowledge of what human beings are like – not knowledge of what Greeks or Frenchmen or Chinese are like, but of humanity as such. We are the heirs of this objectivist tradition, which centers around the assumption that we must step outside our community long enough to examine it in the light of something which transcends it, namely, that which it has in common with every other actual and possible human community. This tradition dreams of an ultimate community which will have transcended the distinction between the natural and the social, which will exhibit a solidarity which is not parochial because it is the expression of an ahistorical human nature. Much of the rhetoric of contemporary intellectual life takes for granted that the goal of scientific inquiry into man is to understand "underlying structures," or "culturally invariant factors," or "biologically determined patterns."

Those who wish to ground solidarity in objectivity – call them "realists" – have to construe truth as correspondence to reality. So they must construct a metaphysics which has room for a special relation between beliefs and objects which will differentiate true from false beliefs. They also must argue that there are procedures of justification of belief which are natural and not merely local. So they must construct an epistemology which has room for a kind of justification which is not merely social but natural, springing from human nature itself, and made possible by a link between that part of nature and the rest of nature. On their view, the various procedures which are thought of as providing rational justification by one or another culture may or may not really *be* rational. For to be truly rational, procedures of justification *must* lead to the truth, to correspondence to reality, to the intrinsic nature of things.

By contrast, those who wish to reduce objectivity to solidarity – call them "pragmatists" – do not require either a metaphysics or an epistemology. They view truth as, in William James' phrase, what is good for *us* to believe. So they do not need an account of a relation between beliefs and objects called "correspondence," nor an account of human cognitive abilities which ensures that our species is capable of entering into that relation. They see the gap between truth and justification not as something to be bridged by isolating a natural and transcultural sort of rationality which can be used to criticize certain cultures and praise others, but simply as the gap between the actual good and the possible better. From a pragmatist point of view, to say that what is rational for us now to believe may not be *true*, is simply to say that somebody may come up with a better idea. It is to say that there is always room for improved belief, since new evidence, or new hypotheses, or a whole new vocabulary, may come along.[1] For pragmatists, the desire for objectivity is not the desire to escape the limitations of one's community, but simply the desire for as much intersubjective agreement as possible, the desire to extend the reference of "us" as far as we can. Insofar as pragmatists make a distinction between knowledge and opinion, it is simply the distinction between topics on which such agreement is relatively easy to get and topics on which agreement is relatively hard to get.

"Relativism" is the traditional epithet applied to pragmatism by realists. Three different views are commonly referred to by this name. The first is the view that every belief is as good as every other. The second is the view that "true" is an equivocal term, having as many meanings as there are procedures of justification. The third is the view that there is nothing to be said about either truth or rationality apart from descriptions of the familiar procedures of justification which a given society – *ours* – uses in one or another area of inquiry. The pragmatist holds the ethnocentric third view. But he does not hold the self-refuting first view, nor the eccentric second view. He thinks that his views are better than the realists', but he does not think that his views correspond to the nature of things. He thinks that the very flexibility of the word "true" – the fact that it is merely an expression of commendation – insures its univocity. The term "true," on his account, means the same in all cultures, just as equally flexible terms like "here," "there," "good," "bad," "you," and "me" mean the same in all cultures. But the identity of meaning is, of course, compatible with diversity of reference, and with diversity of procedures for assigning the terms. So he feels free to use the term "true" as a general term of commendation in the same way as his realist opponent does – and in particular to use it to commend his own view.

However, it is not clear why "relativist" should be thought an appropriate term for the ethnocentric third view, the one which the pragmatist *does* hold. For the pragmatist is not holding a positive theory which says that something is relative to something else. He is, instead, making the purely *negative* point that we should drop the traditional distinction between knowledge and opinion, construed as the distinction between truth as correspondence to reality and truth as a commendatory term for well-justified beliefs. The reason that the realist calls this negative claim "relativistic" is that he cannot believe that anybody would seriously deny that truth has an intrinsic nature. So when the pragmatist says that there is nothing to be said about truth save that each of us will commend as true those beliefs which he or she finds good to believe, the realist is inclined to interpret this as one more positive theory about the nature of truth: a theory according to which truth is simply the contemporary opinion of a chosen individual or group. Such a theory would, of course, be self-refuting. But the pragmatist does not have a theory of truth, much less a relativistic one. As a partisan of solidarity, his account of the value of cooperative human inquiry has only an ethical base, not an epistemological or metaphysical one. Not having *any* epistemology, *a fortiori* he does not have a relativistic one.

The question of whether truth or rationality has an intrinsic nature, of whether we ought to have a positive theory about either topic, is just the question of whether our self-description ought to be constructed around a relation to human nature or around a relation to a particular collection of human beings, whether we should desire objectivity or solidarity. It is hard to see how one could choose between these alternatives by looking more deeply into the nature of knowledge, or of man, or of nature. Indeed, the proposal that this issue might be so settled begs the question in favor of the realist, for it presupposes that knowledge, man, and nature *have* real essences which are relevant to the problem at hand. For the pragmatist, by contrast, "knowledge" is, like "truth," simply a compliment paid to the beliefs which we think so well justified that, for the moment, further justification is not needed. An inquiry into the nature of knowledge can, on his view, only be a sociohistorical account of how various people have tried to reach agreement on what to believe.

The view which I am calling "pragmatism" is almost, but not quite, the same as what Hilary Putnam, in his recent *Reason, Truth, and History*, calls "the internalist conception of philosophy."[2] Putnam defines such a conception as one which gives up the attempt at a God's eye view of things, the attempt at contact with the nonhuman which I have been calling "the desire for objectivity." Unfortunately, he accompanies his defense of the antirealist views I am recommending with a polemic against a lot of the other people who hold these views – e.g., Kuhn, Feyerabend, Foucault, and myself. We are criticized as "relativists." Putnam presents "internalism" as a happy *via media* between realism and relativism. He speaks of "the plethora of relativistic doctrines being marketed today"[3] and in particular of "the French philosophers" as holding "some fancy mixture of cultural relativism and 'structuralism.' "[4] But when it comes to criticizing these doctrines all that Putnam finds to attack is the so-called "incommensurability thesis": vis., "terms used in another culture cannot be equated in meaning or reference with any terms or expressions *we* possess."[5] He sensibly agrees with Donald Davidson in remarking that this thesis is self-refuting. Criticism of this thesis, however, is destructive of, at most, some incautious passages in some early writings by Feyerabend. Once this thesis is brushed aside, it is hard to see how Putnam himself differs from most of those he criticizes.

Putnam accepts the Davidsonian point that, as he puts it, "the whole justification of an interpretative scheme . . . is that it renders the behavior of others at least minimally reasonable by *our* lights."[6] It would seem natural to go on from this to say that we cannot get outside the range of those lights, that we cannot stand on neutral ground illuminated only by the natural light of reason. But Putnam draws back from this conclusion. He does so because he construes the claim that we cannot do so as the claim that the range of our thought is restricted by what he calls "institutionalized norms," publicly available criteria for settling all arguments, including philosophical arguments. He rightly says that there are no such criteria, arguing that the suggestion that there are is as self-refuting as the "incommensurability thesis." He is, I think, entirely right in saying that the notion that philosophy is or should become such an application of explicit criteria contradicts the very idea of philosophy.[7] One can gloss Putnam's point by saying that "philosophy" is precisely what a culture becomes capable of when it ceases to define itself in terms of explicit rules, and becomes sufficiently leisured and civilized to rely on inarticulate know-how, to substitute *phronesis* for codification, and conversation with foreigners for conquest of them.

But to say that we cannot refer every question to explicit criteria institutionalized by our society does not speak to the point which the people whom Putnam calls "relativists" are making. One reason these people are pragmatists is precisely that they share Putnam's distrust of the positivistic idea that rationality is a matter of applying criteria.

Such a distrust is common, for example, to Kuhn, Mary Hesse, Wittgenstein, Michael Polanyi, and Michael Oakeshott. Only someone who did think of rationality in this way would dream of suggesting that "true" means something different in different societies. For only such a person could imagine that there was anything to pick out to which one might make "true" relative. Only if one shares the logical positivists' idea that we all carry around things called "rules of language" which regulate what we say when, will one suggest that there is no way to break out of one's culture.

In the most original and powerful section of his book, Putnam argues that the notion that "rationality . . . is defined by the local cultural norms" is merely the demonic counterpart of positivism. It is, as he says, "a scientistic theory inspired by anthropology as positivism was a scientistic theory inspired by the exact sciences." By "scientism" Putnam means the notion that rationality consists in the application of criteria.[8] Suppose we drop this notion, and accept Putnam's own Quinean picture of inquiry as the continual reweaving of a web of beliefs rather than as the application of criteria to cases. Then the notion of "local cultural norms" will lose its offensively parochial overtones. For now to say that we must work by our own lights, that we must be ethnocentric, is merely to say that beliefs suggested by another culture must be tested by trying to weave them together with beliefs we already have. It is a consequence of this holistic view of knowledge, a view *shared* by Putnam and those he criticizes as "relativists," that alternative cultures are not to be thought of on the model of alternative geometries. Alternative geometries are irreconcilable because they have axiomatic structures, and contradictory axioms. They are *designed* to be irreconcilable. Cultures are not so designed, and do not have axiomatic structures. To say that they have "institutionalized norms" is only to say, with Foucault, that knowledge is never separable from power – that one is likely to suffer if one does not hold certain beliefs at certain times and places. But such institutional backups for beliefs take the form of bureaucrats and policemen, not of "rules of language" and "criteria of rationality." To think otherwise is the Cartesian fallacy of seeing axioms where there are only shared habits, of viewing statements which summarize such practices as if they reported constraints enforcing such practices. Part of the force of Quine's and Davidson's attack on the distinction between the conceptual and the empirical is that the distinction between different cultures does not differ in kind from the distinction between different theories held by members of a single culture. The Tasmanian aborigines and the the British colonists had trouble communicating, but this trouble was different only in extent from the difficulties in communication experienced by Gladstone and Disraeli. The trouble in all such cases is just the difficulty of explaining why other people disagree with us, of reweaving our beliefs so as to fit the fact of disagreement together with the other beliefs we hold. The same Quinean arguments which dispose of the positivists' distinction between analytic and synthetic truth dispose of the anthropologists' distinction between the intercultural and the intracultural.

On this holistic account of cultural norms, however, we do not need the notion of a universal transcultural rationality which Putnam invokes against those whom he calls "relativists." Just before the end of his book, Putnam says that once we drop the notion of a God's-eye point of view we realize that:

> we can only hope to produce a more rational *conception* of rationality or a better *conception* of morality if we operate from *within* our tradition (with its echoes of the Greek agora, of Newton, and so on, in the case of rationality, and with its echoes of scripture, of the philosophers, of the democratic revolutions, and so on...in the case of morality.) We are invited to engage in a truly human dialogue.[9]

With this I entirely agree, and so, I take it, would Kuhn, Hesse, and most of the other so-called "relativists" – perhaps even Foucault. But Putnam then goes on to pose a further question:

> Does this dialogue have an ideal terminus? Is there a *true* conception of rationality, an ideal morality, even if all we ever have are our conceptions of these?

I do not see the point of this question. Putnam suggests that a negative answer – the view that "there is only the dialogue" – is just another form of self-refuting relativism. But, once again, I do not see how a claim that something does not exist can be construed as a claim that something is relative to something else. In the final sentence of his book, Putnam says that "The very fact that we speak of our different conceptions as different conceptions of *rationality* posits a *Grenzbegriff*, a limit-concept of ideal truth." But what is such a posit supposed to do, except to say that from God's point of view the human race is heading in the right direction? Surely Putnam's "internalism" should forbid him to say anything like that. To say that *we* think we're heading in the right direction is just to say, with Kuhn, that we can, by hindsight, tell the story of the past as a story of progress. To say that we still have a long way to go, that our present views should not be cast in bronze, is too platitudinous to require support by positing limit-concepts. So it is hard to see what difference is made by the difference between saying "there is only the dialogue" and saying "there is also that to which the dialogue converges."

I would suggest that Putnam here, at the end of the day, slides back into the scientism he rightly condemns in others. For the root of scientism, defined as the view that rationality is a matter of applying criteria, is the desire for objectivity, the hope that what Putnam calls "human flourishing" has a transhistorical nature. I think that Feyerabend is right in suggesting that until we discard the metaphor of inquiry, and human activity generally, as converging rather than proliferating, as becoming more unified rather than more diverse, we shall never be free of the motives which once led us to posit gods. Positing *Grenzbegriffe* seems merely a way of telling ourselves that a nonexistent God would, if he did exist, be pleased with us. If we could ever be moved solely by the desire for solidarity, setting aside the desire for objectivity altogether, then we should think of human progress as making it possible for human beings to do more interesting things and be more interesting people, not as heading towards a place which has somehow been prepared for humanity in advance. Our self-image would employ images of making rather than finding, the images used by the Romantics to praise poets rather than the images used by the Greeks to praise mathematicians. Feyerabend seems to me right in trying to develop such a self-image for us, but his project seems misdescribed, by himself as well as by his critics, as "relativism."[10]

Those who follow Feyerabend in this direction are often thought of as necessarily enemies of the Enlightenment, as joining in the chorus which claims that the traditional self-descriptions of the Western democracies are bankrupt, that they somehow have been shown to be "inadequate" or "self-deceptive." Part of the instinctive resistance to attempts by Marxists, Sartreans, Oakeshottians, Gadamerians and Foucauldians to reduce objectivity to solidarity is the fear that our traditional liberal habits and hopes will not survive the reduction. Such feelings are evident, for example, in Habermas' criticism of Gadamer's position as relativistic and potentially repressive, in the suspicion that Heidegger's attacks on realism are somehow linked to his Nazism, in the hunch that Marxist attempts to interpret values as class interests are usually just apologies for Leninist takeovers, and in the suggestion that Oakeshott's skepticism about rationalism in politics is merely an apology for the status quo.

I think that putting the issue in such moral and political terms, rather than in epistemological or metaphilosophical terms, makes clearer what is at stake. For now the question is not about how to define words like "truth" or "rationality" or "knowledge" or "philosophy," but about what self-image our society should have of itself. The ritual invocation of the "need to avoid relativism" is most comprehensible as an expression of the need to preserve certain habits of contemporary European life. These are the habits nurtured by the Enlightenment, and justified by it in terms of an appeal of Reason, conceived as a transcultural human ability to correspond to reality, a faculty whose possession and use is demonstrated by obedience to explicit criteria. So the real question about relativism is whether these same habits of intellectual, social, and political life can be justified by a conception of rationality as criterionless muddling through, and by a pragmatist conception of truth.

I think that the answer to this question is that the pragmatist cannot justify these habits without circularity, but then neither can the realist. The pragmatists' justification of toleration, free inquiry, and the quest for undistorted communication can only take the form of a comparison between societies which exemplify these habits and those which do not, leading up to the suggestion that nobody who has experienced both would prefer the latter. It is exemplified by Winston Churchill's defense of democracy as the worst form of government imaginable, except for all the others which have been tried so far. Such justification is not by reference to a criterion, but by reference to various detailed practical advantages. It is circular only in that the terms of praise used to describe liberal societies will be drawn from the vocabulary of the liberal societies themselves. Such praise has to be in *some* vocabulary, after all, and the terms of praise current in primitive or theocratic or totalitarian societies will not produce the desired result. So the pragmatist admits that he has no ahistorical standpoint from which to endorse the habits of modern democracies he wishes to praise. These consequences are just what partisans of solidarity expect. But among partisans of objectivity they give rise, once again, to fears of the dilemma formed by ethnocentrism on the one hand and relativism on the other. Either we attach a special privilege to our own community, or we pretend an impossible tolerance for every other group.

I have been arguing that we pragmatists should grasp the ethnocentric horn of this dilemma. We should say that we must, in practice, privilege our own group, even though there can be no noncircular justification for doing so. We must insist that the fact that nothing is immune from criticism does not mean that we have a duty to justify everything. We Western liberal intellectuals should accept the fact that we have to start from where we are, and that this means that there are lots of views which we simply cannot take seriously. To use Neurath's familiar analogy, we can *understand* the revolutionary's suggestion that a sailable boat can't be made out of the planks which make up ours, and that we must simply abandon ship. But we cannot take his suggestion seriously. We cannot take it as a rule for action, so it is not a live option. For some people, to be sure, the option *is* live. These are the people who have always hoped to become a New Being, who have hoped to be converted rather than persuaded. But we – the liberal Rawlsian searchers for consensus, the heirs of Socrates, the people who wish to link their days dialectically each to each – cannot do so. Our community – the community of the liberal intellectuals of the secular modern West – wants to be able to give a *post factum* account of any change of view. We want to be able, so to speak, to justify ourselves to our earlier selves. This preference is not built into us by human nature. It is just the way *we* live now.[11]

This lonely provincialism, this admission that we are just the historical moment that we are, not the representatives of something ahistorical, is what makes traditional Kantian liberals like Rawls draw back from pragmatism.[12] "Relativism," by contrast, is merely a red herring. The realist is, once again, projecting his own habits of thought upon the pragmatist when he charges him with relativism. For the realist thinks that the whole point of philosophical thought is to detach oneself from any particular community and look down at it from a more universal standpoint. When he hears the pragmatist repudiating the desire for such a standpoint he cannot quite believe it. He thinks that everyone, deep down inside, *must* want such detachment. So he attributes to the pragmatist a perverse form of his own attempted detachment, and sees him as an ironic, sneering aesthete who refuses to take the choice between communities seriously, a mere "relativist." But the pragmatist, dominated by the desire for solidarity, can only be criticized for taking his own community *too* seriously. He can only be criticized for ethnocentrism, not for relativism. To be ethnocentric is to divide the human race into the people to whom one must justify one's beliefs and the others. The first group – one's *ethnos* – comprises those who share enough of one's beliefs to make fruitful conversation possible. In this sense, everybody is ethnocentric when engaged in actual debate, no matter how much realist rhetoric about objectivity he produces in his study.[13]

What is disturbing about the pragmatist's picture is not that it is relativistic but that it takes away two sorts of metaphysical comfort to which our intellectual tradition has become accustomed. One is the thought that membership in our biological species carries with it certain "rights," a notion which does not seem to make sense unless the biological similarities entail the possession of something nonbiological, something which links our species to a nonhuman reality and thus gives the species moral dignity. This picture of rights as biologically transmitted is so basic to the political discourse of the Western democracies that we are troubled by any suggestion that "human nature" is not a useful moral concept. The second comfort is provided by the thought that our community cannot wholly die. The picture of a common human nature oriented towards correspondence to reality as it is in itself comforts us with the thought that even if our civilization is destroyed, even if all memory of our political or intellectual or artistic community is erased, the race is fated to recapture the virtues and the insights and the achievements which were the glory of that community. The notion of human nature as an inner structure which leads all members of the species to converge to the same point, to recognize the same theories, virtues, and works of art as worthy of honor, assures us that even if the Persians had won, the arts and sciences of the Greeks would sooner or later have appeared elsewhere. It assures us that even if the Orwellian bureaucrats of terror rule for a thousand years the achievements of the Western democracies will someday be duplicated by our remote descendants. It assures us that "man will prevail," that something reasonably like *our* world-view, *our* virtues, *our* art, will bob up again whenever human beings are left alone to cultivate their inner natures. The comfort of the realist picture is the comfort of saying not simply that there is a place prepared for our race in our advance, but also that we now know quite a bit about what that place looks like. The inevitable ethnocentrism to which we are all condemned is thus as much a part of the realist's comfortable view as of the pragmatist's uncomfortable one.

The pragmatist gives up the first sort of comfort because he thinks that to say that certain people have certain rights is merely to say that we should treat them in certain ways. It is not to give a *reason* for treating them in those ways. As to the second sort of comfort, he suspects that the hope that something resembling *us* will inherit the earth is impossible to eradicate, as impossible as eradicating the hope of surviving our individual deaths through some satisfying transfiguration. But he does not want to turn this hope into a theory of the nature of man. He wants solidarity to be our *only* comfort, and to be seen not to require metaphysical support.

My suggestion that the desire for objectivity is in part a disguised form of the fear of the death of our community echoes Nietzsche's charge that the philosophical tradition which stems from Plato is an attempt to avoid facing up to contingency, to escape from time and chance. Nietzsche thought that realism was to be condemned not only by arguments from its theoretical incoherence, the sort of argument we find in Putnam and Davidson, but also on practical, pragmatic, grounds. Nietzsche thought that the test of human character was the ability to live with the thought that there was no convergence. He wanted us to be able to think of truth as:

a mobile army of metaphors, metonyms, and anthromorphisms – in short a sum of human relations, which have been enhanced, transposed, and embellished poetically and rhetorically and which after long use seem firm, canonical, and obligatory to a people.[14]

Nietzsche hoped that eventually there might be human beings who could and did think of truth in this way, but who still liked themselves, who saw themselves as *good* people for whom solidarity was *enough*.[15]

I think that pragmatism's attack on the various structure-content distinctions which buttress the realist's notion of objectivity can best be seen as an attempt to let us think of truth in this Nietzschean way, as entirely a matter of solidarity. That is why I think we need to say, despite Putnam, that "there is only the dialogue," only *us*, and to throw out the last residues of the notion of "transcultural rationality." But this should not lead us to repudiate, as Nietzsche sometimes did, the elements in our movable host which embody the ideas of Socratic conversation, Christian fellowship, and Enlightenment science. Nietzsche ran together his diagnosis of philosophical realism as an expression of fear and resentment with his own resentful idiosyncratic idealizations of silence, solitude, and violence. Post-Nietzschean thinkers like Adorno and Heidegger and Foucault have run together Nietzsche's criticisms of the metaphysical tradition on the one hand with his criticisms of bourgeois civility, of Christian love, and of the nineteenth century's hope that science would make the world a better place to live, on the other. I do not think that there is any interesting connection between these two sets of criticisms. Pragmatism seems to me, as I have said, a philosophy of solidarity rather than of despair. From this point of view, Socrates' turn away from the gods, Christianity's turn from an Omnipotent Creator to the man who suffered on the Cross, and the Baconian turn from science as contemplation of eternal truth to science as instrument of social progress, can be seen as so many preparations for the act of social faith which is suggested by a Nietzschean view of truth.[16]

The best argument we partisans of solidarity have against the realistic partisans of objectivity is Nietzsche's argument that the traditional Western metaphysico-epistemological way of firming up our habits simply isn't working anymore. It isn't doing its job. It has become as transparent a device as the postulation of deities who turn out, by a happy coincidence, to have chosen *us* as their people. So the pragmatist suggestion that we substitute a "merely" ethical foundation for our sense of community – or, better, that we think of our sense of community as having no foundation except shared hope and the trust created by such sharing – is put forward on practical grounds. It is *not* put forward as a corollary of a metaphysical claim that the objects in the world contain no intrinsically action-guiding properties, nor of an epistemological claim that we lack a faculty of moral sense, nor of a semantical claim that truth is reducible to justification. It is a suggestion about how we might think of ourselves in order to avoid the kind of resentful belatedness–characteristic of the bad side of Nietzsche–which now characterizes much of high culture. This resentment arises from the realization, which I referred to at the beginning of this chapter, that the Enlightenment's search for objectivity has often gone sour.

The rhetoric of scientific objectivity, pressed too hard and taken too seriously, has led us to people like B. F. Skinner on the one hand and people like Althusser on the other – two equally pointless fantasies, both produced by the attempt to be "scientific" about our moral and political lives. Reaction against scientism led to attacks on natural science as a sort of false god. But there is nothing wrong with science, there is only something wrong with the attempt to divinize it, the attempt characteristic of realistic philosophy. This reaction has also led to attacks on liberal social thought of the type common to Mill and Dewey and Rawls as a mere ideological superstructure, one which obscures the realities of our situation and represses attempts to change that situation. But there is nothing wrong with liberal democracy, nor with the philosophers who have tried to enlarge its scope. There is only something wrong with the attempt to see their efforts as failures to achieve something which they were not trying to achieve – a demonstration of the "objective" superiority of our way of life over all other alternatives. There is, in short, nothing wrong with the hopes of the Enlightenment, the hopes which created the Western democracies. The value of the ideals of the Enlightenment is, for us pragmatists, just the value of some of the institutions and practices which they have created. In this essay I have sought to distinguish these institutions and practices from the philosophical justifications for them provided by partisans of objectivity, and to suggest an alternative justification.

Notes

1 This attitude toward truth, in which the consensus of a community rather than a relation to a nonhuman reality is taken as central, is associated not only with the American pragmatic tradition but with the work of Popper and Habermas. Habermas' criticisms of lingering positivist elements in Popper parallel those made by Deweyan holists of the early logical empiricists. It is important to see, however, that the pragmatist notion of truth common to

James and Dewey is not dependent upon either Peirce's notion of an "ideal end of inquiry" nor on Habermas' notion of an "ideally free community."

2   Hilary Putnam, *Reason, Truth, and History* (Cambridge: Cambridge University Press, 1981), pp. 49–50.

3   Ibid., p. 119.

4   Ibid., p. x.

5   Ibid., p. 114.

6   Ibid., p. 119. See Davidson's "On the very idea of a conceptual scheme," in his *Inquiries into Truth and Interpretation* (Oxford: Oxford University Press, 1984) for a more complete and systematic presentation of this point.

7   Putnam, p. 113.

8   Ibid., p. 126.

9   Ibid., p. 216.

10   See, e.g., Paul Feyerabend, *Science in a Free Society* (London: New Left Books, 1978), p. 9, where Feyerabend identifies his own view with "relativism (in the old and simple sense of Protagoras)." This identification is accompanied by the claim that " 'Objectively' there is not much to choose between anti-semitism and humanitarianism." I think Feyerabend would have served himself better by saying that the scare-quoted word "objectively" should simply be dropped from use, together with the traditional philosophical distinctions which buttress the subjective-objective distinction, than by saying that we may keep the word and use it to say the sort of thing Protagoras said. What Feyerabend is really against is the correspondence theory of truth, not the idea that some views cohere better than others.

11   This quest for consensus is opposed to the sort of quest for authenticity which wishes to free itself from the opinion of our community. See, for example, Vincent Descombes' account of Deleuze in *Modern French Philosophy* (Cambridge: Cambridge University Press, 1980), p. 153: "Even if philosophy is essentially demystificatory, philosophers often fail to produce authentic critiques; they defend order, authority, institutions, 'decency,' everything in which the ordinary person believes." On the pragmatist or ethnocentric view I am suggesting, all that critique can or should do is play off elements in "what the ordinary person believes" against other elements. To attempt to do more than this is to fantasize rather than to converse. Fantasy may, to be sure, be an incentive to more fruitful conversation, but when it no longer fulfills this function it does not deserve the name of "critique."

12   In *A Theory of Justice* Rawls seemed to be trying to retain the authority of Kantian "practical reason" by imagining a social contract devised by choosers "behind a veil of ignorance" – using the "rational self-interest" of such choosers as a touchstone for the ahistorical validity of certain social institutions. Much of the criticism to which that book was subjected, e.g., by Michael Sandel in his *Liberalism and the Limits of Justice* (Cambridge: Cambridge University Press, 1982), has centered on the claim that one cannot escape history in this way. In the meantime, however, Rawls has put forward

a meta-ethical view which drops the claim to ahistorical validity. Concurrently, T. M. Scanlon has urged that the essence of a "contractualist" account of moral motivation is better understood as the desire to justify one's action to others than in terms of "rational self-interest." See Scanlon, "Contractualism and Utilitarianism," in A. Sen and B. Williams, eds., *Utilitarianism and Beyond* (Cambridge: Cambridge University Press, 1982). Scanlon's emendation of Rawls leads in the same direction as Rawls' later work, since Scanlon's use of the notion of "justification to others on grounds they could not reasonably reject" chimes with the "constructivist" view that what counts for social philosophy is what can be justified to a particular historical community, not to "humanity in general." On my view, the frequent remark that Rawls' rational choosers look remarkably like twentieth-century American liberals is perfectly just, but not a criticism of Rawls. It is merely a frank recognition of the ethnocentrism which is essential to serious, nonfantastical, thought.

13 In an important paper called "The Truth in Relativism," included in his *Moral Luck* (Cambridge: Cambridge University Press, 1981), Bernard Williams makes a similar point in terms of a distinction between "genuine confrontation" and "notional confrontation." The latter is the sort of confrontation which occurs, asymmetrically, between us and primitive tribespeople. The belief-systems of such people do not present, as Williams puts it, "real options" for us, for we cannot imagine going over to their view without "self-deception or paranoia." These are the people whose beliefs on certain topics overlap so little with ours that their inability to agree with us raises no doubt in our minds about the correctness of our own beliefs. Williams' use of "real option" and "notional confrontation" seems to me very enlightening, but I think he turns these notions to purposes they will not serve. Williams wants to defend ethical relativism, defined as the claim that when ethical confrontations are merely notional "questions of appraisal do not genuinely arise." He thinks they *do* arise in connection with notional confrontations between, e.g., Einsteinian and Amazonian cosmologies. (See Williams, p. 142.) This distinction between ethics and physics seems to me an awkward result to which Williams is driven by his unfortunate attempt to find *something* true in relativism, an attempt which is a corollary of his attempt to be "realistic" about physics. On my (Davidsonian) view, there is no point in distinguishing between true sentences which are "made true by reality" and true sentences which are "made by us," because the whole idea of "truth-makers" needs to be dropped. So I would hold that there is *no* truth in relativism, but this much truth in ethnocentrism: we cannot justify our beliefs (in physics, ethics, or any other area) to everybody, but only to those whose beliefs overlap ours to some appropriate extent. (This is not a theoretical problem about "untranslatability," but simply a practical problem about the limitations of argument; it is not that we live in different worlds than the Nazis or the Amazonians, but that conversion from or to their point of view, though possible, will not be a matter of inference from previously shared premises.)

14   Nietzsche, "On Truth and Lie in an Extra-Moral Sense," in *The Viking Portable Nietzsche*, Walter Kaufmann, ed. and trans., pp. 46–7.

15   See Sabina Lovibond, *Realism and Imagination in Ethics* (Minneapolis: University of Minnesota Press, 1983), p. 158: "An adherent of Wittgenstein's view of language should equate that goal with the establishment of a language-game in which we could participate ingenuously, while retaining our awareness of it as a specific historical formation. A community in which such a language-game was played would be one . . . whose members understood their own form of life and yet were not embarrassed by it."

16   See Hans Blumenberg, *The Legitimation of Modernity* (Cambridge, Mass.: MIT Press, 1982), for a story about the history of European thought which, unlike the stories told by Nietzsche and Heidegger, sees the Enlightenment as a definitive step forward. For Blumenberg, the attitude of "self-assertion," the kind of attitude which stems from a Baconian view of the nature and purpose of science, needs to be distinguished from "self-foundation," the Cartesian project of grounding such inquiry upon ahistorical criteria of rationality. Blumenberg remarks, pregnantly, that the "historicist" criticism of the optimism of the Enlightenment, criticism which began with the Romantics' turn back to the Middle Ages, undermines self-foundation but not self-assertion.

Index